THE IRWIN SERIES IN
INSURANCE AND ECONOMIC SECURITY

DAVIS W. GREGG

Consulting Editor

PENSION PLANNING

Pensions, Profit Sharing, and Other Deferred Compensation Plans

JOSEPH J. MELONE, Ph.D., C.L.U.
Research Director
McCahan Foundation for Basic Research in
Security, Risk and Insurance

EVERETT T. ALLEN, Jr., LL.B.
Manager, Pension Plans Department
Provident Mutual Life Insurance Company
of Philadelphia

1966
RICHARD D. IRWIN, INC.
Homewood, Illinois

First Printing, September, 1966
Second Printing, June, 1967
Third Printing, May, 1968
Fourth Printing, July, 1969
Fifth Printing, August, 1970
Sixth Printing, June, 1971

Printed in the United States of America

Library of Congress Catalog Card No. 66–27459

To my parents

D. W. MELONE and BEATRICE M. MELONE

—for the many sacrifices they made for me.

J.J.M.

———————————————————————

To my mother, EDNA E. ALLEN,

and to the memory of my father, EVERETT T. ALLEN

—whose death deprived him of the satisfaction

of seeing this completed text.

E.T.A., Jr.

PREFACE

The objective of this text is to present a comprehensive treatment of deferred compensation programs. While primary emphasis has been given to *qualified* pension plans, the text includes extensive coverage of other methods of deferring compensation such as profit sharing, tax-sheltered annuities, informal or nonqualified plans, and plans for the self-employed (H.R. 10).

In an attempt to make the fundamentals of these plans more understandable, examples and practical applications are emphasized throughout the text. In view of the importance of tax considerations in deferred-compensation planning, two separate chapters have been devoted to this subject. Moreover, tax consequences and implications are noted, wherever appropriate, in the balance of the material. Although the text was designed to meet the needs of all parties interested in the area of deferred compensation, emphasis is given to insured plans and the needs of small and medium-size employers.

We believe that there is a definite need for a collegiate-level pension text oriented in this direction. Our opinions were confirmed by members of the staff of the American College of Life Underwriters who informed us of the need for such a text in their educational programs. Indeed, it was the response and enthusiasm of the American College which served as the catalyst for our undertaking the writing of this book.

We are deeply indebted to a number of individuals for their assistance and advice which has been most valuable in the preparation of this book. We would like to acknowledge the assistance of the following for their review of portions of the manuscript: Frank L. Griffin, Jr., F.S.A., Vice-President, The Wyatt Company; Adam Hess, Assistant Secretary, Group Division, Aetna Life & Casualty; and Milton J. Neale, Vice-President, Girard Trust Bank. We would also like to express our appreciation to the following members of the staff of the Provident Mutual Life Insurance Company of Philadelphia for their many helpful suggestions: B. Franklin Blair,

F.S.A., Vice-President and Actuary; Robert H. Carey, Associate Underwriting Officer; Gerald R. Cook, F.S.A., Pension Research Assistant; Robert F. Maguire, Supervisor, Pension Plans Administration; Charles B. Strome, Jr., Assistant Counsel; Thomas S. Tomlinson, Senior Pension Underwriter; and Donald C. Wagner, Pension Underwriter.

Substantial portions of the manuscript were reviewed by James E. Pangburn, Senior Pension Trust Officer, Girard Trust Bank, and by Edwin E. Weller, Vice-President and General Counsel, Provident Mutual Life Insurance Company. Their comments and suggestions were most valuable and are gratefully acknowledged.

Two significant topics included in this book are nonqualified deferred compensation plans and tax-sheltered annuities, which are covered in Chapters 15 and 16. These chapters were contributed by Bernhart R. Snyder, C.L.U., Director of Estate Planning Services, New England Mutual Life Insurance Company. The comprehensive and outstanding treatment of these topics by Mr. Snyder constitutes an important contribution to this text for which the authors are deeply grateful.

Special recognition is due John B. St. John, F.S.A., Consulting Actuary, for his excellent review of the entire manuscript. It is hard to express, in any adequate fashion, our appreciation for his detailed review, extensive criticisms, and constructive suggestions. The entire manuscript has been vastly improved as a result of Mr. St. John's contributions.

We would also like to extend our appreciation to Blanche Lanneaux, Louise Morrison and Anne Sgro for their secretarial assistance in preparing the manuscript. Lastly, a special word of thanks to our families for their patience and understanding during the past year.

Bryn Mawr, Pennsylvania   Joseph J. Melone
Philadelphia, Pennsylvania   Everett T. Allen, Jr.
August, 1966

TABLE OF CONTENTS

DEVELOPMENT OF
PRIVATE PENSION PLANS

Man is constantly seeking means by which to enhance his economic security. One cause of economic insecurity is the probable reduction of an individual's earning power at an advanced age. In this country, this risk is met through one or more of the following means: personal savings (including individual insurance and annuities), private pensions, and government-sponsored programs. The dramatic growth of private pensions since the 1940's has focused considerable interest on this form of income maintenance.

GROWTH OF PRIVATE PLANS[1]

The beginnings of industrial pension plans in the United States date back to the establishment of the American Express Company plan in 1875.[2] The second formal plan was established in 1880 by the Baltimore and Ohio Railroad Company. During the next half century, approximately 400 plans were established. These early pension plans were generally found in the railroad, banking, and public utility fields. The development of pensions in manufacturing companies was somewhat slower, due largely to the fact that most manufacturing companies were still relatively young and therefore not confronted with the superannuation problems of the railroads and public utilities.

[1] Private plans, as used in this text, refers to plans established by private agencies, including commercial, industrial, labor, and service organizations, and nonprofit religious, educational, and charitable institutions. Social Security and public plans for governmental employees are not covered in this text.

[2] Murray Webb Latimer, *Industrial Pension Systems* (New York: Industrial Relations Counselors, Inc., 1932), p. 21.

Insurance companies entered the pension business with the issuance of the first group annuity contract by the Metropolitan Life Insurance Company in 1921.[3] The second contract was issued by the Metropolitan in 1924 to an employer who already had a retirement plan on a "pay-as-you-go" basis.[4] In 1924 the Equitable Life Assurance Society announced its intention of offering a group pension service, thus becoming the second company to enter the field.[5]

Although the beginnings of private pensions date back to the 1800's, the significant growth in these programs has come since the 1940's. As recently as 1940, less than one fifth of all employees in commerce and industry were covered under pension plans.[6] As indicated in Table 1–1, these programs now cover about 28 million persons, representing about 40% of all persons employed in commerce and industry. The assets of pension funds are currently about $76 billion and are growing at the average rate of about $6.5 billion a year.

TABLE 1–1

GROWTH OF PRIVATE PENSION PLANS IN THE UNITED STATES

Year	Number of Persons Covered (In Thousands)			Assets and Reserves (In Millions)		
	Insured Plans	Noninsured Plans	Total	Insured Plans	Noninsured Plans	Total
1930	100	2,700	2,800	$ 100	$ 700	$ 800
1935	285	2,525	2,810	350	950	1,300
1940	695	3,565	4,260	1,000	1,400	2,400
1945	1,470	5,240	6,710	2,550	2,850	5,400
1950	2,755	7,500	10,255	5,600	6,100	11,700
1955	4,105	12,290	16,395	11,325	15,300	26,625
1960	5,475	17,940	23,415	18,850	31,100	49,950
1961	5,635	18,840	24,475	20,250	35,100	55,350
1962	5,770	19,860	25,630	21,625	39,000	60,625
1963	6,060	20,000	26,060	23,300	43,000	66,300
1964	6,710	21,000	27,710	25,200	51,000	76,200

SOURCE: Years 1930–62, *Private and Public Pension Plans in the United States* (New York: Institute of Life Insurance, n.d.), p. 3; years 1963–64, *Life Insurance Factbook*, 1964, pp. 33–35, and 1965, pp. 35–37.

ECONOMIC PROBLEM OF OLD AGE

Longevity is a source of economic insecurity in that an individual may outlive his financial capacity to maintain himself and his de-

---

[3] Kenneth Black, Jr., *Group Annuities* (Philadelphia: University of Pennsylvania Press, 1955), p. 9.

[4] *Ibid.*, p. 11.

[5] *Ibid.*

[6] *Private and Public Pension Plans in the United States* (New York: Institute of Life Insurance, n.d.), p. 2.

pendents. The extent to which an aged person will have the financial capacity to meet self-maintenance costs and those of dependents depends upon the standard of living desired during retirement years, his employment opportunities, and the prior provisions made to meet this contingency.

Standard of Living after Retirement

The assumption is usually made that the financial needs of an individual decrease after retirement. To some extent, this assumption is valid. The retired individual generally has no dependent children, and a home and its furnishings generally have been acquired by retirement age. However, the actual aggregate reduction in the financial needs of a person upon retirement has probably been overstated. Social pressures discourage any drastic change in one's standard of living upon retirement. There is an increasing tendency for retired persons to remain fairly active, particularly in terms of civic, social, travel, and other recreational activities. Furthermore, urbanization and its corollary, apartment living, minimize the prospect of retired parents moving in with their children.

The authors are not suggesting that retired workers require income benefits equal to their earnings levels immediately preceding retirement, nor even the level of preretirement take-home pay. Presumably, at least at the higher income levels, these individuals were allocating a portion of their take-home pay to individual savings. However, it is suggested that the reduction in standard of living after retirement is not very great; and, more importantly, the trend in social thinking seems to be in the direction of not expecting retired workers to have to take much of a reduction in standard of living after retirement. Therefore, it is questionable whether one should assume any significant decrease in basic financial needs upon retirement, at least for individuals in the low- and middle-income categories.

Employment Opportunities

It has been estimated that only 25% of those 65 and over had some income from employment in 1962, and this percentage has been decreasing steadily in recent years.[7] To catalog all of the many factors which account for the reduction in the percentage of the aged in the labor force is an impossible task. A large number of

---

[7] Erdman Palmore, "Work Experience and Earnings of the Aged in 1962," *Social Security Bulletin*, Vol. XXVII, No. 6 (June, 1964), p. 3.

older workers voluntarily retire from the labor force. If one has the necessary financial resources, he may wish to withdraw from active employment and live out his remaining years at a more leisurely pace. Others find it necessary for reasons of health to withdraw from the labor force at an advanced age. The aging process takes its toll, and many individuals are physically unable to operate at the level of efficiency attainable at the younger ages. Disabilities at the older ages tend to be more frequent and of longer duration.

Voluntary retirement and the physical inability to continue employment are undoubtedly important reasons for the decrease in the percentage of older persons participating in the labor force. However, these are probably not the most important factors affecting employment opportunities for the aged. The effects of industrialization and the development of the federal Old-Age, Survivors, and Disability Insurance program (OASDI), private pensions, and other employee benefit programs probably have had a more significant impact on this problem.

The rapid pace and dynamic evolution of industrial employment operate to the disadvantage of older persons. Automation and the mass-production assembly lines put a premium on physical dexterity and mental alertness. Employers generally are of the opinion, justifiable or not, that the younger workers are better suited to the demands of industrial employment. In an agricultural economy the able-bodied older person could continue to work, at least on a part-time basis.

The OASDI program and private pension plans, although created to alleviate the financial risk associated with excessive longevity, have aggravated the problem, in that these programs have tended to institutionalize age 65 as the normal retirement age. Also, some employers may hesitate to hire older workers on the assumption that these employees would increase pension and other employee benefit plan costs. It is difficult to generalize as to the impact of the older worker on employee benefit plan costs. Nevertheless, it must be recognized that an employer's attitude toward the hiring of older workers may be influenced by the assumption, justified or not, that fringe benefit costs will be adversely affected.

Self-employed members of the labor force have greater control as to the timing of their retirements from active employment. For example, physicians and lawyers frequently continue in practice, at least on a part-time basis, until advanced ages. Owners of businesses also continue to be active in the firm until relatively old ages. The fact remains, however, that employment opportunities for the majority of older workers are becoming more and more limited.

Individual Savings of Aged

If employment opportunities for the aged are decreasing and financial needs are still substantial at advanced ages, the need for savings becomes quite apparent. Although data on the extent of savings among the aged are relatively sparse, some research studies have been performed in this area.[8] In these studies it was found that home ownership constitutes the single most important asset. Assets other than the equity in a home of those aged 65 and over were relatively small.

Some experts argue that the economic data developed in studies of the above type do not present an accurate picture of the resources available to the aged in time of need.[9] It is argued that the role of both the immediate and the extended family (i.e., children away from home, relatives, friends, and neighbors) is ignored in these studies. However, it does appear reasonable to conclude that the accumulated individual savings alone of many aged persons are not adequate to provide even a subsistence level of income for their retirement years.

The long-range trend in net personal savings as a percent of national income has been fairly constant. However, the distribution of savings by savings media has changed considerably over the years. The change that is most pertinent to this discussion is the relative increase in private pension reserves in relation to purely individual forms of saving. Annual contributions to private pension funds now amount to about $6.5 billion, representing about 20% of current personal savings.[10] The tremendous increases in disposable income over the last quarter century, therefore, have not resulted in any increase in the proportion of personal savings. There have been many forces at work that have restricted the growth of savings. Advertising, installment credit, and the media of mass communications encourage individuals to set their sights on a constantly

---

[8] Some data on the income and asset position of the aged are presented in an article by Walter Williams, "The Implications of Retirement Security Systems for Consumer Behavior," *Journal of Risk and Insurance*, Vol. XXXII, No. 3 (September, 1965), pp. 352–55.

[9] See, for example, Mortimer Spiegelman, *Ensuring Medical Care for the Aged* (Homewood, Ill.: Richard D. Irwin, Inc., 1960), p. 38. Chapter 2 of this volume includes a good discussion of various studies pertaining to the extent of savings among the aged.

[10] President's Committee on Corporate Pension Funds and Other Private Retirement and Welfare Programs, *Public Policy and Private Pension Programs* (Washington, D.C.: U.S. Government Printing Office, January, 1965), p. i.

increasing standard of living. This competition from consumption goods for current income dollars results in a lower priority being placed on the need for accumulating savings for old age. Also, the high levels of federal income tax rates reduce an income earner's capacity to save. In recent decades, inflation has been an additional deterrent to increased levels of saving. Inflation is a particularly serious threat to the adequacy of savings programs of persons who are already retired. For employed persons, increases in the cost of living may be offset, in part or in whole, by increases in current earnings; that possibility does not exist for most aged persons. Therefore, the aged are faced with the alternatives of accepting a lower standard of living or more rapidly liquidating their accumulated savings.

The proportion of individual (as opposed to group) savings, then, is decreasing at a time when the pattern of living of the aged is becoming increasingly more costly. Under such circumstances, the tremendous importance of pension programs in meeting the economic risk of old age is obvious.

Increasing Longevity

Still another dimension to the overall economic problem of old age is the number of aged in the population. The fact that life expectancy has been increasing is well recognized. However, that this increase in longevity is a recent and quite dramatic development is often not appreciated. Within the last 60 years, the life expectancy at birth has increased from 47 years to approximately 70 years. This result has been achieved in spite of the limited gains in life expectancy in the last decade. The rates of mortality at the earlier ages are now so low that further improvements in mortality at these ages would have little impact on further extensions of the average length of life. If additional improvements in longevity are to be realized, reductions in mortality at the older ages are required. This impediment to further extensions in life expectancy may be overcome if medical advances result from the current concentration of research in the areas of the chronic and degenerative diseases.

One effect of the improvements in longevity in the twentieth century has been an absolute and relative increase in the population of persons age 65 and over. In 1900, there were approximately 3 million persons age 65 and over, whereas there were about 18 million such persons in 1965. By 1975 and 1985, it is estimated that persons age 65 and over will number about 21 million and 25 million, respectively.[11] The proportion of the U.S. population age 65 and over is currently about 9% whereas the proportion of the population in these age brackets in 1900 was about 4%.

The problem of old-age economic security, therefore, is of concern to an increasing number and percentage of the U.S. population.

REASONS FOR GROWTH OF PRIVATE PENSIONS

In the above discussion, the point was made that the problem of economic security for the aged is a serious and increasingly important problem. However, the mere existence of the problem does not explain the phenomenal growth of private pensions. In other words, given the existence of the old-age economic problem, why did employers and employees choose to meet the need, at least in part, through the vehicle of private pension programs? In a broad sense, the major reason is the fact that private pensions offer substantial advantages to both employers and employees. Without this foundation of mutual benefit, the private pension movement could not have achieved the prolonged and substantial growth that it has enjoyed. In addition, government officials have recognized the social desirability of pension programs and have acted to encourage the growth of these plans.

The specific factors generally considered as having influenced the growth of private pensions are discussed below. It must be recognized that the reasons that give rise to the establishment of one plan might be quite different in the case of another plan.

Increased Productivity

A systematic method of meeting the problem of superannuated employees can be easily justified on sound management grounds. Practically every employee eventually reaches a point where, due to advanced age, he is a liability rather than an asset to the employer. That is to say, at some advanced age, an employee's contribution to the productivity of the firm is less than the compensation he is receiving.

The employer has several courses of action open to him when an employee reaches this point. One, the employee can be terminated without any further compensation or any retirement benefits as soon as the value of his services is less than the salary he is

---

[11] *Statistical Bulletin* (New York: Metropolitan Life Insurance Company), Vol. XLVI (November, 1965), p. 1.

receiving. For obvious reasons, this course of action is seldom followed by employers. Two, the employer can retain the superannuated employee in his current position and at his current level of compensation. The difference between the employee's productivity and salary is absorbed by the employer as a cost of doing business. This alternative is also undesirable. Such an approach would undoubtedly prove to be the most costly method of meeting the problem of superannuated employees. Furthermore, the longer-range indirect costs that would be incurred from the resultant inefficiencies and poor employee morale among the younger workers would be indeed significant. Three, the employer could retain the superannuated worker, but transfer him to a less demanding job at the same or a reduced level of compensation. In the former case, the direct costs would be similar to alternative two, but the indirect costs would be reduced in that a younger and more capable person would now be staffing the more demanding position. If the employee's salary is reduced, the direct costs of superannuation would also be reduced.

Most employers who do not have a pension plan generally handle the problem of the older worker in the latter manner. The effectiveness of this approach to the problem has certain important limitations. First of all, a firm usually has only a limited number of positions to which aged workers can be transferred. For a larger or even medium-sized firm, only a fraction of the superannuated employees can be efficiently employed. With automation and the increasingly higher levels of skill required in most jobs, the limitations of this solution are apparent. Furthermore, the superannuated employee is generally still overpaid in the less demanding jobs since, for practical purposes, reductions comparable to the decrease in employee productivity are seldom made. Lastly, this approach does not solve the problem of superannuation; it merely defers it, since a point will be reached where the employee's productivity is considerably below even a minimum level of wage.

The fourth alternative available to the employer in meeting the problem of superannuation is to establish a formal pension plan. A pension plan permits employers to terminate superannuated employees in a humanitarian and nondiscriminatory manner. The inefficiencies associated with retaining employees beyond their productive years are, therefore, eliminated. Employees will know that they are expected to retire by a certain age, and they can make the necessary provisions for their retirement. Furthermore, the sense of security derived from the knowledge that provision is made, at least in part, for their retirement income needs should increase the morale and productivity of employees. Also, systematic retirement of older workers will keep the channels of promotion open, thereby offering opportunity and incentive to the young, ambitious employees—particularly those aspiring to executive positions. Therefore, a pension plan should permit an employer to attract and keep a better caliber of employee.

The problem of superannuation, then, exists in all business firms. Any solution, except the unlikely alternative of arbitrary termination of older workers without any retirement benefit, results in some cost, direct and/or indirect, to the employer. Unfortunately, some employers assume that the pension plan solution is the only approach that carries a price tag. The hidden costs of the other alternatives must be recognized. The decision, therefore, is which solution is best suited to the needs and financial position of the employer. For a large number of employers, the formal pension plan approach has proved to be the superior solution.

Tax Considerations

The bulk of the growth in private pension plans has occurred since 1940. One reason for the growth of these plans during the World War II and Korean War periods was the fact that normal and excess profits tax rates imposed on corporations during these years were extremely high. Since the employer's contributions to a *qualified* pension plan are deductible for federal income tax purposes, a portion of the plan's liabilities could be funded with very little effective cost to the firm. Furthermore, the investment income earned on pension trust assets is exempt from federal income taxation.[12]

The tax advantages of qualified pension plans are even more impressive from the standpoint of employees covered under the plan. For example, the employer's contributions to a pension fund do not constitute taxable income to the employee in the year in which contributions are made. The pension benefits derived from employer contributions are taxed when distributed or made available to the employee. However, the employee is expected to be in a lower tax bracket when retirement benefits are received. In addition, under certain circumstances, lump sum distributions from a pension plan are taxed at capital gain rates rather than at ordinary income rates. Also, favorable estate tax treatment is accorded death benefits paid under a qualified plan.

Therefore, qualified pension plans offer significant tax advantages to participants generally, and in particular, to employees

---

[12] For a complete discussion of the tax aspects of qualified pension plans, see Chapters 5 and 6.

currently in high income tax brackets. For such employees, deferred compensation schemes are favored over equivalent cash wage increases. Since the high-salaried senior officers of corporations often make the decision regarding the establishment and design of employee benefit plans, their role as participants under the plan may influence their decisions on these matters. However, in the case of large corporations, cost and other considerations minimize, or eliminate, the personal tax situations of key employees as factors influencing the establishment or design of a pension plan. In the case of a small, closely held corporation, on the other hand, one can readily see how the tax implications for stockholder-employees may be a decisive factor in the establishment and design of a pension plan. Lastly, tax considerations are certainly one reason, although not the most important, why some labor leaders negotiate for establishment and liberalization of employee benefit programs in lieu of further wage increases.

Wage Stabilization

The second wartime development that helped to stimulate the growth of pensions was the creation of a wage stabilization program as part of a general price control scheme. Employers, in competing for labor, therefore, could not offer the inducement of higher wages. Under these conditions, union leaders found it difficult to prove to their membership the merits of unionism. Therefore, the War Labor Board attempted to relieve the pressure on management and labor for higher wage rates by permitting the establishment of fringe benefit programs, including pensions. This policy further stimulated the growth of pension plans during this period.

Union Demands

Labor leaders have had mixed emotions over the years regarding the desirability of employer financed pension plans. In the 1920's, labor generally did not favor such plans for its membership. It held the view that pensions represented an additional form of employer paternalism and were instituted to encourage loyalty to the firm. Labor leaders felt that the need would be best met through the establishment of a government-sponsored universal social security system; and in the absence of that solution, unions should establish their own pension plans for their members. The former objective was achieved with the passage of the Social Security Act of 1935. By the 1930's, several unions had established their own plans.

However, many of these plans were inadequately financed; a condition which became quite apparent during the depression years. Recognition of the financial burden of a pension program and enactment of wage controls led some labor leaders, in the early 1940's, to favor establishment of employer-supported pension plans.

From 1945 to 1949 the rate of growth of new plans fell off markedly. During this postwar period, employee interest centered upon cash wage increases in an attempt to recover the lost ground suffered during the period of wage stabilization. In the latter part of the decade of the 1940's, union leaders once again began expressing an interest in the negotiation of pension programs. The renewal of interest in pensions was probably due to two factors. First, there was increasing antagonism on the part of the public against what were viewed by many persons as excessive union demands for cash wage increases. The negotiation of fringe benefits was one way of possibly reducing pressures from this quarter. Second, some union leaders argued that Social Security benefits were inadequate, and a supplement in the form of private pension benefits was considered to be necessary. Also, certain labor officials believed that the negotiation of employer-supported pensions would weaken the resistance of the latter toward liberalizations of Social Security benefit levels. Thus, pension demands became a central issue in the labor negotiations in the coal, automobile, and steel industries in the late forties. Although unions had negotiated pension benefits prior to this period, it was not until the late forties that a major segment of labor made a concerted effort to bargain for private pensions.

Labor's drive for pension benefits was facilitated by a National Labor Relations Board ruling in 1948 that employers had a legal obligation to bargain over the terms of pension plans. Until that time, there was some question as to whether employee benefit programs fell within the traditional subject areas for collective bargaining, i.e., wages, hours, and other conditions of employment. The issue was resolved when the National Labor Relations Board held that pension benefits constitute wages and the provisions of these plans affected conditions of employment.[13] Upon appeal, the court upheld the NLRB decision, although it questioned the assumption that such benefits are wages.[14] The result of these decisions was that an employer cannot install or terminate or alter the terms of a pension plan covering organized workers without the approval of the authorized bargaining agent for those em-

---

[13] *Inland Steel Company* v. *United Steelworkers of America*, 77 NLRB 4 (1948).

[14] *Inland Steel Company* v. *National Labor Relations Board*, 170 F.(2d) 247, 251 (1949).

ployees. Furthermore, management has this obligation regardless of whether the plan is contributory or noncontributory, voluntary or compulsory, and regardless of whether the plan was established before or after the certification of the bargaining unit.

Labor was quick to respond to these decisions, and the 1950's were marked by union demands for the establishment of new pension plans, liberalization of existing plans, and the supplanting of employer-sponsored programs with negotiated plans. Undoubtedly, labor's interest in private pensions has been an important factor in the tremendous growth in plans since 1949.

Business Necessity

Employers hire employees in a free, competitive labor market. Therefore, as the number of plans increase, employees come to expect a pension benefit as part of the employment relationship. Employers who do not have such a plan are at a competitive disadvantage in attracting and holding personnel. Therefore, some employers feel they must install a plan even if they are not convinced that the advantages generally associated with a pension plan outweigh the cost of the benefit. Admittedly, this is a negative reason for instituting a plan. In other words, these employers feel that there is little evidence that pension plans truly result in improved morale and efficiency among their work force; but they feel that there would clearly be an adverse employee reaction if they did not offer a pension. Also, in contrast to situations where a plan is established in response to labor demands, an employer may offer a pension plan as part of an employee relations objective of keeping the union out of the firm.

Reward for Service

There is a tendency to argue that employers never provide any increase in employee benefits unless they can expect an economic return in some form. Although this philosophy must prevail generally in a capitalistic system, the fact remains that many employers have established plans out of a sincere desire to reward employees who have served the firm well over a long period of service. Also, some employers may feel a moral responsibility to make some provision for the economic welfare of employees during their retirement years.

Efficiency of Approach

Part of the growth of private pensions must be attributed to the fact that a formal group savings approach has certain inherent advantages. The advantages are not such that they eliminate the need for individual savings; but the merits of private pensions as a supplement to Social Security benefits and individual savings programs are indeed significant. First of all, the economic risk of old age derives from the fact that a point is reached when an employee is unable or unwilling to continue in active employment. A formal plan as an integral part of compensation arrangements and employment relationships, therefore, is quite logical. There is no additional wage cost to the employer to the extent that pension benefits are provided in lieu of other forms of compensation. If pension benefits are provided in addition to prevailing wage rates, the employer's extra wage costs resulting from the pension plan can generally be passed on to the consuming public in the form of higher prices.

It has been argued that from a broad social point of view, the private pension system is the lowest-cost method of providing economic security for the aged. In addition to the administrative efficiency of group saving arrangements, it is argued that the small increase in consumer prices that might be required to provide pension benefits is a relatively painless method of meeting the risk. In other words, the burden of retirement security is spread over a large number of people and over a long period of time. The economic principle of marginal utility would support the conclusion that the disutility of the small increase in prices for all consumers would be less than the burdens that would be borne by those individuals who would have inadequate retirement resources in the absence of pension benefits. Still another aspect to the argument is the assumption that private pensions increase consumption levels among the aged, which in turn helps to maintain a high level of economic activity.

Lastly, private pensions constitute a form of forced savings. This advantage is extremely important in view of the apparent desire of many people to maintain a relatively high standard of living during their active employment years. Although it can be argued that employees would, in the absence of private pension programs, make equivalent provision for old age through increased levels of individual savings, the evidence seems to point to the conclusion that a number of people would not do so. Thus, it might be economically more efficient if at least part of the risk is met through a forced saving private pension scheme.

Sales Efforts of Funding Agencies

For all of the above-mentioned reasons, there has been a considerable demand over the years for private pensions. However, in many instances, the advantages of these programs had to be called to the attention of specific employers. This function of creating effective demand for the pension product has been aggressively performed by those parties interested in providing services in this area. Insurance companies, through agents, brokers, and salaried representatives, were undoubtedly instrumental in the growth of pensions, particularly in the decades of the twenties and thirties. The trust departments of banks are also equipped to handle pension funds, and many corporate trustees have been actively soliciting pension business, particularly since the early 1950's.

RATIONALE OF PRIVATE PENSIONS

The growth of private pensions is attributable, as seen above, to a variety of reasons. It is difficult to determine the extent to which each factor contributed. Indeed, it seems reasonable to conclude that the dominant reasons leading to the establishment of specific plans vary depending on the circumstances surrounding each case. In other words, productivity considerations were dominant forces leading to the creation of some plans, while labor pressures, tax considerations, or other factors encouraged establishment of still other plans. With such variety of motivation, it is difficult to characterize private pensions in terms of a single philosophy or rationale. Nevertheless, attempts have been made over the years to explain private pensions in terms of an underlying concept or philosophy.[15]

Early industrial pension plans were viewed as gratuities or rewards to employees for long and loyal service to the employer. Closely related to this view is the concept that private pensions constitute a systematic and socially desirable method of releasing employees who are no longer productive members of the employer's labor force. Regardless of the view taken, the fact remains that these early plans were largely discretionary, and management made it quite clear that employees had no contractual rights to benefits under the plan. Continuation of the pension plan was dependent upon competitive conditions and management policy. Furthermore, management reserved the right to terminate benefit payments to pensioners for misconduct on the part of the beneficiary or for any other reasons justifying such action in the opinion of the employer.

Thus, the growth of early pensions might be best categorized by

---

[15] For an excellent discussion of pension philosophies, see Jonas E. Mittelman "The Vesting of Private Pensions" (Unpublished dissertation, University of Pennsylvania, 1959), chap. ii.

a single concept: *business expediency*. Business expediency, by the very nature of the concept, implies that the establishment of a plan is a management prerogative and that the primary motivation for the creation of such plans was the economic benefit, direct or indirect, that accrued to the employer. But as the economy became more and more industrialized and pension plans became more prevalent, there was increasing interest in the view that employers had a moral obligation to provide for the economic security of retired workers. This point of view was expressed as early as 1912 by Lee Welling Squier, as follows: "From the standpoint of the whole system of social economy, no employer has a right to engage men in any occupation that exhausts the individual's industrial life in 10, 20 or 40 years; and then leave the remnant floating on society at large as a derelict at sea."[16] This rationale of private pensions has come to be known as the *human depreciation concept*. It was the point of view taken by the United Mine Workers of America in their 1946 drive to establish a welfare fund:

The United Mine Workers of America has assumed the position over the years that the cost of caring for the human equity in the coal industry is inherently as valid as the cost of the replacement of mining machinery, or the cost of paying taxes, or the cost of paying interest indebtedness, or any other factor incident to the production of a ton of coal for consumers' bins. . . . [The agreement establishing the Welfare Fund] recognized in principle the fact that the industry owed an obligation to those employees, and the coal miners could no longer be used up, crippled beyond repair and turned out to live or die subject to the charity of the community or the minimum contributions of the state.[17]

This analogy between human labor and industrial machines was also made in the report of the President's "fact-finding" board in the 1949 steelworkers' labor dispute in support of its conclusion that management had a responsibility to provide for the security of its workers: "We think that all industry, in the absence of adequate Government programs, owes an obligation to workers to provide for maintenance of the human body in the form of medical and similar benefits and full depreciation in the form of old-age retirement—in the same way as it does now for plant and machinery."[18] The report continues as follows: "What does that mean in terms of

---

[16] Lee Welling Squier, *Old Age Dependency in the United States* (New York: Macmillan Co., 1912), p. 272.

[17] United Mine Workers of America Welfare and Retirement Fund, *Pensions for Coal Miners* (Washington, D.C., n.d.), p. 4.

[18] Steel Industry Board, *Report to the President of the United States on the Labor Dispute in the Basic Steel Industry* (Washington, D.C.: U.S. Government Printing Office, September 10, 1949), p. 55.

steelworkers? It should mean the use of earnings to insure against the full depreciation of the human body—say at age 65—in the form of a pension or retirement allowance."[19]

The validity of the human depreciation concept of private pensions has been challenged by many pension experts.[20] The process of aging is physiological and is not attributable to the employment relationship. Admittedly, the hazards of certain occupations undoubtedly shorten the life span of the employees involved. In those instances the employer can logically be held responsible only for the increase in the rate of aging due to the hazards of the occupation. More importantly, the analogy between men and machines is inherently unsound. A machine is an asset owned by the employer, and depreciation is merely an accounting technique for allocating the costs of equipment to various accounting periods. Employees, on the other hand, are free agents and sell their services to employers for a specified wage rate. An employee, unlike a machine, is free to move from one employer to another. The differences between men and machines are so great that one must question the value of the analogy as a basis for a rationale of private pensions. As Dearing notes: "Any economic or moral responsibility that is imposed on the employer for the welfare of workers after termination of the labor contract should be grounded on firmer reasoning than is supplied by the machine-worker analogy."[21]

In recent years a view of private pensions that has achieved broader acceptance is the *deferred wage concept*. This concept views a pension benefit as part of a wage package which is composed of cash wages and other employee fringe benefits. The deferred wage concept has particular appeal with reference to negotiated pension plans. The assumption is made that labor and management negotiators think in terms of total labor costs. Therefore, if labor negotiates a pension benefit, the amount of funds available for increases in cash wages are reduced accordingly. This theory of private pensions was expressed as early as 1913:

In order to get a full understanding of old-age and service pensions, they should be considered as a part of the real wages of a workman. There is a tendency to speak of these pensions as being paid by the company, or, in cases where the employee contributes a portion, as being paid partly by the employer and partly by the employee. In a certain sense, of course,

---

[19] *Ibid.*, p. 65.

[20] For example, see Dan M. McGill, *Fundamentals of Private Pensions* (2d ed.; Homewood, Ill.: Richard D. Irwin, Inc., 1964), p. 16. See also Charles L. Dearing, *Industrial Pensions* (Washington, D.C.: Brookings Institution, 1954), pp. 62–63 and 241–43; and Mittelman, *op. cit.*, pp. 28–34.

[21] Dearing, *op. cit.*, p. 243.

this may be correct, but it leads to confusion. A pension system considered as part of the real wages of an employee is really paid by the employee, not perhaps in money, but in the foregoing of an increase in wages which he might obtain except for the establishment of a pension system.[22]

The deferred wage concept has also been challenged on several grounds. First, it is noted that some employers who pay the prevailing cash wage rate for the particular industry also provide a pension benefit. Thus, it can be argued that in these cases the pension benefit is offered in addition to, rather than in lieu of, a cash wage increase. Second, the deferred wage concept ignores the possible argument that the employer is willing to accept a lower profit margin in order to provide a pension plan for employees. Third, it is sometimes argued that if pension benefits are a form of wage, then terminating employees should be entitled to the part of the retirement benefit that has been earned to the date of termination. In practice, one finds that only a small proportion of the plans provide for the full and immediate vesting of all benefits. However, it can be argued that the deferred wage concept does not necessarily require the full and immediate vesting of benefits. Proponents of this concept view the pension benefits as a wage, the receipt of which is conditioned upon the employee remaining in the service of the employer for a specified number of years. This view of the pension benefit is similar, conceptually, to the pure endowment, the consideration of the employee being the reduction in cash wages accepted in lieu of the pension benefit.

In spite of the appeal of the deferred wage theory, it is questionable whether the private pension movement can be explained solely in terms of this concept. Indeed, there is probably no one rationale or theory that fully explains the "reason for being" of private pensions. This conclusion is not surprising in view of the fact that these plans are *private*, and the demands or reasons that give rise to one plan may be quite different from those leading to the introduction of another plan.

FUTURE GROWTH OF PRIVATE PLANS

The future growth of private pension plans depends on many variables that make predictions in this area rather difficult. However, the President's Cabinet Committee report sets forth some projections of growth up to 1980,[23] based in part on studies being

---

[22] Albert de Roode, "Pensions as Wages," *American Economic Review*, Vol. III, No. 2 (June, 1913), p. 287.

[23] President's Committee on Corporate Pension Funds, *op. cit.*, Appendix A, Table 1.

performed by the National Bureau of Economic Research. According to these projections, it is expected that private plans will cover about 43 million employees by 1980, or more than three out of five of the employees projected for private nonfarm establishments. Annual contributions are expected to increase from their current level of about $6.5 billion to almost $11 billion a year, with pension reserves increasing to an estimated $225 billion by 1980.

These estimates assume a high-employment economy and a continuation of the current interest in retirement. No significant changes are assumed in the present legal or legislative framework affecting private plans. A considerable variation in either direction would be possible, depending on such factors as new arrangements regarding coverage or pooling, developments in the public programs, and economic conditions.[24]

Since plans have been established by most large employers, the future extension of private pension coverage depends largely on the extent to which programs are started by smaller employers. The fact that smaller employers generally do not have pension plans is understandable. The costs of a pension program are fairly substantial; and many small firms are unable, or at least hesitant, to assume a financial obligation of such magnitude. Also, there is probably less pressure on small employers to establish pension plans. The employees of these firms are often not represented by a union, and this source of pressure to establish plans is nonexistent. Even if the employees are organized, the high rates of turnover among employees or the economic condition of the employers or the industry may reduce the prospects for negotiating a retirement benefit. Furthermore, small employers do not seem to have the personnel problem of larger firms, that is, the need to match the employee benefit programs being offered by competing firms.

However, small employers must compete with the large firms for qualified employees; and as pensions become more common, it may be increasingly necessary for small firms to provide pension benefits. Also, the problem of establishing pension plans in industries characterized by small employers and high rates of employee turnover has been partially met by the recent growth of multiemployer pension plans. A multiemployer pension plan is a plan that covers the employees of two or more financially unrelated employers. Pension contributions are payable into one common fund, and benefits are payable to all employees from the pooled assets of the fund. Employees are free to transfer from one participating employer to another without loss of earned pension credits. These plans gener-

---

[24] *Ibid.*, p. 9.

ally require uniform contribution rates and uniform benefit provisions. Although there are a few nonnegotiated multiemployer plans in operation, these plans have been established almost exclusively as a result of collective bargaining. These plans cover more than three million employees and account for one third of the employees covered under collectively bargained plans of all types and about one sixth of the total coverage of private plans.[25] In recent years, there has been increasing interest in the possibilities of pooling arrangements as funding vehicles for nonnegotiated plans of small employers.

Another factor which probably to some extent discouraged the establishment of pension plans by small employers has been the unfavorable federal income tax treatment, prior to 1962, accorded plans established by sole proprietorships and partnerships. A sole proprietorship or a partnership can deduct for federal income tax purposes the contributions to a qualified pension plan made on behalf of employees. But no tax deduction was permitted for contributions under those plans made on behalf of the sole proprietors or partners. The Keogh Act, passed by Congress in 1962, amended the Internal Revenue Code to permit tax deductions for contributions made to pension plans on behalf of sole proprietors and partners. In order to be entitled to these deductions, the plan must meet the requirements set forth in the 1962 amendment. There are limitations on the amount of deductions for contributions made on behalf of the self-employed owners, and the Act requires that all employees who have a specified number of years' service with the firm must be included in the plan.[26]

Although it is difficult to determine to what extent these developments will encourage the growth of pension plans among smaller employers, it seems reasonable to conclude that the number of new plans established each year will continue to grow for some years to come, but at a slower rate than experienced in the past.

---

[25] Joseph J. Melone, *Collectively Bargained Multi-Employer Pension Plans* (Homewood, Ill.: Richard D. Irwin, Inc., 1963), p. 13.

[26] See Chapter 14 for further analysis of pension and profit sharing plans for self-employed individuals.

2

BASIC FEATURES
OF A PENSION PLAN

An employer who is adopting a qualified pension plan must make a number of decisions as to the basic features to be included in the plan. He must, for example, determine the class of employees to be covered; when and under what conditions these employees will be eligible for participation; what benefits they will receive upon retirement, death, disability, or severance of employment; how and when these benefits will be paid; and whether or not employees will contribute toward the cost of these benefits.

The employer's actual circumstances as well as his objectives as to benefit and cost levels are of paramount importance when making these decisions, although a number of other factors must often be taken into account. The funding instrument to be employed, for example, might influence the choice of certain features of the plan (or, as is more often the case, the employer's desire for a specific benefit or plan provision will suggest the choice of funding instrument). The employer's existing fringe benefit program should also be considered if unnecessary duplication or overlapping of benefits is to be avoided. Demands by a collective bargaining unit will also have an impact on the employer's decisions, as might the benefit patterns established by competing business organizations.

The requirements of the Internal Revenue Code and appropriate Regulations are of vital importance if the employer wishes to obtain the favorable tax benefits that flow from having a "qualified" plan. While the requirements for qualification are discussed at greater length in Chapter 5, it might be observed, at this point, that such a plan must not discriminate in any way (i.e., in benefits, contributions, or coverage) in favor of officers, stockholders, supervisors, or highly compensated employees—often called the *prohibited* group of employees. Thus, the employer, if he is to have a qualified plan, cannot pick and choose the employees to be covered nor can he determine their benefits in a selective manner.[1] Instead, he must adopt a plan which treats employees fairly and equitably and which does not produce discrimination in favor of this prohibited group of employees.

The design of a pension plan for a particular employer should reflect a thorough evaluation of the needs and circumstances of that employer. It is possible, of course, that a given combination of plan benefits and features will work out quite well for a number of different employers. As a practical matter, however, each employer has his own specific objectives as well as his own specific circumstances. Thus, a plan provision that might be quite satisfactory for one employer could be completely inadequate for another. For this reason, it is most important that the plan developed for any employer be designed to accomplish his particular objectives while taking into account his own particular problems. All too often, an employer will abruptly adopt a "package" plan only to find, at a later date, that his plan is deficient in some respect. Unfortunately, the remedy to this type of problem frequently involves considerable expense and effort on the part of all concerned.

This chapter discusses the various factors which bear on an employer's decisions as to the design of the more prominent features to be included in a pension plan. While much of this material applies equally well to profit sharing plans, it is specifically oriented toward *qualified pension* plans established by *corporate* employers.[2] The features discussed include: eligibility requirements, retirement ages and benefits, death and disability benefits, severance-of-employment benefits, and employee contributions. The chapter also touches upon some of the other provisions which are essential to any pension plan (such as the employer's right to amend or terminate the program), but which are more or less straightforward in nature and do not require any major consideration by the employer.

ELIGIBILITY REQUIREMENTS

In the generally accepted sense, eligibility requirements are those conditions an employee must meet in order to become a participant in the plan. In noncontributory plans, an employee who meets the eligibility requirements will automatically become a participant

---

[1] These requirements do not apply in the case of nonqualified deferred compensation plans. See Chapter 15.

[2] For a full discussion of profit sharing plans, see Chapter 13, and for a full discussion of plans established by self-employed individuals, see Chapter 14.

when first eligible. In contributory plans, the employee usually has the option of participating and must take some affirmative action before becoming a participant. Thus, he must usually sign an application for participation under which he agrees to make contributions and also designates his beneficiary.

There are two broad types of eligibility requirements—those which defer an employee's participation until some stipulated conditions are met, and those which exclude an employee from participation on a permanent basis (or, at least, until the employee has had some change in his employment classification). An example of an eligibility requirement that defers participation would be a requirement that the employee must attain some minimum age before becoming eligible. On the other hand, provisions which exclude hourly employees or which prevent participation if an employee has attained some maximum age are illustrative of requirements that exclude certain employees from ever participating in the plan.

Those eligibility requirements which defer participation are often indicated for administrative cost considerations. Inclusion of employees who are still in what might be termed the "high turnover" stage of their employment will involve the creation and maintenance of records and, depending upon the funding instrument involved, could create additional and unnecessary costs for the employer. For example, an employee who terminates employment shortly after becoming a participant under an individual policy plan creates a cost to the employer which is measured in terms of the difference between the premiums paid for the employee's coverage and the cash surrender value (including any dividends) which is available from the insurer under the employee's insurance or annuity contract. However, care must be exercised so that the eligibility requirements are not too stringent. Much of the psychological effect of the plan may be lost if a number of employees find that they are not yet eligible to participate. The selection of appropriate eligibility requirements balances these factors so that within the employer's objectives as many employees as possible are eligible, while financial losses and administrative difficulties are kept to a minimum.

Those eligibility requirements which permanently exclude employees from participation are generally dictated by the employer's objectives, by bargaining agreements or, as is very often the case, by cost considerations. For example, it is rarely desirable for an employer to include part-time or seasonal employees in a pension plan. Similarly, if a bargaining unit is negotiating for a pension plan, coverage is generally confined to employees represented by the bargaining unit. Perhaps the most difficult of the eligibility requirements is the maximum age established for the plan. The employer may have many employees who have accumulated a record of long and faithful service with the employer, and, to the extent possible, these employees should be included in the plan. Unfortunately, however, the inclusion of employees who have attained some specified age could present definite and immediate cost problems for the employer.

Requirements of the Internal Revenue Code are an extremely important consideration in the establishment of eligibility provisions. The Code requires that: (1) at least 70% of all employees be covered; or (2) in a plan requiring employee contributions at least 80% of all eligible employees be covered, provided that 70% of all employees are eligible. Employees with less than the years of service specified by the plan (not to exceed five years) and part-time and seasonal workers may be excluded in determining "all employees." In lieu of the foregoing, the law also permits eligibility to be determined by special classifications of employees if such classifications do not discriminate in favor of officers, stockholders, supervisors, or highly compensated employees.

The most common eligibility requirements involve the use of a minimum age and/or a minimum period of service. In the broad sense, there are other eligibility requirements that may also be considered. These include the use of a maximum age, a minimum earnings requirement, and employment classifications.[3]

One further point to note is that eligibility requirements which defer participation might also affect the employee's benefit and the ultimate cost of the plan since, for example, they could limit the time during which he may accrue credited service. Many plans, however, and particularly those negotiated by collective bargaining units, give credit for total service or give credit for all service up to some maximum such as 30 years.

In designing eligibility requirements, it is often helpful to prepare a chart which shows the distribution of employees by age and service. It may be desirable to prepare different charts for males and females, or to show a distribution which takes earnings into account. This type of chart will often indicate the proper choice of eligibility requirements and, when compared with the employer's

---

[3] It might also be mentioned that if an unallocated funding instrument is being employed for the plan, it is possible to make all employees eligible but to use years of service and minimum age requirements in determining the employer's contributions. In other words, all employees are eligible, but the employer does not make contributions with respect to employees who have not been employed for some stipulated period and/or who have not attained some stipulated age.

prior employment levels, will give a graphic picture of the employer's turnover. Table 2–1 shows how such a chart might be prepared.

TABLE 2–1

ANALYSIS OF EMPLOYEES BY AGE AND SERVICE

Age	Under 1 Year	1	2	3	4	5–9	10–14	15–19	20 or More	Total
Under 20	1									1
20–24		1								1
25–29	1		1							2
30–34			1	1	1	2				5
35–39	1					1	3			5
40–44	2	2	1				1	1		7
45–49	1			5	1	3	1	2		13
50–54			1		1		1		1	4
55–59						1	2		1	4
60–64			1				1			2
65–69						1	1			2
70 & over							1			1
Total	6	3	4	7	3	8	11	3	2	47

With the above discussion as general background, it is now appropriate to consider certain specific types of eligibility requirements in greater detail.

Years of Service

In almost all situations, it is possible to demonstrate that an employer's highest rate of turnover occurs among employees who have been with the firm for a relatively short period of time. It is generally desirable that any minimum service requirement of the plan be set so as to provide that only those persons who have been employed beyond this period will be eligible. The particular period will vary from employer to employer and with the type of industry and employee involved, but a period of from one to three years is most common. It should be noted that the Internal Revenue Service generally will not permit the years-of-service requirement to exceed five years.[4]

---

[4] Often, the Internal Revenue Service will require that the minimum service requirement be less than five years to prevent discrimination in a specific plan. The President's Committee on Corporate Pension Funds has also recommended that the maximum permissible waiting period for a qualified plan be reduced to three years. President's Committee on Corporate Pension Funds and other Private Retirement and Welfare Programs, *Public Policy and Private Pension Programs* (Washington, D.C.: U.S. Government Printing Office, January, 1965), p. xiii.

Many plans employ a dual service requirement which establishes a longer period of minimum service for individuals who become employees after the effective date of the plan. This type of provision will be acceptable to the Internal Revenue Service only if employees in the prohibited group (i.e., officers, stockholders, supervisors, and highly compensated employees) can, at the time the plan is established, meet the more stringent requirements set for future employees.

A word of caution is indicated for newly incorporated firms that are considering the adoption of a pension plan. Under federal tax law, any employee of the corporation who was formerly a partner or the proprietor of the predecessor business organization may measure his service only from the date of incorporation. Thus, the period of service chosen for eligibility purposes is usually set low enough to permit stockholder-employees to participate at the time the plan is established.

A minimum service requirement for participation is rarely found in negotiated plans; however, these plans frequently require that an employee, to be eligible for retirement benefits, must have completed some minimum period of service (such as 10 or 15 years) by the normal retirement age specified in the plan.

Minimum Age

Most employers will be able to establish that turnover is highest among employees who have not attained a certain age. Thus, many plans, in addition to having a years-of-service requirement, also require that an employee must have attained some minimum age (such as 25 or 30) before he will be eligible to participate. Since the rate of turnover among young female employees is usually quite high, different eligibility requirements, particularly as to minimum age, are often established for male and female employees.[5] Gener-

---

[5] Treating male and female employees differently for the purpose of eligibility requirements will generally not be objectionable to the Internal Revenue Service, although the authors know of some plans where a local office of the Service has insisted, as a condition of qualification, that the same eligibility requirements be applied to both male and female employees. There are further questions as to whether or not the different treatment of male and female employees for eligibility purposes would be in violation of either the Equal Pay provisions of the Fair Labor Standards Act or the Federal Fair Employment Practices law. As yet, there has been no specific or authoritative determination of these questions, although early indications are that different eligibility requirements for male and female employees will not be objectionable in the case of plans where the different requirements will not affect benefit and contribution levels.

The complete exclusion of female employees, of course, would not be acceptable to the Internal Revenue Service. It also appears that such an exclusion

ally, the Internal Revenue Service will not permit the minimum age to be higher than 30.

Occasionally, a plan will establish a higher minimum age requirement for future employees, but, as is the case with a minimum service requirement, employees in the prohibited group must have attained the age required for future employees if the plan is to be approved by the Internal Revenue Service.

Minimum age requirements are rarely found in collectively bargained plans.

Maximum Age

As previously stated, the use of a maximum age as an eligibility requirement is of considerable significance, primarily from the viewpoint of costs. A typical maximum age provision would exclude individuals over some age such as 55, 60, or 65.

The cost of including older employees in the plan might prove to be prohibitive. This is particularly true for fully insured individual policy or group permanent plans since, in the absence of some form of postretirement funding, the time in which the necessary funds must be accumulated for an older employee is relatively short. This situation is alleviated somewhat in plans using a different funding instrument, where postretirement funding is available, or where the normal retirement schedule for older employees is staggered so as to give the maximum period possible for accumulating the necessary funds. Even here, however, cost considerations may dictate that certain older employees be excluded from the plan. The problem is further complicated because these older employees may be the very reason that the employer is considering the adoption of a pension plan.

Just what should be done will vary from case to case, keeping in mind the desires of the employer, the actual cost problems involved, the actuarial cost method used for the plan, and the funding instrument being employed. Many plans are established with a high maximum age for employees on the effective date of the plan but with a lower maximum age for future employees. Another approach would be to exclude employees who were *hired* after some maximum age. The effect of such a provision would be to include older employees with long service, while at the same time excluding those with short service. In any event, where employees are excluded from the plan because of a maximum age provision, the employer often provides some benefit for them on an informal pay-as-you-go basis.

would be in violation of the Equal Pay provisions of the Fair Labor Standards Act and the Federal Fair Employment Practices law.

In some plans, particularly those which have been collectively bargained, the equivalent of a maximum age is included by requiring that an employee must have completed some stipulated number of years of service (15, for example) by the normal retirement age specified in the plan. Under this type of provision, an employee will be excluded if he is hired after he has reached the age when he can no longer accumulate the required years of service.

Earnings Requirements

Some plans require that an employee, in order to be eligible to participate in the plan, must be earning in excess of some amount such as the amount subject to Social Security tax. These plans, as well as those plans which provide a greater benefit for earnings over the Social Security taxable wage base than is provided for earnings under this amount, may qualify under the Internal Revenue Code. When a plan is limited in this fashion, it is required that the plan benefits must *integrate* with the benefits under the Social Security Act. The specific requirements for integrating plan benefits with Social Security benefits are discussed in the portion of this chapter which deals with benefit formulas.

It is also possible to use an earnings level other than the Social Security taxable wage base in determining whether or not an employee will be eligible to participate in the plan. However, such an earnings level is infrequently used.

Employment Classifications

At one time, it was quite common to establish plans with participation limited to salaried employees only. However, it has become increasingly more difficult to qualify plans with this limitation. As a general rule, if the salaried employees are all earning more than the hourly employees, the plan will not be acceptable to the Internal Revenue Service. The acceptability of such a plan increases, however, when the hourly employees earn substantially the same as some of the salaried employees.[6]

Salaried-only plans may also be acceptable where the employer is

[6] For a more detailed discussion of the position of the Internal Revenue Service on this subject, see pp. 111–13. It might also be noted that the President's Committee on Corporate Pension Funds has recommended that "salaried-only" plans should not be permitted to qualify unless special circumstances are shown. The report indicated that such a plan might be justified if there is a showing that the other employees preferred not to be covered or preferred to be covered under separate plans, or that differences in working conditions warranted differences in pension treatment. President's Committee on Corporate Pension Funds, *op. cit.*, pp. 60–61.

already making contributions for the hourly employees as, for example, under a union-negotiated plan. Thus, if the salaried-only plan would not qualify on its own, i.e., it would not meet the requirements discussed above, it may still qualify if the plan covering the hourly employees provides contributions or benefits which are comparable to those being provided for salaried employees.

A closely related question is whether or not a plan could be limited to employees who are not represented by a collective bargaining unit. Here, the National Labor Relations Act must be considered. In the absence of a plan providing comparable benefits for the employees represented by the bargaining unit, such an exclusion would apparently constitute an unfair labor practice under Section 8(a) of the Act.

It is possible for a plan to be established for only those employees who work in a specific plant or at a specific location, or who work in a specific occupation. These classifications are not used too frequently and, when used, must not produce discrimination in favor of the prohibited group of employees.

RETIREMENT AGES

Normal Retirement Age

The normal retirement age in most plans is 65. The choice of this age is influenced not only by the fact that this is the age at which full Social Security benefits commence but also by the fact that retiring employees before age 65 and with full benefits often produces prohibitive costs. Occasionally, an earlier age such as 60 will be chosen as the normal retirement age although, to a great extent, this practice is confined to public, quasi-public, and charitable institutions. Also, in industries in which an employee's working career is shorter than in most other occupations, some plans provide for a normal retirement age which is lower than 65.

A few plans retire female employees at age 60 and male employees at age 65.[7] In the absence of a special occupational problem, however, there would seem to be little justification for retiring females earlier than males—particularly since annuity tables show that females have a longer life expectancy than males.

---

[7] The Wage-Hour Administrator has ruled that the choice of an employer to require a different retirement age for male and female employees is not within the scope of the Fair Labor Standards Act. Letter signed by Clarence T. Lundquist, Administrator, Wage and Hour and Public Contracts Divisions, U.S. Department of Labor, dated August 6, 1964, *Pension and Profit Sharing Tax Service* (Englewood Cliffs, N.J.: Prentice-Hall, Inc., n.d.), ¶ 12,036. However, a different retirement schedule for male and female employees might be in violation of the Federal Fair Employment Practices law, although this issue has yet to be ruled upon.

A "floating normal retirement age" is sometimes used in negotiated plans. Under this type of arrangement, the employee has the right to retire with full benefits upon attaining some minimum age —usually 65; however, the employer does not have the right to retire the employee until he attains some maximum age—usually 68. At any time in the interim, the employee has the right to retire with full benefits credited up to his actual retirement.

As previously mentioned, in certain situations it is quite common to provide a staggered normal retirement schedule for older employees at the time the plan is established. A typical schedule would state that anyone over age 55 will retire at the end of 10 years of participation in the plan or, if earlier, at age 70. Thus, an employee 56 years old at entry into the plan would retire at 66, while a person 61 would retire at 70. The use of a staggered normal retirement schedule accomplishes several things. First, the cost of providing a given amount of pension will decrease as the employee's normal retirement age increases. Second, it enables the employer to accumulate the cost of an older employee's pension over a longer period of time. Third, if the plan bases benefits on service or uses a defined contribution (money purchase) formula, the employee will have an additional period of time in which to accrue benefits. Finally, both the employer and employee are given an adequate period of time in which to plan for the employee's retirement.

Early Retirement Age

Most plans provide that an employee may choose early retirement on a reduced pension, although a few plans limit this feature to cases of total and permanent disability. If an early retirement provision is to be included, it is customary to establish some requirements which an employee must fulfill before he will be allowed to elect early retirement.

A typical requirement for early retirement would be that the employee must have attained at least age 55 and must have completed at least 10 years of participation in the plan. Requirements such as these limit the option to situations where the employee is actually retiring, as opposed to changing jobs. They also tend to create a situation in which the employee will receive a reasonable benefit.

Employer consent is generally not required for early retirement. If employer consent is required, the Internal Revenue Service requires that the value of the benefit payable at early retirement be not greater than the value of the benefit which the employee would have received under the plan's vesting schedule had he terminated employment on the date of his retirement.

The benefit payable at early retirement is reduced for two reasons. First, the employee's full benefit will not have accrued by his early retirement date. Second, the benefit, because it is starting several years earlier than anticipated, will be paid over a longer period of time. Thus, an actuarial reduction factor is usually applied to the value of the employee's accrued benefit in order to determine his early retirement benefit.

Determining the value of the employee's accrued benefit is relatively simple under an allocated funding instrument. In a fully insured individual policy plan, for example, the value of the accrued benefit is generally the cash surrender value of the employee's insurance or annuity contract at the time of his retirement. In this type of plan, the actuarial reduction is accomplished by the use of the settlement option rates contained in the contract. The employee's benefit is generally that amount which may be provided by applying the cash surrender value under the option at the employee's attained age on his retirement date.

In plans using an unallocated funding instrument, and where the benefit formula reflects the employee's service, his benefit is generally measured in terms of his accrued service to the date of his retirement. If the plan uses another type of formula, however, the determination of the value of the employee's accrued benefit is more difficult. One approach, which is used quite often, is to multiply the value of the employee's projected benefit at normal retirement date by a fraction, the numerator being the years of participation he has completed to his early retirement date and the denominator the years of participation he would have completed at his normal retirement date.

The reduction factor applied to the value of the employee's accrued benefit might be something as simple as a reduction of $\frac{1}{2}$ of 1% for each month by which early retirement precedes normal retirement or, as is usually the case in plans funded with some form of group pension contract, an actuarial reduction factor is determined from a table included in the plan or group contract. Table 2–2 shows a typical set of actuarial reduction factors which are based upon the 1951 Group Annuity Table and which apply where the normal form for the payment of benefits is a pure life annuity.

Late Retirement Age

A great many plans also include a provision which allows an employee to defer his retirement. This feature could also be important to the employer, since it permits a greater degree of flexibility in scheduling the actual retirement of a key employee when there is a problem in obtaining or training his replacement.

The right to elect late retirement is usually subject to the employer's consent. While late retirement may be permitted on an unlimited basis as to point of time, it is frequently limited to some period of time after his normal retirement date, such as five years.

The benefit payable at late retirement may be the same as would have been payable had the employee retired on his normal retirement date (with the employer in some fashion receiving a credit toward his next contributions under the plan by reason of the

TABLE 2–2

EARLY RETIREMENT FACTORS*

Years Prior to Normal Retirement Date†	Percentage	
	Male	Female
1	90.1%	91.7%
2	81.5	84.4
3	74.0	77.9
4	67.4	72.0
5	61.7	66.8
6	56.6	62.1
7	52.0	57.8
8	48.0	53.9
9	44.4	50.4
10	41.2	47.2

* Based on a normal retirement date of 65.
† Years prior to normal retirement date means years and complete months from early retirement date to normal retirement date. Allowance for such months is made by interpolating in the table.

excess values created by this provision), or the benefit may be an increased actuarial equivalent. It is even possible to provide that the employee may accrue additional pension credits with respect to service performed between his normal and late retirement dates. However, many pension authorities feel that if a pension plan is to accomplish its real purpose, the election of late retirement should not be made attractive to employees. These authorities feel that it is generally desirable that there be no increase in benefits at late retirement or, at the most, that the benefit at late retirement be no more than an actuarial equivalent of the benefit that would have been payable at normal retirement age; otherwise, there is too much of an incentive for the employee to remain employed.

RETIREMENT BENEFITS

The formula selected for determining an employee's retirement benefit is a vital provision in a pension plan. The employer's financial capacity, his general philosophy concerning the desired level of retirement benefits, and his specific objectives as to the distribution of benefits among his employees all play an important role in selecting such a formula.

Many employers feel that a plan should be designed so as to provide an employee with an income after retirement which, when Social Security benefits are included, will range between 50% and 60% of his earnings just before retirement. For lower-paid employees, the percentage might be higher. From the employer's viewpoint, the benefit formula selected should in no event result in a plan which produces costs so high as to endanger the continuation of the plan when corporate earnings may be decreased or when current tax advantages may be reduced.

Basically, there are two types of benefit formulas for the employer to consider. The first is called a *defined contribution* or a *money purchase* formula. Under this type of formula, contribution rates are fixed, and an employee's benefit will vary depending upon such factors as the amount of the contributions made and the employee's age, sex, and normal retirement age. The second type is called a *defined benefit* or an *annuity purchase* formula. Here, a definite benefit is established for each employee, and contributions are determined to be whatever is necessary to produce the desired benefit results. Defined benefit formulas are far more popular than defined contribution formulas and, in themselves, may be subdivided into several different classifications.[8]

Determination of Earnings

Since the amount of benefit under most formulas is based on an employee's compensation, it is important, before discussing specific formulas, to have a clear idea of the different considerations involved in selecting the earnings base to which the benefit formula will be applied.

Normally, only basic compensation will be considered for benefit purposes. Thus, overtime payments, bonuses, and other forms of extraordinary compensation are not included. As a matter of fact, the inclusion of these additional items of compensation will receive special attention from the Internal Revenue Service since the inclusion of bonus and incentive pay could very easily lead to a plan which discriminates in favor of the prohibited group of employees. Under a discretionary bonus formula, for example, employees in

---

[8] It has been said that a third type of benefit formula is emerging—one where the employee's benefit will vary, depending upon the performance of the common stock market or upon changes in a cost-of-living index. Actually, this is not so, since variable benefit plans involve either a defined contribution or a defined benefit formula. These plans are discussed on pp. 41–42.

the prohibited group may tend to receive proportionately greater
bonus payments than other employees. Thus, although the plan
benefit formula otherwise appears acceptable when applied to base
earnings, it could produce disproportionate benefits for key employees when applied to total earnings.

Determining the earnings of commission salesmen can be a difficult problem because of the variation in their total earnings from
year to year. Where the salesman is paid a basic salary plus commissions, some plans apply the benefit formula only to his basic
salary. This approach, however, often produces inequitable results
since the salesman's true compensation and worth to the employer
is reflected by his total earnings, and not by his basic salary.
Another frequently used solution is to consider a salesman's compensation in any year to be equal to the annual average of the total
compensation paid to him over the preceding three- or five-year
period. In plans where salesmen constitute a major portion of the
total employees covered, this problem often dictates the selection of
a defined contribution formula where the amount contributed each
year for each employee is a percentage of what he has actually
earned in that year. In any event, it is customary to exclude any
portion of the salesman's compensation which is allowed for expenses.

Another aspect of the problem of determining the earnings to be
used for the benefit formula is the question of whether plan benefits
should be based on the average of the employee's earnings over the
entire period of his participation in the plan or on an average of his
earnings during some shorter period of time which is near his
normal retirement age. The latter type of provision, often called a
"final-pay" provision, would base benefits on the employee's earnings averaged, for example, over the last five years of his employment or over the five-year period which ends five years before his
normal retirement date.

The advantage of a final-pay plan is that it relates an employee's
benefit to his earnings and standard of living during a period just
preceding his retirement. As a result, his benefits keep pace with
any inflationary or deflationary trends. This type of plan, however,
is usually more expensive than one which bases benefits on "career
average" earnings. It also could create funding problems under
certain funding instruments if additional benefits for an employee
must be paid for in the short time before he retires. Many employers feel that it is best to use a career average earnings plan and to
make periodic adjustments in the benefit formula when economic
trends justify such an action.

While a final-pay plan has the disadvantage of committing an employer to increased costs during an extended inflationary period, it should be remembered that in many situations the employer's capacity to absorb these increases will also be increased. Moreover, a final-pay plan will generally produce more favorable results for key employees than will the career average approach.

Defined Contribution Formulas

As previously noted, a defined contribution formula does not provide a fixed benefit for employees. Instead, the rate of contribution of the employer is fixed, usually as a percentage of the employee's earnings, and this contribution is applied (together with the employee's contribution under a contributory plan) to provide whatever pension benefits can be purchased. Since the cost of a given amount of benefit varies by age, sex, and normal retirement age, the benefits which any employee will receive depends upon these factors.

Defined contribution plans are often contributory. In this case, the employer's contribution either matches or is a multiple of the employee's contribution. For example, the plan could call for employer and employee each to contribute 5% of the employee's compensation; or the employee's contribution could be set at 3% of compensation with the employer contributing 6%. In fully insured individual policy plans, these contributions are usually applied as a level premium to purchase the amount of insurance available based on the employee's age, sex, and normal retirement age. If the plan utilizes a group deferred annuity contract, these contributions are applied each year to purchase a unit of paid-up deferred annuity for whatever amount can be provided under the insurer's rates, depending upon these same factors. In plans using other funding instruments, the contributions are usually accumulated and are applied at retirement, together with investment earnings, to provide such benefit as may then be available, depending upon the manner of payout contemplated by the plan.

The defined contribution formula has been employed primarily by nonprofit organizations where there is often a need, because of cost considerations, to be able to predict future plan liabilities with some degree of certainty. It has had little popularity otherwise, because of several inherent limitations. The first of these is that an employee who joins the plan at an older age will have only a short period of time in which to accumulate funds, with the result that his benefit will often be inadequate. Since the owners of a business are often advanced in years when a plan is being established, and since a defined benefit formula will generally produce more favorable results for them, it is not hard to see why they often find little appeal in a defined contribution formula. It is possible, of course, to include a past service benefit at the time the plan is established; on balance, however, most firms will still find a defined benefit formula to be more desirable from this point of view. Table 2–3 indicates the results which could flow under a defined contribution formula and the disparity in benefits that is often produced in such a plan. This table assumes that the compensation shown for each employee will continue until normal retirement; that the contribution made by the employer each year is 10% of the employee's compensation; that this contribution will accumulate at 4% compound interest until retirement; and that the fund accumulated at retirement will be applied under representative annuity purchase rates to provide a monthly retirement benefit.

TABLE 2–3

ILLUSTRATION OF DEFINED CONTRIBUTION FORMULA

Age at Entry	Sex	Normal Retirement Age	Compensation	Contribution	Fund at Retirement	Monthly Benefit	Benefit as a Percent of Compensation
25....F		65	$ 4,000	$ 400	$39,530.80	$229.28	68.8
30....M		65	6,000	600	45,958.80	316.20	63.2
40....M		65	10,000	1,000	43,312.00	297.99	35.8
45....M		65	6,500	650	20,129.85	138.49	25.6
45....F		65	6,500	650	20,129.85	116.75	21.6
53....M		65	20,000	2,000	31,254.00	215.03	12.9
55....M		65	6,000	600	7,491.60	51.54	10.3

As Table 2–3 shows, younger employees who have a much longer time to accumulate funds will receive a proportionately larger benefit. Moreover, the defined contribution plan has an additional weakness since, due to the effect of compound interest, greater weight is given to the employee's lower compensation at his younger age than will be given to the higher compensation he is likely to receive when he is older.

This table also indicates the difference in results due to the sex of the employee. The two employees shown in the table who are age 45 have identical compensation and thus have accumulated identically the same amount by retirement. However, the female employee will receive a smaller monthly benefit due to the fact that she is expected to live longer under the annuity table employed to determine benefits. While it is true that the benefits are equivalent in value, it is questionable, from a pension planning viewpoint, that there should be a difference in benefits due to the sex of the employee. It would seem reasonable that benefit levels should be the same, regardless of sex, and that cost differences due to this factor should be absorbed by the employer.

One final observation that should be made with respect to the deficiencies of a defined contribution formula is that with many types of funding instruments and actuarial cost methods, the employee's benefit under this formula can only be estimated. This lack of certainty as to benefits could prove to be an unsatisfactory employee relations feature of such a plan.

Union-negotiated plans, particularly multiemployer plans, possess characteristics of both defined contribution and defined benefit plans. In many of these situations, an employer's contribution to the plan is fixed, most frequently as a contribution of so many cents for each hour worked by each covered employee or as a percentage of compensation. An actuarial cost method, with appropriate actuarial assumptions, is then employed to make an estimate as to the benefit levels the aggregate employer contributions will provide. The plan is then established with a defined benefit formula, even though funds are received on a defined contribution basis. Only rarely will it turn out that the contribution level will precisely support the benefit level so determined, with the result that future contributions or benefits, or both, are periodically adjusted to conform with the actual experience of the plan.

Defined Benefit Formulas

Broadly speaking, there are four basic defined benefit formulas. These include: (1) a flat amount formula which provides a flat benefit unrelated to an employee's earnings or service; (2) a flat percentage of earnings formula which provides a benefit related to the employee's earnings but which does not reflect his service; (3) a flat amount per year of service formula which reflects an employee's service but not his earnings; and (4) a percentage of earnings per year of service formula which reflects both an employee's earnings and his service. Defined benefit formulas may also be integrated with Social Security benefits; however, since the requirements for integrated formulas are detailed and specific, they are discussed separately in this chapter.

Flat Amount Formula. As indicated above, this type of formula provides for a flat benefit which treats all employees alike, regardless of their service, age, or earnings. A typical benefit might be $50 or $75 a month. The flat amount formula, since it is considered to produce inequitable results, is seldom used by itself, although it is still found in many negotiated plans, particularly in the case of multiemployer plans. The likelihood of fairly comparable wage rates for all employees in the bargaining unit minimizes the potential problem of inequities produced by a flat amount formula. On occasion, this formula is used in conjunction with some other type of formula. For example, a plan may provide a flat benefit of $50 a month for a covered employee, plus a percentage of his earnings in excess of $400 a month.

While the employee's length of service is not reflected directly in this type of formula, service is in effect recognized since most plans require that an employee, by his normal retirement age, must have been employed for some period of time, such as 25 years. Plans which include such a requirement frequently provide for a proportionately reduced benefit if the employee has accumulated less than the required number of years, thus creating, in effect, a formula which is weighted for service.

Flat Percentage of Earnings Formula. This type of formula is used frequently today, particularly in plans which cover salaried or clerical employees. Some percentage of earnings, usually ranging from 20% to 40%, is selected as the measure of the pension benefit. It may be used with either career average or final average earnings, although it is used most frequently in final pay plans.

This type of formula does not take an employee's service into account, except in those plans which require that the employee must have completed a minimum period of service by his normal retirement date and which provide for a proportionately reduced benefit if his service is less than the required number of years.

An administrative device that can be used with many formulas, but which is frequently employed with the flat percentage of earnings formula, is the "earnings bracket" schedule. Instead of using actual earnings under the benefit formula, the benefit is determined by an earnings bracket approach and is expressed as a dollar amount per bracket of earnings. Table 2–4 shows a typical earnings bracket schedule. Actually, a 30% of earnings formula has been applied to the midpoint of each earnings bracket.

Flat Amount per Year of Service Formula. This type of formula is often found in negotiated plans. It provides a flat dollar amount for each year of service accumulated by the employee. The dollar amount varies from plan to plan, but a benefit of $2, $2.50 or even as much as $4.50 or $5 a month for each year of service is not uncommon. Thus, in a plan which provides for a benefit of $2 a month for each year of service, an employee with 27 years of employment would receive a monthly pension of $54.

This type of formula frequently requires that an employee must have worked for a minimum number of hours during a plan year in order to receive a full benefit credit for such year. A minimum often used for this purpose is 1,600 hours. If the employee works less than the required number of hours in a given year, he will usually receive some proportionate credit for the actual hours he has worked.

Some plans limit benefits to service performed after the plan was made effective, although in most cases credit is given for service prior to the inception of the plan. When this is done, credit may or may not be given for service needed to meet any eligibility requirements of the plan. Also, it is not uncommon to include a provision

TABLE 2–4

ILLUSTRATIVE EARNINGS BRACKET SCHEDULE

Earnings	Monthly Pension
$350–$383	$110
384– 416	120
417– 449	130
450– 483	140
484– 516	150

which limits the total service which may be credited for benefit purposes to a period such as 30 years.

Percentage of Earnings per Year of Service Formula. A formula which gives specific recognition for service as well as earnings is considered by many pension practitioners to produce the most equitable results in terms of a benefit formula that provides benefits for employees in relation to their value or contributions to the firm. A formula producing this result is often called a "unit credit" or "past and future service" formula. Under such a formula, an employee receives a benefit credit equal to a percentage of his earnings for each year that he is a participant under the plan. This benefit credit is called his "future service" or "current service" benefit. The percentage of earnings credited varies from plan to plan, but a typical percentage would be 1% or 1¼%. It may be used with either career average or final earnings, and works particularly well with career average plans.

Many plans also include a "past service" benefit for employees who enter the plan on its effective date. In a plan which bases future service benefits on career average earnings, the past service benefit is usually expressed as a fixed percentage of the employee's earnings on the effective date of the plan multiplied by his years of past service. In determining his past service, however, it is customary to exclude the service he would have been required to complete in order to join the plan had it always been in effect. It is also possible to limit the total years of past service credited. For example, past service could be limited to a given number of years (such as 10), to service completed after a certain calendar year (such as the year in which the firm was acquired by the current ownership interests), to service completed after attaining a certain age (such as 30), or to a combination of these factors. The percentage applied to earnings to determine past service benefits is usually a lower rate than is applied for future service benefits. The reason for this is that the earnings of an employee on the effective date of the plan are generally higher than the average of his earnings over his period of past service. Rather than determine his actual average earnings during his past service, which is often difficult or even impossible because of the lack of records, a rough approximation is made by reducing the percentage applicable to the employee's higher earnings at the time the plan is established.

If the plan bases benefits on final earnings, a distinction is usually not made between past and future service benefits. Here, the employee's total service (subject to any limitations such as excluding service needed to meet eligibility requirements or such as a maximum service credit provision) is applied to the percentage of final earnings to determine his total retirement benefit.

TABLE 2–5

PAST AND FUTURE SERVICE FORMULA

(1) Years of Total Past Service	(2) Years of Credited Past Service	(3) Monthly Earnings	(4) Past Service Benefit $(2) \times (3) \times \frac{1}{2}\%$	(5) Years of Future Service	(6) Future Service Benefit $(3) \times (5) \times 1\%$	(7) Total Benefit $(4) + (6)$
20	17	$600	$51	25	$150	$201

To illustrate the operation of a past and future service formula in a career average earnings plan, assume that the benefit formula of a plan provides a monthly pension of $\frac{1}{2}$ of 1% of a participant's earnings on the effective date of the plan multiplied by his years of past service, and a future service benefit of 1% of earnings during each year that he is a participant. The plan has an eligibility requirement of three years of service, and service needed to meet this requirement is excluded when determining the employee's total past service. Normal retirement under the plan will occur at 65. Table 2–5 shows how the monthly pension benefit would be calculated for a 40-year-old employee who joined the plan at its inception date and after he had completed 20 years of service. This table assumes, for illustrative purposes, that the employee's monthly earnings are $600 and that his earnings remain constant at this level during his period of future service.

A formula that weights both earnings and service is used in a great many plans today. However, if a firm is considering the adoption of a plan shortly after incorporation, and if the former partners or the former proprietor is advanced in years, this formula might produce inadequate results since the service of such an employee may be measured only from the date of incorporation. In this situation, a flat percentage of earnings formula is often adopted if it would produce more substantial benefits for the stockholder employees.

Variable Benefit Formulas. Variable benefit plans are a relatively recent development in the pension field. These plans are designed to protect against the effects of inflation on a retired employee's pension benefit. They take either of two general forms: (a) the benefit varies to reflect changes in the value of a specific portfolio of common stocks and similar investments, or (b) the benefit varies to reflect changes in a recognized cost-of-living index such as that published by the Bureau of Labor Statistics. In either case, the plan attempts to adjust a retired employee's benefit to keep his purchasing power on a relatively level basis.

Plans which relate an employee's benefit to the performance of common stocks, i.e., the so-called "variable annuity" plans (although the term "equity annuity" seems more appropriate), credit an employee with a number of shares or units in the total assets of the plan. Defined contribution plans usually credit an employee with a given number of shares or units depending upon the amount of the contribution and the value of a unit when the contribution is made. Defined benefit plans usually convert, at retirement, the dollar benefit then credited into shares or units, determined by the value of these shares or units on the employee's retirement date. As the value of these units increases or decreases because of investment performance, the employee's pension benefit increases or decreases, as the case may be. Adjustments in the value of units are made at least annually. The underlying theory of these plans is that there is a parallel between the cost of living and the performance of common stocks, although experience has shown that at any given time, there can be a marked deviation between changes in the cost-of-living index and changes in the common stock market. A number of insurance companies have entered this field during recent years, and many states have recently enacted legislation authorizing the sale of variable annuity contracts (at least in conjunction with qualified plans). However, there are still relatively few of these plans in existence, and it is still too early to measure the impact these plans will have on pension planning.

Plans which relate an employee's benefits to a cost-of-living index adjust an employee's benefit when the cost-of-living index varies by more than a specified percentage from the index level in effect when the employee retired or when the last adjustment in his pension was made, as the case may be. Unquestionably, a plan which adjusts benefits in relationship to a cost-of-living index is more responsive to changes in the employee's purchasing power than is a variable annuity plan. However, some difference of opinion exists regarding the question of whether a cost-of-living index is an accurate reflection of the expenditure pattern of retired employees. In any event, cost-of-living plans have not received the publicity or attention that variable annuity plans have attracted in recent years.

Integrated Formulas

For many individuals, retirement income will be derived from both Social Security benefits and private pension plans. Since the employer bears part of the cost of Social Security benefits, it is only logical that he might wish to recognize these benefits in the benefit formula of his plan. Thus, it is not uncommon for an employer to establish his retirement plan on a basis which excludes employees whose earnings are less than the Social Security taxable wage base. An alternative and more prevalent approach is to provide a greater level of benefits for earnings above this taxable wage base than are provided for earnings below this amount. While at first glance such a plan would appear to discriminate in favor of highly paid employees, federal tax law expressly permits this type of plan provided the benefit formula *integrates* with Social Security benefits. The basic concept of integration is that the benefits of the employer's plan must be dovetailed with Social Security benefits in such a manner that employees earning over the taxable wage base will not receive combined benefits under the two programs which are proportionately greater than the benefits for employees earning less than this amount. Therefore, although the benefit formula under the private plan may favor the higher-paid employees, the combined Social Security and private plan benefits must produce a total retirement income that is a relatively equal percentage of compensation for all employees. Thus, the integration requirements are designed to prevent discrimination in favor of the prohibited group of employees.[9]

These requirements take the form of establishing the maximum benefits which may be provided for employees under various circumstances. In arriving at these maximums, a value is placed on the employee's Social Security benefits. Essentially, these benefits are valued at 150% of the employee's maximum primary benefit of $127 in recognition of the spouse's benefit. Therefore, the employee's Social Security benefits are considered to be worth $190.50 This amount is 47⅝% of $400—the maximum monthly wage subject to Social Security tax. However, the integration rules reflect the fact that employees also pay a Social Security tax. While the tax rate is divided equally among employer and employees, it has been assumed that until the Social Security program matures, an employee will not, in fact, bear half of the cost of his benefit. For this reason, the employee is considered to have contributed approximately 22% of the cost of his Social Security benefits.[10] The 47⅝% figure, then, is reduced by 22%, with the result that Social Security benefits, after rounding, are considered to be 37½% of the maximum taxable wage base of $400. The employer could thus establish a plan which excludes all employees earning under $400 a month and which provides a monthly pension benefit of up to 37½% of earnings in excess of this amount. This percentage, however, applies only to a pure life annuity plan without death benefits. If the plan includes death benefits, either before or after retirement, this maximum percentage is reduced.

The following is by no means an exhaustive discussion of the integration requirements of federal tax law. It does, however, point out the major requirements for typical integrated formulas. It also assumes that normal retirement under the plan will not occur before 65 and that employees will not make contributions.[11]

---

[9] Final Regulations concerning the integration of plans at the $6,600 level had not been released at the time this material was prepared. As a result, the following discussion relates to plans integrated at the $4,800 level. Until such Regulations are released, the rules for $4,800 plans continue to apply to plans integrated at this level and, if it is desired to integrate a plan at the $6,600 level, it will be permissible to use 48/66 of the maximum percentages arrived at for a $4,800 plan.

[10] It should be noted that the President's Committee on Corporate Pension Funds has recommended that the integration requirements be changed to value an employee's contributions as providing one half of his Social Security benefits. President's Committee on Corporate Pension Funds, *op. cit.*, pp. 62–63.

[11] A decrease in the allowable benefit is required when normal retirement may occur before 65, and an increase in the allowable benefit is permitted when

Flat Percentage—Excess. In plans of this type, benefits are provided only on earnings in excess of $400 a month. In a plan which provides no death benefits before or after retirement (other than a return of employee contributions), the maximum percentage that can be provided on earnings in excess of $400 a month is 37½%. If the plan provides for a death benefit before retirement, but none after retirement, the maximum is 33⅓%. If the plan provides a death benefit before retirement and guarantees that the monthly pension benefit will be continued for at least 10 years (as is common in individual policy plans), the maximum is 30%. Variations in the allowable percentage are made for plans which provide for different levels of death benefits after retirement, but the foregoing should serve as a general guide.

In order for an employee to qualify for the maximum percentage, he must have completed at least 15 years of total service with the employer (not necessarily as a participant in the plan). For an employee with less than 15 years of service, a proportionate reduction in benefits must be made.

Flat Percentage—Stepped Up. If some benefits are being provided on the first $400 of earnings, the rate which can be credited on earnings in excess of $400 may be increased. For example, if the plan provides for no death benefit either before or after retirement, and provides a benefit of 10% of the first $400 of monthly earnings, the maximum percentage applicable to monthly earnings in excess of $400 would be 47½%. In effect, the percentage applicable to earnings under $400 a month is considered a base plan applicable to all earnings. Only the excess portion must integrate, and this portion must meet the requirements previously discussed. Thus, in the example cited, there would be a base plan of 10% of earnings, plus a supplemental plan of 37½% of earnings in excess of $400 a month, which is within the permissible limits.

The 15 years of service requirement for full benefits also applies to plans of this type.

Unit Credit—Excess. Determining the limit for a unit credit excess formula is largely a matter of dividing what the flat percentage limitation would be for an excess plan by the years of credited service. However, an important factor is whether the plan bases benefits on career average or final earnings.

In a career average plan, the divisor is always 30. Thus, in a career average plan which has no death benefit, either before or after retirement, the maximum percentage of earnings over $400

employees contribute. These points have not been covered, however, since few plans permit normal retirement before 65 and since the allowable increase for employee contributions, as it is relatively small, is rarely taken into account.

a month that may be credited for each year of service would be $1\frac{1}{4}\%$ ($37\frac{1}{2}\%$ divided by 30). If the plan includes a death benefit before retirement and the life annuity after retirement is guaranteed for at least 10 years, the maximum percentage on excess earnings would be 1% (30% divided by 30).

In a final-pay plan, the divisor is the maximum number of years of credited service, but need not be greater than 45. For example, if an employee could enter the plan at age 25 and if normal retirement were 65, there would be 40 years of possible service credit, which means that the divisor would have to be 40. If such a plan had no death benefit, either before or after retirement, the maximum percentage of earnings that could be credited for each year of service would be .9375% ($37\frac{1}{2}\%$ divided by 40). Also, an acceptable variation in a final-pay plan would be to limit credited service to 30 years. This would result in a divisor of 30 and would produce the percentage limitations applicable to a career average plan.

If the plan bases future service benefits on career average earnings after the effective date of the plan and past service benefits on earnings as of the effective date, the divisor for future service benefits is 30, and for past service benefits it is the maximum number of years of credited service, but this divisor for past service benefits cannot be less than 30 nor need it be greater than 45.

Unit Credit—Stepped Up. In plans of this type, one rate is credited on monthly earnings up to $400, with a higher rate being credited to earnings in excess of this amount. The technique here is the same as that described for a flat percentage—stepped-up formula in that the maximum percentage applicable to earnings in excess of $400 a month is determined by adding the maximum percentage permissible for an excess plan to the rate applicable to the first $400 of earnings. Thus, in a career average plan with no death benefits either before or after retirement, if the rate credited to the first $400 of monthly earnings is $\frac{1}{2}$ of 1%, the maximum rate that could be credited to monthly earnings in excess of $400 would be $1\frac{3}{4}\%$ ($\frac{1}{2}$ of 1% plus $1\frac{1}{4}\%$).

Social Security Offset. Many plans provide a retirement benefit inclusive of benefits payable under the Social Security Act. This type of formula deducts all or a part of the employee's primary Social Security benefit from the pension benefit which would otherwise be payable under the plan. In other words, any of the earlier described benefit formulas can be used, with Social Security benefits being deducted from the amount of benefit the formula would otherwise provide. Only the employee's primary insurance amount (i.e., exclusive of dependent's benefits) is taken into account for this purpose. The integration limit in these plans applies not to the percentage of compensation being credited, but to the percentage of the permissible Social Security offset. Table 2–6 indicates the maximum offset permissible, depending upon the form of the death benefit both before and after retirement.

The 15 years of service requirement for full benefits does not apply to Social Security offset formulas.

Defined Contribution Formulas. It is also possible to integrate defined contribution formulas with Social Security benefits. If no contribution is being made with respect to the first $400 of monthly earnings, the maximum percentage which may be contributed with

TABLE 2–6

SCHEDULE OF MAXIMUM SOCIAL SECURITY OFFSETS

Death Benefit before Retirement*	Normal Form for the Payment of Retirement Benefits	Maximum Offset†
None	Life annuity (no certain period)	117%
None	Life annuity, five years certain	113
None	Life annuity, 10 years certain	105
Yes	Life annuity (no certain period)	104
Yes	Life annuity, five years certain	100
Yes	Life annuity, 10 years certain	93

* In addition to a return of employee contributions.
† Rounded to the lowest whole number.

respect to monthly earnings in excess of $400 is 9⅜%. If a contribution is being made with respect to the first $400 of monthly earnings, the percentage applicable to earnings in excess of $400 a month may be increased by the amount of this contribution. Thus, for example, if the formula requires a contribution of 3% of the first $400 of monthly earnings, it would be permissible to contribute 12⅜% of earnings in excess of this amount. In plans of this type, no adjustment is made in the limit for the inclusion of death benefits, either before or after retirement, or for service of less than 15 years, etc. The reason, essentially, is that since the contribution is fixed, these features automatically affect the amount of the employee's retirement benefit.

Minimum and Maximum Benefits

Closely related to the choice of an adequate benefit formula is the question of whether or not provision for a minimum or a maximum pension, or both, should be included in the plan.

A minimum pension provision is generally a desirable feature for any pension plan. It is often possible for a benefit formula to produce a very small pension benefit as applied to certain employees. The use of a minimum pension can result in the payment of at least a minimum amount to these employees, while at the same time avoiding the embarassment and ill-will that might otherwise be generated in these situations. Apart from these considerations, if the plan is insured, the insurer may insist on the inclusion of a minimum pension provision as a part of its general underwriting requirements—particularly in the case of a plan funded with individual policies.

The minimum most frequently used is $20 a month and this, incidentally, is the highest permissible minimum in an integrated excess plan. However, many other plans establish a minimum in the vicinity of $25 or $30 a month.

The use of a maximum pension provision can be important in limiting the cost of a pension plan. In addition, in certain cases, it may be necessary to have a maximum provision so as to avoid discrimination in favor of the prohibited group of employees or to avoid the objections of stockholders. The general trend, however, appears to be away from the inclusion of a maximum pension provision.

When necessary or desirable to include a maximum pension provision, there are several ways in which this can be accomplished. Perhaps the most common method involves the use of a maximum dollar amount of pension, such as $1,000 a month. Another method would be to specify that earnings in excess of some stipulated amount, such as $20,000 a year, will not be considered for benefit purposes. A third method would be to limit the total years of credited service that may be counted for benefit purposes.

DEATH BENEFITS

A death benefit other than a return of employee contributions is an optional benefit under a pension plan; however, a great many plans include such a benefit. Broadly speaking, such a death benefit may take either of two forms—the first consists of life insurance which is provided under some form of individual policy or group life insurance contract issued by an insurer, and the second consists of a cash distribution from plan assets. Death benefits may also be classified as being payable in the event of death either before or after retirement.

Death benefits provided under individual policy plans and death benefits which are provided from plan assets are considered to be a part of the plan and, as such, are subject to the requirement of the Internal Revenue Service that the death benefit must be "incidental." In a defined benefit plan, the incidental test is satisfied if the benefit does not exceed 100 times the expected monthly pension benefit or, if greater, the reserve for the pension benefit. In a defined contribution plan which includes life insurance benefits, this test is satisfied if: (1) the aggregate of the premiums paid for a participant's life insurance is *less than* one half of the contributions allocated to him at any particular time; and (2) the plan requires the trustee to convert the entire value of the life insurance contract at or before retirement into cash or to provide periodic income so that no portion of such value may be used to continue life insurance protection beyond retirement or to distribute the contract to the participant.

While it is possible to have a group term life insurance contract issued to the trustee of a pension trust and thereby make it a part of the plan, the customary procedure is to issue the contract directly to the employer. When this is done, the death benefit under the group term life insurance contract is not considered to be a part of the plan for federal tax purposes, even though the benefit might have been initiated concurrently with the pension plan and even though the amount of the benefit is provided only for participants in the plan or is in some way related to the amount of their pension benefits.

Death Benefits before Retirement. In fully insured individual policy plans (i.e., plans which employ retirement income or annuity contracts), the death benefit under the plan is generally expressed in terms of the contract benefits. The standard death benefit under a retirement income contract is an amount equal to 100 times the expected pension it will provide or the reserve for the latter benefit, if greater. If the employee is insurable only on an extra-premium basis, the plan may provide for his receiving the full benefit and for the employer to pay any additional premium involved. The most common practice, however, is to give the employee the option of paying the additional premium if he wants the full benefit; his benefit otherwise is provided by a retirement annuity contract or, if available from the insurer, by a graded or graduated death benefit contract under which the life insurance benefit is reduced to reflect the degree of the employee's impairment.

If retirement annuity contracts are employed, either for the plan as a whole or for individuals who are uninsurable or insurable only on an extra-premium basis, the death benefit is equal to the premiums paid for the coverage or the cash value of the contract, whichever is greater.

In individual policy combination plans (i.e., plans which employ some form of whole life insurance and a conversion fund), the death benefit is usually the same as would be applicable in an individual policy fully insured plan—100 times the employee's expected monthly pension. However, it is possible to develop a schedule of death benefits under such a plan which is related to the earnings of an employee (similar to the schedules frequently employed in group term life insurance contracts), provided the requirements of the "incidental" test of the Internal Revenue Service are met.

Plans funded with group permanent coverages generally provide the same level of death benefits as are provided in comparable individual policy plans.

In plans funded with group pension contracts or in trust fund plans, the death benefit is frequently provided by means of a group term life insurance contract issued to the employer. Subject to any limitations imposed by state law as to group term life insurance, the schedule of death benefits under such a contract can be anything the employer wishes (and the insurer is willing to underwrite), although the schedules most frequently employed relate the death benefit to the employee's current earnings. Typically, the benefit will be equal to the employee's annual earnings (often rounded to the nearer $500) or it might be an amount such as one and one-half or two times the employee's annual earnings.

Group pension and trust fund plans also provide for a return of an employee's contributions, usually accrued at some rate of interest, in the event of his death prior to retirement. On occasion, there is also provision for paying some cash death benefit out of employer contributions. However, such a benefit, when it is provided, is usually limited in amount. If a cash death benefit is provided from employer contributions, it should be correlated with the severance-of-employment benefits of the plan so as to provide consistency in the form and amount of the two benefits.

There has been increasing interest in the inclusion of "widow's benefits" in group pension and trust fund plans. One reason for this interest is that the benefit is restricted to the widow only, and the employer is not paying for an "across-the-board" benefit which might ultimately be paid to the employee's estate or to individuals in whom the employer has little or no interest and to whom, as a result, the employer feels little or no obligation.

A widow's benefit usually takes the form of a life annuity payable to the widow of an employee who dies after having met certain minimum requirements. The amount of the benefit may be that amount which can be provided by a part of the reserve accumulated for the employee's pension benefit at the time of his death, depending upon the age of the widow at that time or, as is more commonly the case, the amount may be all or a percentage of the pension credits accrued by the employee at the time of his death. Usually, there is a requirement that the employee must have attained some minimum age, such as 50 or 55, and must have completed some minimum period of service or participation in the plan, such as 10 years, before the widow will be entitled to receive such a benefit.

While interest in widow's benefits has been increasing in recent years, it is still a relatively rare form of benefit in this country. The social problems involved in this type of benefit may be one reason for its slow growth.[12] The employer, for example, is providing a benefit for the widow of a male employee, but what of the widower of a long-term female employee—particularly if the widower has been totally and permanently disabled and is dependent upon his wife's income for support? And what of the widower or unmarried employee, male or female, who has accumulated a long period of service with the employer and who has a dependent child or parent to support? Some employers feel that a pure widow's benefit produces inequitable results in situations such as these.

Other social aspects to the problem of including a widow's benefit concern the eligibility of the widow to receive benefits. Should there be a provision requiring that the marriage must have been in effect for a minimum period of years before the widow will be eligible to receive the benefit? Should the benefit be paid if there has been a final decree of divorce before death? What if divorce proceedings have been instituted but have not yet been finalized when death occurs? While situations involving divorce might seem to indicate definite answers, legal separations present a slightly different problem. Thus, should the benefit be paid if the employee and his wife were legally separated? And, what if the employee and his wife were simply living apart without benefit of any legal proceeding? A further question for the employer to consider is whether the benefit should be terminated if the widow remarries.

These questions, of course, do not present insurmountable problems. However, a conscientious employer will want to give them serious consideration before adopting a widow's benefit for his pension plan.

---

[12] There is a further problem in that a widow's benefit may be in violation of the Fair Labor Standards Act or the Federal Fair Employment Practices law. The Wage-Hour Administrator has already ruled that when benefits are furnished for employees, either the benefits or the cost of providing the benefits must be equal for male and female employees, and that a plan providing family hospital insurance for male employees and individual hospital insurance for female employees would be in violation of the Fair Labor Standards Act. Letter signed by Clarence T. Lundquist, Administrator, Wage and Hour and Public Contracts Divisions, U.S. Department of Labor, dated October 14, 1965, *Pension and Profit Sharing Tax Service* (Englewood Cliffs, N.J.: Prentice-Hall, Inc., n.d.), ¶ 12,054.

Death Benefits after Retirement. The death benefit payable in the event of death after retirement generally depends upon the type of annuity normally used for the payment of retirement benefits. Most plans funded with individual policies or group permanent coverage typically provide that the monthly payments will be paid for life with a guaranteed certain period of 5 or 10 years. Thus, if the retired employee dies within this period, the value of the guaranteed payments will be paid to his beneficiary. It is possible, of course, to arrange an individual policy or group permanent plan so that the provision for the payment of retirement benefits is a pure life annuity, with no benefits paid in the event of death after retirement. This practice, however, is relatively uncommon.

Most group pension and trust fund plans provide that retirement benefits are payable on a pure life annuity basis with no death benefit payable in the event of death after retirement. If employees have contributed, however, the normal form is usually the so-called "modified cash refund annuity" under which a death benefit is provided if the employee dies before having received total payments which equal his own contributions (usually with interest at some rate credited up to the time of his retirement). The death benefit is the amount by which his contributions (with interest) exceed the total payments he has received. Group pension and trust fund plans, of course, may be established on a basis which includes some other type of death benefit under the normal form for the payment of retirement benefits.

Apart from the death benefit included in the normal form, it is also possible to provide some amount of death benefit under various optional forms of payment which are generally made available to a retired employee. If the employee creates or increases his death benefit by making such an election, he will, of course, reduce his retirement benefit. The reason is that in total, the value of the retirement and death benefits under the optional form of payment should be equal to the value of these benefits under the normal form. The most common optional form of payment is the joint and survivor option under which the employee may arrange to have all or a portion of his retirement benefit continued after his death to his wife or some other person.

DISABILITY BENEFITS

While most employers recognize the possibility of short-term disabilities and usually provide a reasonable level of benefits for this contingency through their wage continuation plans, such is not generally the case in the area of total and permanent disabilities. With the increased availability of insured long-term disability programs, however, more employers are seeking to provide benefits in the event of total and permanent disability via this device, and on a basis which is completely apart from any benefits available under the employer's pension plan.

In the pension area, disability benefits, even in insured plans, have generally been provided on a self-insured basis—i.e., the benefits are paid in some form directly from plan assets, and the employer's experience in this regard is immediately reflected in the cost level of the plan.

A number of pension plans, particularly those funded with individual policies, provide for full vesting if an employee becomes totally and permanently disabled. Other plans treat such a disability as an early retirement if the employee has completed some minimum period of service or participation in the plan and has attained some minimum age. Unfortunately, the disability benefits provided under such provisions either are nonexistent or inadequate for disabilities occurring at younger ages.

Some group pension and trust fund plans, however, and particularly those which have been union negotiated, provide for a separate and distinct benefit in the event of total and permanent disability. The benefit provided under such plans is sometimes a specified dollar amount, a specified percentage of earnings, or an amount equal to the employee's accrued pension credits (with or without actuarial reduction). Often, the disability benefit under the plan is integrated with benefits available under government plans such as Workmen's Compensation or Social Security benefits. Frequently, the plan provides that the disability benefit will terminate when the employee reaches his normal retirement age, at which time his accrued normal pension benefit will be payable.

Even in these plans, however, it is common to require that the employee must have attained some minimum age (such as 50) and/or must have completed some minimum period of service or participation (such as 10 years) if he is to qualify for the plan disability benefit. For this reason, most pension plans, including those which provide a separate disability benefit, fail to provide adequate benefits for employees becoming disabled at younger ages —yet, a total and permanent disability at a young age could be far more disastrous from a financial point of view than one occuring at a later age when family financial burdens may have somewhat lessened.

From an insurer's point of view, it is not desirable to offer an insured long-term disability program in connection with a pension plan that limits disability benefits to those employees who have attained some minimum age such as 50 and who have completed some minimum service or participation requirement. The insurer's underwriting risk is much more acceptable if younger employees are included in an across-the-board program. Since, from an insurer's viewpoint, it is desirable to include a greater cross section of employees, and from the point of view of the adequacy of benefits this would be desirable, the solution to the problem of providing adequate total and permanent disability benefits would seem to lie in the direction of broader insured programs independent of the employer's pension plan.

SEVERANCE OF EMPLOYMENT BENEFITS

The rights of an employee to the benefits attributable to his employer's contributions under a pension plan in the event of his termination of employment prior to retirement has been a subject of considerable discussion in recent years. Vesting has been defined as "the attainment by a participant of a benefit right, attributable to employer contributions, that is not contingent upon a participant's continuation in specified employment."[13] This definition concerns itself only with the employee's rights with regard to his employer's contributions since, for all practical purposes, most plans provide that a terminating employee will be entitled to a return of his own contributions (with or without a specified rate of interest) or to benefits attributable to his own contributions.

The Internal Revenue Code does not specifically require vesting as a condition for favorable tax qualification of a pension plan.[14] Notwithstanding, there has been a noticeable trend in recent years for the Internal Revenue Service to require some degree of vesting if a plan is to qualify, particularly in the case of plans for smaller employers. Further evidence of this current attitude of the federal government with regard to vesting is found in the January, 1965, report of the President's Committee on Corporate Pension Funds. This Committee observed that vesting is necessary if private pension plans are to serve the broad social purpose which justifies their favored tax status. The broad recommendation of this Committee was that the Internal Revenue Code be amended to require that a qualified plan must provide some reasonable measure of vesting for employees. The report indicated that the vesting requirement might take the form of graded deferred vesting and, as an example, suggested that at least one half of the employee's accrued benefit be

---

[13] *Bulletin of the Commission on Insurance Terminology of the American Risk and Insurance Association*, Vol. I, No. 4.

[14] The Service, however, will generally require vesting, and at a fairly rapid rate, in connection with qualified profit sharing plans. See pp. 295–296.

vested after 15 years of service, with full vesting after 20 years of service. The report specifically observed that no minimum age requirement should be included for eligibility for the vesting of benefits.

The reasons for including vesting in a pension plan are summarized in the Committee's report, part of which reads as follows:

Briefly stated, the advantages which vesting brings to the private pension system are the following:

As a matter of equity and fair treatment, an employee covered by a pension plan is entitled, after a reasonable period of service, to protection of his future retirement benefit against any termination of his employment. Vesting validates the accepted concept that employer contributions to pension plans represent "deferred compensation," which the individual worker earns through service with his employer.

Without vesting, a worker displaced after long years of service is denied all of his accrued pension protection. A worker in a similar position who voluntarily changes his employment has to forfeit his right to a future pension. Both circumstances are charged with inequity.

Vesting also provides special advantages to the employer. The adoption of vesting by two-thirds of all plans indicates that employers, as well as employees, recognize the value of vesting. For employers, vesting provides added flexibility to management's task of meeting manpower requirements and removes a possible source of employee discontent arising from the operation of the pension plan.

By making private pension benefits more widely available, vesting strengthens the Nation's entire program for retirement protection. Without vesting, the employer's contributions under a pension plan go only to those employees remaining in his employ until retirement age. With vesting, the employer's contributions are made available to a higher proportion of his work force. By bringing pension benefits to additional workers with a rightful claim to benefits, vesting strengthens the private pension system and the security function it is expected to perform.

Vesting enhances the mobility of the work force. The effective functioning of the Nation's labor market system rests on the individual worker's freedom to change jobs to parts of the economy where his services can be better utilized. In an earlier section, the Committee concluded that while the effect of private pensions on mobility is significant, it is limited and selective. Although the lack of vesting in private pension plans may not currently constitute a major impediment to labor mobility, it clearly is a deterrent to mobility for important segments of the labor force including highly skilled professional, technical, other white collar, and some manual workers. Moreover, such a deterrent to mobility may well become more serious in the future as technological progress continues and as participants in relatively new pension plans acquire a greater stake in the plans' benefits.[15]

---

[15] President's Committee on Corporate Pension Funds, *op. cit.,* pp. 39–40.

These arguments are persuasive, but are rather broad in scope. The employer, of necessity, must view the question of whether or not his plan should include severance-of-employment benefits from a much narrower point of view. He must take into account the fact that the inclusion of this type of benefit in his plan will ultimately result in higher plan costs—not only because of the benefit itself but also because of the added administrative burdens and expenses such a benefit entails. And, while mobility of labor is desirable from the viewpoint of our national economy, the employer's specific interests are generally better served by a plan provision which encourages employees to remain with his firm.

On balance, it seems desirable that a pension plan should include some measure of vesting for terminated employees, and current trends indicate that vesting provisions are becoming more prevalent. Certainly, the current attitude of the federal government will influence this aspect of pension plans to a great extent in the foreseeable future.[16]

If vesting is to be included in a plan, there are two basic questions involved. The first of these is how much of a benefit will be provided, and the second is in what manner will the benefit be made available to the terminated employee.

As to the first question, a plan might provide for full and immediate vesting so that an employee, upon termination of employment at any time, is entitled to all benefits which have then accrued on his behalf. Or the plan might provide that the employee has no rights until he has attained some minimum age and/or has completed some minimum period of service or participation, at which time his accrued benefits would become fully vested. A common provision is the graded vesting schedule which provides that an employee is entitled to an increasing proportion of his accrued benefits as his length of service or plan participation increases. (On occasion, a graded vesting schedule also reflects the employee's increasing age.) For example, a graded vesting schedule might provide for no vesting during the first three years of participation; 30% vesting after the completion of three full years of participation, increasing by 10% for each full year of participation thereafter, so that 100% vesting is achieved after the employee has been a participant for 10 full years.

Apart from the general level of vested benefits, many plans include a feature which provides that an employee automatically

---

[16] For a detailed discussion of the considerations involved in the desirability or necessity of including vesting in private pension plans, see Joseph J. Melone, "Implications of Vested Benefits in Private Pension Plans," *Journal of Risk and Insurance*, Vol. XXXII, No. 4 (December, 1965), pp. 559–69.

forfeits his rights to any employer contributions if his employment is terminated due to an act of fraud, dishonesty, etc.

As to the second question, the vested benefit is generally made available either in the form of a cash payment (or its equivalent) or as a deferred benefit. To some extent, the form of the vested benefit is influenced by the funding instrument employed to provide plan benefits. In plans that utilize individual policies, the form of vesting is usually cash or its equivalent as an insurance or annuity contract which may be surrendered for cash.[17] In group pension and trust fund plans, the benefit is frequently available only in the form of a deferred benefit, commencing at the employee's normal retirement date. Also, group pension or trust fund plans commonly provide that if an employee has contributed, he will be entitled to vesting of his employer's contributions in the form of a deferred benefit only if he leaves his own contributions in the plan. Under such a provision, if the employee withdraws his own contributions he automatically forfeits any interest he might otherwise have had in the amounts contributed by his employer.

EMPLOYEE CONTRIBUTIONS

A major question that the employer must resolve is whether or not employees will be required to make contributions toward the cost of plan benefits. Sound arguments may be presented for both contributory and noncontributory plans, although the ability of the employer or employees to pay is often the controlling factor.

Arguments advanced in favor of contributory plans include the following:

1. If employees contribute, it will mean a smaller employer contribution to provide the same overall plan benefits.
2. If the employer does not want to use employee contributions to reduce his own contribution, then by making the plan contributory, the overall plan benefits will be larger.
3. Something for nothing is too often taken for granted, and the deductions from current earnings will continually remind employees that the employer is assuming a large share of providing the plan benefits. (It would seem that this argument could be minimized by an effective method of repeatedly publicizing the plan and its value to employees.)
4. Employees are encouraged to save and, in the process, to solve a portion of their own retirement problems. The contributory plan

---

[17] The contract distributed, however, may be endorsed in such a manner that the employee need not consider its cash value as currently taxable income. See pp. 146–47.

also provides an employee with additional funds if he should terminate employment.

The proponents of a noncontributory plan hold that the contributory plan has the following disadvantages:

1. Employer contributions represent dollars which have not been taxed. On the other hand, dollars received by the employee as earnings which are then contributed under the plan are dollars which have been taxed to the employee. Hence, dollar for dollar, employer contributions will provide more than those of an employee.
2. Many deductions from earnings are a source of constant irritation to employees.
3. The employer might be forced to increase salaries in order to compensate for the additional deductions.
4. The number of participants required for a qualified plan (or required by the insurer under certain funding instruments) might not enroll.
5. Some employees may refuse to participate, in which case the employer will still have a problem on his hands when these employees reach retirement age.
6. Additional records must be kept by the employer, thereby increasing administrative work and costs.
7. If employees contribute, the portion of any death benefit attributable to these contributions will be included in the employee's gross estate for federal estate tax purposes.

If the employer decides that employees should make contributions, his next decision will be the amount which employees should contribute. While employee contributions may be related to the cost of benefits, it is generally much more satisfactory to relate these contributions to earnings. In this way, an employee's contributions are geared to his ability to make them. Furthermore, in most plans it is impossible to predict exactly what the cost of an employee's pension will be until he actually retires. Hence, any contributions which are made by him and related to cost are necessarily estimated and do not have an exact relationship.

Employee contribution rates of 2%, 3%, or even 4% of earnings are commonly used. If the plan is to qualify, however, the contribution rate should not exceed 6%. If the plan employs a formula integrated with Social Security benefits, the contribution rate should reflect the different level of benefits as to earnings under and over the Social Security taxable wage base. For example, if the benefit formula provides a 1% future service benefit with respect to earnings under $400 a month and a 2% benefit on earnings in excess of this amount, the corresponding employee contributions could be 2% and 4%.

Contributory plans usually require that an employee, before he may become a participant, must sign a request for participation under which he agrees to make the required contributions and authorizes the employer to withhold his contributions from earnings. If an employee fails to make such an election when first eligible, it is customary to impose some form of penalty. In plans using a unit credit formula, for example, the employee might forfeit his past service benefits as well as the future service benefits that otherwise would have accrued until such time as he joins the plan. If the plan employs a flat percentage of earnings formula, the benefits for a late entrant might be reduced by multiplying the benefit he would otherwise have received by a fraction, the numerator being the years he will have contributed and the denominator the number of years he could have contributed. A few plans are even more severe and provide that if an employee does not join when first eligible, he forfeits for all time his right to participate. Another approach used by some employers is to give employees the option of participating if they are employed when the plan becomes effective, but to require participation as a condition of employment for all future employees.

Another provision to be considered in contributory plans is the right of an employee to suspend or discontinue contributions. Many plans do not give an employee either of these privileges. Others will permit a temporary suspension (for a year or so) without affecting benefits, and some will permit a complete discontinuance at any time. Still others permit only a complete discontinuance. If discontinuance of contributions is permitted, there are further questions such as whether the employee will be permitted to rejoin the plan and, if so, what benefits he will then be entitled to receive. There is also the question of whether a discontinuing employee should be treated in the same manner as a terminating employee or whether his accrued credits should be held under the plan subject to application of the plan's termination-of-employment provisions in the event he subsequently terminates employment.

Regardless of whether or not the plan requires employees to make contributions, it may permit an employee to make voluntary contributions (or additional contributions under a contributory plan) to supplement his benefits. Generally, such a provision will be acceptable to the Internal Revenue Service provided that the voluntary additional contributions do not exceed 10% of earnings. The advantage of such a provision is that the employee will not be required to include the interest earnings on his accumulated contributions as income subject to tax until these earnings are distributed or made available to him. Even then, the favorable tax treatment accorded to distributions from a qualified plan will apply to the earnings on these additional contributions. When employees are permitted to make additional contributions, the plan should also contain provisions concerning the amounts which employees may contribute on this basis, how often (if at all) the rate of contribution may be changed by the employee, the conditions under which these contributions may be withdrawn,[18] whether or not employees may suspend or discontinue these additional contributions, and if so, the effect of a suspension or discontinuance, etc.

GENERAL PLAN PROVISIONS

The preceding portion of this chapter has dealt with the major plan provisions that an employer must consider when establishing a pension plan. There are, of course, a number of other provisions that are a part of any plan and that relate generally to the rights and duties of the interested parties and to the administrative aspects of the program. The following discusses, very briefly, the most significant of these general provisions.

Employer's Right to Amend or Terminate the Plan

While a pension plan is established on an indefinite and presumably permanent basis, an essential plan provision is one which gives the employer the unilateral right to amend or terminate the program at any time. As will be seen, however, the rights reserved to the employer under such a clause are limited to some extent by federal tax law.

The right-to-amend clause is usually straightforward and reserves the right to the employer to make plan amendments without the consent of employees or their beneficiaries. However, if a plan is to maintain its qualified status, an amendment may not reduce benefits related to contributions made prior to the amendment, deprive any employee of his then accrued vested interest, nor permit the employer to recover any funds previously contributed to the plan. Thus, the amendment clause normally restricts the employer's rights to this extent unless the amendment itself is required to make the plan conform to federal or state laws.

The typical right-to-terminate clause gives the employer the uni-

---

[18] If an employee is permitted to withdraw his contributions prior to his severance of employment, he cannot receive the earnings that have accumulated on these amounts. Rev. Rul. 60–323, IRB 1960–41.

lateral right to terminate the plan (or to discontinue contributions) for any reason and at any time. However, for a plan to achieve a qualified status under federal tax law, it must be permanent and, while the Internal Revenue Service will approve a plan with such a termination provision, restrictions are imposed on the employer's right to terminate the program. Thus, if an employer terminates the plan for reasons other than "business necessity" within a few years from its inception, the plan may lose its qualified status for all prior open tax years since this action will be considered by the Service as evidence that the plan, from its inception, was not a bona fide program for the exclusive benefit of employees in general. If business necessity exists, the employer may terminate the plan without adverse tax consequences. Valid reasons for a plan termination include financial incapacity, bankruptcy, insolvency, change of ownership, etc.

The termination-of-plan clause must make provision for the distribution of plan assets if the plan is terminated or contributions are discontinued. Since federal tax law prohibits the return of any funds to the employer on plan termination (other than excess amounts remaining due to "actuarial error" after satisfaction of all plan liabilities), the plan assets must be applied for the benefit of the employees or their beneficiaries. In a fully insured individual policy plan or in a deferred group annuity contract, the procedure on plan termination is relatively simple. Each employee will become entitled to the benefits of the contract in force on his life or under the annuities already purchased on his behalf. In an individual policy combination plan, employees will receive the benefits of their contracts, and the conversion fund will be allocated among them in some equitable fashion. While it is possible to allocate the conversion fund in some order of priorities, most individual policy combination plans are written to allocate this fund among all employees on some proportionate basis—for example, each employee's share of the conversion fund will bear the same ratio to the total fund that the cash value of his contract bears to the total cash values of all contracts held for all employees.

If the plan employs an unallocated funding instrument (as would be the case with a group deposit administration contract or in a trust fund plan), plan assets are usually allocated among employees on the basis of an order of priorities. The first class of priorities would be employee contributions. Thus, there would first be withdrawn from the plan assets an amount equal to the employee contributions (usually with some stipulated rate of interest). Any remaining plan assets would then be applied, in the order of priorities established, to provide accrued benefits for employees in each class of priorities, the benefits of each class being satisfied before proceeding to the next class. If, at any time, the remaining plan assets would be insufficient to provide the accrued benefits for the class in question, the remaining assets would be applied on a pro rata basis within that class, and all subsequent classes would receive no benefit. After providing for employee contributions, the classes of priorities might be as follows: (1) retired employees; (2) employees on a late retirement status; (3) employees receiving disability benefits; (4) employees eligible for early retirement; (5) employees who would have a vested interest if they were to terminate employment on the date of plan termination and former employees who have a vested interest; and (6) all other employees. The allocation of plan assets in a priority order, however, should not result in discrimination in favor of the prohibited group of employees.

In any event, there must be a provision which limits the benefits payable to certain employees in the event of plan termination. The employees affected are the 25 highest paid employees of the employer at the inception of the plan, whose individual annual retirement benefit from employer contributions will exceed $1,500. An employee could be within this group even though he was not a participant when the plan was established. This limitation on benefits applies if the plan is terminated within 10 years after its effective date. (It will also apply to any benefits that become payable with respect to this group during the first 10 plan years even though the plan has not been terminated if, when the distribution is made, the "full current costs" of the plan have not been met. If, at the end of the 10-year period, full current costs have not been met, the 10-year period is extended until such time as full current costs have been met.) Essentially, the limitation is that the benefits payable to any such employee or his beneficiary cannot exceed those purchasable by the greater of: (a) $20,000; or (b) 20% of the employee's annual compensation up to $50,000 multiplied by the number of years since the effective date of the plan. If any employee is affected by this limitation, the value of his excess benefit will be distributed ratably among remaining employees who are not affected by the limitation.

Exculpatory Provisions

The trustee, if a trust is involved, and the insurer, in an insured plan, will want to have provisions which protect them in their relationships with the employer, the employees and their beneficiaries, and with each other. These provisions set forth the rights of the insurer and trustee as well as the limits of their responsibilities and liabilities. The following exculpatory clause for an insurer was taken from a typical individual policy combination plan.

The insurer shall not be deemed to be a party to this agreement for any purpose nor to be responsible for the validity of this agreement; nor shall it be required to look into the terms of this agreement; nor to question any action of the trustees hereunder; nor shall it be responsible to see that any action of the employer or the trustees is authorized by this agreement. The obligations of the insurer shall be measured and determined solely by the terms of its contracts and of any other written agreements entered into by the insurer with the trustees. The insurer shall act only upon the written direction of the trustees, and shall be fully discharged from any and all liability for any amount paid to the trustees or paid in accordance with the direction of the trustees or for any change made or action taken upon such direction; and the insurer shall not be obligated to see that any money paid by it to the trustees or to any other person shall be properly distributed or applied.

Miscellaneous Provisions

The plan must also contain a number of provisions relating to the broad administration of the program, many of these provisions being dictated by the funding instrument employed to provide benefits. The following, while by no means all-inclusive, indicates some of the provisions which must be considered.

Beneficiary Provisions. If the plan contains a death benefit, there must be a provision with regard to the employee's right to name and change his beneficiaries. The provision should also cover such matters as the form which any such designation or change should take; when and under what conditions it will become effective; the rights and duties of the interested parties if payment has been made (or has commenced) before a change has been properly recorded; the distribution of the proceeds in the event the employee dies without having made a beneficiary designation, etc.

Facility of Payment. A related provision is one which permits the trustee or insurer to distribute proceeds to certain individuals if the employee or his beneficiary is in any way incompetent to receive the proceeds.

Trustee Provisions. If a trust is involved, there are several points concerning the trustee which should be covered. For example, there should be a provision covering the details of the resignation or removal of the trustee and the manner in which a successor trustee will be appointed. There should also be a provision authorizing payment of the trustee's expenses and, if applicable, payment of the trustee's fee. The powers and duties of the trustee in connection with the plan should be covered, with special emphasis on his investment authority. If more than one trustee is involved, there should be a provision indicating whether the trustees are required to act unanimously or whether majority action will suffice. If the trustees are to have the right to delegate authority to one or more of their number to sign documents and perform ministerial duties, a provision to this effect should be included.

Small Benefits. Many plans include a provision which permits payment of the employee's retirement benefit in a lump sum if it is less than a certain amount, such as $40 a year. Obviously, the payment of small amounts on a periodic basis is of little value to the retired employee, and the administrative problems involved in maintaining the necessary records and making the small payments could be significant. Thus, payment of the benefit in a lump sum is generally desirable for all concerned.

Leaves of Absence. A well-designed plan should have a provision dealing with the possiblitiy of an employee going on leave of absence and the effect this might have on his benefits. A typical provision would protect an employee's rights while he is on military leave (normally for the period of time his employment rights are protected by law) or while on any other authorized leave for a period not exceeding one or two years. The plan should indicate whether or not time spent on such a leave will be considered as credited service for purposes such as eligibility, retirement benefits, and vested rights on termination of employment. If such time is to be considered as credited service, however, and if the employee fails to return to work within the time allowed, he is usually considered as having terminated employment when the leave began. Also, if such credit is given and if the plan is contributory, there is need for a further provision with regard to any employee contributions that might otherwise have been due during the leave of absence. If, under the funding instrument involved, the employer advances the employee's contribution during the leave, there is usually a feature which allows the employer to recover this amount if the employee fails to return to work within the time allowed.

Governing Law. Most plans include a provision stating that the plan and its provisions will be construed in accordance with the laws of a specific state.

Spendthrift Provision. Almost all plans provide that to the extent permitted by law, benefits are not subject to alienation, assignment, pledge, or encumbrance by the employee or his beneficiary, and that these benefits are exempt from the claims of creditors.

Limitation of Employee's Rights.   A desirable provision in any plan is one which stipulates that the existence of the plan and the employee's participation do not give the employee any right to be retained in the employ of the employer, nor any legal or equitable rights against the employer.

FUNDING CONSIDERATIONS

Pension plan benefits may be funded or they can be financed on a current disbursement basis. The purpose of this chapter is to consider some of the important implications of each of the alternative approaches. Although the terms "funding" and "financing" are normally associated with the notion of contribution payments, it might be best to start this discussion with a brief consideration of the benefit payout pattern under a typical plan.

A pension plan, in its simplest form, is a promise by the employer to pay a periodic benefit (usually for life) to employees who meet the requirements set forth in the plan. For a given pension benefit, the amount of annual benefit payments under the plan depends upon the number of retired workers. The number of retired workers, in turn, depends upon the rate at which already retired workers die and the rate at which new employees are added to the retirement rolls. Since the average life expectancy for a 65-year-old male is about 15 years, it is obvious that for some time after the plan is established, more new members are added to the retired employee group than are removed from the group as a result of death. Therefore, under a typical plan, the aggregate annual benefit payout should increase for a substantial number of years after the inception of the plan. The annual benefit payout continues to increase until a point is reached where the size of the retired employee group tends to stabilize, that is, the point at which the number of retired workers dying is about equal to the number of new additions to the retired group.

Based on the above analysis, the amount of annual *benefit payments* under a plan might resemble the pattern shown in Chart 3-1. Thus, if the employer has made no prior financial provision to meet the periodic benefits promised under the plan, his annual pension outlay will usually follow the benefit payout pattern indicated in this chart. This approach is referred to as the current disbursement method of financing a pension plan. The employer has an alternative to current disbursement financing in that he can fund the benefits promised under the pension plan. If the employer chooses to fund the plan, the pattern of his annual contributions under the plan will differ from the benefit payout pattern indicated in Chart 3–1. However, it should be noted that the benefit payout

CHART 3–1

ANNUAL BENEFIT PAYOUT PATTERN
UNDER A TYPICAL PENSION PLAN

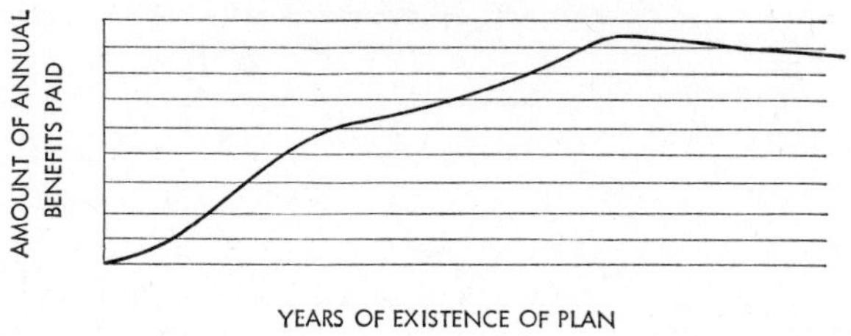

AMOUNT OF ANNUAL BENEFITS PAID

YEARS OF EXISTENCE OF PLAN

pattern is not altered by the choice of financing method. As indicated earlier, the benefit payout pattern for a given level of pension benefit is dependent on the number of retired workers eligible for benefits during each year and will be the same regardless of the manner in which contributions are made. The choice of financing method does, however, affect the amount and timing of annual contributions to the plan.

There are factors, other than the timing of pension contributions, that also must be considered in the choice of a particular financing approach. With the above as background, let us now turn to a more detailed consideration of the pros and cons of the alternative approaches to financing a pension plan.

CURRENT DISBURSEMENT APPROACH

Nature of Approach

Under the current disbursement approach, the employer pays each retired worker his monthly pension as each payment becomes due. There is no accumulation of pension funds in an irrevocable trust or through a contract with an insurance company. Of course, the employer may estimate the pattern of future pension payments and recognize this fact in the cash flow projections of the company. The employer may even establish balance sheet reserves or earmark a part of the firm's cash in a special pension bank account for future pension payments. However, if the funds are still under the employer's control, these funds can be diverted to other business uses at his discretion. Therefore, even where balance sheet reserves or special pension bank accounts are used, the financing of the plan is still considered to be on a current disbursement basis.

An illustration of the current disbursement approach would be a plan under which the employer promises all employees with at least 25 years of service a lifetime pension of $100 a month beginning at age 65. If there are no employees eligible for benefits during the first two years after the plan is established, the employer would not make any pension plan payments during that period. The employer's pension outlay of $100 a month begins with the retirement of the first eligible employee; his outlay increases by that amount as each new retired worker is added to the pension roles, and decreases by $100 a month as each retired worker dies. These monthly pension outlays are provided out of current operating income and, in effect, are treated as a part of wage costs.

Advantages

From the employer's viewpoint, the current disbursement approach might be found attractive in that the initial pension outlay required is very low. Also, the after-tax earnings rate of the firm might be appreciably higher than the tax-free investment return earned by a qualified pension trust. In that case, the employer might prefer to invest all funds in the business and meet his pension obligations on a current disbursement basis. Lastly, the employer may wish to provide benefits on a selective basis or may wish to provide some or all of his employees with additional types or amounts of benefits as a supplement to the benefits already provided under a qualified plan. These benefits may be financed on a current disbursement basis, if the employer does not want to meet the nondiscrimination test and other requirements of the Internal Revenue Service or if he is uncertain as to his future financial capacity to provide these benefits.

From the standpoint of the employee, the current disbursement approach offers even fewer advantages. One possible advantage is that the low initial outlay required under this method probably has encouraged the establishment of some plans that might not have been started or would have been started at a much later date; another is that initial benefit levels under these plans were higher than would have been provided if the benefits had been funded. Supplemental plans have undoubtedly enlarged the benefits made available to covered employees.

Disadvantages

The disadvantages associated with the current disbursement approach far outweigh its advantages. From the standpoint of the employer, a major disadvantage is the loss of the tax advantages available under a qualified pension plan.[1] Pension plans financed on a current disbursement basis do not meet the qualification requirements imposed by the Internal Revenue Code. Indeed, there is no need for a plan of this type to become qualified. As long as the benefit is deemed by the Internal Revenue Service to be reasonable in amount and a necessary business expense, the employer's pension payments are deductible for federal income tax purposes as these benefit payments are made. However, if a plan is not qualified and the employer decides to set aside some funds in an earmarked account, the employer does not have the advantage enjoyed under a qualified pension trust of tax-free investment income on these accumulated funds. Nor would advance payments to the special pension account be treated as deductible expenses.

A second disadvantage for the employer under current disbursement financing is the fact that annual pension outlays, though small in the initial years of the plan, increase rapidly and eventually reach a level (at least for a closed group of employees) that is considerably higher than the annual contributions required under a funded plan. The amount of annual contributions required under the current disbursement approach increases for a considerable number of years and does not level off until the size of the retired group stabilizes, i.e., the number of pensioners dying each year is about equal to the number of workers added each year to the retirement rolls. Since there is generally no advance accumulation of pension funds under the current disbursement approach, annual contributions in later years must be higher under this method as compared with a funded plan. Under current disbursement financing, the pension obligation for each employee is spread only over the years of retirement (i.e., an average of about 15 years); whereas with advance funding, the pension obligation can be spread over the working careers of employees (i.e., a period of possibly 30, 35, or 40 years). Furthermore, the absence of an accumulated fund on which investment income can be earned requires greater total contributions under a current disbursement plan than under a funded plan. The difference in the incidence of employer "contributions" referred to here should not be interpreted as differ-

---

[1] For a complete treatment of the tax aspects of qualified pension plans, see Chapters 5 and 6.

ences in the "cost" of the plan—a point that is discussed at length in the following chapter.

Still another disadvantage of the current disbursement approach is the virtual impossibility of requiring employees to share in the cost of the plan. It is difficult to envision an employee being willing to contribute to a plan under which continuation of benefit payments is completely subject to the discretion of the employer. This would probably be true even if provision were made for a return of employee contributions in the event of plan termination.

Lastly, under current disbursement financing, the employer has little control over the incidence of annual deposits, as compared with his ability to suspend and vary contributions under a funded plan.

From the viewpoint of employees, the major disadvantage under current disbursement financing is the lack of benefit security. Continuation of benefit payments is conditioned upon the financial capacity of the employer and his continued willingness to provide the promised benefit. If the company goes out of business, then both active and retired employees suffer the loss of future pension payments. Likewise, retired employees have no recourse if the employer, although remaining in business, decides to discontinue, for financial or any other reasons, the benefits being provided on a current disbursement basis. Another disadvantage for employees under current disbursement financing is the loss of favorable tax treatment of distributions from a qualified pension trust. Participants under qualified pension plans receive certain estate tax advantages and the opportunity of treating certain lump sum distributions as long-term capital gains.

Extent of Use

Relatively few private pension plans are financed on a current disbursement basis. The U.S. Department of Labor reports that there were, based on the financial reports filed for 1960 under the Welfare and Pension Plans Disclosure Act, 851 unfunded pension plans in existence, covering about 1.4 million workers.[2] However, less than 500,000 of these workers were covered by the 677 unfunded basic plans providing old-age pensions. The other 900,000 workers belonged to unfunded supplementary plans that provided long-term disability, death, or other benefits; virtually all members

---

[2] U.S. Department of Labor, *Unfunded Private Pension Plans* (B.L.S. Bulletin 1394) (Washington, D.C.: U.S. Government Printing Office, May, 1964), p. 1.

of these latter plans also belonged to funded plans providing old-age pensions.[3]

The United Mine Workers of America Welfare and Retirement Plan is probably the best known of the private plans operated on a current disbursement basis. Welfare and pension benefits under the plan are financed solely by employer contributions based on coal production. The original contribution rate negotiated in 1946 was 5 cents per ton, and it was increased to 10 cents per ton in 1947, 20 cents in 1948, 30 cents in 1950, and 40 cents (the current rate) in 1952. Annual welfare and pension benefit disbursements under the plan are currently equal to about 80% of the fund's annual income. Furthermore, the current balance in the trust fund is not quite sufficient to provide one year's benefit payments. The financial adversities experienced under the plan have necessitated occasional reductions in the monthly pension amount paid to retired workers.

The financial difficulties encountered by the UMW plan illustrate the hazards to benefit security associated with the current disbursement approach to the financing of private pension plans. This method of financing is sound if one can be assured that the employing firm (or the industry, in the case of a multiemployer plan) will remain in existence indefinitely and further that the firm (or industry) will always have the financial capacity to provide the promised benefit. Obviously, economic uncertainties are such that one is unable to assume such an optimistic future for any firm. Thus, it seems advisable that employers attempt, whenever possible, to pursue a policy of funding benefits at a rate consistent with the financial capabilities of the firm.

The current disbursement approach is used to a much greater extent in the financing of public pension plans. Political reasons probably account for the use of the current disbursement approach in these plans. It is politically expedient for elected officials to minimize expenditures and thus avoid possible tax increases. Therefore, a financing approach which minimizes initial pension outlays and defers part of the obligation to a later date (and a later governmental administration) offers considerable appeal to incumbent officials at the inception of the plan. The political problem then becomes even more acute for later administrations that might wish to convert the plan to a funded basis. A second possible explanation for the greater prevalence of current disbursement financing under public plans is the taxing power argument which assumes that future governmental administrations can increase tax rates to meet the rising financial obligations under the plan.

----

[3] *Ibid.*

FUNDED APPROACH

An alternative to current disbursement financing is for the employer to set aside funds irrevocably with a trustee or an insurance company prior to the date that each monthly payment is due. There are two basic approaches to funding a pension plan, and they are generally referred to as terminal funding and advance funding.

Terminal Funding

Nature of Approach. Under terminal funding, the employer sets aside for each employee, on the date that the latter retires, a single-premium sum sufficient to provide the monthly pension benefit promised under the plan. (Terminal funding, as used in this text, also includes postretirement funding approaches, under which the employer spreads the cost of retirement benefits over a limited period after the employee's date of retirement, e.g., 5 or 10 years.) The single-premium sum needed to provide the promised benefit is a function of the amount of benefit, the expected benefit period, and the rate of interest expected to be earned on the investment of this principal sum. For example, based on the 1951 Group Annuity Table (for males, projected on a static basis to 1965 in accordance with Scale C) and $3\frac{1}{2}\%$ interest, the sum needed to provide $100 a month for life to a male, age 65, is $13,433.[4] If the mortality and interest assumptions prove to be accurate, the principal plus interest earnings will be sufficient, on the average, to provide the $100-a-month benefit.

The employer, therefore, sets aside the appropriate single-premium sum as each employee retires. Like the current disbursement approach, terminal funding does not require the employer to make any contributions on behalf of the employees who are still actively at work.

The benefits can be funded through the purchase of single-premium annuities from insurance companies, or the employer can transfer the estimated single-premium sums to a trust fund.

The reader should not confuse terminal funding with the prac-

---

[4] An expense assumption is ignored in the above calculation since the authors are interested solely in illustrating the concept of terminal funding. In practice, the expenses of administering the benefit would be taken into account in the single-premium rate charged by an insurance company or in determining the amount to be set aside in a trust fund under noninsured plans, if expenses associated with the plan are paid from the trust fund. Normally, the expenses under trust fund plans are paid directly by the employer, and, therefore, no expense allowance is required.

tice of split funding that is prevalent in the pension field. The term "split funding," as it is commonly used in pension planning, refers to the use of two different funding agencies in administering the assets of a pension plan. For example, a plan may provide that contributions on behalf of active employees are to be administered by a corporate trustee. When an employee retires, the trust agreement may require the corporate trustee to withdraw from the trust fund, and transfer to an insurance company, the single-premium sum needed to purchase a life annuity equal to the monthly pension earned by the employee under the terms of the pension plan. This type of plan would be considered to be an advance-funded plan, unless the employer is paying to the corporate trustee an annual sum exactly equal to the amount of single premiums needed to provide the benefits for workers retiring each year—a highly unlikely situation.

Advantages. Under the terminal funding approach, the employer has the satisfaction of knowing that he has met his full obligation to retired workers. Unlike the current disbursement approach, terminal funding substantially eliminates the possibility of ever having to decrease the benefits payable to workers who have already retired, assuming that annuities are purchased or that the single-premium sums paid to a trust fund prove to be adequate. Thus, the employer avoids the adverse public and employee relations that might result from a reduction in the benefits of retired employees.

Another advantage to the employer is that total contribution outlays under this method are less than under the current disbursement approach. As indicated above, a principal sum of $13,433, on the average, is needed under terminal funding to provide a male, age 65, with a lifetime income of $100 a month. Let us compare this figure with the total outlay required to provide a similar benefit on a current disbursement basis. The 1951 Group Annuity Table (with the same projection) indicates that a male, age 65, has an average life expectancy of 15.13 years. Thus, on a current disbursement basis, the annual pension outlay will be $1,200, and the aggregate outlay for a retired worker will, on the average, be $18,156 ($1,200 times the average life expectancy of 15.13 years). The latter approach, then, requires a total outlay which is $4,723 greater than that required under terminal funding, the difference, of course, being due to the effects of compound interest.

From the standpoint of employees, the major advantage of terminal funding is the high degree of benefit security available to workers once they have retired. Also, a minor advantage, similar to one indicated for the current disbursement approach, is the possibility that the plan itself or the particular level of benefits could not have been provided, if the employer had had to use advance funding.

Disadvantages. The employer's total contribution outlay under terminal funding is larger than the amount that would be required under advance funding. The sum needed to provide the $100-a-month benefit indicated in the earlier illustration can be reduced considerably if periodic contributions are made to the pension fund during the active working years of the employee. The difference in total contribution outlay, once again, is due to the fact that these periodic contributions to the pension fund are invested and the resulting tax-free investment income enlarges the size of the pension fund.

An important disadvantage for the employer is the fact that terminal funding generally produces considerable fluctuation in the annual contributions required in the early years of the plan. As indicated above, the annual contribution under this method is a function of the size of the single-premium sums required and the number of employees retiring in that year. Even if the benefit amount is the same for all employees, the number retiring each year is bound to fluctuate, at least during the early years of the plan. As the plan approaches maturity, the degree of fluctuation in the number of employees retiring will become smaller. At that stage, the annual pension outlay will still fluctuate, but within a much narrower range than will be the case in the early years of the plan.

A related problem is the possibility that terminal funding may require very large contributions during any given year—particularly in the early years of the plan. This may be a serious problem if the employer has a large number of employees at, or near, retirement age at the inception of the plan. If this is the case, it is possible for terminal funding to require larger annual contributions in the early years of the plan than would be required under some form of advance funding. An even more important disadvantage is the fact that the employer has no flexibility in annual contribution payments under terminal-funded plans. However, an element of flexibility can be introduced through postretirement funding over a 5- or 10-year period.

As is true in the case of current disbursement financing, terminal funding discourages (or, more realistically, eliminates) the possibility of making the plan contributory.

From the standpoint of the employee, the major disadvantage of terminal funding lies in the lack of benefit security for active employees. As is the case in current disbursement financing, the nonretired workers under terminal funding have no segregated assets, either in a trust fund or an insurance company, to look to in order to satisfy their pension claims.

Extent of Use. The extent to which terminal funding is used in financing private pension plans is not known. One pension expert points out that this method is being used by a number of steel companies.[5] Also, certain of the plans negotiated by the International Ladies' Garment Workers Union are operating on a terminal funding basis. These latter plans started out on an advance-funded basis, but changes in methods of production and consumer style preferences have adversely affected certain segments of the industry and, therefore, the financial experience of some of their pension funds.

Terminal funding is also used in the case of some negotiated plans where the employer's commitment under the collective bargaining agreement is to provide retirement benefits for those workers retiring during the term of the labor agreement. The Internal Revenue Service has ruled that a plan can be qualified if "the expected contributions will not be less than the full costs of prospective pensions for employees expected to retire under the plan [during the term of the labor agreement]."[6]

Advance Funding

Nature of Approach. Under advance funding, the employer (and the employee, under contributory plans) sets aside funds on some systematic basis prior to the employee's retirement date. Thus, periodic contributions are made on behalf of the group of active employees during their working years. This does not mean that each dollar of contributions is necessarily earmarked for specific employees. As will be noted in subsequent chapters, contributions are not allocated to specific employees under certain funding instruments, for example, trust fund and group deposit administration plans. Thus, it is true that in some plans using unallocated funding instruments, contributions in the early years may only be sufficient to provide lifetime benefits to the first group of employees retiring under the plan. However, if contributions are continued on an advance funding basis, the accumulated assets in the pension fund will soon exceed the aggregate single-premium sums needed to provide benefits to those workers who are already retired. This excess of pension assets, then, represents the advance funding of

---

[5] H. C. Biegel, G. B. Buck, *et al., Pensions and Profit Sharing* (3rd ed.; Washington, D.C.: Bureau of National Affairs, Inc., 1964), p. 156.

[6] Rev. Rul. 55–681, CB 1955–2, 585.

benefits that have been accrued or credited to the active (nonretired) employees.

Pension plans operating on an advance funded basis are invar-
iably qualified with the Internal Revenue Service. An employer is
generally not willing to make advance contributions to an irrevocable trust fund unless he receives the tax advantages of a qualified
plan.

Advantages. The advantages of advance funding are, in effect,
implied in the discussions of the disadvantages of the current disbursement and terminal funding approaches. However, in the interests of clarity and thoroughness, the advantages of this approach
will be spelled out in some detail.

From the standpoint of the employer, an important reason for
the advance funding of pension benefits is the fact that it requires
the smallest outlay of pension contributions for each employee.[7]
This point can be best illustrated with reference to the example
cited earlier, i.e., a lifetime pension of $100 a month for a male age
65. Let us assume further that the person for whom this pension is
to be provided is now age 30. If the pension benefit is to be funded
by annual contributions for the next 35 years, the annual outlay
required (assuming $3\frac{1}{2}\%$ interest and no mortality discount)
would be $195. The aggregate outlays made during this period
would be $6,825 ($195 a year for 35 years). The aggregate outlay
of $6,825 required under advance funding is clearly lower than the
outlays of $13,433 and $18,156 required under terminal funding
and current disbursement financing, respectively. Again, the difference is due solely to the fact that interest is earned under the two
funded approaches, with aggregate interest earnings being greatest
under advance funding.

Secondly, advance funding permits the employer to spread the
costs of a pension plan fairly evenly over the lifetime of the plan.
Chart 3–2 indicates the pattern of annual contributions required
under each financing approach for a typical pension plan. Line (C)
(advance funding) in the chart assumes that the plan's past service
(supplemental) liability is to be funded over 20 years. The increasing pattern of contribution outlays under the current disbursement
approach is based on the assumption that the number of retired
workers will increase for a substantial period of time after the
inception of the plan. Theoretically, a point will be reached where
the number of retired workers dying in a given year will about

---

[7] It is necessary to point out that contribution outlays and pension costs
must not be confused. If the employer can invest his money more profitably in
his business or elsewhere, it may be to his advantage, from a cost point of view,
to finance his pension plan on a current disbursement basis.

equal the number of employees being added to the pension rolls, at which point annual outlays will become somewhat stable. As indicated earlier, the contribution outlay curve and the benefit payout curve are identical under the current disbursement method.

Under terminal funding, assuming a fixed benefit, the annual contributions will vary with the number of workers retiring each

CHART 3-2

ILLUSTRATIVE CONTRIBUTION PATTERNS UNDER
ALTERNATIVE FUNDING APPROACHES

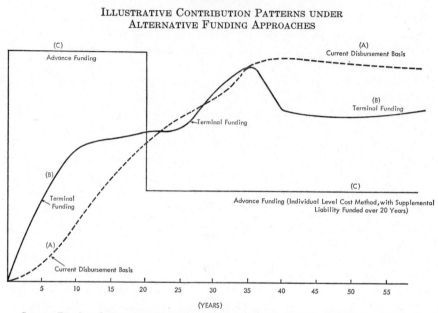

SOURCE: Based on data presented by Charles L. Trowbridge in "Fundamentals of Pension Funding," *Transactions*, Society of Actuaries, Volume IV, No. 8, p. 17.

year, rather than with the size of the total retired group. Once again, when the group matures, a reasonably constant number of new retirements each year can be expected. However, there will almost always be some fluctuation in the number retiring each year and, therefore, some variation in the annual contributions required under terminal funding.

The relatively even distribution of annual pension outlays under advance funding produces a more equitable charge against the firm's profits over the years. The pension is being provided to employees for the years of service rendered to the firm. Thus, it would seem that the financial statements of the employer should reflect, as a charge against operations, pension contributions in an amount approximately equal to the present value of benefits accruing under the plan. It is true that credit for past service, offered at the inception of the plan, creates a problem. Since the plan was not in existence during those past service years, it is difficult to justify pension charges against operating income for that period of time. The next best solution seems to be to charge off past service costs in the first 20 or 25 years after the inception of the plan. Thereafter, annual pension outlays should be related to the benefit credits accruing during each fiscal period.

It is clear that the current disbursement approach seriously understates, in the early years, the magnitude of contributions that will be required in subsequent years. Thus, later generations of stockholders will have to bear a substantially greater burden of pension outlays on behalf of employees whose benefits were earned for previous years of service. The level approach of advance funding produces a much more equitable matching of income and expenditures during the various fiscal years.

The reader should recognize that the relationship discussed here, between the financing approach and the incidence of the pension burden, also applies in the case of the OASDI program. Opponents of the funding policy pursued under OASDI point out that the past and current underfinancing of benefits will impose a greater burden on future taxpayers covered under the program. There are, of course, other issues involved in the case of OASDI, but it is pertinent to the discussion to note that the above relationship applies whether the plan is public or private.

A third advantage of advance funding for employers is the flexibility it permits. This flexibility applies to both the financing and design aspects of pension planning.

The accumulation of assets in a pension fund resulting from the advance funding of benefits serves as a buffer during periods of financial stress. During a period of low earnings or operating losses, an employer may find it advisable to reduce or eliminate pension contributions for a year or even a longer period. This can be done in those cases where the pension fund is of sufficient size, so that a temporary reduction or termination of contributions does not violate the minimum funding requirements imposed by the Internal Revenue Service on qualified plans. It should be noted that this financing flexibility, available under advance-funded plans, does not necessitate any reduction or termination in pension benefits. Under the current disbursement approach, an employer faced with similar financial problems might have to take the drastic action of temporarily reducing or terminating benefits to retired workers.

Advance funding also permits greater flexibility in plan design. For example, advance funding permits the establishment of a plan on a contributory basis, an arrangement that is virtually impossible under the alternative financing approaches. Also, the promise of a vested benefit is much more meaningful if benefits are advance funded.

Still another advantage for the employer is the presumed improvement in employee relations that should result from the personal satisfaction and security that employees experience under advance-funded plans. Indeed, labor leaders are increasingly aware of the advantages to their members of funded pension plans. Some labor contracts require that employers maintain a certain minimum level of funding in those plans.

Also, for small corporations, it might be advantageous to fund pension benefits to minimize possible tax problems associated with unreasonable accumulations of surplus. Lastly, advance funding offers the advantage of placing these funds beyond the reach of creditors of the corporation.

From the standpoint of employees, the major advantage of advance funding is the increased benefit security available under this financing arrangement. If a qualified pension plan is terminated, the accumulated assets in the fund are fully vested for the benefit of covered employees—both active and retired. The assets of a terminated plan are used to provide benefits to employees on the basis of some order of priorities established under the plan.[8] Whether all employees receive the equivalent of their benefits accrued to the date of termination depends on the degree to which benefits have been funded. It is important that the reader recognize that advance funding does not necessarily mean that benefits are fully funded. On a termination-of-plan basis, benefits are fully funded when the accumulated assets in the pension fund are equal to the present value of accrued benefits to date. However, a plan may be advance funded, but may not yet have reached the point where the asset fund is equal to the present value of benefits accrued as of a given date. The reason that this is true in many plans is the fact that a part of the past service (supplemental) liability may still be unfunded or contributions may have been skipped in some previous years. The fund may also be inadequate in those cases where the actual experience under the plan varied adversely from the actuarial assumptions used in calculating prior contributions to the plan. Thus, the security of benefits of covered employees under advance-funded plans depends on the degree of funding achieved as of a given date and, for specific employees, the priority class in which they belong if the plan were to be terminated.[9] Therefore, it is

---

[8] See pp. 60–61 for a discussion of the typical procedures followed upon termination of a plan.

[9] This statement assumes that the investments of the pension fund are sound and can be converted into cash without any capital losses being sustained.

possible that some workers, particularly the younger active employees, may not receive any benefits if a plan is terminated, even if the plan has been advance funded.[10]

In spite of the above qualification, the fact remains that advance funding is far superior to the alternative financing approaches in enhancing the security of benefits of covered employees.

Lastly, it should be noted that both the employer and the employee enjoy certain tax advantages associated with qualified pension plans. Practically all advance-funded plans are qualified.

Disadvantages. The disadvantages of advance funding to the employer are minimal. However, these factors may be significant in a few isolated instances. For example, it might be difficult to convince an employer to set aside funds in a pension trust when, in fact, capital invested in the business is earning more, even after federal income taxes, than the return that can be reasonably expected on trust investments. This is particularly true in the case of a growing company where additional capital is still required. The argument that advance funding reduces the total contribution outlays required under the plan has little force in this case. The employer will have to be convinced of the merits of the other advantages offered in favor of advance funding.

Another possible disadvantage of advance funding results from a misunderstanding by employees or labor union officials of the nature of the benefit payout pattern under pension plans. As indicated earlier, the amount of annual benefit payments tends to increase continuously, leveling out as the plan matures. Thus, advance funding requires a substantial accumulation in the early years to offset the heavy drains on the fund in subsequent years. This accumulation of assets might be improperly interpreted as evidence that the plan is overfunded and that benefit improvements can be provided without any additional cost. Although this was a serious problem some time ago, it appears that labor leaders are becoming quite sophisticated in the area of pension funding. In fact, labor seems to be increasingly concerned with the problem of inadequately financed pension plans. The problem can be minimized further if pension experts fully inform their clients of the nature of pension funding. The concept is rather complex, and both management and labor would benefit from educational efforts in this direction.

Lastly, a disadvantage of an advance-funded plan is the inconvenience, restrictions, and expense associated with qualifying the plan with the Internal Revenue Service.

---

[10] The closing of the Studebaker Corporation's auto works in South Bend, Indiana, in December, 1963, washed away the accumulated pension rights of practically every man on the work force under age 60. *New York Times*, August 16, 1964, p. 1.

From the standpoint of the employee, there are no disadvantages of advance funding, unless the financial requirements imposed on the employer are such that a plan would not be established or that benefits would be lower than those offered under an alternative financing arrangement.

Extent of Use. Advance funding is used under most private pension plans. This fact is due largely to the convincing nature of the advantages of this approach. However, although most plans are advance funded, there has been increasing concern among governmental officials and some pension experts that the degree of funding under many plans is inadequate. In March, 1962, President John F. Kennedy appointed a Cabinet Committee to review the "implications of the growing retirement and welfare funds for the financial structure of the economy, as well as a review of the role and character of the private pension and other retirement systems in the economic security system of the nation, and consideration of how they may contribute more effectively to efficient manpower utilization and mobility."[11]

The Committee report recommends, among other things, that the

. . . present minimum standard for funding needs strengthening to provide more adequate funding. In addition, there is a basic need for strengthening the enforcement of the minimum standard to assure that it is met, both when a plan qualifies and periodically during its existence. The Committee believes that full funding is a desirable goal for pension plans and that minimum standards of funding, assuming continued operation, should be set with this objective in mind. It does recognize, however, that improved standards for funding may involve increased costs for some plans but believes that this impact can be minimized by providing for an adequate transition period.[12]

More specifically, the Committee recommends, as a minimum standard of funding, that past service liabilities under defined benefit plans "be funded fully over a period that roughly approximates the average work life of employees, but not more than 30 years from the inception of a new plan or (with reference to existing plans) from enactment of this requirement."[13] For defined contribution (money purchase) plans, the recommendation is that the benefits promised be realistically related to the contribution commitment under the plan.[14]

---

[11] President's Committee on Corporate Pension Funds and Other Private Retirement and Welfare Programs, *Public Policy and Private Pension Programs* (Washington, D.C.: U.S. Government Printing Office, January, 1965), Appendix C.

[12] *Ibid.*, p. 51.

[13] *Ibid.*, p. 52.

[14] *Ibid.*, p. 52.

Whether the above recommendations will ever be enacted into law is uncertain. Furthermore, it is difficult to assess the probable impact on the private pension movement if legislation as recommended above were in fact enacted. Many private plans now in existence have achieved a degree of funding substantially in excess of the suggested minimum standard. On the other hand, several negotiated multiemployer plans could not meet the above requirement unless benefits were drastically reduced or contribution rates substantially increased. This would clearly be the case for the United Mine Workers' plan and several of the plans negotiated by the International Ladies' Garment Workers union. Furthermore, some pension experts are concerned that enactment of the recommendations set forth in the Committee's report might encourage some employers to establish their plans on (or switch existing plans to) a current disbursement basis of financing. This possibility exists, in view of the fact that legislation in this area would apply only to qualified plans.

The basic assumption underlying the Committee's recommendations is that employees expect to receive the promised pension benefit upon retirement. Therefore, the pattern of funding should be such that sufficient assets are available to assure payment of these benefits. The objective of the recommendation, then, is to enhance the protection of the pension rights of employees. However, this increased protection of employee pension expectations is achieved (if legislation is enacted) by infringing on the existing prerogatives of management, and also on the freedom of management and labor to contract on terms that they deem to be mutually satisfactory. Furthermore, some individuals question the desirability of further governmental intervention in the area of private pension planning, regardless of the merits of the recommendations. Thus, it is likely that such recommendations will receive mixed reactions.

COST CONSIDERATIONS

If an employer chooses to fund his pension plan, he must have some idea of the cost of the program in order to determine the amount of periodic contribution payments under the plan. Even if the employer decides against advance funding, he should be aware of the expected long-term cost of the plan. If one were to choose the most complex and least understood aspect of pension planning from the viewpoint of the employer, a logical candidate would be the area of cost projections.

The objective of this chapter is to acquaint the reader with the factors affecting the *ultimate cost* of a pension plan, apart from specific plan provisions and benefits, with particular reference to the various actuarial assumptions and cost methods that can be used in determining the incidence and amount of pension costs. Thus, the remainder of the discussion in this chapter assumes a fixed set of plan specifications. The discussion also assumes, for the purpose of simplicity, that the plan is noncontributory.

ESTIMATED COST VERSUS ULTIMATE COST OF PLAN

The point that pension cost projections are *estimates* and not *actual cost* figures cannot be overstressed. A moment's reflection regarding the nature of a pension plan should make this point quite clear. Assume, for example, that a pension plan provides employees with a retirement benefit only after attainment of age 65 and completion of a minimum of 25 years of continuous service with the employer. It is obvious that not all current employees of the firm will be entitled to a benefit under the plan. Some employees may die and others may quit, be laid off, or become disabled prior to age 65. Other employees may defer their retirement beyond age 65; and, also, the number of years that retired workers will live cannot be predicted with certainty. Furthermore, in the case of funded plans, the rate of investment income to be earned in the future on accumulated assets in the pension fund can only be estimated.

The point is sometimes made in pension sales presentations that all of these cost uncertainties facing the employer can be eliminated by using a fully insured individual policy approach to funding the plan. The reader should recognize the weakness in this argument. It is true that individual policies offer very important guarantees as to mortality, interest, expense, and annuity options. However, this is not the same as arguing that the employer's ultimate outlay or cost under the plan is known with certainty. The guarantees under individual policy plans pertain only to contracts that have already been purchased. Future premium commitments will be reduced by dividends and other employer credits.[1] On the other hand, future premium commitments will be increased by the addition of newly covered employees and benefit increases to which currently covered employees may become entitled. Even under individual policy plans, then, projections of employer costs are estimates rather than firm, long-run cost commitments.

The conclusion, therefore, is that the ultimate cost of a pension plan cannot be determined until the last retired worker dies, and all benefit payments under the plan are thereby terminated. Under current disbursement financing, the ultimate cost of the plan will be the total of the benefits paid to all retired workers plus the expenses of operating the plan. Under funded plans, the ultimate cost of the plan will equal total benefit payments plus administrative expenses less investment income earned on the plan assets.

However, no business firm would ever establish a pension plan if the cost of the plan were completely uncertain until the plan is terminated at some date in the distant future. The obvious solution lies in the fact that although the specific ultimate cost is unknown, actuaries are able to estimate the ultimate cost of the plan with reasonable accuracy and thus arrive at a level of estimated plan contributions. To do this, assumptions must be made regarding the factors that affect the plan's ultimate cost. In subsequent years, adjustments in the estimated amounts of contributions required may have to be made, based on comparisons between the actual experience under the plan and the assumed experience. Experience more favorable than expected permits a reduction in future contributions or, alternatively, results in a more rapid amortization of past service (supplemental) liabilities. Conversely, adverse experience under the plan requires an increase in future contributions or

---

[1] For a full discussion of employer credits under individual policy plans, see pp. 166–168.

a lengthening of the period over which past service (supplemental) liabilities will be amortized.[2]

CHOICE OF ASSUMPTIONS

Two important points should be made regarding the choice of assumptions for the calculation of estimated pension costs.

First, the flexibility available in choosing a particular set of actuarial assumptions depends in large part on the funding instrument involved. The greatest flexibility is available under trust fund plans, under the conversion fund portion of individual policy combination plans, and under unallocated group pension contracts such as a group deposit administration contract. If the employer has competent advice, the assumptions used will be reasonable for the type of plan and the characteristics of the employee group covered. Fully insured individual policy plans, the individual policy portion of combination plans, and group permanent and group deferred annuity instruments offer the employer the least choice in cost assumptions, since the insurance company effectively establishes the assumptions to be used by its premium rates.

Second, the choice of a particular set of assumptions does not normally alter the ultimate cost of the plan. Obviously, the ages at which employees retire or the rate at which they die or leave their jobs is not conditioned by the assumptions in these areas made by the pension actuary. The relative magnitude of actuarial gains and losses under the plan will vary, given different original assumptions, but the end result will be an approximately similar ultimate cost picture except to the extent investment earnings are affected by the incidence of contributions produced by the funding assumptions chosen. This conclusion does not apply fully in the case of plans funded with individual policies. In the case of individual contracts, there is a certain degree of pooling of experience among the whole class of business. For example, the mortality or expense experience under a particular plan is not reflected directly in the insurance company's dividends paid to that group, since the dividend scale for individual policies is determined by the experience

---

[2] The situation is somewhat analogous to the pricing of individual life insurance policies sold on a participating basis. Participating life insurance premium rates are based on assumptions as to mortality, interest and expenses. If the actual experience in future years with respect to these factors proves to be more favorable than expected, the cost of the coverage is adjusted through dividend payments. On the other hand, if experience proves to be adverse, policyholders with assessable policies may have to pay an additional premium; or, in the more typical case of nonassessable policies, the losses are made up out of the surplus of the insurer.

for that class of business as a whole. There is also an element of pooling in some group plans.

It must be remembered, however, that the greater the freedom in choosing actuarial assumptions, the greater is the responsibility imposed on the employer for the adequacy of the pension fund.

COST ASSUMPTIONS

One method of approach in considering the factors affecting the cost of a pension plan is to relate these factors to the formula for determining the ultimate cost of the plan, i.e., benefits paid plus administrative expenses less investment earnings.

Benefits Paid

Number of Employees Retiring. The amount of benefits paid under a plan depends upon several factors. The first factor is the number of workers that will ultimately be entitled to receive benefits under the plan. The number of employees that will be eligible for benefits will depend on four factors: (1) mortality rates among active employees; (2) rates and duration of disabilities among active employees under a plan that offers a disability benefit; (3) layoffs and voluntary terminations of employment; and (4) rate of retirement. Let us now turn to a consideration of each of these cost factors.

A. Mortality. The higher the rate of mortality among active employees, the lower will be the cost of retirement benefits under the plan. However, if the plan provides a preretirement death benefit, this will increase the cost of the plan, as additional benefits are being provided.

Mortality among active employees can be an important cost-reducing factor in those plans providing little or no death benefit. This is particularly true for small plans where a few deaths can have a significant impact on the cost of the plan. Also, this factor becomes more important as the normal retirement age under the plan is increased beyond age 65, resulting in the occurrence of higher ages among the active employee group.

Actuaries generally use the same mortality table in projecting mortality among both active and retired employees.[3] Several mor-

---

[3] One exception is individual policy combination plans. Here, an annuity table is used for mortality after retirement and, often, a Commissioners Standard Ordinary (CSO) mortality table for mortality prior to retirement. CSO tables are based on the mortality experience of purchasers of life insurance and generally indicate higher rates of mortality at all ages in comparison with the rates indicated in annuity tables. Conservatism in the construction of mortality tables suggests the use of higher-than-expected mortality rates for insurance tables and lower-than-expected mortality for annuity tables.

tality tables are available for pension cost calculations, the most popular probably being the 1951 Group Annuity Table. Several projections have also been developed to reflect the probable continuing improvements in mortality. Thus, as improvements in mortality occur, or are expected to occur, the actuary can use the 1951 table with the projection that he believes to be appropriate for the given case. Mortality gains or losses will develop from year to year, and the actuary can keep abreast of the experience through subsequent modifications of the mortality assumption. Table 4–1 shows the

TABLE 4–1
PROBABILITY OF SURVIVING TO AGE 65—MALES

Age	1937 Std. Annuity	1937 Std. Annuity (−1)*	1951 GAT	1951 GAT (−1)*	1951 GAT Proj.C(Static) to 1965	1951 GAT Proj.C(Gen.) as of 1965
20	.698	.716	.776	.793	.809	.871
25	.703	.721	.779	.796	.811	.866
30	.709	.727	.782	.799	.814	.861
35	.718	.735	.787	.803	.818	.856
40	.730	.747	.793	.809	.823	.854
45	.749	.765	.803	.819	.832	.854
50	.778	.792	.822	.836	.849	.863
55	.821	.833	.856	.867	.878	.885
60	.890	.897	.910	.918	.924	.926

* Indicates an age setback of one year.

probability of surviving to 65 under the 1937 Standard Annuity Table and the 1951 Group Annuity Table, with the modification indicated. Obviously, the results are considerably different, which indicates the impact on estimated costs caused by the mortality assumption chosen by the actuary.

The question is often raised as to whether a mortality assumption should be used in calculating the amount of contributions that should be paid into a conversion fund under combination plans— particularly those plans covering a small group of employees. Pension practitioners seem to be divided in their opinions on this point. Some planners prefer to use a mortality assumption in these cases, while others believe that the size of the covered group generally involved in plans of this type is too small to permit the law of averages to work. If the expected mortality among a small group of employees does not materialize, the employer will be faced with the need for additional contributions in future years. Those favoring the use of a mortality assumption in these situations argue that its use results in a lower initial contribution requirement, which might be best suited to the current financial needs of some employers, and that any actuarial losses due to the use of such an assumption will be offset by actuarial gains due to severance of employment. Furthermore, it is argued that if the expected mortality is realized, the use of a mortality assumption produces a more realistic projection of future costs. Although there is merit in the latter position, the pension planner should clearly point out to the employer the full implications of using a mortality assumption with relatively small groups.

B. Rate and Duration of Disability. If a pension plan offers a disability benefit, cost projections for that plan should include a disability assumption. The plan actuary must establish two sets of probabilities in evaluating the cost of providing a disability benefit. First, he must estimate a rate of occurrence (frequency) of disabilities of the nature entitling the disabled employee to a benefit under the plan. The rates of disability will vary with the plan's definition of disability, the age and sex composition of the covered employee group, the nature of the employment, and the general level of economic activity. In the beginning, the disability experience projected for a particular plan may be based on insurance company data, or on the actual experience of the employer, or on the experience of a large company in the same, or a comparable, industry. Ultimately, the plan's own experience may be used as a yardstick.

Having determined the probable incidence of disability, the actuary must then project the duration of the disability. The duration of the disability will be affected by reemployment opportunities, which in turn are related to the nature of the employment and general economic conditions. The duration of the benefit period will also be affected by the mortality rates among disabled workers.

It can be seen, then, that the ability to project future disability rates is a difficult task. The actuary must keep a careful check on the actual disability experience evolving under the plan.

C. Turnover. Employees who voluntarily quit or who are laid off represent a cost-reducing factor to a pension fund, assuming the absence of full vesting. Also, as indicated above, in plans that do not provide death or disability benefits, terminations of employment due to these causes also represent cost-reducing factors. In the latter case, separate assumptions may be made regarding mortality, disability, and turnover, or, as is quite common, the plan actuary may use one set of termination rates covering all causes of termination of employment among nonretired workers.

Table 4–2 shows the effect on costs using three different turnover assumptions. The yearly withdrawal rates under Scale A and Scale B are as follows:

Male Age	Scale A	Scale B
25................	5.00%	10.00%
35................	2.50	5.00
45................	0.75	1.50
50................	0	0

As indicated in the above examples, most turnover tables assume a greater withdrawal rate at the younger ages than at the older ages, which is what normally would be the case.

The problems of developing accurate termination rates for a

TABLE 4–2

PRESENT VALUE OF $1 OF MONTHLY BENEFIT
BEGINNING AT AGE 65

Male Age	No Turnover	Scale A	Scale B	Ratio (2) ÷ (1)	Ratio (3) ÷ (1)
25............	$28.96	$16.13	$8.81	56%	30%
35............	41.20	34.09	28.11	83	68
45............	59.12	57.80	56.50	98	96

SOURCE: Based on 1951 GAT, Projection Scale C to 1965, 3½% interest and 5% loading.

specific plan are obvious. Future withdrawal rates will vary among employers and industries, and with changing economic conditions. The age and sex composition of the covered group have a significant impact on turnover rates. It is generally recognized that termination rates for female employees and younger workers are very high. Turnover rates also vary depending on the length of service of employees. Furthermore, working conditions and the personnel policies and benefit programs of a particular employer may affect turnover rates in that firm. Lastly, economic recessions or periods of prosperity may significantly alter termination rates. During periods of recession, employees will be less likely to quit, while the rate of layoffs will probably increase. The opposite situation will generally prevail during periods of economic prosperity.

The concept of turnover is broader for multiemployer plans than it is for single-employer pension funds. In the former, the employee terminates his coverage only if he fails to be reemployed by a participating employer within a specified time period, usually one or two years. In the skilled trades, withdrawal from the industry is less likely than separation from an individual employer. One of the basic assumptions justifying the existence of a multiemployer pension arrangement is the high degree of job mobility of the covered employees. But it is also assumed that there is a tendency for employees to be reemployed within the scope of coverage of the plan.

It is not surprising, therefore, that two actuaries may recommend considerably different withdrawal rates for the same plan. The choice of turnover assumption must rest, in the final analysis, on the sound judgment of the actuary. This judgment is based on the characteristics of the employee group, the factors discussed above, and the actuary's overall experience in pension cost projections. Some turnover tables have been developed to guide pension consultants.[4] These tables are of assistance for initial cost calculations, and adjustments in assumed turnover rates can be made as the actual experience under the plan evolves.

The question arises as to whether a turnover assumption should be used in calculating the level of annual contributions to be made under a plan using an unallocated funding instrument (including the conversion fund under a combination plan) when the plan covers a relatively small number of employees. The arguments for and against the use of a turnover assumption in these cases are somewhat similar to the arguments set forth earlier regarding the advisability of a mortality assumption under these plans. There is one more argument against use of a turnover assumption and that is the fact that turnover is even less predictable than mortality for relatively small groups of employees. Furthermore, the use of an eligibility requirement may well operate to eliminate the bulk of the high turnover employees in these cases. Therefore, it seems reasonable to conclude that a turnover assumption should be used only in larger cases. It certainly seems inadvisable to use both a turnover and a mortality assumption in smaller plans. If a mortality assumption is used, possible funding deficits due to this factor may be offset by the gains from employee terminations (assuming no vesting and a zero turnover assumption).

D. Rate of Retirement. In estimating the cost of pension benefits, one must make an assumption regarding the retirement age under the plan. Obviously, the higher the retirement age, the lower will be the cost of a given amount of retirement benefit. For example, if a plan has a retirement age of 70 rather than 65, there is an additional five-year period during which an employee may die, with the resulting possibility that he will never receive retirement benefits. More importantly, the requirement of retiring at 70 will reduce the length of the benefit period.

---

[4] See, for example, T. F. Crocker, H. M. Sarason, and B. W. Straight, *Actuaries Handbook* (Los Angeles: Pension Publications, 1955).

Regardless of the normal retirement age specified in the plan, the actuary may use an assumed average retirement age which is higher than the specified normal retirement age. Unless the plan requires that employees retire no later than at normal retirement age, it is not unusual to find that some employees defer retirement beyond the normal retirement age. Thus, it may be logical to assume in cost estimates that the actual average retirement age is higher than the normal retirement age. Although not typical, some plans provide actuarially equivalent (larger) benefits to persons deferring retirement beyond normal retirement age. In these plans, there should be no discount reflected in the cost calculations for postponed retirements.

One generally should not use a retirement age assumption lower than the normal retirement age specified in the plan. Even if an early retirement benefit is offered, the amount of the benefit is usually the actuarial equivalent (smaller in this case) of the normal retirement benefit.

Length of Benefit Period. In addition to the number of employees retiring, the amount of benefits paid under the plan is affected by the length of time that retired workers receive their pension benefits (or the length of time payments will be continued under the normal form to a beneficiary of the retired worker after his death). The length of the benefit period depends on the longevity of retired workers and the normal annuity form, since most plans provide life income benefits, frequently with a guaranteed certain period. Therefore, an assumption must be made regarding mortality among retired lives. As indicated earlier, the mortality table used for retired lives is generally identical to the table used for active lives, except in the case of individual policy plans.

Benefit Formula. The last factor affecting the total amount of pension benefits paid under the plan is the amount of pension paid to each retired worker. It goes without saying that the higher the benefit level, the greater will be the cost of the plan.

However, projecting benefit levels is more difficult under some benefit formulas than under others. The least difficult formula is one that provides a flat benefit for all retired workers, for example, a $100-a-month benefit. On the other hand, if the benefit formula calls for a pension benefit related to compensation, cost projections may include an assumption regarding expected future increases in the salaries of covered employees. For example, if a plan provides a pension benefit of 1% of salary per year of covered service, future increases in salary will increase benefit levels and, therefore, the cost of the plan.

There is some difference of opinion among pension practitioners regarding the advisability of using salary progressions in cost projections. The major argument in favor of using salary scale projections is the fact that their use results in more accurate estimates of future costs. The major argument opposing the use of salary progressions is the substantial increase in the current cost of the plan. The substantial impact on a cost estimate that results from use of a salary progression has been illustrated by one pension expert as follows: "The current rates of salary progression exhibited by statistics drawn from current records of salaried employees are so substantial that their effect is the equivalent of the assumption that every employee hired at age 20 for $4,000 a year would be receiving at least $32,000 a year immediately before retirement, in 45 years' time at the age of 65."[5] Part of the wage increase is due to an employee's advancement in the firm, and part is due to inflationary pressures on wage levels. Employers are generally unwilling to make current contributions based on cost estimates that reflect the *full* impact of projected salaries, although some recognition is given to this cost factor under most final-pay plans, except for individual policy plans. For example, it is quite common to use a scale based on expected increases in salary due to normal job advancement only. However, in the case of individual policy plans, contracts are almost always purchased on the assumption that the employee's pension benefit is based on his current compensation. As his compensation increases, additional policies are purchased to fund the increase in benefits to which he then becomes entitled.

Also, in the case of negotiated plans providing a flat benefit per year of service, there is generally no advance provision for future increases in the unit benefit amount. It is generally recognized that benefit levels will be increased periodically due to inflationary pressures, but recognition is not given to this fact in cost projections until increases are actually negotiated.

Expenses

The expenses of administering the pension plan must be added to the amount of benefits paid in arriving at the ultimate cost of the plan. The expense assumption used depends on the type of administration and the funding instrument involved. Under individual policy plans and some group pension contracts, the insurance company includes a loading for expenses in the gross premiums charged for purchased benefits. The expense loading is largest under individual

---

[5] William F. Marples, *Actuarial Aspects of Pension Security* (Homewood, Ill.: Richard D. Irwin, Inc., 1965), p. 61.

policy plans and decreases considerably under group pension contracts.

In the case of trust fund plans, the employer may pay the actuarial, legal, and investment expenses associated with the plan separately from the contribution payments to the plan. Nevertheless, these expenses must be added to the amount of benefit payments in arriving at the ultimate cost of the plan, even though they are not included in the actual cost estimates.

Possible differences in the handling of expenses, then, must be recognized in comparisons of cost projections involving different funding instruments.

Interest

The investment income earned on the accumulated assets of a funded pension plan reduces the ultimate cost of the plan. Thus, the higher the interest rate assumption, other things being equal, the lower will be the projected cost of the plan. For example, the single-premium sum required for a 45-year-old male to purchase a pure life annuity of $1 a month beginning at age 65 is $63.36, using a $3\frac{1}{4}\%$ interest assumption, as compared with a single premium of $59.12, using a $3\frac{1}{2}\%$ interest assumption.[6] Thus, in this example, an increase of $\frac{1}{4}$ of 1% in the interest rate assumption results in a reduction of almost 7% in the estimated cost of the plan. For a given plan, the impact of a change in the interest assumption on the estimated cost of the plan will depend on the age distribution of participants and their relative benefit credits.

The interest assumption used should take into account the size of the fund, the anticipated investment policy of the plan trustees, current and projected long-term rates of return, and any other factors that might affect the future pattern of investment earnings of the fund. The choice of an appropriate rate of interest is particularly difficult if a sizable portion of the assets are invested in common stocks, since these investments are subject to significant fluctuations in value. Also, investments in equities raise the rather difficult issue of how to handle unrealized capital gains.[7]

Summary

The choice of actuarial assumptions, then, has a significant impact on the *estimated* costs of a pension plan. It must be repeated,

---

[6] Premiums are based on the 1951 Group Annuity Table projected by Scale C to 1965 and a 5% loading.

[7] For an excellent discussion of this problem, see Marples, *op. cit.*, pp. 63–66 and 106–10.

however, that the choice of a particular set of assumptions generally has little effect on the *ultimate* cost of the plan. Table 4–3 illustrates the impact of varying sets of assumptions on the cost *estimates* for an actual plan. The plan provides a benefit of 1% of compensation per year of service, with a normal retirement age of 65. The individual level cost method with a supplemental liability

TABLE 4–3

Effect of Varying Sets of Actuarial Assumptions
on Estimated Cost of a Pension Plan

Assumptions	Estimated Annual Cost	
1. (a) 3½% interest	1. Normal cost	$18,690
(b) No turnover	Initial Supplemental	
(c) 1951 GAT, projection	Liability ($57,913)	3,040
Scale C to 1965	Total cost	$21,730
(d) Average normal		
retirement age: 65		
2. (a) 4% interest	2. Normal cost	$16,820
(b) No turnover	ISL ($52,887)	2,940
(c) 1951 GAT, 1965	Total cost	$19,760
(d) ANRA: 65		
3. (a) 4% interest	3. Normal cost	$15,375
(b) Heavy turnover	ISL ($52,753)	2,935
(c) 1951 GAT, 1965	Total cost	$18,310
(d) ANRA: 65		
4. (a) 4% interest	4. Normal cost	$13,270
(b) Heavy turnover	ISL ($45,272)	2,515
(c) 1951 GAT, 1965	Total cost	$15,785
(d) ANRA: 67		
5. (a) 4% interest	5. Normal cost	$12,220
(b) Heavy turnover	ISL ($41,613)	2,315
(c) 1951 GAT, no projection	Total cost	$14,535
(d) ANRA: 67		

was used to project the cost of the plan. It is assumed that the supplemental liability will be funded over a 30-year period. The nature of the various actuarial cost methods are discussed in detail in the remainder of this chapter.

Unfortunately, an employer is sometimes unduly influenced by these cost estimates in his choice of a funding instrument. In the case illustrated in Table 4–3, proposal 5 may be misinterpreted as the lowest-cost arrangement available to the employer. It may well turn out that one of the other cost projections is in fact closer to the cost that is eventually experienced under the plan. The important factors that an employer should consider in the choice of a funding instrument are examined at length in Chapter 10.

BUDGETING PENSION COSTS

The above discussion sets forth the various factors that will affect the ultimate cost of the plan. What is still needed, however, is some actuarial technique to determine how these estimated costs of the plan are to be spread over future years. These techniques are referred to as actuarial cost methods. More specifically, an *actuarial cost method* is a particular technique for establishing the amount and incidence of the normal costs, supplemental costs, and actuarial liabilities pertaining to the benefits (or benefits and expenses) of a pension plan.[8]

The plan actuary, then, uses a set of assumptions and an actuarial cost method in estimating the annual cost of a plan. Annual contribution payments are usually based on these estimated annual costs. However, it should be noted that actual annual contribution payments need not be identical to the estimated annual costs generated by a given actuarial cost method. As will be noted in later chapters, the employer has considerable flexibility in the timing of contribution payments under unallocated funding instruments (for example, deposit administration and trust fund plans). However, under certain insured funding instruments (for example, individual contracts), the actuarial cost method does effectively determine the amount of annual premiums due under the plan. The reader should also recognize that the meaning of the term "cost" as used in the context of this chapter may not be identical to the meaning of pension cost from an accountant's point of view.[9]

There are several different actuarial cost methods, each producing different patterns of annual costs under the plan. Having different actuarial cost methods to calculate annual pension costs is analogous to having different methods for determining the annual amount of depreciation of plant and equipment to charge against operations. The depreciation methods that can be used may produce different annual charges, but the total value of the building and

---

[8] The terminology pertaining to the actuarial aspects of pension planning reflects, wherever possible, the thinking of the Committee on Pension and Profit Sharing Terminology, sponsored jointly by the American Risk and Insurance Association and the Pension Research Council, University of Pennsylvania.

[9] The accounting profession seems to be increasingly of the opinion that accounting principles must be established regarding the reporting of pension costs; and, furthermore, that contribution payments are not necessarily the best measure of the amount of pension costs to be charged to a particular accounting period. (See, for example, *Accounting for the Cost of Pension Plans* [American Institute of Certified Public Accountants, 1965]).

equipment to be depreciated is constant regardless of the depreciation formula used. Similarly, the various actuarial cost methods will produce different levels of annual cost, but the choice of a particular actuarial cost method will not affect the ultimate cost of the plan. One important exception to the latter conclusion is the fact that if an actuarial cost method is chosen that produces higher initial contributions than other methods, then the asset accumulation will be greater in the early years of the plan, thereby producing greater investment income. An increase in investment income will decrease the ultimate cost of the plan.[10]

If the choice of actuarial cost method usually has little effect on the ultimate cost of a pension plan (after taking into consideration interest, etc.), what factors determine which method will be used in calculating the amount and incidence of pension contributions? The answer to this question will become more apparent after the following discussion of the specific cost methods. However, the reader may find it helpful to keep in mind that the choice of a specific actuarial cost method is influenced to a great degree by the degree of flexibility in annual contribution payments desired by the employer and available under the particular funding instrument used.

ACTUARIAL COST METHODS[11]

Actuarial cost methods can be broadly classified into (1) accrued benefit and (2) projected benefit cost methods. As further explained below, the class into which a particular cost method falls depends upon whether, for cost determination purposes, an employee's benefits under the pension plan are deemed to "accrue" in direct relation to years of service or are viewed as a single "projected" total.

Accrued Benefit Cost Method

An accrued benefit cost method is one under which the actuarial costs are based directly upon benefits accrued to the date of cost determination, such benefits being determined either by the terms of the plan or by some assumed allocation of total prospective

---

[10] More precisely, the timing of contribution payments has additional cost implications if federal income tax rates change; or if alternative uses of capital vary over time; or if investment return rates vary over the life of the plan; or if the plan is terminated prior to full provision having been made for all accrued benefits.

[11] Parts of the material in this section were drawn from Joseph J. Melone, "Actuarial Cost Methods—New Pension Terminology," *Journal of Insurance,* Vol. XXX, No. 3 (September, 1963).

benefits to years of service. With respect to the determination of the actuarial cost of the plan for a given year, the method assumes that a precisely determinable unit of benefit is associated with such year of a participant's credited service.

This method of calculating the actuarial costs of pension plans has also been referred to as the single-premium, unit credit, unit cost, or step-rate method.

The accrued benefit method is best adapted to those plans that provide a unit benefit type of formula based on career average compensation (for example, a percentage of each year's compensation), or a specified dollar amount for each year of credited service. Under these benefit formulas, a precisely determinable unit of benefit is associated with each year of a participant's credited service. Although best adapted to those plans that use a unit benefit type of formula, the accrued benefit cost method can also be used when the plan provides a composite benefit based on the participant's total period of credited service. For example, the plan may provide a $100 monthly pension benefit at age 65 after 25 years service, or the plan may use a benefit formula based on final average compensation. In these instances, the accrued benefit method requires that a portion of the prospective benefit be imputed to each year of credited service. This requires some arbitrary basis of allocating total prospective benefits to particular years of service. Thus, it is generally deemed advisable to use one of the projected benefit cost methods for plans of this type.

Most actuarial cost methods break down the total actuarial cost into the normal cost and supplemental cost of the plan. The *normal cost* of the plan is the amount of annual cost, determined in accordance with a particular actuarial cost method, attributable to the given year of the plan's operation. More specifically, the normal cost of the plan is the amount (determined in accordance with a particular actuarial cost method) needed for the year on the assumptions that: (1) the plan has been in effect from the earliest date of credited service of each then included employee; (2) the normal costs for all previous years of the plan have been paid or accrued; (3) there has been no retroactive change in benefit formulas; and (4) the assumptions used in calculating normal costs have in fact been realized.

However, most plans provide credit for service rendered prior to the inception date of the plan. If the normal cost is calculated on the assumption that annual costs have been paid or accrued from the earliest date of credited service (when in fact they have not), the plan starts out with a supplemental liability. At the inception of the plan, the supplemental liability arises from the fact that credit for past service is granted or part of the total benefit is imputed to years prior to the inception of this plan. The annual contribution will normally be equal to the normal cost of the plan plus at least interest on the supplemental liability. If the employer wishes to fund this supplemental liability, then annual contributions in addition to this amount will be required. The portion of the annual cost that is applied toward the reduction of the supplemental liability is referred to as the plan's supplemental cost. As the plan continues in operation, the size of the supplemental liability will normally change. These changes in the size of the supplemental liability result from prior supplemental cost payments, possible changes in benefit formulas, deviations of actual from expected experience, and changes in the actuarial assumptions or in the actuarial cost method used in subsequent normal cost calculations. A supplemental liability arises, then, whenever the present value of total normal costs is less than the present value of total projected benefits under the plan.

The first step in the calculation of the normal cost under the accrued benefit cost method is to determine the present value of each participant's benefit credited during the year for which costs are being calculated. The cost per $1 of benefit is a function of the participant's age and sex, and of the mortality, interest, and other assumptions used. Thus, the normal cost per $1 of benefit under the accrued benefit cost method increases with the age of the participant, assuming that all other assumptions are held constant. For example, using the 1951 Group Annuity Table projected by Scale C to 1965, a 3½% interest assumption and a 5% loading, the normal cost per $1 of monthly benefit beginning at age 65 for a male employee at various ages would be as follows:

Male Age	Present Value of $1 of Monthly Benefit Beginning at Age 65 (Normal Cost)
25	$ 28.96
30	34.52
35	41.20
40	49.26
45	59.12
50	71.60
55	87.94
60	110.03

If the benefit formula is related to salary, then increases in compensation would also increase the normal cost for a given participant.

The normal cost for the plan as a whole is simply the sum of the separate normal costs for the benefits credited for each participant during that particular year. Although the normal cost for a given participant increases over time under the accrued benefit cost method, the normal cost for the plan as a whole generally does not increase as rapidly or may even remain fairly constant or decrease. The reason for this is that some older employees will die or terminate, and they will probably be replaced by much younger workers. If the distribution of current service benefit credits by age and sex remains constant, the total normal cost of the plan will remain constant.

At the inception of the plan, the supplemental liability under the accrued benefit cost method arises either from the fact that past service credits have been granted or from the fact that a part of the benefits of the plan are imputed to past service. An exact relationship between the supplemental liability and the past service liability exists under the accrued benefit cost method, if the plan specifically provides benefits on account of past service. After the inception of the plan, this precise relationship between the supplemental liability and the past service liability may no longer exist, since the supplemental liability is affected, as indicated earlier, by factors other than credited past service. Therefore, the supplemental liability at the inception of the plan under the accrued benefit cost method is simply the present value of the accrued past service benefits credited as of that date. Using the single-premium rates indicated above, the supplemental liability for a male employee, age 40, as of the inception date of the plan, would be $49.26 per $1 a month of past service benefit payable beginning at age 65. If the benefit formula provides a $4-a-month benefit per year of service and the employee has 10 years of credited past service, the supplemental liability for that individual would be $1,970.40 ($49.26 × $40 past service benefit). The supplemental liability for the plan as a whole at the inception of the plan would be the sum of the supplemental liabilities for each of the covered employees.

It should now be clear as to why the accrued benefit method is readily adaptable to unit benefit formula plans. Also, this method is generally used under group deferred annuity plans, since a unit of benefit is usually purchased for each year of credited future service under these contracts. The employer has considerable flexibility in funding the supplemental liability. However, if the plan is funded through a group annuity contract, insurers usually require that the past service benefit of each employee be purchased by retirement date. The requirement that the past service benefits of employees be fully funded by their retirement dates imposes a substantial financial burden on the employer in those cases where there is a large number of older workers at the inception of the plan. To meet this objection, most insurers permit postretirement funding of some of the past service benefits under group annuity plans.

Terminal funding may be construed as a special case of the accrued benefit cost method under which the entire benefit is deemed to accrue at retirement.

Projected Benefit Cost Methods

Rather than costing the benefits credited during a specific period, one can project the total benefits that will be credited by retirement date and spread these costs evenly over some future period. These costing techniques are referred to as projected benefit cost methods. More specifically, a *projected benefit cost method* is one under which the actuarial costs are based upon total prospective benefits, whether or not they are attributed to any specific periods of service. The actuarial cost determination assumes regular future accruals of normal cost, generally level in amount or as a percentage of earnings, whose actuarial present value is equal to the present value of prospective benefits less the value of plan assets and un-funded supplemental liabilities.

From the above definition one can see that projected benefit cost methods differ from accrued benefit cost methods in two important respects. First, the normal cost accrual under a projected benefit cost method is related to the total prospective benefit rather than the benefit for a particular year. The projected benefit methods are almost always used when the plan provides a composite benefit based upon the participant's total period of credited service, such as $100 per month or 30% of average earnings for the last five years of service. These latter formulas do not allocate benefits to any particular year. However, it may be necessary, in the case of early retirement or termination of service with vested rights, to allocate the total potential benefit to actual years of service or to define the accrued benefit in terms of the amount purchasable by the accrued level annual cost. A projected benefit cost method can be, and is, used with benefit formulas that do allocate units of benefit to partic-ular years of service. When so used, the normal cost accruals are still calculated on the basis of total projected benefits rather than annual units of benefit. For example, if a plan provides a retire-ment benefit of $6 a month per year of service, the normal cost computation is based on a projected monthly retirement benefit of $6 times the expected number of years of credited service as of normal retirement age. If the employee is age 35 upon entry into the plan and the normal retirement age is 65, then the total pro-jected benefit is $180 a month.

A second distinguishing characteristic of projected benefit cost methods is that these techniques generally are applied with the objective of generating a normal cost which is level in amount or as a percentage of earnings with respect to either the individual participants or to the participants as a group. Therefore, these methods can be characterized as level cost methods. A cost method is characterized as level if it is based on an actuarial formula designed to produce a constant year-to-year accrual of normal cost (either in amount or as a percentage of payroll or other index) if (a) the experience conforms with the actuarial assumptions, (b) there are no changes in the plan, and (c) certain characteristics of the employee group remain unchanged.

However, the actual experience of the plan seldom conforms precisely with the actuarial assumptions used, and it is likely that there will be changes in the composition of the group for which cost accruals are assumed. Nevertheless, these methods are characterized as level cost methods, since the theoretical objective of most of these methods is to produce a level normal cost. By contrast, the accrued benefit cost method theoretically should produce increasing annual costs until the plan matures. However, as noted earlier, changes in the composition of the group may, in practice, result in fairly level normal costs under the accrued benefit cost method.

Projected benefit cost methods may be subdivided into (1) individual level cost methods and (2) aggregate level cost methods.

Individual Level Cost Methods. The *individual* subcategory of projected benefit cost methods is characterized by the assumed allocation of the actuarial cost for each individual employee, generally as a level amount or percentage of earnings, over all or a part of his period of service, over his period of coverage under the plan, or some other appropriate period uniformly applied. Under individual cost methods, the total actuarial cost is generally separable as to the various participants, i.e., costs are individually calculated for each employee, or are calculated by group methods in such a way as to produce essentially the same total result as though individually calculated.[12] The individual level cost methods may be further sub-

---

[12] It should be noted, however, that this does not mean that it is possible, at any given time, to identify a participant's "share" in the plan assets. For example, a turnover assumption reduces the normal cost attributable to each participant. However, this normal cost figure is too low for the participant who does not terminate and eventually retires under the plan. Likewise, this normal cost figure is excessive for those participants who subsequently terminate with no vested benefits. For the plan as a whole, however, this normal cost figure may be entirely appropriate. This point should be kept clearly in mind, particularly in those sections of the chapter illustrating the calculations of normal costs under the various actuarial cost methods in terms of an individual participant. The authors recognize the weakness of this approach but feel that the basic nature of each method is illustrated more clearly through use of individual participant examples.

divided as to whether or not a supplemental liability is created.

A. Without Supplemental Liability. As indicated above, projected benefit cost methods have as their objective the spreading of the costs of total projected benefits evenly over some future period. One logical period over which costs can be spread is the period from the attained age of the employee at the time he entered the plan to his normal retirement age under the plan.

The normal cost accruals are determined by distributing the present value of an individual's total projected benefits as a level amount or percentage of earnings over his assumed future period of coverage under the plan. Total projected benefits include past service benefits, if any, as well as future service benefits to be credited by retirement age. Thus, there is no supplemental liability created under this cost method at the inception of the plan, since the present value of future benefits is exactly equal to the present value of future normal cost accruals. Thereafter, there is still no supplemental liability if contribution payments have been made equal to the normal costs that have accrued in prior years. It must be reemphasized that a supplemental liability may be created for other reasons. The point to be made here is that this actuarial cost method, other things equal, does not of itself generate a supplemental liability.

This actuarial cost method requires, then, a projection of total benefits distributed by age at inception of coverage, and calculation of the normal cost based on a set of level premium deferred annuity rates.[13] The latter may be determined by dividing the present value of an annuity at normal retirement age by the present value of a temporary annuity running to normal retirement age. For example, assume that the total projected benefit for a participant, age 35 at the inception date of the plan, is $200 a month beginning at age 65. The normal cost for this participant's benefit would be equal to the present value at age 35 of an annuity of $200 a month beginning at age 65, divided by the present value of a temporary annuity due of $1 for 30 years.

If there is no change in the projected benefits of any employee

---

[13] Regardless of which actuarial cost method is used, there is the question of whether to include in the cost calculations employees who have not yet met the plan participation requirements. One view is that a certain percentage of the currently noneligible employees will eventually qualify for participation in the plan and, therefore, the cost calculations should recognize this fact. Some actuaries, however, project costs only for those employees who are actually eligible for participation in the plan. The latter approach generally produces lower cost estimates. Either approach can be justified, but the reader should recognize that differences in cost projections may be due, at least in part, to the approach used.

and the covered group remains constant, the normal cost under the plan will remain constant (subject to adjustment to the extent that actual experience deviates from the assumptions employed). Obviously, this will not prove to be the case in most plans. For example, if the benefit formula is related to compensation, employees will be entitled to larger projected benefits as they receive salary increases. Where salary scales have not been used in the original cost calculations, the increase in projected benefits due to salary increases is spread evenly over the period from the year in which compensation is increased to the year in which the employee reaches normal retirement age. This, of course, results in an increase in annual contributions for the plan as a whole. Also, new employees will become eligible for participation in the plan, and some currently covered workers will terminate their participation under the plan. Since the age and sex distribution and the benefit levels of new employees are not likely to be identical to those of terminated participants, there are bound to be variations in the annual contributions for the plan as a whole.

The reader will recognize that the individual level cost method without supplemental liability is, in effect, the actuarial cost method used under fully insured individual policy and group permanent plans. Indeed, this cost method is analogous to the level premium concept used in individual life insurance premium calculations. For this reason, this actuarial cost method is sometimes referred to as the individual level premium method or the attained age level contribution method.

B. *With Supplemental Liability.* This cost method is similar to the previous method except that the assumption is made, with respect to the initial group of participants, that the period over which costs are spread begins with the first year they could have joined the plan, had it always been in effect. For an employee who enters after the inception date of the plan, the normal cost under this method is the same as would be generated by the previous method.[14] This follows since that employee's entry year coincides with the year in which he becomes a participant. In the case of the initial group of participants, a supplemental liability is automatically created because of the assumption that normal cost payments have been made prior to the inception date of the plan.

Using the example cited above, assume that an employee is entitled to a total projected benefit at age 65 of $200 a month. He is age 35 at the inception of the plan but would have been eligible when he was 30, had the plan been always in effect. Under the

---

[14] This statement assumes that the normal cost is calculated in a consistent manner for both the original group and subsequent entrants.

individual level cost method with supplemental liability, the normal cost for this participant's benefit would be equal to the present value at age 30 (rather than age 35, as is the case under the previous cost method) of an annuity of $200 a month beginning at age 65, divided by the present value of a temporary annuity due of $1 for 35 years (rather than 30 years). In the above example, the numerator is smaller and the denominator is larger than the corresponding values calculated under the individual cost method without a supplemental liability. The result, of course, is that the normal costs are lower under the individual cost method with a supplemental liability. However, since the normal costs have not been paid for the prior years, there is a supplemental liability on behalf of this employee. Unlike the accrued benefit cost method, the initial supplemental liability under the individual cost method does not bear a precise relationship to past service benefits.

The difference between the two indiviudal level cost methods can be made clear by reference to a situation in the individual life insurance field. Let us assume that an individual, age 25, purchased a 10-year convertible term life insurance contract. At age 30, the insured decides to convert the policy to an ordinary life insurance policy. If the conversion is made as of issue age (25), the ordinary life premium for age 25 can be viewed conceptually as the annual normal cost under the individual level cost method with supplemental liability. The sum of the annual premiums from issue date (age 25) to conversion date (age 30), improved at the assumed rate of interest, and adjusted to reflect the insurance cost, would be analogous to the supplemental liability under this method. If the conversion was made as of attained age, then the annual premium for age 30, adjusted to reflect the insurance cost, would be analogous to the annual cost required under the individual cost method without supplemental liability.

The individual level cost method, with supplemental liability, cannot be used under a fully insured individual policy or group permanent plan. However, this method can be used for the conversion fund portion of a combination plan and under most forms of group pension contracts and trust fund plans.

The individual level cost method with a supplemental liability has generally been referred to as the entry age normal method.

Aggregate Level Cost Methods.   The distinguishing characteristic of aggregate level cost methods is that the normal cost accruals are calculated for the plan as a whole without identifying any part of such cost accruals with the projected benefits of specific individuals. The cost accruals are expressed as a percentage of compensation or as a specified dollar amount.

The normal cost accrual rate under an aggregate method can be determined by dividing the present value of future benefits for all participants by the present value of the estimated future compensation for the group of participants. This accrual rate is then multiplied by the total annual earnings to determine the initial normal cost of the plan. If the normal cost accrual rate is to be expressed in terms of a dollar amount, then the present value of aggregate future benefits is divided by the present value of $1 per employee for each year of future service. Since there is no assumption that any normal costs have been accrued prior to the inception date of the plan, the above method does not create a supplemental liability.

In the determination of cost accruals after the inception of the plan under the above method, recognition must be given to the plan assets that presumably have been accumulated to offset prior normal cost accruals. Thus, for those years subsequent to the establishment of the plan, the accrual rate is determined by dividing the present value of aggregate future benefits, less any plan assets, by the present value of future compensation.

The normal cost accrual can be calculated under an aggregate method so as to produce a supplemental liability. This can be done in many ways, but the most clearly understood approach to creating a supplemental liability under the aggregate method is to exclude past service benefits in the projection of aggregate future benefits. This decreases the numerator of the fraction, thereby producing a smaller normal cost accrual rate. Or the actuary may simply use a supplemental liability that is generated by one of the individual cost methods. However the supplemental liability is calculated, it must be subtracted (along with plan assets) from the present value of aggregate future benefits in the calculation of subsequent accrual rates.

The aggregate level cost method without supplemental liability has been variously referred to as the percentage of payroll, the aggregate, or the remaining cost method. When there is a supplemental liability in connection with this method, it has sometimes been referred to as the attained age normal or entry age normal method.

Amortization of Supplemental Liability

The actuarial cost methods that create a supplemental liability offer the employer greater flexibility in annual contribution payments than is available under the cost methods without supplemental liability. Under the former cost methods, the employer has the alternative of paying interest only on the supplemental liability, or funding a portion of the supplemental liability in addition to the annual normal costs under the plan. In most cases, the employer makes some contribution toward the amortization of the supplemental liability. The length of the period over which the supplemental liability should be funded varies with the circumstances surrounding each plan. However, amortization periods of 20, 25, 30, and 35 years are quite common. Under federal tax law, the maximum payment for this purpose which may be made in any one year and for which a deduction may be claimed is 10% of the initial supplemental liability. Funding the supplemental liability at the maximum rate of 10% requires a funding period of about 12 years, since the supplemental liability figure reflects a discount for interest.

DEFINED CONTRIBUTION PLANS

The discussion thus far in this chapter has been concerned primarily with the role of actuarial assumptions and actuarial cost methods in calculating the annual cost of a plan. The question arises as to the degree to which this discussion is pertinent in the case of defined contribution (money purchase) plans. In these plans, the employer's contribution commitment is fixed and is usually expressed as a specified percentage of the compensation of covered employees. Thus, it would seem that there is little need for actuarial assumptions and cost methods to determine annual costs under these plans. However, if the employer wishes to have an estimate of future costs or benefits under the plan, the projection would require the choice of appropriate actuarial assumptions and a specific actuarial cost method. In estimating ultimate costs under a defined contribution plan, the actuary could use either the accrued benefit method or a projected benefit cost method, depending on how benefits are defined. Also, under traditional defined contribution plans, the annual contribution on behalf of each employee is viewed as a single-premium payment for a unit of deferred annuity to begin upon attainment of normal retirement age. Indeed, many of the defined contribution plans are funded through group deferred annuity contracts. Thus, the sex of the employee and mortality and interest assumptions determine the amount of benefits being credited each year. The amount of benefit credited each year for a given employee will vary with the size of the contribution payment and the number of years to retirement age.

A variation of the traditional defined contribution plan is found in some negotiated plans that have both a fixed contribution and a fixed benefit. Negotiated multiemployer plans are established on this basis. The union negotiates a fixed pension contribution rate with all participating employers, and the rate is usually expressed in terms of cents per hour worked or as a percentage of the compensation of covered employees. The contributions are paid into a single trust fund, and a uniform benefit schedule applicable to all covered employees is established. Actuarial assumptions and an actuarial cost method are needed in order to determine the level of benefits that can be supported by the fixed contribution commitment. In these plans, there is an additional assumption that must be made in actuarial computations which was not mentioned earlier in the chapter, i.e., the expected level of future contributions. Since the contribution commitment is usually related to compensation or hours worked, changes in levels of economic activity affect the contribution income of the plan. The actuary, therefore, must project the future flow of contribution income in order to determine an appropriate benefit formula for the plan.

The cost method normally used in actuarial computations for fixed contribution–fixed benefit plans is the projected benefit cost method with a supplemental liability. This method is used for several reasons. One, this method tends to produce annual normal costs that may be expected to remain fairly stable as a percentage of payroll or in terms of cents per hour, if the actuarial assumptions are in fact realized; and this is consistent with the contribution commitment under these plans which is normally expressed as a percentage of payroll or in cents per hour of work. Two, the existence of a supplemental liability permits some flexibility in annual contribution income. As indicated above, changes in levels of employment will result in fluctuations in the annual aggregate contribution income of the plan, which may not match fluctuations in the amount of benefits credited. During periods of prosperity, the excess of actual over expected contribution income can be applied toward amortizing the supplemental liability at a rate faster than anticipated; likewise, periods of recession would result in extensions of the period over which the supplemental liability is to be amortized. Lastly, other things being equal, the projected benefit method with supplemental liability will usually generate the highest benefit level for a given rate of contribution.

EVALUATING PENSION PROPOSALS

The reader should now be fully aware of the reasons why competing proposals in pension cases often present significantly different cost projections. There is no simple solution to this problem.

Sound decision making by the employer and professional advising by the pension practitioner requires these individuals to possess a thorough understanding of the many factors affecting ultimate and estimated costs of a pension plan.

The first step in evaluating pension proposals is to be sure that all proposals are based on similar plan provisions; or, where plan design differences exist, recognition should be given to the cost implications of these differences. If the proposals are limited to fully insured individual policy or group permanent plans, net cost illustrations and annuity guarantees should be important factors in the employer's final decision. The quality of service that the competing underwriters and their respective home offices can provide should also be taken into account.

If the proposals involve unallocated funding instruments, there are many factors that might explain the possible differences in cost estimates. Differences in actuarial assumptions, cost methods, and the assumed period over which supplemental liabilities, if any, are to be amortized have little effect on the ultimate cost of the plan. Therefore, in these cases, the final decision should rest largely on an evaluation of the probable future performance of the competing funding agencies in the areas that do affect the ultimate cost of the plan, i.e., investment earnings and expense factors. In addition, consideration should be given to annuity rate guarantees and the quality of service to be rendered by each funding agency. The employer must decide upon the relative importance to be assigned to each of these factors.

5

PLAN QUALIFICATION
AND DEDUCTIBILITY OF
EMPLOYER CONTRIBUTIONS

The tax advantages provided under the Internal Revenue Code with respect to qualified pension and profit sharing plans are most significant—both to an employer and to his employees. The principal tax advantages of such a plan are:

1. Contributions made by the employer, within the limitations prescribed, are deductible as a business expense.
2. Investment income on these contributions is not normally subject to federal income tax.
3. An employee is not considered to be in receipt of taxable income until benefits are distributed or made available to him.
4. Death benefits paid on behalf of an employee are not considered as part of his gross estate for federal estate tax purposes to the extent attributable to employer contributions and to the extent paid to a named personal beneficiary.
5. A lump sum distribution to an employee on account of his severance of employment may be taxed as a long-term capital gain.

To obtain these tax benefits, the plan must achieve a qualified status by meeting the requirements of the Internal Revenue Code and appropriate Regulations and Rulings issued by the Commissioner of Internal Revenue. This chapter, while not intended as an exhaustive treatise of the tax aspects of qualified plans, should serve as a general guide to the major requirements of federal tax law which a plan must meet if this qualified status is to be obtained. This chapter also includes a summary of the procedures involved in submitting a plan to the Internal Revenue Service for the purpose of obtaining an advance determination letter, as well as a brief discussion of the provisions of federal tax law relating to trust investments for a qualified plan and the deductibility of employer contributions.

QUALIFICATION REQUIREMENTS

Coverage Requirements

One of the most important requirements of a qualified plan is that it must be for the exclusive benefit of employees or their beneficiaries.[1] Officers of a corporation and stockholders may participate in the plan if they are bona fide employees.[2] However, a plan cannot be structured so that it discriminates in any fashion in favor of officers, stockholders, supervisors, or highly compensated employees, commonly referred to as the *prohibited* group of employees.[3]

It is possible for an attorney or other professional person to be a bona fide employee and, as such, to participate in a qualified plan. The mere fact that a professional employee has income other than from the employer is immaterial. If such an individual is an employee for all purposes, including coverage for Social Security benefits, and his income from the employer is subject to withholding for income tax purposes, he may be considered as an employee under the plan.[4]

The Code requires that a plan, if it is to qualify, must meet *either* of the two following requirements:

1. It must cover 70% or more of all employees or, if the plan requires employee contributions and if 70% or more of all employees are eligible to participate in the plan, at least 80% of those eligible must elect to participate.[5] Under this latter provision, if 70% of the employees are eligible only 56% of the total employees have to be covered (80% × 70%). In applying this requirement, those employees who have been employed for less than the minimum eligibility period prescribed by the plan (not exceeding five years) need not be taken into consideration. Also, it is not necessary to

---

[1] I.R.C. 401(a)(2); Reg. 1.401–1(a)(3)(ii).

[2] Reg. 1.401–1(b)(3).

[3] I.R.C. 401(a)(4); Reg. 1.401–1(b)(3). Before enactment of the Self-Employed Individuals Tax Retirement Act, better known as H.R. 10, sole proprietors and partners could not participate in a qualified plan, although they could establish such a plan for their employees. H.R. 10 gave these individuals the status of "employees" for the purpose of participating in a qualified plan, but under certain restrictions and limitations. The requirements for H.R. 10 plans are considerably different from those of a regular qualified plan and are beyond the scope of this chapter. They are, however, discussed in Chapter 14.

[4] Rev. Rul. 65–178, Part 2(j)(4), IRB 1965–28.

[5] I.R.C. 401(a)(3)(A); Reg. 1.401–3(a).

take into consideration those employees whose customary employment is for not more than 20 hours in any one week or for not more
than five months in any calendar year.
2. It will benefit such employees as qualify under a classification set
up by the employer and found by the Internal Revenue Service not
to be discriminatory in favor of officers, stockholders, supervisors,
or highly compensated employees.[6]

In actual practice, the second of these two requirements is the
one most frequently used in small and medium-sized firms. Under
this provision, it is possible to establish a plan solely for hourly or
salaried employees or for those employees who work in certain
designated departments or in other classifications, so long as it does
not discriminate in favor of the prohibited group of employees. The
Code itself states that a classification shall not be considered discriminatory merely because it excludes employees who earn no
more than wages taxable under the Social Security Act or merely
because it is limited to salaried or clerical employees.[7] It should be
noted, however, that this Code provision does not mean that a
"salaried-only" plan will automatically be acceptable. Such a plan
must still meet the overriding requirement that there cannot be
discrimination in favor of the prohibited group of employees.

The question of whether or not a plan may qualify if limited to
only salaried employees has been of considerable significance in
recent years. At one time, advance determination letters were readily granted for such plans by the Internal Revenue Service if all
other factors were acceptable. It has, however, become increasingly
difficult to qualify plans with this type of eligibility requirement,
and the attitude of the Service appears to be that for a salaried-only
plan to qualify, it must cover a fair cross section of employees.
Thus, for example, if the salaried employees of an employer are all
earning more than his hourly employees, it is quite likely that the
Service will find the plan objectionable. On the other hand, if the
earnings of covered salaried employees, as compared to the earnings of all the employees, reflect both the lowest pay ranges and a
satisfactory portion of the intermediate pay levels, it is quite possible that the plan will qualify if all other factors are acceptable.

In an effort to clarify this area, the Internal Revenue Service has
issued four Revenue Rulings which deal with specific fact situations
and which give an indication of the circumstances under which a
salaried-only classification will be acceptable. The first of these
Rulings involved an employer with 109 full-time employees.[8] Of this

---

[6] I.R.C. 401(a)(3)(B); Reg. 1.401–3(b).

[7] I.R.C. 401(a)(5).

[8] Rev. Rul. 66–12, IRB 1966–3.

number, 83 employees were classified as hourly and were excluded. Of the 26 salaried employees, 11 were officers, stockholders, supervisors, or highly paid employees. A significant fact in this Ruling was that the compensation of the remaining 15 salaried employees was substantially the same as the compensation of the excluded hourly employees. On these facts, the Service found the salaried-only classification to be acceptable. The Ruling also pointed out that when such a classification is acceptable under circumstances comparable to the above, it is immaterial as to whether or not the excluded employees are covered under a similar or comparable plan.

The second Ruling involved an employer with 20 employees.[9] Of this number, 17 were hourly employees and were excluded from participation. One of the remaining three employees was excluded by the age or service requirements of the plan. The two salaried employees who were participating were officers and supervisors and earned substantially more than the hourly employees. The hourly employees were not covered under any similar plan toward which the employer was making contributions. Here, the Service found the salaried-only classification to be discriminatory.

In the third Ruling, the hourly employees were represented by a union which had made demands for certain benefits but had not made demands for a qualified plan of deferred compensation.[10] The firm employed a total of 60 employees, 54 of whom were classified as hourly employees and were represented by the union. Of the six salaried employees, five were officer-stockholders who earned $25,000 a year. The sixth salaried employee had an annual salary of $6,160. The compensation of the hourly employees was considerably less than the amount paid to the officer-stockholders. In this situation, the Service found the salaried-only classification to be discriminatory, notwithstanding the employer's contention that it had a strict obligation to bargain in good faith and that it could not unilaterally include union employees in the plan.

Even if a salaried-only plan does not meet the requirements of the Service, as outlined above, it may still qualify if the employer is providing comparable contributions or benefits for the hourly employees under another plan. The most frequent example of this situation is where the hourly employees are represented by a collective bargaining unit and where the employer is making contributions to a negotiated plan. It should be noted, however, that contributions to a negotiated welfare fund are not sufficient for this purpose—there must be contributions to a pension or a profit shar-

[9] Rev. Rul. 66–13, IRB 1966–3.
[10] Rev. Rul. 66–14, IRB 1966–3.

ing plan, and the contributions or benefits under this plan must be comparable to the contributions or benefits contemplated for the salaried employees.

The fourth Ruling involved this question of comparable contributions or benefits.[11] The employer established a profit sharing plan for its six salaried employees. Contributions could be made out of profits up to a maximum of 15% of compensation. Three of the six salaried employees were officers, stockholders, or supervisors and the remaining three were highly compensated employees. There were 56 hourly employees who were provided with retirement benefits under a collectively bargained contract. Under this contract, the employer contributed approximately 9% of compensation, 4% being allocated to an industry-wide pension plan and 5% being paid into a fund used to provide vacation, health, and welfare benefits. While the coverage requirements of the Code were met, viewing the two plans as a whole, the Service found the *potential* 15% contribution under the profit sharing plan to be discriminatory when compared with the 4% contribution for the hourly employees. It is interesting to note that the ruling did not explore the possibility of whether or not the plans provided comparable benefits. It could be that under some circumstances the actual benefits being provided under two such plans would be comparable, when expressed as a percentage of compensation, even though contributions were at a different level. It would seem that when this is the case, the plan for the salaried employees should be acceptable.

The coverage requirements of federal tax law also limit the employer's choice of eligibility requirements (for example, minimum service, minimum and maximum ages, minimum compensation, etc.) to the extent that the requirements chosen must not produce discrimination in favor of the prohibited group of employees. Here, as in other areas, the question of whether or not a particular plan provision is discriminatory will depend upon the facts of the particular case and the judgment of the local reviewer of the Internal Revenue Service.

Some employers might want to establish a plan with a provision that those persons employed on the effective date of the plan will be eligible immediately but that future employees will have to meet some stipulated eligibility requirements. Dual eligibility requirements of this type will generally be acceptable if employees in the prohibited group, at the time they are eligible, can also meet the more restrictive requirements set for future employees.[12]

---

[11] Rev. Rul. 66–15, IRB 1966–3.
[12] Rev. Rul. 65–178, Part 4(e), IRB 1965–28.

The coverage requirements are also significant in the area of employee contributions. For example, while a plan may require employees to contribute, the employee contribution rate cannot be so high as to make the plan unattractive except to highly compensated employees.[13] As a general rule, an employee contribution rate of 6% or less will not be considered burdensome.[14]

The coverage requirements need be met on only one day in each quarter of the plan's taxable year.[15]

Contribution and Benefit Requirements

Another major requirement of a qualified plan is that the contributions or benefits provided cannot discriminate in favor of officers, stockholders, supervisors, or highly compensated employees—i.e., the prohibited group of employees.[16]

A plan will not be discriminatory merely because it excludes individuals who earn less than the maximum taxable wage for Social Security purposes, nor does the law prohibit the use of a benefit formula which provides a larger percentage of benefit for earnings in excess of the Social Security taxable wage base than it does for earnings under this amount. However, if the benefit formula is in any way "integrated" with Social Security benefits, certain requirements are imposed to prevent discrimination in favor of the prohibited group of employees.[17] The basic concept of these requirements is that the benefits from the employer's plan must be dovetailed with Social Security benefits in such a manner that employees earning over the taxable wage base will not receive combined benefits under the two programs which are proportionately greater than the combined benefits for employees earning under this amount.

These integration requirements take into account the type of benefit formula employed, whether or not a death benefit is included prior to retirement, and whether or not there is any death benefit

---

[13] Reg. 1.401–3(d).

[14] Rev. Rul. 65–178, Part 4(g), IRB 1965–28.

[15] I.R.C. 401(a)(6); Reg. 1.401–(3)(g).

[16] I.R.C. 401(a)(4); Reg. 1.401–4.

[17] I.R.C. 401(a)(5); Reg. 1.401–3(e); Rev. Rul. 65–178, Part 4(j), IRB 1965–28. Final Regulations concerning the integration of plans at the $6,600 level had not been released at the time this material was prepared. As a result, the following discussion relates to plans integrated at the $4,800 level. Until such Regulations are released, the rules for $4,800 plans continue to apply to plans integrated at this level and, if it is desired to integrate a plan at the $6,600 level, it will be permissible to use 48/66 of the maximum percentages arrived at for a $4,800 plan.

(and the form thereof) after retirement. Other factors such as the normal retirement age specified in the plan, the manner of determining earnings, and the presence or absence of employee contributions are also considered. The following discussion should serve as a general guide to the integration requirements of a plan with a normal retirement age not lower than 65 and under which employees do not make contributions.[18]

In a flat percentage excess plan (where the benefit is a percentage of monthly earnings in excess of $400), the maximum percentage that may be applied to excess earnings, if there is no death benefit either before or after retirement, is 37½%. If there is a death benefit before retirement, but none after retirement, the maximum would be 33⅓%. With a death benefit before retirement and with benefits payable for life with five years certain, the percentage becomes 32⅓% and if payments are to be made for life with 10 years certain, the maximum percentage would be 30%.

In a flat percentage stepped-up plan (where a higher percentage is applied to earnings in excess of $400 a month than is applied to earnings below this amount), the maximum percentage applied to monthly earnings in excess of $400 may be increased by the percentage applicable to the first $400. In effect, the percentage applicable to the first $400 of monthly earnings is considered a base plan applicable to all earnings. Only the excess portion must integrate, and this portion must meet the requirements discussed for an excess plan. Thus, for example, if a plan has no death benefit (either before or after retirement), and provides a benefit of 15% of the first $400 of monthly earnings, the maximum percentage applicable to the excess compensation would be 52½% (15% plus 37½%). If the plan had a death benefit before retirement and if retirement benefits were payable for life with 10 years certain, the maximum percentage applicable to excess earnings in this example would be 45% (15% plus 30%).

Regardless of the presence or absence of death benefits, it is required, when integrating a flat percentage plan, that an employee must have completed at least 15 years of service with the employer (not necessarily as a participant) in order to receive the full benefit. For an employee retiring with less than 15 years of service, a proportionate reduction in benefit is made.

To determine the maximum percentage for a unit credit plan (where service and earnings are both reflected), it is first necessary to determine the maximum that would otherwise be applicable if

---

[18] The integration requirements for various benefit formulas are discussed in greater detail in Chapter 2. See pp. 42–46.

the plan had a flat percentage formula. If the plan bases benefits on career average earnings, this percentage is then divided by 30. If the plan bases benefits on final earnings, the divisor will be the maximum number of years of credited service but in any event, need not exceed 45.

To illustrate, in a unit credit excess plan which provides for no death benefit (either before or after retirement) and which bases benefits on career average earnings, the maximum percentage per year of service applicable to excess earnings would be 1¼% (37½% divided by 30). If such a benefit formula based benefits on final earnings and the plan had a minimum age requirement for participation of 25 with a normal retirement age of 65, with no credit for past service, the maximum percentage would be .9375% (37½% divided by 40). If the plan had a death benefit prior to retirement and retirement benefits were payable for life with 10 years certain, the corresponding percentages in this example would be 1% (30% divided by 30) and ¾% (30% divided by 40). If the plan bases future service benefits on career average earnings after the effective date of the plan and past service benefits on earnings as of the effective date, the divisor for future service benefits would be 30, and for past service benefits it would be the maximum number of years of credited service, but this divisor for past service benefits could not be less than 30 nor would it need to be greater than 45.

In a unit credit stepped-up plan (where a higher percentage is applied to earnings in excess of $400 a month than is applied to earnings below this amount), the maximum percentages are determined in the same manner as for a flat percentage stepped-up plan. Thus, the percentage applicable to the first $400 of monthly earnings is considered a base plan applicable to all earnings, and only the excess portion must integrate. To illustrate, if a career average plan provides no death benefit either before or after retirement and a 1% benefit for each year of service with respect to the first $400 of monthly earnings, the maximum percentage applicable to excess earnings would be 2¼% (1% plus 1¼%).

Another type of integrated formula is the "offset" formula, which subtracts all or a portion of the employee's primary Social Security benefit from his benefit under the plan. The integration limit in these plans applies not to the percentage of compensation being credited but to the percentage of the Social Security offset. In a plan which has no death benefit either before or after retirement, the maximum offset would be 117% of the employee's primary Social Security benefit. In a plan with a death benefit before retirement and which provides that retirement benefits will be paid for life with 10 years certain, the maximum offset would be 93.6% of the employee's primary Social Security benefit.[19]

Defined contribution (money purchase) pension plans and profit sharing plans may also be integrated. Here, the integration rules are relatively simple, and adjustments are not made for the inclusion of death benefits, either before or after retirement, or for service of less than 15 years, etc. The reason, essentially, is that since the contribution is fixed in these plans, these features automatically affect the amount of the employee's retirement benefit. If the first $400 of monthly earnings is to be excluded under this type of plan, the maximum percentage that may be contributed with respect to excess earnings is 9⅜%. If a stepped-up formula is used, the percentage may be increased by the percentage applicable to the first $400 of monthly earnings. Thus, for example, if a contribution of 3% is being made with respect to the first $400 of monthly earnings, the maximum contribution that may be made with respect to excess earnings would be 12⅜%.

Other Requirements

Must Be in Writing. A qualified plan must be in writing and must set forth all the provisions necessary for qualification.[20] This is normally accomplished by means of a trust agreement, a plan instrument, or both. In group pension programs, the plan provisions are often contained in the group contract, and, in this event, neither a trust agreement nor a plan instrument is necessary.

A trust agreement is generally required for trust fund plans and for plans using individual insurance or annuity contracts.[21] This allows the employer to make irrevocable contributions on a basis which will permit the employee to defer including these contributions as taxable income until the time they are distributed or made available to him. If a group pension contract is employed, an intervening trust is usually not necessary since the same results can be achieved through the group contract itself—i.e., the contract can be written so that employer contributions are irrevocably made without the employees being considered in receipt of these contributions until they are distributed or made available.

Communication to Employees. The plan must also be communicated to employees.[22] An announcement letter or booklet is frequently

---

[19] For a more extensive table of permissible offsets, see Table 2–6, p. 46.

[20] Reg. 1.401–1(a)(2); Rev. Rul. 65–178, Part 2(f), IRB 1965–28.

[21] A trust agreement is not necessary for some fully insured individual policy plans that employ nontransferable contracts. However, a plan instrument of some type would still be required so that the plan provisions can be set forth in writing.

[22] Reg. 1.401–1(a)(2); Rev. Rul. 65–178, Part 2(i), IRB 1965–28.

used for this purpose, although a conspicuously posted bulletin board announcement will suffice. If employees are not given a copy of the actual plan, they should be told that a copy is available for inspection at a certain place (usually at the corporate office) and at certain times.

Nondiversion of Contributions. The trust must specifically provide that it is impossible for the employer to divert or recapture his contributions before the satisfaction of all plan liabilities—funds contributed must be used for the exclusive benefit of employees or their beneficiaries.[23] One exception to this rule may occur at termination of a pension plan if any funds then remain because of "actuarial error" and all fixed and contingent obligations of the plan have been satisfied. In this event, such excess funds may be returned to the employer.[24] A second exception makes it possible to establish a plan on a conditional basis so that employer contributions are returnable if the plan is not approved by the Internal Revenue Service.[25]

Definitely Determinable Benefits. A qualified *pension* plan must provide definitely determinable benefits.[26] A defined contribution pension plan meets this requirement since the employer's contribution formula is definite and, for this reason, benefits are considered as being actuarially determinable. Also, variable annuity plans or plans under which the benefit varies with a cost-of-living index will be acceptable.

Because of the definitely determinable benefit requirement, any amounts forfeited by terminating employees may not be used to increase benefits for the remaining participants under a pension plan—instead, these forfeitures must be used to reduce employer contributions next due.[27] Under this requirement, the question often arises as to whether dividends under insurance or annuity contracts must be used to reduce employer contributions or whether they may be applied to provide additional benefits. If the benefit formula specifically calls for the use of these dividends to increase benefits and discrimination in favor of the prohibited group of employees does not result, use of dividends in this manner will be permissible under plans funded with individual insurance or annuity contracts.[28] However, if the plan is funded with a group

---

[23] I.R.C. 401 (a) (2) ; Reg. 1.401–2.

[24] Reg. 1.401–2 (b) ; Rev. Rul. 65–178, Part 3 (d), IRB 1965–28.

[25] Rev. Rul. 65–178, Part 3 (c), IRB 1965–28.

[26] Reg. 1.401–1 (b) (1) (i) ; Rev. Rul. 65–178, Part 2 (m), IRB 1965–28.

[27] I.R.C. 401 (a) (8) ; Reg. 1.401–7.

[28] PS 45, *Pension and Profit Sharing Tax Service* (Englewood Cliffs, N.J.: Prentice-Hall, Inc., n.d.), ¶ 12,543. However, additional benefits that result from applying dividends in this manner must be taken into account if the plan is integrated with Social Security benefits.

pension contract, dividends must generally be used to reduce employer contributions.[29]

The definitely determinable benefit requirement does not apply to qualified profit sharing plans. Here, there is a requirement that the plan must provide for participation in the profits of the employer by the employees or their beneficiaries.[30] While it is not required that there be a definite formula for determining the amount to be contributed to the profit sharing plan, it is required that there be a definite predetermined formula for allocating contributions among participants and for distributing funds after a fixed number of years, the attainment of a stated age, or upon the happening of some event such as layoff, illness, disability, retirement, death, or severance of employment.

Permanency.   The plan must be a permanent one.[31] While the employer may reserve the right to amend or terminate the plan at any time, it is expected that the plan will be established on a permanent basis. Thus, if a plan is terminated for any reason other than business necessity within a few years after it has been in force, this will be considered as evidence that the plan, from its inception, was not a bona fide one for the benefit of employees.

In the profit sharing area, as previously noted, it is not necessary that the employer make contributions in accordance with a definite predetermined formula. However, merely making a single or an occasional contribution out of profits will not be sufficient to create a permanent and continuing plan. The Regulations require that "substantial and recurring" contributions must be made out of profits.

Inclusion of Life Insurance Benefits.   Life insurance benefits may be included in a qualified plan but only to the extent that these benefits are "incidental."[32]

In a qualified pension plan (other than one using a defined contribution formula), the incidental test is satisfied if the life insurance benefit does not exceed 100 times the expected monthly retirement benefit or, if greater, the reserve for this benefit. For profit sharing plans and pension plans using a defined contribution (money purchase) formula, the incidental test is satisfied if: (1) the aggregate of the premiums paid for a participant's life insurance is *less than* one half of the contributions allocated to him at any particular time; and (2) the plan requires the trustee to con-

---

[29] I.R.C. 403 (a) (2) (A) (ii) ; I.R.C. 404 (a) (2) ; Rev. Rul. 65–178, Part 3 (f), IRB 1965–28.

[30] Reg. 1.401–1 (b) (1) (ii).

[31] Reg. 1.401–1 (b) (2) ; Rev. Rul. 65–178, Part 2 (h), IRB 1965–28.

[32] Reg. 1.401–1 (b) (1) (i) ; Rev. Rul. 65–178, Part 2 (n) (1), IRB 1965–28; Rev. Rul. 60–83, IRB 1960–10.

vert the entire value of the life insurance contract at or before retirement into cash or to provide periodic income so that no portion of such value may be used to continue life insurance protection beyond retirement, or to distribute the contract to the participant.[33]

Vesting. A plan will not qualify unless it provides for "ultimate" vesting when an employee attains his normal retirement age (or a stated age or some other event in the case of a profit sharing plan) and unless it provides for fully vested rights in all participants upon termination of the plan.[34] Beyond this, there are no specific requirements as to vesting other than the general prohibition against discrimination in favor of employees in the prohibited group. Because of this prohibition against discrimination, the Internal Revenue Service will, on occasion, require some degree of vesting under a pension plan before it will issue an advance determination letter—particularly in connection with plans being instituted by small closely held corporations.

The prohibition against discrimination has particular application in connection with profit sharing plans. Here, unlike the situation with respect to pension plans, forfeitures may be reallocated among remaining participants to increase their benefits. Since a profit sharing plan with no vesting provision could, in operation, result in all of the employer's contributions ultimately being allocated for key employees, it could produce discrimination in favor of the prohibited group of employees. Therefore, the Service will generally require vesting in connection with profit sharing plans and at a relatively rapid rate.

U.S. Trust. If a trust is used, it must be one which is organized or created in the United States and maintained at all times as a domestic trust.[35] The earnings of a trust created outside of the United States will be taxable, although if the trust would otherwise qualify, the employer will be allowed to take appropriate deductions for his contributions, and the beneficiaries of the trust will be allowed the same tax treatment with respect to distributions as if the trust had been qualified.[36]

---

[33] Rev. Rul. 65–178, Part 2(n), IRB 1965–28; Rev. Rul. 66–143, IRB 1966–22; Private letter ruling dated May 28, 1965 to American Life Convention, Life Insurance Association of America, signed by John W. Littleton, Director, Tax Rulings Division, Internal Revenue Service, *Pension and Profit Sharing Tax Service* (Englewood Cliffs, N.J.: Prentice-Hall, Inc., n.d.), ¶ 12,042.

[34] I.R.C. 401(a)(7); Reg. 1.401–6; Rev. Rul. 65–178, Part 5(c), IRB 1965–28.

[35] I.R.C. 401(a); Reg. 1.401–1(a)(3); Rev. Rul. 65–178, Part 2(d), IRB 1965–28.

[36] Special rules exist with regard to the taxation of distributions to nonresident aliens. Rev. Rul. 65–178, Part 2(d), IRB 1965–28.

OBTAINING AN ADVANCE DETERMINATION LETTER

The federal tax law does not require an employer to submit his plan to the Internal Revenue Service for an advance determination that the plan meets the requirements of the Code and has achieved a qualified status. As a convenience to the taxpayer, however, the Internal Revenue Service will issue advance determination letters (often called "approval" letters) as to the qualified status of a plan.[37] Most taxpayers take advantage of this and obtain such a ruling.

One reason for taking advantage of this procedure is the possibility that the Service will find some feature or features of the plan to be unacceptable. The Code permits a retroactive change in the plan (to its effective date) if the change is made by the 15th day of the third month following the close of the employer's taxable year.[38] If changes are necessary, the employer may make the appropriate amendments to the plan within this period and thus preserve the deductions he wishes to claim for the taxable year involved.

In contrast, if the employer does not file for an advance determination letter, the qualified status of the plan will be examined by the Service at the time the employer's tax return is audited. Any changes then required by the Service will, in all probability, be at a time which is beyond the period allowed for making a retroactive change. Thus, there would be the possibility of the employer losing at least one year's deduction.

The information required is filed with the local District Director of Internal Revenue. While there are no particular government forms for this purpose, most insurance companies and consulting firms have forms available to aid the employer's tax counsel in organizing the material for submission.

The Regulations set forth the material and information that should be filed for obtaining an advance determination letter.[39] This includes:

1. The name of the plan and the name and address of the employer (and trustee, if applicable).
2. Verified copies of any trust agreement involved.
3. Verified copies of any plan instrument involved.

---

[37] Rev. Proc. 62–31, IRB 1962–47.

[38] I.R.C. 401(b); Reg. 1.401–5. It should be noted that although extensions granted for the filing of a tax return extend the time in which an accrual basis taxpayer may make his contributions to a plan, they do not extend the time during which a retroactive plan change may be made.

[39] Rev. Proc. 62–31, Section 4, IRB 1962–47; Reg. 1.404(a)–2.

4. Verified copies of any group pension contract involved.
5. Specimen copies of any individual life insurance or annuity contracts involved.
6. Specimen copies of the formal announcement and detailed description made available to employees.
7. Verified or specimen copies of any amendments to any of the above items.
8. A detailed description of the plan (effective dates, eligibility requirements, employer and employee contribution levels, retirement dates and provisions, vesting and death benefit provisions, rights of the employer to amend or terminate and employee benefits upon termination, funding instrument, method of distributing benefits, etc.)
9. A summary concerning the salaries, benefits, contributions, and other information relating to the 25 highest-paid participants.[40]
10. A schedule concerning the total nondeferred compensation paid or accrued to employees and the total amount allocated by the employer under the plan.
11. A classification of all employees, with reasons indicated as to why certain employees are not eligible to participate.
12. A detailed description of all methods, factors, and assumptions used in determining and adjusting costs.
13. A statement of applicable limitations on deductions.
14. Certain information concerning the employer—the type of organization, the nature of the employer's business, when it was incorporated or when the business commenced, whether or not there was a predecessor business and if so, the name of the predecessor, the date the transfer took place, and whether or not the predecessor business was a sole proprietorship, a partnership, or a corporation.

If all factors are acceptable, an advance determination letter will be issued by the local District Director, although all such letters are subject to post review by the National Office of the Internal Revenue Service. If the District Director is unwilling to issue an advance determination letter, it is customary for him to notify the employer and to arrange for a conference at the local office in order to work out mutually acceptable changes. If the employer is unwilling to accept the changes required by the District Director, he may request the District Director to refer the issue to the National Office for technical advice. If the District Director does not refer the matter to the National Office, the employer may request direct consideration by the National Office if he can show one of the following:

---

[40] While in most cases the employees affected are the same, this listing of the 25 highest-paid participants should not be confused with the 25 highest-paid employees on the effective date of the plan who are or who may become participants and whose benefits would be restricted in the event of early termination of the plan.

1. The position of the district office is contrary to the law or Regulations.
2. The position of the district office is contrary to the position of the Service as set forth in a Revenue Ruling currently in effect.
3. The position of the district office is contrary to a court decision which is followed by the Service.
4. The contemplated district office action is in conflict with a determination made in a similar case in the same or another district.
5. The issues arise because of unique or novel facts which have not previously been passed upon in any published Revenue Ruling or announcement.

TRUST INVESTMENTS

As previously noted, a qualified plan must be for the exclusive benefit of employees or their beneficiaries, and this primary purpose must be maintained with respect to the investment of trust funds as well as in other activities of the trust. Generally, the trustee may purchase any investments permitted by the trust agreement to the extent permitted by local law.[41]

This requirement does not prevent others from benefiting from a transaction with the trust as, for example, when the sale of securities at a profit benefits the seller, provided that the applicable investment requisites have been met. These requisites are:

1. The cost of the investment must not exceed fair market value at the time of purchase.
2. A fair return commensurate with the prevailing rate must be provided.
3. Sufficient liquidity is to be maintained so as to permit distributions in accordance with the terms of the plan.
4. The safeguards and diversity that a prudent investor would adhere to are present.[42]

The question quite logically arises as to whether or not lending money to the employer or purchasing the stock of the employer corporation would meet the requirement that funds must be invested for the exclusive benefit of the employees or their beneficiaries.[43] Such an investment may be made; however, the trustee must notify the District Director of Internal Revenue of such an investment, making a full disclosure of the reasons for such investment and the conditions under which it is being made, so that a determi-

---

[41] Reg. 1.401–1 (b) (5) (i).

[42] Rev. Rul. 65–178, Part 2 (k) (1), IRB 1965–28.

[43] There is also the question of whether or not such an investment would constitute a prohibited transaction. See pp. 124–127.

nation may be made as to whether the trust serves any purpose other than constituting part of a plan for the exclusive benefit of employees.[44] Such investments must be reported on Form 990-P, which the trustee must file annually.

It should be noted that these requirements also apply to loans made to other related or controlled interests, including a corporation controlled by the employer, and to the purchase of the stock of such a controlled corporation. A corporation is controlled by the employer when the employer owns, directly or indirectly, at least 50% of the total combined voting power of all classes of stock entitled to vote or at least 50% of the total value of shares of all classes of stock of the corporation.[45]

The information that must be submitted to the District Director with respect to such an investment includes the following:

1. Balance sheets of the employer (and controlled corporation, if involved) as of the close of the last two taxable years.
2. Comparative statements of income and profit and loss for the last five taxable years.
3. Analysis of surplus for the last five years, specifically showing the amount and rate of dividends paid on each class of stock.
4. A statement accounting for all material changes from the latest dates of the foregoing information to the date of filing the information.
5. A schedule showing the nature and amounts of the various assets in the trust fund.
6. A statement setting forth the amount to be invested in the stock or securities of the employer or a controlled corporation (or both), the nature of the investment, the present rate of return, collateral or type of security for the loan, if any, and the reasons for the investment.[46]

This information must be certified to by the accounting or other responsible officer of the employer.

The trustee may also obtain an advance determination letter from the District Director as to the investment by filing the same information with an appropriate request.[47]

Prohibited Transactions

A trust may lose its tax-exempt status if it engages in a prohibited transaction.[48] A prohibited transaction means any transaction

---

[44] Reg. 1.401–1 (b) (5) (ii) ; Rev. Rul. 65–178, Part 2 (k) (1), IRB 1965–28.

[45] Reg. 1.401–1 (b) (5) (ii) ; I.R.C., 503 (c).

[46] Rev. Proc. 62–31, Section 4.05, IRB 1962–47.

[47] Rev. Rul. 65–178, Part 2 (k) (1), IRB 1965–28.

[48] I.R.C., 503 (a) ; Reg. 1.401–1 (b) (5) (1).

in which the trust engages in any one or more of the following:

1. Lends any part of its funds to the employer without the receipt of adequate security and a reasonable rate of interest.
2. Pays any compensation to the employer in excess of a reasonable allowance for salaries or other compensation for personal services actually rendered.
3. Makes any part of its services available on a preferential basis to the employer.
4. Makes any substantial purchase of securities or any other property from the employer for more than adequate consideration.
5. Sells any substantial part of its securities or other property to the employer for less than adequate consideration.
6. Engages in any other transaction which results in a substantial diversion of its funds to the employer.[49]

Also prohibited are similar transactions with other related or controlled interests, including a corporation controlled by the employer by ownership, either directly or indirectly, of at least 50% of the total combined voting power of all classes of stock entitled to vote or at least 50% of the total value of shares of all classes of stock of the corporation.

If a trust engages in a prohibited transaction, it will lose its exemption only for taxable years after the one in which the trust is notified by the Commissioner of Internal Revenue that it has engaged in the transaction. However, if the transaction was entered into intentionally for the purpose of diverting funds from the exempt purpose of the trust and if a substantial amount was involved, the exemption will be lost starting with the year in which the transaction occurred, and notification from the Commissioner is not necessary.[50] The loss of exemption will continue until the Commissioner is satisfied that the trust will not knowingly engage in such a transaction again. This requires that the trust file a claim for exemption with the District Director of Internal Revenue along with a letter claiming exemption, a sworn statement that the trust will not again knowingly engage in a prohibited transaction, and the information otherwise required to obtain an advance determination letter as to the qualified status of the plan. If the Commissioner is satisfied and the plan otherwise qualifies, the trust will be notified in writing, and its exempt status will be restored for taxable years *following* the one in which the claim is filed.[51]

For all practical purposes, the prohibition against loans without

---

[49] I.R.C., 503(c).

[50] I.R.C. 503(a)(2); Reg. 1.503(a)–1(b).

[51] I.R.C. 503(d); Reg. 1.503(d)–1.

adequate security and without a reasonable rate of interest is of most significance to qualified trusts. The Regulations define adequate security as

. . . something in addition to and supporting a promise to pay, which is so pledged to the organization that it may be sold, foreclosed upon, or otherwise disposed of in default of repayment of the loan, the value and liquidity of which security is such that it may reasonably be anticipated that loss of principal or interest will not result from the loan.[52]

The Regulations stipulate that stock of the borrowing corporation does not constitute adequate security. However, the law permits the trust to invest in unsecured debentures of the employer without the purchase being considered a prohibited transaction from the viewpoint of adequate security if certain requirements are met.[53] The first of these requirements relates to the purchase price of the obligation and is satisfied if any one of the following three tests is met:

1. The obligation is acquired on the market either at the price of the obligation prevailing on a national securities exchange which is registered with the Securities and Exchange Commission, or at a price not less favorable to the trust than the offering price as established by current bid and asked prices quoted by persons independent of the issuer.
2. The obligation is acquired from an underwriter at a price not in excess of the public offering price for the obligation as set forth in a prospectus or offering circular filed with the Securities and Exchange Commission if a substantial portion of the same issue is acquired by persons independent of the issuer at the same price.
3. The obligation is acquired directly from the issuer at a price not less favorable to the trust than the price paid currently for a substantial portion of the same issue by persons independent of the issuer.

The second requirement which must be satisfied is that immediately following the acquisition of the obligation, not more than 25% of the aggregate amount of obligations issued in such issue and outstanding at the time of acquisition is held by the trust and that at least 50% of such amount is held by persons independent of the issuer. A third requirement provides that immediately following such acquisition, not more than 25% of the assets of the trust is invested in obligations of the employer or related or controlled interests.

It is still necessary, of course, that the obligations produce a

---

[52] Reg. 1.503(c)–1(b).

[53] I.R.C. 503(h) ; Reg. 1.503(h).

reasonable rate of interest payable to the trust.[54] In this respect, and with regard to any type of loan that might otherwise be a prohibited transaction, the Regulations suggest that the prevailing rate of interest charged by financial institutions in the community where the transaction takes place and for the same type of loan be taken into account.[55]

UNRELATED BUSINESS INCOME

Generally, the income of a qualified trust is exempt under Section 501(a) of the Code. However, even though such a trust does not lose its qualified status, all or a part of its income may be subject to tax if such income is considered to be unrelated business income.[56]

Unrelated business income is the gross income derived from *any* unrelated trade or business regularly carried on by the trust, less allowable deductions which are directly connected with the carrying on of such trade or business.[57] An unrelated trade or business means any trade or business the conduct of which is not substantially related to the exempt purpose of the trust.[58]

It should be noted that only income resulting from the direct operation of the business is subject to tax. Thus, if the trust owns all of the stock of a corporation and the corporation directly operates the business, the dividend income received by the trust will not be subject to tax.[59]

The following income is *not* considered as unrelated business income: dividends, interest, annuities, royalties, rents from real property (including personal property leased with the real property), and gains from the sale or exchange of capital assets.[60]

However, rental income from a "business lease" must be considered as unrelated business income.[61] The law defines a business lease as the lease of real property for a term of more than five years if

---

[54] Also, the fact that a particular transaction is not considered a prohibited transaction does not mean that the requirement that investments must be for the "exclusive benefit of employees" has been met. This test must be satisfied independently.

[55] Reg. 1.503(c)–1(c).

[56] I.R.C. 501(b); I.R.C. 511, et seq.

[57] I.R.C. 512(a); Reg. 1.512(a)–1.

[58] I.R.C. 513(a).

[59] Reg. 1.512(b)–1.

[60] I.R.C. 512(b); Reg. 1.512(b)–1. Note, however, that income from the rental of personal property not leased with real property is considered as unrelated business income. Rev. Rul. 60–206, IRB 1960–21.

[61] I.R.C. 512(b)(4); I.R.C. 514.

there is a business-lease indebtedness against the property at the end of the trust's taxable year.[62] A business-lease indebtedness, in turn, is defined as an indebtedness incurred by the trust to acquire or improve the real property leased for a term of more than five years, whether incurred before or after the acquisition of the property.[63] It also includes the amount of indebtedness secured by a mortgage or similar lien to which the property was subject when acquired by the trust, even though the trust did not assume such indebtedness.[64] If only a portion of the property is subject to the business lease, the indebtedness is allocated proportionately.[65]

Thus, if the trust does not borrow money, even the income from a long-term lease would not be taxable, and if the trust does borrow money, the income will not be taxable if a short-term lease of five years or less is involved. It should be noted, however, that when figuring the term of the lease, any period for which the lease may be extended or renewed by reason of an option is considered as part of the term.[66]

If the rent from a business lease is to be taxed to a trust, the unrelated business income is that part of the rent which bears the same relationship to the total rent as the business-lease indebtedness at the end of the taxable year bears to the adjusted basis of the property at that time.[67] The same proportion of interest, depreciation, taxes, etc., will be allowed as a deduction to the trust.[68]

When a trust has unrelated business income, this must be reported by the trustee on Form 990-T. This return must be filed on or before the 15th day of the fourth month following the close of the trust's taxable year. Generally speaking, most qualified trusts will be taxed at personal income tax rates, although a specific deduction of $1,000 is allowed.[69]

DEDUCTIBILITY OF EMPLOYER CONTRIBUTIONS

Apart from the specific provisions of the Internal Revenue Code dealing with the deductibility of employer contributions to a qualified plan, it is first required that if such a contribution is to be deductible, it must otherwise be deductible as an ordinary and

---

[62] I.R.C. 514(b)(1); Reg. 1.514(b)–1.

[63] I.R.C. 514(c)(1); Reg. 1.514(c)–1.

[64] I.R.C. 514(c)(2); Reg. 1.514(c)–1(c).

[65] I.R.C. 514(c)(6); Reg. 1.514(c)–1(g).

[66] I.R.C. 514(b)(2)(A); Reg. 1.514(b)–1(b)(1).

[67] I.R.C. 514(a)(1); Reg. 1.514(a)–1.

[68] I.R.C. 514(a)(2) and (3); Reg. 1.514(a)–2.

[69] I.R.C. 511(b)(1); I.R.C. 512(b)(12).

necessary business expense under Code Sections 162 (relating to trade or business expenses) or 212 (relating to expenses for the production of income).[70] Also, a deduction will not be allowed for any portion of the contribution for any employee which, together with other deductions allowed for compensation for such employee, exceeds a reasonable allowance for services he has actually rendered.

The employer's contributions to a qualified plan are generally deductible under Section 404 of the Internal Revenue Code. Expenses such as actuary's and trustee's fees which are not provided for by contributions under the plan are deductible under Sections 162 or 212 to the extent they are ordinary and necessary expenses.[71]

Employer contributions are generally deductible only in the year in which paid, even though the employer is on an accrual basis.[72] However, an accrual basis employer accruing the liability for a plan contribution in a given taxable year will be deemed to have made the contribution during this taxable year if it is in fact paid by the time prescribed for filing his return for such taxable year (including extensions).

It is most important that the liability to make contributions be established by the close of the employer's taxable year. This is of special significance for the taxable year in which the plan is made effective. In the case of a plan which involves a trust, there must be a valid existing trust, complete in all respects and recognized as such under the applicable local law, in effect by the close of such taxable year. If the employer is on an accrual basis, there need be no trust *corpus* prior to the close of such taxable year; however, the corpus must be furnished no later than the due date of the employer's tax return for such taxable year (including extensions).[73]

In a group pension program without a trust, the plan will be considered to be in effect if, by the close of the taxable year, the contract has been applied for by the employer and accepted by the insurance company, a contract or abstract has been prepared in sufficient detail outlining all of the terms of the plan, a part payment of premiums has been irrevocably made, the plan has been communicated to employees, and an appropriate resolution of the board of directors has been passed setting forth and authorizing a definite plan for the purchase of annuities and under which a liability is created to provide the benefits.[74] If these steps are taken by the close of the taxable year in question, the actual contract need

---

[70] I.R.C. 404(a) ; Reg. 1.404(a)–1(b).

[71] Reg. 1.404(a)–3(d).

[72] I.R.C. 404(a) ; Reg. 1.404(a)–1(c).

[73] Rev. Rul. 65–178, Part 2(f), IRB 1965–28.

[74] *Ibid.*

not be executed and issued until the due date of the employer's tax return for such taxable year (including extensions).

Apart from the aspect of first-year deductions, it is also important to establish the employer's liability, when necessary, for subsequent years. For example, if the actuarial cost method used to determine annual contributions to a pension plan allows a degree of flexibility from year to year (for instance, it contemplates the payment of the normal cost of the plan plus a payment ranging from interest only on the initial supplemental liability up to 10% of this amount), it would seem advisable for an accrual basis employer who is going to make his contribution within the grace period permitted after the close of the taxable year in question to pass a resolution by the board of directors prior to the close of such taxable year. This resolution would establish a liability to contribute the amount which will be paid for such taxable year within the grace period allowed. Similarly, in a profit sharing plan without a definite formula for determining the employer's contribution each year, it is necessary that prior to the close of the taxable year in question an appropriate resolution be passed under which the amount of the contribution (or the formula by which it will be determined) is established.

Basically, there are three provisions which determine the maximum amount that an employer can contribute and take as a deduction to a qualified pension plan in any one taxable year. The first of these rules is that the employer is allowed to make contributions up to an amount not in excess of 5% of the compensation paid or accrued during the taxable year to all employees who are participating in the plan.[75] For the first taxable year, the employer need not submit actuarial data in support of the deduction claimed. For the second year and each fifth year thereafter, however, an actuarial certification is required. Under this rule, the Commissioner of Internal Revenue has the right to reexamine the plan periodically at not less than five-year intervals and has the right to reduce the 5% figure if he finds that this is more than is reasonably necessary to provide the unfunded cost of the past and current service credits of all employees who are participating in the plan.

The second rule allows a contribution up to the maximum determined under the first rule, plus any excess amount which must be contributed to provide, for all employees who are participating in the plan, the unfunded cost of their past and current service credits distributed as a level amount or as a level percentage over the remaining future service of each such employee.[76] If this rule is

---

[75] I.R.C. 404(a)(1)(A); Reg. 1.404(a)–4.

[76] I.R.C. 404(a)(1)(B); Reg. 1.404(a)–5.

followed, and if the remaining unfunded cost with respect to any three individuals is more than 50% of the total unfunded cost, the unfunded cost attributable to such individuals must be distributed over a period of at least five taxable years. It might be mentioned that contributions under most individual policy pension plans are claimed under the first two rules.

The third rule, while occasionally used with individual policy plans, is primarily used in group pension and trust fund plans. This third rule permits the employer to deduct the normal cost of the plan plus, if past service or other supplementary pension or annuity credits are provided, an amount not in excess of 10% of the cost which would be required to fund completely or purchase such credits as of the date when they are included in the plan.[77]

If amounts contributed in any taxable year are in excess of the amounts allowed as a deduction for that year, the excess may be carried forward and deducted in succeeding taxable years, in order of time, to the extent the amount carried forward to any such succeeding taxable year plus the amount contributed during such succeeding taxable year does not exceed the deductible limit for such succeeding taxable year.[78]

For profit sharing plans, the maximum deductible contribution is equal to 15% of the compensation paid or otherwise accrued during the employer's taxable year to all covered employees.[79] If the contribution to the profit sharing plan is less than this amount, the difference between the amount actually paid in and the 15% limit (called a "credit carry-over") can be contributed and deducted in succeeding years. However, the credit carry-over contribution in any later year cannot exceed 15% of the compensation paid or otherwise accrued during such later year. Thus, it is possible for a credit carry-over to result in a deduction equal to 30% of compensation in a succeeding taxable year—15% for the current contribution and 15% for the credit carry-over contribution.

Carry-over provisions also apply in profit sharing plans when the contribution in one taxable year is greater than 15% of the compensation paid or otherwise accrued to employees during such taxable year. This type of carry-over is called a "contribution carry-over." Thus, if a contribution is made in a given year which is in excess of the allowable deduction for such year, the employer will be allowed to take a deduction for such excess payment in a succeeding taxable year, if it does not bring the deduction of the succeeding year to over 15% of the participating payroll for such succeeding year.

---

[77] I.R.C. 404(a)(1)(C); Reg. 1.404(a)–6.

[78] I.R.C. 404(a)(1)(D); Reg. 1.404(a)–7.

[79] I.R.C. 404(a)(3); Reg. 1.404(a)–9.

If there is both a pension plan and a profit sharing plan in existence, the total amount deductible in any taxable year under both plans cannot exceed 25% of the compensation paid or accrued to covered employees for that year.[80] When excess payments are made in any taxable year, the excess may be carried forward to succeeding taxable years, subject to the limitation that the total amount deducted for such succeeding taxable year (including the deduction for the current contribution) cannot exceed 30% of the compensation paid or accrued for such subsequent year.

The 25% limitation does not eliminate the requirement that a currently deductible profit sharing contribution must not exceed 15% of the payroll of the participating employees and that a currently deductible pension contribution must not exceed the amount which would have been the limit had only a pension plan been in effect.

---

[80] I.R.C. 404(a)(7); Reg. 1.404(a)–13.

6

TAXATION OF DISTRIBUTIONS

Unquestionably, a major advantage of a qualified pension or profit sharing plan is that an employer's contributions, although currently deductible, will not be considered as taxable income to an employee until they are distributed or made available to him. Moreover, when a distribution does represent taxable income to the employee or his beneficiary, it is generally received under very favorable tax circumstances.

Broadly speaking, distributions from a qualified plan are taxable in accordance with the annuity rules of Section 72 of the Internal Revenue Code. If a lump sum distribution is made on account of the employee's severance of employment, however, it may be treated as a long-term capital gain if certain conditions are met. Although these general principles apply regardless of the contingency which gives rise to the distribution, this chapter discusses the tax aspects of a distribution in terms of the contingency which has brought it about. Thus, this chapter briefly explores the tax situation of an employee during his employment, as well as his tax situation (or his beneficiary's) when distributions are made because of his retirement, death, severance of employment, or disability, or because of termination of the plan.

With a view toward achieving some degree of simplicity, the discussion has been confined to the federal taxation of typical forms of distribution under corporate plans which have a qualified status when the distributions are made.[1]

---

[1] For a discussion of the taxation of distributions under H.R. 10 plans, see pp. 323–325. The tax aspects of nonqualified deferred compensation plans are discussed in Chapter 15.

TAXATION DURING EMPLOYMENT

Even though employer contributions may be fully vested in an employee under a qualified plan, the employee will not have to report these contributions as taxable income until such time as they are distributed or made available to him.[2] Thus, employer contributions made on behalf of an employee will generally not be considered as taxable income to the employee during the period of his employment.

If the plan includes a life insurance benefit for employees, however, the employee is considered to have received a distribution each year equal to the portion of the employer's contribution (or the portion of the trust earnings) which has been applied during such year to provide the pure insurance in force on his life.[3] The pure insurance is considered to be the excess, if any, of the face amount of the employee's life insurance contract over its cash value.[4] The amount which the employee must include as taxable income for each year is the one-year term insurance rate for his attained age multiplied by the amount of pure insurance involved. This insurance cost is often called the PS 58 cost because the original Treasury Department Ruling on the subject was so numbered.

Since the term insurance rate will increase each year with the employee's increasing age, this factor will tend to increase the amount which the employee will have to include as taxable income each year. An offsetting factor, however, is the increasing cash value of the contract, which reduces the amount of pure insurance in effect each year. For plans which employ some form of whole life insurance, or its equivalent, the insurance cost will tend to rise each year, the reduction in the amount of pure insurance being insufficient to offset the increase in the term insurance rate caused by the employee's advancing age. If the plan is funded with retirement

---

[2] I.R.C. 402(a); I.R.C. 403(a); Reg. 1.402(a)–1; Reg. 1.403 (a)–1.

[3] I.R.C. 72(m); Reg. 1.72–16; PS 58; Rev. Rul. 55–747, CB 1955–2, 228; Rev. Rul. 66–110, IRB 1966–20. Note that the amount applied during any year to provide life insurance will often cover a period extending into the following year. The employee, however, will not be permitted to apportion this insurance cost between the two years and will be required to include this amount as taxable income in the year in which it is applied, even though the period of protection extends into the subsequent year. Letter, signed E. I. McLarney, Deputy Commissioner, dated April 30, 1946, *Pension and Profit Sharing Tax Service* (Englewood Cliffs, N.J.: Prentice-Hall, Inc., n.d.), ¶ 12,707–A.

[4] Reg. 1.72–16(b) (3).

income contracts, the yearly increase in cash value is more substantial and, ultimately, the cash value will exceed the face amount of the contract. Under this type of contract, the insurance cost (after the first few years) will tend to decrease and will ultimately disappear.

Normally, the term insurance rates employed to determine the cost of the employee's insurance coverage are the rates contained in PS 58 (reissued as Rev. Rul. 55–747, as amplified by Rev. Rul. 66–110). However, the insurer's own rates may be used if they are lower than the rates set forth in these Rulings. If an employee is insurable only on an extra-premium basis and the employer contributes the extra premium necessary to obtain full coverage (and follows the same practice for all employees in similar circumstances), the employee's insurance cost will be determined on the basis of the standard rates, and the extra premium paid due to the rating need not be taken into account.[5]

If employees are making contributions, the plan may provide that an employee's contribution will first be applied toward the cost of his insurance coverage. This provision makes it possible to reduce or completely eliminate having any portion of the employer's contribution considered as taxable income to the employee during his employment.

If the death benefit is being provided outside of the qualified plan by a group term life insurance contract issued to the employer rather than to the trustee of the pension trust (the usual situation in a plan using some form of group pension contract), the employee is not required to consider any part of the premium paid for him by the employer as taxable income, except to the extent that the coverage on his life in excess of $50,000 is attributable to employer contributions.[6] However, if the trustee of a qualified trust purchases the group term life insurance instead of the employer, the value of the insurance attributable to employer contributions will be considered as taxable income to the covered employees, regardless of the amounts of coverage involved.[7]

---

[5] Letter to Guardian Life Insurance Company, New York, signed E. I. McLarney, Deputy Commissioner, dated March 12, 1948. *Pension and Profit Sharing Tax Service* (Englewood Cliffs, N.J.: Prentice-Hall, Inc., n.d.), ¶ 12,711. If the contract is issued on a graded or graduated death benefit basis, i.e., a standard premium is paid but there is a reduction in the amount of insurance due to the extra mortality risk involved, the employee's insurance cost will be lower since he is receiving less insurance protection.

[6] I.R.C. 79.

[7] Rev. Rul. 54–52, CB 1954–1, 150, amplified by Rev. Rul. 56–634, IRB 1956–50.

DETERMINATION OF COST BASIS

Before discussing the taxation of benefits, it is important to have a clear idea of the elements that constitute an employee's cost basis (or his "investment in the contract"), if any, since the employee's cost basis is an important factor in the taxation of distributions under the plan.

Briefly, Section 72 of the Internal Revenue Code provides that an employee's cost basis includes:

1. The aggregate of any amounts he has contributed as an employee.
2. The aggregate of the prior insurance costs he has reported as taxable income. (If the employee has made contributions and the plan provides that his contributions will first be used to pay any cost of insurance, his reportable income for any year is the excess, if any, of the insurance cost of his protection over the amount of his contribution for the year and not the full cost of his insurance protection.)
3. Other contributions made by the employer which have already been taxed to the employee. An example of this would be where the employer has maintained a nonqualified plan that was later qualified.

There is also provision for the inclusion of other items in an employee's cost basis, such as contributions made by the employer after 1950 but before 1963 while the employee was a resident of a foreign country. For the most part, however, the items listed above will constitute an employee's cost basis in the typical situation.

TAXATION OF RETIREMENT BENEFITS

Lump Sum Distributions

If an employee takes his benefit under a qualified plan in the form of a lump sum benefit at retirement, he may treat the excess of the distribution over his cost basis, if any, as a long-term capital gain if the following conditions are met:

1. The distribution is on account of the employee's separation from the employer's service (which includes the employee's actual retirement).
2. The distribution represents the full amount then credited to the employee's account and the entire distribution is received within one taxable year of the employee.[8]

_____

[8] I.R.C. 402(a)(2); I.R.C. 403(a)(2); Reg. 1.402(a)–1(a)(6); Reg. 1.403(a)–2.

Separation from Employer's Service. The requirement that there be an actual separation from the employer's service is most important. If the employee continues to work for the same employer in the same or in a different capacity, the distribution will not qualify for long-term capital gains treatment.[9] While the question of whether or not an employee relationship continues is generally determined under rules applicable to federal employment taxes, the fact that the individual no longer receives compensation does not necessarily mean there has been a severance of employment. If, in fact, he continues to act in some capacity as an employee, even though without compensation, the long-term capital gains treatment may be denied to any distribution he has received under the employer's plan.[10] Also, if an employee agrees to remain available as a consultant after his retirement, this relationship may, depending upon all the facts and the actual services he performs, produce the same result.

Distribution of Full Amount within One Taxable Year of Employee. The distribution must represent the full amount then credited to the employee's account if long-term capital gains treatment is to be available. Where the distribution consists of a cash payment of the employee's entire account, or of an annuity contract which is then surrendered by the employee or which is otherwise immediately taxable to the employee, this presents no problem. Where, however, the distribution consists of two or more annuity contracts and the value of these contracts would not otherwise be immediately taxable to the employee, the long-term capital gains treatment will be lost if the employee elects to receive income payments under one contract and surrenders the other(s) in the year of separation.[11] For the long-term capital gains treatment to apply, it is necessary that all such contracts be surrendered at the time of separation from service.[12] If the total distribution consists of annuity con-

---

[9] Rev. Rul. 56–214, CB 1956–1, 196; *Estate of Frank B. Fry*, 19 TC 461, aff'd. 205 F. 2d 517.

[10] Rev. Rul. 57–115, IRB 1957–12.

[11] Reg. 1.403(a)–2(b)(2). The discussion in this portion of the chapter assumes the distribution of an annuity contract which, by reason of its date of issue or contract provisions, does not require the employee to consider its total value as taxable income in the year of distribution. The section on distributions on severance of employment (see p. 146) discusses this area in more detail and indicates the circumstances under which an annuity contract must be endorsed or rewritten as "nontransferable" so as to avoid current tax liability at the time of distribution.

[12] Note, however, that if the employee has surrendered one or more contracts and is receiving payments under another and subsequently dies, any lump sum death benefit paid under the annuity contract may be treated by his beneficiary as a long-term capital gain.

tracts, the value of which are not immediately taxable to the employee, and they are surrendered in a subsequent year, the proceeds would be considered as ordinary income in such subsequent year in accordance with the annuity rules of Section 72 of the Internal Revenue Code.[13] However, if the total distribution consists of such an annuity contract for part and cash for the balance, and the annuity contract is not surrendered in the year of severance, the cash portion may be treated as a long-term capital gain in the year it is distributed even though the value of the annuity contract will not be taxable income to the employee until some later year.[14]

It is important to note that the foregoing relates to the full amount standing to the employee's account at the time of his separation from service. Thus, if an employee receives such a distribution, it will qualify for long-term capital gains treatment even though he receives an additional amount, attributable to his last year of service, in a later taxable year.[15] The amount paid in the later taxable year, however, will be taxed as ordinary income.[16]

It appears that as long as the total distribution is made to the employee within one taxable year, it need not be made during the year in which his retirement occurs for the long-term capital gains treatment to apply.[17] However, any part of the total distribution which consists of an increment to the employee's account that accrued after his severance of employment will be taxed to him as ordinary income unless the delay in distribution was occasioned by "administrative problems" of the plan. There is, of course, a question of how much time may elapse between the severance of employment and the year in which the employee receives his distribution and still have the distribution treated as a long-term capital gain. Rev. Rul. 60–292, cited above, dealt with a situation where the distribution was deferred for four years under a plan provision which permitted deferment for a maximum period of five years. Whether or not the Internal Revenue Service would be willing to permit the long-term capital gains treatment to apply to distributions which follow the date of severance of employment by longer periods remains to be seen.

Distributions in the Form of Periodic Payments

If a retiring employee receives his distribution in the form of periodic payments, these payments will be taxed to him as ordinary

---

[13] Rev. Rul. 55–298, CB 1955–1, 394.

[14] Rev. Rul. 65–267, IRB 1965–47.

[15] Reg. 1.402(a)–1(a)(6)(ii).

[16] Rev. Rul. 56–558, IRB 1956–45.

[17] Rev. Rul. 60–292, IRB 1960–37.

income in accordance with the annuity rules of Section 72 of the Internal Revenue Code.[18]

Thus, in a plan where the employee has no cost basis, periodic payments will be subject to ordinary income tax as received. If the employee has a cost basis, his tax treatment will depend upon the length of time it takes him to recover an amount equal to his cost basis.

If the employee will receive, within three years of the first payment, total payments which equal or exceed his cost basis, then all payments will be excluded from his taxable income until the payments he has received equal his cost basis. Thereafter, the payments will be subject to ordinary income tax as received.[19] To illustrate, take the case of an employee who has contributed $5,400 under his employer's retirement plan and who will receive an annual payment, for life, of $2,400. Since his payments for the first three years ($7,200) exceed his cost basis, he will not have to report any part of his payments as taxable income for the first two years. At the end of the second year, he will have recovered $4,800 of his cost basis, and will still have $600 of this amount left to recover. Thus, during his third year of retirement, he will exclude $600 of his payments from taxable income and will report only $1,800 as income subject to tax. Thereafter, the full $2,400 will be subject to tax each year as ordinary income.

If it will take longer than three years for the employee to recover his cost basis, then the regular annuity rules of Section 72 apply. First, an exclusion ratio is determined for the employee. The exclusion ratio is the ratio of the employee's cost basis (his "investment in the contract") to his "expected return." The resulting percentage represents the portion of each income payment which is excluded from taxable income.[20]

For example, assume that a male employee retiring at age 65 is entitled to an annual income of $2,400 for life (with no death benefit payable in the event of his death after retirement) and that the employee has a cost basis of $9,000. The first step would be to determine the employee's "expected return." This would be done by obtaining his life expectancy under the tables included in the Regulations and multiplying this figure by the amount of the annual

---

[18] The retirement income tax credit provided by Section 37 of the Internal Revenue Code will apply to these payments. However, the impact of this credit is generally not significant since the credit is applied only with respect to a maximum of $1,524 of retirement income ($2,286 for a married couple filing a joint return), and since this maximum is reduced by Social Security benefits and by earned income of the type which would, in itself, reduce the employee's Social Security benefits.

[19] I.R.C. 72 (d) ; Reg. 1.72–13.

[20] I.R.C. 72 (b) ; Reg. 1.72–4 (a).

payment. In this example, the employee's life expectancy under these tables would be 15. Multiplying 15 by the annual payment of $2,400 produces an expected return of $36,000. The next step would be to divide the employee's cost basis ($9,000) by his expected return ($36,000), which yields an exclusion ratio of 25%. Consequently, $600 of each year's payment (25% of $2,400) would be excluded from the employee's taxable income, and the balance of $1,800 would be subject to tax as ordinary income.

The exclusion ratio, once established, will apply to all future payments, regardless of the length of time the employee actually lives and receives payments. If he lives longer than the average life expectancy assumed in the tables included in the Regulations, he will still continue to receive a portion of each payment free of income tax, even though by that time he will have recovered his cost basis.

If payments are made to the employee for a period certain or with a refund feature, his cost basis will be adjusted, when determining his exclusion ratio, to reflect the value of the refund or period certain feature.[21] In the example described above, if the retirement benefit of $2,400 were payable for life with a guarantee that payments would be made for at least 10 years, it would be necessary to reduce the employee's cost basis of $9,000. Under the tables included in the Regulations, the value of the 10-year guarantee for a male, age 65, is 15%. Consequently, the $9,000 would be reduced by 15% ($1,350) and the employee's adjusted cost basis would be $7,650. His exclusion ratio would then be determined in the regular fashion.

If retirement payments are being made under some form of joint and survivor annuity, the expected return, rather than the cost basis, would be adjusted to reflect the value of the survivorship feature.[22]

TAXATION OF DEATH BENEFITS

Lump Sum Distributions

A lump sum distribution to the employee's beneficiary from a qualified plan which is made on account of the employee's death (either before or after severance of employment), will be taxed to the beneficiary as a long-term capital gain if the distribution represents the full amount then credited to the employee's account and if it is received within one taxable year of the beneficiary.[23]

---

[21] I.R.C. 72 (c) (2) ; Reg. 1.72–7.

[22] I.R.C. 72 (c) (3) ; Reg. 1.72–5 (b).

[23] I.R.C. 402 (a) (2) ; I.R.C. 403 (a) (2) ; Reg. 1.402 (a)–1 ; Reg. 1.403 (a)–1.

In determining the net amount of gain subject to tax, the beneficiary's cost basis will be the same as the employee's (i.e., the aggregate of the employee's contributions and any amounts, such as insurance costs, on which the employee has previously been taxed) plus, unless otherwise used, the employee death benefit exclusion provided by Section 101(b) of the Internal Revenue Code up to a maximum of $5,000. It should be noted that in the case of a lump sum distribution that otherwise qualifies for the long-term capital gains treatment, this exclusion under Section 101(b) applies regardless of whether the employee's rights were forfeitable or nonforfeitable.[24]

If any portion of the distribution consists of life insurance proceeds and the employee either paid the insurance cost or reported this cost as taxable income, the pure insurance, i.e., the difference between the face amount of the contract and its cash value, will pass to the beneficiary free of income tax under Section 101(a) of the Internal Revenue Code. The beneficiary will only have to treat the cash value of the contract, plus any other cash distributions from the plan, as income subject to tax.[25]

The following example illustrates how the death benefit under a typical retirement income contract would be taxed if the employee died before retirement and the face amount of the contract were paid to the beneficiary in a lump sum.

Face amount of contract	$25,000
Cash value of contract	11,000
Amount of pure insurance excludable under Section 101(a)	$14,000
Cash value of contract	$11,000
Amount excludable under Section 101(b) (assuming not otherwise utilized)	5,000
Balance subject to income tax	$ 6,000
Beneficiary's cost basis (aggregate of prior insurance costs which employee reported as taxable income)	940
Balance taxable to beneficiary as long-term capital gain	$ 5,060

The beneficiary would, therefore, receive $19,940 of the total distribution free of income tax, and only $5,060 would be considered as a taxable long-term capital gain.

If there is more than one beneficiary and each includes the lump sum payment as income in the same taxable year, each may treat

---

[24] I.R.C. 101(b)(2)(B); Reg. 1.101–2(d)(3). Briefly, Section 101(b) permits a beneficiary to exclude from gross income any payments made by the employer of a deceased employee up to a maximum of $5,000. Except as noted, this exclusion is available only to the extent the employee's rights to the amounts were forfeitable immediately prior to death.

[25] I.R.C. 72(m)(3)(C); Reg. 1.72–16(c)(2).

the lump sum payment as a long-term capital gain.[26] However, if one beneficiary elects to take the lump sum payment and the other makes a timely election to receive his share in the form of income over a period of years, the long-term capital gains treatment will not apply to either beneficiary.[27]

It is important to note that the Regulations provide that if the employee did not pay the insurance cost of his contract, or did not report the cost of insurance as taxable income, the portion of the insurance proceeds consisting of pure insurance will be considered as taxable income to the beneficiary.[28]

When an employee dies after retirement and after he has received periodic payments, a lump sum death payment to his beneficiary, if it meets the requirements previously noted, will be taxed to the beneficiary as a long-term capital gain. The beneficiary's cost basis, however, will be reduced by any amount which the employee had recovered free from income tax.[29]

Distributions in the Form of Periodic Payments

Death before Retirement. If an employee dies before retirement and the plan provides for the distribution of his death benefit over a period of years (including payments based upon the life expectancy of the beneficiary), these payments will be taxed in accordance with the annuity rules of Section 72 of the Internal Revenue Code.[30]

The beneficiary's cost basis will consist of the amount which would have been the employee's cost basis, had he lived and received payments himself, plus, if applicable, the exclusion allowed under Section 101(b) of the Internal Revenue Code up to the maximum of $5,000. While the question of whether or not the employee's rights were forfeitable is immaterial for the application of Section 101(b) to a lump sum distribution from a qualified plan on death, the same is not so when the distribution is in the form of periodic payments. Here, the exclusion under Section 101(b) is applicable only to amounts to which the employee's rights were forfeitable immediately prior to his death.[31]

If any part of the periodic payments arises from pure life insurance, the proceeds are divided into two parts:

---

[26] Reg. 1.402(a)–1(a)(6)(iv); Reg. 1.403(a)–2(b)(4).
[27] *Ibid.*
[28] Reg. 1.72–16(c)(4).
[29] Reg. 1.402(a)–1(a)(5) and (6).
[30] I.R.C. 402(a); I.R.C. 403(a); Reg. 1.402(a); Reg. 1.403(a).
[31] I.R.C. 101(b)(2)(B); Reg. 1.101–2(d).

1. The cash value of the contract immediately before death.
2. The pure insurance (the excess of the face amount of the contract over its cash value).

That portion of each periodic payment which is attributable to the cash value of the contract will be taxed to the beneficiary under the annuity rules. The balance of each payment which is attributable to the pure insurance will be treated as insurance proceeds under Section 101(d) of the Internal Revenue Code.[32]

To illustrate, if the face amount of the employee's contract was $25,000, and if the proceeds were paid to his beneficiary in 10 annual payments of $3,000 each, the following would be the manner in which the payments would be taxed to the beneficiary, assuming that the contract had a cash value at death of $11,000, that the employee had forfeitable interests to the extent of $5,000, and that the aggregate of the insurance costs which he previously reported as taxable income is $940.

The portion of each annual payment of $3,000 which is attributable to the cash value is $1,320 ($11/25$ of $3,000). The beneficiary's cost basis for this portion would be $5,940 (the $5,000 exclusion under Section 101(b) plus his aggregate insurance costs of $940). The expected return under this portion would be $13,200 (the annual payment of $1,320 multiplied by the 10 years of payments). Since the beneficiary's cost basis would not be recovered within the first three years, the three-year rule would not apply. Therefore, an exclusion ratio would be determined by dividing the cost basis ($5,940) by the expected return ($13,200). This produces an exclusion ratio of 45% which would be applied to the portion of each annual payment attributable to the cash value of the contract. As a result, $594 (45% of $1,320) would be excluded from income each year, and the balance of $726 would be taxed to the beneficiary as ordinary income.

The portion of each annual payment of $3,000 attributable to the pure insurance is $1,680 ($14/25$ of $3,000). Of this amount, $1,400 ($1/10$ of $14,000) is excludable from gross income as Section 101 proceeds, and only the balance of $280 would be taxable as ordinary income to the beneficiary. Moreover, the $1,000 interest exclusion would be applicable if the beneficiary were the surviving spouse of the employee. The interest exclusion, of course, would not be applicable to any portion of the annual payment attributable to the cash value of the contract.

If the beneficiary in this example were the spouse of the employee, she would consider only $726 of each annual payment as

---

[32] Reg. 1.402(a)–1(a)(4); Reg. 1.72–16(c).

ordinary income. The balance of $2,274 would be received by her free of income tax. A beneficiary other than the spouse of the employee would include $1,006 ($280 plus $726) in taxable income each year, and $1,994 of each annual payment would be received free of income tax.

Death after Retirement. The taxation of payments to the beneficiary of an employee who dies after retirement and after periodic payments have begun will depend upon whether or not the employee had a cost basis (and if so, whether it had been recovered by the employee), as well as upon the method of payment involved. If the employee had no cost basis or had recovered his cost basis under the three-year rule, each payment would be considered as taxable income to the beneficiary as received. However, where the payments are being continued under a joint and survivor annuity form, the exclusion ratio established when the annuity became effective would apply for the balance of the survivor's lifetime.[33] If payments are being continued under a period certain life annuity or under a refund annuity, and the employee had not recovered his cost basis at the time of his death, the beneficiary could exclude all payments from gross income until the total of the portion of the cost basis the employee had recovered and the payments the beneficiary has received equal the employee's cost basis. Thereafter, all payments would be taxed as ordinary income to the beneficiary.[34]

Estate Tax

The foregoing discussion has covered only the income tax liability of the beneficiary. There is also the matter of the federal estate tax to be considered.

Briefly, any amounts distributed from a qualified plan to a named personal beneficiary of the employee will be excluded from the employee's gross estate for federal estate tax purposes to the extent that the amount distributed is attributable to employer contributions.[35] This includes the proceeds of a life insurance contract.

This exclusion applies to any such payment made pursuant to a qualified plan even though the individual's death occurs subsequent to his separation from the employer's service or even if the benefit is in the form of continued payments to a survivor. Suppose, how-

---

[33] Reg. 1.72–4(a)(4).

[34] Reg. 1.72–11(c).

[35] I.R.C. 2039(c) ; Reg. 20.2039–2. Presumably, the estate tax exclusion will also apply if the proceeds are paid to an *inter vivos* trust. See Rev. Rul. 58–423, IRB 1958–34, which states that a lump sum distribution to an *inter vivos* trust qualifies for long-term capital gains treatment, and see discussion in *Pension and Profit Sharing Tax Service* (Englewood Cliffs, N.J.: Prentice-Hall, Inc., n.d.), ¶ 5,502.

ever, that the individual severed his employment with the employer and received a distribution of his life insurance contract from the plan under circumstances such that its cash value was then included in his gross income. Here, the distribution would have become a part of his personal assets and, upon his subsequent death, the proceeds of the contract would be includable in his gross estate for federal estate tax purposes in accordance with the regular rules.

It should be noted that the exclusion does not apply if the benefit is paid to the employee's estate. Also, the exclusion applies only to amounts attributable to employer contributions.[36] If the employee has contributed, the amount excludable from his gross estate would be that percentage of the total benefit which is determined by dividing the employer's contributions on behalf of the employee by the total contributions for his benefit.[37] If the actuarial method used under the plan is such that the employer's contribution cannot be readily ascertained, the value of the benefit at the time of death (or, if death occurs after retirement, as of the employee's retirement date) will be considered to be the total contribution.[38] The employee contributions are then subtracted from this amount, and the balance is considered to be the employer's contribution.

If the death benefit consists of the proceeds of a group term life insurance policy which is owned by the trustee of the pension trust (total premiums having been paid by the employer), the full proceeds would fall within the estate tax exclusion. However, if the policy was issued directly to the employer, as is usually the case, the proceeds would be includable in the employee's gross estate.[39]

[36] In *Comm'r.* v. *Est. of Albright*, USCA–2, No. 29594, 2/9/66, the beneficiary received a return of the employee's contributions under two separate group annuity contracts. Under one contract, the amount paid also included interest on the employee's contributions. The Tax Court held that only a portion of the distributions was includable in the employee's gross estate. The Court of Appeals, however, held that the entire distributions under both contracts were includable, as such distributions were solely attributable to the employee's own contributions.

[37] Under the Income Tax Regulations, the aggregate of the insurance costs which an employee has included in his gross income are considered as "having been contributed by the employee" and thus form a part of his cost basis in determining the net amount of any subsequent distribution which is subject to income tax. For estate tax purposes, however, insurance costs are not considered as having been contributed by the employee, and in a noncontributory plan, the full amount of the death proceeds may be excluded from the employee's gross estate even though his beneficiary may consider the aggregate of the prior insurance costs as a part of her cost basis in determining the portion of the cash value of the contract to be excluded from her gross income.

[38] Reg. 20.2039–2(c)(2).

[39] It might be possible under some state laws for the employee to assign his interest in the group life insurance and thus have the proceeds excluded from his gross estate. See *First Nat. Bank of Birmingham* v. *U.S.*, USCA–5, No. 22,075, 3/29/66. However, many authorities consider this procedure to be questionable.

Gift Tax

It is appropriate, in a discussion of the tax aspects of the death benefits payable under a qualified plan, to cover the gift tax aspects of an irrevocable designation by an employee of a beneficiary to receive the benefit payable under the plan at his death.

The provisions of the federal gift tax law are similar to those dealing with the federal estate tax. In a noncontributory plan, the employee will not have to pay a gift tax if he makes such an irrevocable designation.[40] If, however, the employee has made contributions, the gift tax exclusion will apply only to the part of the beneficiary's interest attributable to employer contributions. The methods followed to determine the portion of the beneficiary's interest attributable to employer contributions are the same as the methods outlined in determining the estate tax exclusion.

TAXATION OF SEVERANCE-OF-EMPLOYMENT BENEFITS

For the most part, the discussion in this chapter on the taxation of distributions at retirement is equally applicable to the taxation of distributions on severance of employment. If the distribution is in the form of periodic payments, the taxation of payments to the employee will be governed by the annuity rules after taking the employee's cost basis, if any, into account. So, also, a lump sum distribution, provided that the necessary conditions are met, may qualify for long-term capital gains treatment.[41]

If the distribution is in the form of a life insurance contract, its cash value less the employee's cost basis, if any, will be considered as taxable income in the year in which the employee receives the contract, even though he does not then surrender the contract for its cash value. The distribution may be taken as a long-term capital gain if all necessary conditions are met. On the other hand, the employee may avoid any current tax liability by making an irrevocable election, within 60 days of the distribution, to convert the contract to a "nontransferable" annuity which contains no element of life insurance.[42] If the employee would otherwise receive a cash

---

[40] I.R.C. 2517; Reg. 25.2517–1.

[41] I.R.C. 402(a)(2); I.R.C. 403(a)(2); Reg. 1.402(a); Reg. 1.403(a).

[42] Reg. 1.402(a)–1(a)(2); Rev. Rul. 57–191, IRB 1957–19. The Regulations spell out what is meant by "nontransferable," and the language of the Regulations has been used as a guide by many insurers in endorsing their contracts. Such an endorsement might read approximately as follows: "This contract is not transferable except to the ABC Insurance Company. It may not be sold, assigned, discounted or pledged as collateral for a loan or as security for the

distribution but has the option under the plan of electing, within 60 days, to receive a nontransferable annuity in lieu of the cash payment, he may also avoid current tax liability by making a timely exercise of this option.[43]

If current tax liability is avoided by such an election, the employee will not pay any tax until payments are made from the annuity contract. At that time, the payments will be considered as ordinary income under the annuity rules.

If the distribution is in the form of an annuity contract, the tax situation will be governed by the date of issue of the contract.[44] If issued after December 31, 1962, the distribution will be treated exactly the same as the distribution of a life insurance contract unless the annuity is endorsed or rewritten on a "nontransferable" basis within the 60 days allowed. If issued before January 1, 1963, the employee will not have to include any amount as taxable income until payments are actually received. At that time, payments will be considered as ordinary income under the annuity rules.

TAXATION OF DISABILITY BENEFITS

Many qualified pension plans provide for a monthly benefit if an employee becomes totally and permanently disabled. Typically, the benefit is payable for life (subject to the continuance of the disability) but only with respect to a disability that occurs after the employee has attained some minimum age, such as 50 or 55, and/or has completed some minimum period of service, such as 15 or 20 years. The benefit may or may not be related to his accrued or projected pension. Frequently, the amount of the benefit will be adjusted if disability continues until the employee attains the normal retirement age specified in the plan.

Generally speaking, disability benefits of this type will be taxed to the employee in accordance with the annuity rules of Section 72 of the Internal Revenue Code; however, such disability benefits may qualify for the "sick pay" exclusion provided for in Section 105 (d) of the Code.[45]

---

performance of an obligation or for any other purpose to any person other than this Company; provided, however, that notwithstanding the foregoing, the owner may designate a beneficiary to receive the proceeds payable upon death, and may elect a joint and survivor annuity."

[43] Rev. Rul. 59–94, IRB 1959–12.

[44] Reg. 1.401–9 (b) ; Reg. 1.402 (a)–1 (a) (2).

[45] Reg. 1.72–15; Reg. 1.105–4. Briefly, the Code provides that after an absence from work of 30 days due to sickness or injuries, an employee may exclude from income, up to a rate of $100 per week, payments which are wages or which are in lieu of wages. During the first 30 days he can exclude up to $75

The sick pay exclusion applies only to the benefits provided by employer contributions. If the plan is contributory, however, the disability benefit will be presumed to have been financed by the employer's contributions unless the plan specifically provides otherwise.[46]

The sick pay exclusion is available only with respect to disability payments made prior to the employee's retirement age; thereafter, all payments will be taxed in accordance with the annuity rules.[47] The Internal Revenue Service has considered retirement age to be the lowest age under the plan at which the employee could have otherwise retired without the employer's consent and with full benefits accrued to the time of retirement without actuarial reduction.[48]

TAXATION OF BENEFITS UPON TERMINATION OF PLAN

Generally speaking, distributions on account of the termination of a qualified plan are taxed under the annuity rules of Section 72 of the Internal Revenue Code, and the preceding discussion applies to the taxation of these benefits. The most notable difference, however, concerns the treatment of lump sum distributions (whether in the form of cash, life insurance contracts, or "transferable" annuity contracts issued after 1962). If such a lump sum distribution is made on account of termination of the plan, the long-term capital gains treatment will not apply.

It is possible, under some forms of corporate mergers or reorganizations, that severance of employment could take place at the same time. In such an event, a lump sum distribution might qualify for long-term capital gains treatment. Whether a particular distribution has been made on account of severance of employment can be a difficult problem to resolve. The question is greatly influenced by the facts in each particular case and by the timing of events. A number of cases and Rulings have dealt with this particular point,

---

per week if the sick pay does not exceed 75% of his regular wages. If the employee was hospitalized for at least one day, this exclusion starts from the first day of disability; otherwise, there is no exclusion for the first seven days of disability.

[46] Reg. 1.72–15(c)(2).

[47] Reg. 1.105–4(a)(2)(i) and (3)(i).

[48] Rev. Rul. 57–76, IRB 1957–9, modified by Rev. Rul. 61–6, IRB 1961–1; Rev. Rul. 58–544, IRB 1958–45. But see *Winter* v. *Comm'r*. 303 F. 2d 150, affirming 36 TC 14 (Comm'r. non acq. IRB 1962–37), where the court held that the normal retirement age specified by the plan could be used even though the plan permitted earlier retirement with full accrued benefits to the time of early retirement and without actuarial reduction. The Service is now reconsidering its position on this question. See TIR No. 822, 5/31/66.

and a brief survey of some of the more significant of these cases and Rulings is of value.

1. In one situation a corporation sold all of its assets, discontinued all former activities and invested all of its funds in securities. The employment of all employees was terminated. The firm's profit sharing plan was also terminated, and a lump sum distribution was made to each participant. An officer-employee, who was also a participant, continued to act as an uncompensated officer and director with services limited to attendance at board meetings and other services not of a substantial nature. The lump sum distribution to this officer was taxed at ordinary income tax rates since there had not been a severance of employment.[49]

2. In another situation, a corporation sold all of its assets and selected one of its officer-employees to serve, without compensation, as liquidator of the corporation. The employment of all employees was terminated, and each participant received a lump sum distribution of his profit sharing account. Here, it was held that the officer-employee, even though acting as liquidator, had severed his employment, and long-term capital gains treatment was allowed.[50]

3. Buckley was an employee of Scharff-Koken Mfg. Co. In 1946 all of the assets of Sharff-Koken were turned over to International Paper Co. Buckley then became an employee of International Paper. International Paper continued the Scharff-Koken pension plan until 1951, at which time the plan was terminated. Buckley then received a lump sum distribution from the terminated Scharff-Koken plan. Two years later Buckley terminated employment with International Paper. It was held that the distribution to Buckley in 1951 was taxable as ordinary income since it was not made on account of his separation from service.[51]

4. A company was engaged in the sale of swimming apparel. It discontinued this activity and became an investment company. The firm had a pension plan which was terminated at the time of the change in the nature of its business. The president then received a distribution of his annuity contract and surrendered the contract for its cash value. It was held that there had been no severance of employment, and long-term capital gains treatment was denied.[52]

5. The profit sharing plan of a parent corporation covered employees of wholly-owned subsidiaries. The parent corporation sold its stockholdings in one of its wholly-owned subsidiaries, with the result that employees of the former subsidiary were no longer eligible to participate in the parent corporation's plan. The employees received a distribution of their accounts in the profit sharing plan. Long-term capital gains treatment was denied since there had only been

---

[49] Rev. Rul. 57–115, IRB 1957–12.
[50] Rev. Rul. 63–22, IRB 1963–8.
[51] *Clarence F. Buckley*, 29 TC 455.
[52] *Est. of E. K. Rieben*, 32 TC 1205.

a change in stockholder makeup and there had not been a severance of employment.[53]

6. M corporation transferred all of its assets and liabilities to P corporation in exchange for common stock in the P corporation. P corporation then transferred the assets and liabilities to S corporation (its wholly-owned subsidiary) in exchange for stock in the S corporation. Employees of M corporation became employees of S corporation. M corporation terminated its plan, and distribution was made to former employees. It was held that there had been a severance of employment, and that long-term capital gains treatment would apply.[54]

7. M corporation purchased all of the stock in O corporation. M corporation operated O corporation as a wholly-owned subsidiary for four months, after which M corporation took over all of the assets and liabilities of O corporation and O corporation was completely liquidated. Employees of O corporation became employees of M corporation, and the pension plan of O corporation was terminated. It was held that there had been severance of employment and that long-term capital gains treatment would apply to lump sum distributions that had been made.[55]

8. Incident to a plan of complete liquidation, a corporation sold its assets and transferred most of the employees of one of its two divisions to another corporation. Transferred employees received a distribution of their total interests in the selling corporation's profit sharing plan. These distributions were on account of separation from service and could be treated as long-term capital gains.[56]

9. Control of a subsidiary corporation was transferred from the parent corporation to other interests. The subsidiary corporation continued as a separate taxable entity under the control of these other interests. A pension plan had been established by the parent and subsidiary corporations. The plan was discontinued as to the subsidiary and distributions were made from the plan to employees. However, there was no separation from service, and the distributions did not qualify for long-term capital gains treatment.[57]

It would appear, from a study of the cases and Rulings, that the Internal Revenue Service will require something more than a nominal or technical change in employment relationship if there is to be separation from the employer's service so as to qualify lump sum distributions for long-term capital gains treatment. It would also appear that if a plan termination is being contemplated, especially

---

[53] *McGowan, P. J.* v. *U.S.*, 277 F. 2d 613, aff'g. 175 F. Supp. 364.

[54] Rev. Rul. 58–94, IRB 1958–11.

[55] Rev. Rul. 58–95, IRB 1958–11.

[56] Rev. Rul. 58–97, IRB 1958–11.

[57] Rev. Rul. 58–99, IRB 1958–11.

in conjunction with a corporate merger or reorganization, extreme care should be taken during the planning stages to assure the most favorable tax treatment for all concerned. Consideration might be given to the possibility of distributing assets in the form of non-transferable annuities so as not only to defer tax liability until some future time but also to spread its impact over a period of years.

7

INDIVIDUAL POLICY PLANS

One of the first financial decisions to be made in pension planning is to determine whether benefits are to be funded or whether the plan is to be financed on a current disbursement basis, although the tax advantages of funded qualified plans have all but made the current disbursement plan obsolete. Having chosen one of these alternatives, the broad *financing policy* of the plan has been established. Assuming that agreement is reached on a financing policy of funding benefits, then several decisions must be made under the general heading of *funding policy*.

The first of these decisions is the choice of a funding agency. A *funding agency* is an organization or individual that provides facilities for the accumulation or administration of assets to be used for the payment of benefits under a pension plan. Funding agencies include life insurance companies, corporate fiduciaries, and individuals acting as trustees. These funding agencies have several different contracts or instruments through which pension benefits are funded. Insured pension plans, for example, may be funded through individual policies, deferred group annuities, deposit administration contracts, and so forth. These various contracts are referred to as funding instruments. A *funding instrument* is an agreement or contract governing the conditions under which assets are accumulated or administered by a funding agency for the payment of benefits under a pension plan. Funding instruments include contracts with life insurance companies and trust agreements with corporate fiduciaries or individuals acting as trustees. A trust agreement is generally used in connection with a fully insured individual policy plan and, on occasion, in a plan where all assets are being accumulated under a group pension contract. However, in these cases, the insurance or annuity contracts are viewed as the principal funding instruments.

Funding instruments have also been classified on the basis of whether contributions are *allocated* to provide the benefits of specific employees or whether contributions are accumulated in an *unallocated* fund to provide benefits for employees.[1] Allocated funding instruments include individual insurance and annuity contracts, group permanent contracts, and group deferred annuity contracts; deposit administration contracts, immediate participation guarantee contracts, and trust fund plans are unallocated funding instruments.

An *insured plan*, then, is a pension plan for which the funding agency is a life insurance company; all contributions are paid directly or indirectly to the insurer, which pays all benefits to individual participants. A *trust fund plan* is a plan for which the funding agency is a corporate fiduciary or individual(s) acting as trustee(s), the responsibilities of the funding agency for investment of funds, and for any other functions, generally being provided for in a trust agreement. A *combination plan* is an arrangement under which two funding instruments are used, with a portion of the contributions placed in a trust fund (or a conversion fund held by an insurer) and the balance paid to an insurance company as contributions under a group annuity contract or as premiums on individual life insurance or annuity contracts. The entire pension for each participant is generally paid by the insurance company, with transfers from the trust fund or conversion fund being made as required.

This chapter is concerned solely with insured plans that are fully funded through the use of individual life insurance or annuity contracts and with combination plans utilizing both individual contracts and a conversion fund.

The individual policy plan has proved to be a very popular funding arrangement for relatively small employers. About 65% of all insured plans currently in force use individual contracts, at least in part, to fund benefits.[2] However, the average size individual policy plan is only about 20 participants per plan.[3] This is not to say that the individual policy arrangement cannot be used for larger firms. However, the group approaches normally offer cost savings and a greater degree of flexibility and, therefore, are generally preferred over the individual policy arrangement by large employers.

Since most large employers have already established pension

---

[1] Dan M. McGill, *Fundamentals of Private Pensions* (2d ed.; Homewood, Ill.: Richard D. Irwin, Inc., 1964), pp. 111–12.

[2] *Life Insurance Fact Book* (New York: Institute of Life Insurance, 1965), p. 37.

[3] *Ibid.*

plans for their employees, future expansion in pension coverage must come from the further establishment of such plans among smaller employers. The future market for individual policy plans, then, should be particularly good in view of the advantages that they offer in the case of the smaller firm.

FULLY INSURED PLAN

Type of Contract

The major objective of a pension plan is to provide a periodic income to retired workers. In the case of an insured plan, the insurance company generally requires that a specified sum of money be on hand as of the date of the employee's retirement to provide the periodic benefit to which he is entitled under the plan. Under individual policy plans, the cash value under the contract as of the retirement date of the employee can be used as the single-premium sum needed to provide the annuity benefit. Thus, in theory, any permanent life insurance or any annuity contract can be used to fund a pension benefit. However, under a fully insured plan, the policy cash values at retirement must be sufficient to provide the full benefit, since no other source of funds is contemplated under the plan. In order to generate sufficient cash values under the ordinary life type of policies, the face amount of the policy would be considerably in excess of 100 times the monthly retirement benefit—the maximum permitted under qualified plans. Thus, retirement income or retirement annuity contracts must be used, since they are specifically designed by insurers to provide the proper ratio of insurance to income and to generate the cash values needed to provide a specified monthly income as of a given retirement age.

Table 7–1 sets forth the cash values at quinquennial ages available under various participating individual policies offered by one insurance company for a male, age 30 as of issue date.

The insurance company whose policy values are described in Table 7–1 currently requires a net sum of $1,608 to provide a male, age 65, with a life annuity of $10 a month, with annuity payments guaranteed for 10 years. It is obvious, therefore, that a retirement income contract is the only *insurance* contract that provides sufficient cash values at age 65 to provide monthly income at the rate of $10 for each $1,000 of face value.

General Characteristics

The retirement income and retirement annuity contracts used by some insurance companies for pension cases are identical to the contracts issued to nonpension individual policyholders. Other companies have developed a special series of retirement income and retirement annuity contracts to be used solely for pension cases. Although both lines of policies would be essentially similar, the special pension series policies may provide for different commission scales, premium rates, cash values, death benefits, underwriting standards, and dividend scales. In either case, these contracts are

TABLE 7–1

ILLUSTRATIVE CASH VALUES AT QUINQUENNIAL AGES PER $1,000 OF FACE VALUE
UNDER VARIOUS PARTICIPATING INDIVIDUAL POLICIES, FOR A MALE, AGE 30,
AS OF ISSUE DATE

Age	Ordinary Life	Paid-Up at 65	Endowment at 65	Retirement Income	Retirement Annuity*
30..........	4	5	9	15	20
35..........	59	68	95	133	134
40..........	136	157	214	301	299
45..........	214	248	339	487	489
50..........	297	348	475	701	710
55..........	384	456	626	955	966
60..........	472	573	797	1,257	1,263
65..........	559	701	1,000	1,608	1,608

* Retirement annuity contracts are expressed in terms of units of annuity benefit as of a specified age. The cash values indicated above are for a retirement annuity contract that will provide a life income of $10 a month with a 120 payments certain.

essentially standard forms that have been modified to the extent possible to meet the needs of a pension plan. However, the standard forms cannot be tailored perfectly for this purpose and, therefore, certain plan provisions must be designed to conform to the structure of individual contracts, for example, minimum units of benefit and retirement dates expressed as the policy anniversary nearest to normal retirement age.

The retirement annuity contract is an individual deferred annuity contract and is expressed in units of $10-a-month annuity benefit payable beginning at a specified age, usually the normal retirement age under the plan. The retirement income policy is expressed in terms of $1,000 of face value of life insurance for each $10-a-month annuity benefit. The normal annuity form under individual policy plans is generally a life income with 120 payments certain, although a pure life annuity or a life annuity with 60 payments certain or other annuity forms may be used as the basic annuity form under the plan. In addition, participants generally have the right to elect annuity options other than the normal annuity under the plan.

Individual policy plans require that separate contracts be issued on the life of every covered employee. In most cases, a trust agreement is executed between the employer and the trustee, and the trustee serves as custodian of the individual contracts. The trustee normally applies for the insurance or annuity contracts and pays the premiums due. The insured employee, of course, must sign the application for the contract. Legal ownership of the contracts is vested in the trustee, either through the use of an ownership clause or by attachment of an appropriate rider to each of the contracts. The use of a trustee under individual policy plans is required under the Internal Revenue Code.[4] This requirement is imposed in order to preclude the possibility of the employer recovering funds that must be irrevocably committed to the trust. Also, the use of a trust assures that funds will not be currently distributed to employees, except in accordance with the provisions set forth in the plan.

The use of a trustee under individual policy plans has resulted in the use of the term "pension trust" to describe these plans. This terminology is unfortunate, since plans employing funding instruments other than individual policies quite often use a trust agreement. In the case of a noninsured plan, for example, a trust agreement is a necessary condition to qualification of the plan. Thus, the term "pension trust" should not be used unless it is quite clear as to what type of funding instrument is involved. Indeed, it would probably be best if the term disappeared entirely from pension terminology.

Employees covered under retirement income contracts must furnish the insurance company with evidence of insurability, since these contracts offer a substantial element of life insurance protection. The evidence of insurability required under these contracts is similar to that required under regular individual policies, i.e., filling out an application and taking a physical examination. Retirement annuity contracts, on the other hand, do not require evidence of insurability, since these contracts provide no element of pure life insurance protection as such. Thus, these latter contracts can always be used to fund the benefits of employees who are not insurable.

The question of the insurability of employees, however, is not generally a serious problem in fully insured individual policy plans. First of all, most companies are willing, under specified conditions, to issue retirement income contracts up to given amount without evidence of insurability.[5] Furthermore, insurers are generally will-

---

[4] See p. 117. It is possible in fully insured plans with full vesting to purchase "nontransferable" retirement income or annuity contracts directly from an insurer without an intervening trust. A complete plan instrument is still necessary, however, and it is expected that this device will generally be confined to H.R. 10 plans.

[5] The nature of the requirements generally imposed by insurance companies under guaranteed issue underwriting are discussed in Chapter 11.

ing to issue retirement income contracts at substandard rates for employees who are insurable, but not standard, risks. Also, many insurance companies now offer retirement income contracts with graded or graduated death benefits for substandard risks, or even for uninsurable risks in some cases, the pure life insurance protection being very low at the issue date of the contract and increasing each year that the contract stays in force. Ultimately, the death benefit under a graded death benefit retirement income contract is identical to that available under a standard contract, since the cash values build up at the same rate under both contracts and eventually exceed the face value. Finally, retirement annuity contracts can be used, and the death benefit will ultimately be about the same as under the other contracts. At any rate, the trust agreement should clearly specify the approach that will be used in funding the benefits of impaired lives, i.e., substandard rating, retirement annuity contracts, or graded death benefit contracts.

The use of retirement annuity contracts solely for the uninsurable employees under a plan is becoming less and less prevalent. Whenever possible, the benefits of all employees under the plan should be funded with one type of individual contract; the retirement annuity contract is most desirable in those cases where life insurance coverage is not needed or desired or where the lower premium cost of these policies is a critical factor. This is particularly true in those cases where there are a number of older workers to be included in the plan, thereby presenting a sizable life insurance benefit cost. The fact remains, however, that in most instances life insurance protection is desired and the net premium differential is not normally significant enough to be a major issue. Therefore, one finds that retirement income contracts are by far the most popular type of contract used under fully insured individual policy plans.

Benefit Structure

Retirement Benefits. Under retirement income and retirement annuity contracts, a given level of benefit is funded through level periodic contribution payments made on behalf of each covered employee. Thus, it is desirable, whenever possible, that the level of retirement benefit be capable of projection with a reasonable degree of accuracy. However, firm projections of retirement benefits are difficult except for plans that provide a fixed benefit ($100 a month, for example) or a unit benefit of, say, $4 a month per year of service. Even in the cases of these plans, the benefit formula is likely to be amended in future years.

The most difficult benefit formula to use under an individual policy plan is one that relates retirement benefits to the average of the employee's compensation over the entire period of his participation in the plan, i.e., a career average provision. In this case, estimates of the amount of ultimate benefits are quite uncertain in view of the tremendous possible variation in future salary levels. Furthermore, because of minimum-size policy requirements, substantial increases in compensation are required before additional amounts of insurance can be purchased. Thus, this benefit provision is seldom found in individual policy plans.

The benefit formula under most fully insured plans generally specifies that the percentage be applied to the participant's average earnings during some period near his normal retirement date, such as the first 5 of the last 10 years of employment before his normal retirement age or his compensation during the fifth year preceding his normal retirement date; in other words, a final-pay provision. Final-pay provisions that base benefits on a participant's average earnings during a period, say five years, immediately preceding retirement are seldom used under individual policy plans. It is obviously too difficult to predict what a participant's earnings will be during this period. Furthermore, most insurance companies will not issue an individual retirement income contract of less than five year's duration. Therefore, if retirement benefit increases were granted for increases in compensation during the last few years of employment, there would not be sufficient time prior to retirement to fund the additional policy amounts that would have to be purchased. This problem has been minimized somewhat by those insurers that permit a degree of postretirement funding of individual contracts. Theoretically, the problem can also be minimized by use of salary projections. Nevertheless, most individual policy plans do not permit increases in retirement benefits due to increases in compensation during the five-year period immediately preceding retirement.

Salary projections are generally not used in individual policy plans, even though final-pay provisions are quite prevalent in these plans.[6] The approach normally used is to assume that the current level of compensation for each participant will remain in effect until normal retirement age. If amendments of the plan or changes in compensation result in an increase in a participant's level of benefits, then additional policies must be purchased. Likewise, a decrease in salary which results in a decrease in benefits requires that part or all of one or more policies be canceled.

---

[6] The pros and cons of using salary projections in actuarial cost estimates is discussed in Chapter 5. See pp. 91–92.

The requirement generally imposed by insurance companies that benefits under individual policy plans be funded over a minimum of five years also has an impact on the setting of a normal retirement age. It is not unusual for an employer to have employees who are approaching age 65 at the inception of the plan. Furthermore, in future years, the employer may wish to cover employees who are over 55 years old as of the date they become eligible for coverage. Thus, it is quite common to find in individual policy plans that the normal retirement age is 65 or 10 years after entry date for those participants entering the plan after age 55.

It should also be noted, as mentioned earlier, that individual contracts mature on a policy anniversary date which seldom coincides with the date that a participant reaches normal retirement age. Therefore, it is quite common in an individual policy plan to define the normal retirement date as the policy anniversary nearest the participant's 65th birthday. An alternative provision is to set the normal retirement date as the January 1 nearest the participant's 65th birthday. This is an unfortunate feature of individual contracts in that the actual retirement dates for two participants who are only a few days apart in age may vary by as much as a full year.

As indicated earlier, retirement income contracts are expressed in terms of $10-a-month pension benefit per $1,000 face value of life insurance. After a period of years from issue date, the cash value exceeds the face of the contract; thereafter, the cash value rather than the face value is the sum that is payable upon the death of the employee. The amount of retirement income coverage that is purchased depends on the level of pension benefit to which the employee is entitled under the benefit formula. For example, if the benefit formula provides a benefit of 40% of compensation, an employee currently earning $500 a month would be entitled to a retirement benefit at age 65 of $200 a month. The trustee would purchase a retirement income contract in the amount of $20,000, since this contract provides $10-a-month annuity benefit at age 65 for each $1,000 face amount of insurance. The cash value under this contract, at age 65, would be $32,160, the amount required by one insurance company to provide $200 a month with 120 payments certain to a male beginning at age 65.

If the participant's salary at some future date is increased to $525 a month, his projected retirement benefit would then be $210 a month. Another retirement income contract in the amount of $1,000 would be purchased as of that date, so that sufficient cash values would be available at age 65 to provide the annuity benefit of $210 a month. There would be no increase in the monthly pension benefit of the employee for compensation increases between $500 and $525 a month, since most insurers will not generally issue a retirement income contract unless the additional monthly benefit is at least $10. The relatively high administrative costs of issuing contracts for less than $10 of monthly benefit is the primary reason for this limitation. Thus, the benefit provision normally provides that increases in compensation will only be recognized when they result in an increase in benefit at least equal to the minimum-size contract issuable by the insurer. The exact amount of coverage will be issued once the minimum-size requirement is met.

The retirement annuity contract is similar to the retirement income contract except that the former provides no pure life insurance protection. The contract is expressed in terms of $10 units of monthly income benefit, although some insurance companies issue units of $5 a month or even as low as $2.50 a month. Where units of benefit of less than $10 a month are available, adjustment in monthly pensions may be required for relatively small increases in compensation. However, the smaller the available units of benefit, the greater will be the number of contracts that the trustee must buy and hold until retirement date. Regardless of the size of the unit of benefit, it is characteristic of individual policy plans that the trustee will generally own a number of contracts for each participant.

Early retirement benefits are often provided under fully insured plans. A typical provision provides such benefits for employees who have attained their 60th birthday and have completed at least 10 years of continuous service as a participant under the plan. The amount of the benefit is almost always expressed as the annuity amount that can be purchased with the accrued cash value for the sex and attained age of the participant under the settlement option rates in the contract or contracts.

Defined contribution (money purchase) formulas may also be used in fully insured individual policy plans. Under these formulas, the contributions are normally expressed as a fixed percentage of compensation with the amount of benefits varying with the age, sex, and retirement date of each covered employee. Defined contribution formulas are particularly popular in the H.R. 10 plans.

Death Benefits. As indicated above, the preretirement death benefit under retirement income contracts is the greater of the face amount or the cash value of the contract as of the date of death of the employee. The face amount of the contract is usually 100 times the monthly pension benefit on the normal form (for example, $1,000 face value per $10-a-month pension benefit payable for life with 120 payments certain). The point at which the cash value exceeds the face of the contract depends on the sex of the employee, the age at issue of the contract, the retirement date, and the actuarial assumptions used by the insurance company in calculating the premium rate and cash value scales. In most cases, the cash value will exceed the face of the policy at an age in the mid- to late-fifties. It should be noted, however, that the plan can restrict death benefits to the face amount of the contract. In those instances in which the cash value exceeds the face value, the difference would constitute an employer credit. As a practical matter, however, fully insured individual policy plans generally pay a death benefit equal to the larger of the face amount or cash value under the contract.

In the case of retirement annuity contracts, there is no element of pure insurance protection built into the contract. Thus, upon the death of an employee prior to retirement, the death benefit would equal the larger of the reserve under the contract or the premiums paid to date under the contract without interest. The reserve under the contract will exceed the accumulated premiums under the contract a few years after its issue date. If no death benefit is provided by the plan, the greater of the reserve or accumulated premiums is returned to the trustee of the plan. This is an unlikely situation, however, and in a plan which provides for no preretirement death benefits, individual retirement annuity contracts would be a poor choice of funding instrument.

Some insurance companies offer double indemnity coverages and family income riders for contracts used to fund a pension plan. The availability of these benefits are particularly valuable when additional amounts of life insurance are desired. Since these additional benefits normally result in amounts of life insurance in excess of the maximum permitted under qualified plans (i.e., 100 to 1), double indemnity and family income coverages are generally paid for by the participant. Thus, these benefits are considered for tax purposes to be outside the scope of the plan. The availability to participants of these extra coverages is advantageous in that it may prove convenient for employees to be able to obtain a more complete package of insurance protection through the one underwriting process.

Disability Benefits. Most insurance companies offer waiver-of-premium and disability income coverages with retirement income contracts. However, the latter benefit is seldom provided under these plans, primarily because of the additional cost and the more stringent underwriting by insurers of this benefit. Under either provision, determination of whether a participant is disabled is made by the insurance company.

Waiver of premium, although not providing immediate cash income, does permit the buildup of cash values so that the full pension benefit will be available at normal retirement age. If a disability income rider is used, the typical benefit of $10 a month per $1,000 of insurance is paid during the period of disability, with the normal pension commencing as of normal retirement age. In those cases where waiver of premium is provided, the general practice is to have employees pay for these additional benefits.

Some plans provide that the cash value of the contract is fully vested in the employee in cases of total and permanent disability. This provision does offer the employee some immediate cash benefits. However, to the extent that part or all of the cash values are withdrawn, benefits available at death or normal retirement age are reduced or eliminated.

Vested Benefits. Upon separation from employment for reasons other than retirement, death, or disability, the cash values accumulated under contracts issued on behalf of the terminating employee are available for distribution to the employer, employee, or both. The disposition of cash values of separating employees depends on the plan provisions.

If the plan is contributory, most plans provide for a return of employee contributions (with or without some stated rate of interest) upon withdrawal from the plan. However, it should be noted that there is no legal requirement that employee contributions be returned if employment is terminated. The cash values for the first few years under an individual contract may not be sufficient to cover the accumulated contributions of the employee. The employer is not required to make up the difference between the cash value and the total of employee contributions, although many plans provide that this be done.[7] However, the cash values soon exceed the amount of employee contributions, and plans generally provide, as a minimum, for the return of employee contributions for separating employees.

Whether the participant is entitled to any part or all of the cash values in excess of his own contributions depends on the availability and type of vested benefit under the plan. If the plan provides no vested benefit, then any excess of the cash value over the employee's contributions is credited to the trustee and serves to reduce future employer contributions. If the plan offers full and immediate vesting, the employee is entitled to the full amount of the cash values under the contracts. The more typical vesting provision, however, entitles the employee to a specified portion (for example,

---

[7] This is one very good reason why appropriate eligibility requirements for participation are particularly desirable for contributory individual policy plans.

10% per year of covered service) of such excess cash value. In this latter case, the number of years of employment or participation in the plan up to the date of separation usually determines the portion of the cash values to which the employee is entitled.

Assuming that the employee is entitled to part or all of the cash values upon termination, the plan can establish one or more of several different methods of providing this benefit to the employee. If the cash values are fully vested, the trustee can transfer the contract to the terminating participant, and the latter can keep the contract in full force through the payment of the required periodic premiums. If the cash values are only partially vested, the participant may choose paid-up life insurance or a paid-up deferred annuity in an amount that can be purchased with the vested portion of the cash value. Another alternative in the latter case is for the trustee to borrow from the insurance company the amount of the nonvested portion of the cash value and assign the contract, subject to the loan, to the terminating participant. The employee is then free to pay the full premium under the contract and keep the full amount of insurance in force, subject to the loan outstanding. Of course, the employee can amortize or pay off the loan in full, thereby reducing or eliminating the encumbrance against the contract. Finally, the trustee may surrender the contract and use the cash surrender value to pay the terminating participant his vested interest, retaining any excess to be applied to reduce employer contributions next due under the plan.

Where the employee fails to exercise any of the options available to him, the automatic nonforfeiture option generally found in contracts issued to pension cases is reduced paid-up insurance.

In a few plans, the vested cash values are not available until the normal retirement age of terminating employees. The trustee elects paid-up insurance or a paid-up deferred annuity and holds the contract in the trust until the employee's normal retirement date. In these cases, the employee is generally required to leave his own contributions, if any, in the plan until his retirement date; failure to leave his own contributions in the plan could result in a forfeiture of vested benefits, depending upon the plan provisions.

Contributions

Premium Rate. The premium rate for retirement income and retirement annuity contracts is based on the participant's sex and issue age. The premium rate is level from date of issue to retirement date. If an employee becomes entitled to an increase in benefits, an additional contract is purchased at a level rate appropriate for the participant's then attained age.

The premium rates for these contracts are generally based on the same mortality, interest, and expense assumptions used in the calculation of rates for regular retirement income and retirement annuity contracts. If the insurance company offers a special series of contracts for pension plans, it often uses a different set of actuarial assumptions in calculating premium rates for these contracts. Different assumptions for pension plan contracts can be justified on the basis of the special tax credit for investment income earned on pension reserves; differences in acquisition costs and administrative expenses associated with pension business; and possible differences in mortality experience due to guaranteed issue underwriting or due to differences in experience among pension plan annuitants as compared with regular annuitants. Some insurers who offer a special series of pension contracts base their premium rates for these contracts on the same assumptions used in rate calculations for regular individual policies and reflect differences in experience in the computation of dividends on the pension contracts.

The insurance company guarantees the premium rates and annuity option rates on contracts that have been purchased. Thus, the employer is guaranteed a minimum rate of interest and, in addition, capital depreciation or adverse mortality and expense experience under purchased contracts must be borne by the insurance company. Likewise, the annuity rate guarantees protect the employer from additional costs due to possible improvement in longevity. The insurance company does not, of course, guarantee the rates at which individual contracts will be purchased in the future for new employees or for additional benefits earned by currently covered employees. Future contracts will be purchased at the premium and option rates in effect at the time these contracts are purchased.

Annual Contributions. The gross annual premium required under the plan is determined by simply adding up the premiums required to fund the amounts of life insurance to which each participant is entitled in accordance with the plan's benefit formula. For example, Table 7–2, page 166, sets forth the gross annual premium required under a hypothetical retirement income policy plan which provides a normal retirement benefit at age 65 of 30% of monthly earnings. The employer informs the trustee as to the amount of monthly pension to which each participant is entitled, and the trustee then purchases a retirement income contract equal to 100 times the

monthly benefit. The gross premium required for each participant
is a function of the age, sex, and amount of the contract. Thus, the
sum of the annual gross premiums for each employee in this example is $21,263.15.

The annual contribution required of the employer is equal to the
gross annual premiums for the plan less: (1) employee contributions, if any; (2) dividends under participating contracts; and
(3) the nonvested cash values of contracts of terminating employees.

TABLE 7–2

HYPOTHETICAL FULLY INSURED PLAN
Illustrative Gross Annual Premium
(Normal Retirement Benefit Formula = 30% of Salary)

Participant	Sex and Age	Monthly Earnings	Monthly Retirement Benefit	Face Amount— Retirement Income Contract	Gross Annual Premium
J. A. Wenhold............	M 54	$2,000	$600.00	$60,000	$ 8,778.90
R. C. Goshay............	M 50	1,800	540.00	54,000	5,509.26
S. W. Cain..............	M 46	1,000	300.00	30,000	2,292.00
R. M. Crowe............	M 43	925	277.50	27,750	1,756.36
A. F. Clark.............	M 34	650	195.00	19,500	771.24
W. C. Black............	M 31	525	157.50	15,750	545.36
F. X. Basile............	M 28	450	135.00	13,500	412.74
P. A. Zerby............	M 27	400	120.00	12,000	352.86
A. G. Luger............	M 25	375	112.50	11,250	306.23
B. E. Savastio..........	F 25	300	90.00	9,000	269.10
G. M. Sarf.............	F 25	300	90.00	9,000	269.10
Total Gross Annual Premium for Plan......................					$21,263.15

The advantages and disadvantages of requiring employee contributions were discussed at length in Chapter 2. If employee contributions are required, the commitment is generally expressed as a
fixed percentage of salary, such as 3% of annual earnings. However, where employee contributions are required to finance special
benefits (such as family income riders, double indemnity benefits,
waiver-of-premium or disability income benefits), each employee
generally pays the required premium for his particular set of extra
benefits. Lastly, employee contributions are usually applied toward
meeting the premium cost of the pure life insurance portion of the
contract, thereby minimizing or eliminating the employee's PS 58
cost.

If participating contracts are used, then dividends are available,
at least after the first or second year, to reduce the amount of
annual contributions required under the plan. Dividends are almost

always used to reduce the employer's contribution requirement for the following year. This practice is generally followed even in the case of contributory plans. Crediting the employer with the full amount of dividends is reasonable in view of the fact that he generally bears a substantial portion of the cost of the plan. Furthermore, administrative difficulties discourage the alternative procedure of allocating dividends between the employer and covered employees. The use of dividends to purchase additional amounts of benefits is permissible if specified in the terms of the plan and if such procedures do not discriminate in favor of stockholders, executives, supervisors, or highly compensated participants.

The employer's annual contribution requirement is reduced further whenever a covered employee terminates without full vesting. The employer does not know which employees will terminate employment in the future and, therefore, he must purchase the necessary amount of insurance for all currently covered employees. The reduction in cost due to turnover, then, is recognized only when the actual terminations take place. At that time, the nonvested portion of the cash value under the contract is held by the trustee and is used to reduce the amount of the employer's next premium payment. The Internal Revenue Code does not permit the trustee of the plan to reallocate the nonvested cash values among the remaining covered employees.[8] Such a practice would often result in discrimination in favor of the highly compensated employees and would also violate the Internal Revenue Code requirement that benefits be actuarially determinable.

The effect of employee contributions and expected dividends on the employer's annual cost under the hypothetical plan set forth in Table 7-2 can now be illustrated. The following projections are based on employee contributions of 3% of salary, and an estimate of average annual dividends expected to be paid over the next 10 years under the insurer's retirement income contracts.

Gross annual premium.................		$21,263.15
Less: Employer credits:		
Employee contributions............	$3,141.00	
Average annual dividends..........	2,029.28	5,170.28
Average annual employer contribution....		$16,092.87

The above illustration does not represent an actuarial projection of the long-range cost of the plan, since the effects of salary increases, new participants, and employee turnover are not reflected in these calculations.

Thus, it should now be clear why the statement, sometimes

[8] See p. 118.

heard, that individual policy plans have a level cost is seldom, if ever, true. The level annual gross premiums for a given set of purchased contracts are not descriptive of the contribution pattern for the plan as a whole. The gross premiums for the plan will change with increases in benefit levels and with additions and terminations among covered employees. Furthermore, annual dividends and termination credits will vary over time, thus producing some variation in the amount of employer contributions required in future years.

Contribution Flexibility.   One of the major disadvantages of fully insured individual policy plans is the fact that the employer has little flexibility in determining the timing and amount of contribution payments. The trustee is expected to have sufficient funds to meet premium payments as they become due. Furthermore, the insurance company chooses the actuarial assumptions used in the calculation of appropriate premium rates. Nor can the employer discount in advance for expected turnover among covered employees. It is true that deviations of actual from expected mortality, investment, and expense experience under these contracts are eventually reflected in the insurance company's dividend scale. Also, employer credits are received for terminations among employees who do not have fully vested benefits. Nevertheless, these cost-reducing factors cannot be discounted by the employer in advance of the date that they are actually realized.

The allocation of contributions to pay the premiums for contracts on specific employees creates inflexibility in meeting the costs of benefits for those employees who are at advanced ages at the inception of the plan. The employer will have only a relatively short period over which to fund the benefits of these older workers. The relatively high premiums for these employees plus the premium payments due for younger employees may produce a substantial contribution commitment in the early years of the plan. This problem is reduced somewhat if the insurance company permits a degree of postretirement funding of the benefits of older participants. Under unallocated funding instruments, plan contributions could be applied to provide the benefits of those at or near retirement age, the benefits of younger workers being provided for by future contributions.

There is one element of flexibility in employer contributions available under fully insured individual policy plans. If an employer finds it impossible to pay part or all of the premium due under issued contracts in a given year, the trustee can be directed to borrow on their cash values in order to meet the premium payments due. If the trustee does borrow to pay premiums, the loan must be charged against all contracts in the trust in a manner that precludes discrimination in favor of the highly compensated employees. In other words, the loan would be distributed in the proportion that the premium for each contract bears to the total premium for all contracts. If the trustee borrows on the cash value, it should be recognized that the actuarial cost method employed is in effect changed from an individual level cost method without a supplemental liability to an individual level cost method with a supplemental liability. Thus, the Internal Revenue Service requirements pertaining to minimum and maximum limitations on funding must be observed. For example, employer contributions in future periods applied toward repayment of the loans are deductible only to the extent that the annual repayment amounts do not exceed 10% of the supplemental liability created by the loans.

An alternative to having the trustee borrow to pay premiums would be for the employer to borrow the needed sums directly from a bank without using plan assets as collateral. The employer could then pay the required premiums to the plan trustee and take the normal tax deduction for annual pension contributions. Also, the interest charged on the loan would be deductible as a necessary and reasonable business expense. Furthermore, since the borrowing takes place outside of the scope of the plan, there would be no resultant change in actuarial cost method. Thus, the employer could repay the loan at any rate permitted by the bank without reference to pension plan tax Regulations. This approach would be particularly useful if the employer was faced with temporary financial difficulties, while at the same time having some older employees who are to be retired in a relatively short period of time. The employer may also wish to borrow the needed premium sums in a period of operating losses, in order to increase his carry-over loss for tax purposes.

The relative inflexibility of the employer's contribution commitment under fully insured individual policy plans may be viewed as an advantage of this funding instrument from the viewpoint of the employee. To the extent that the employer views the periodic premiums due as a fixed commitment, the long-run effect might be a greater degree of funding of benefits than might result if a more flexible funding instrument were used.

COMBINATION PLANS

General Characteristics

The term "combination plan" can be used to describe any funding arrangement that employs two or more different funding instruments. However, the term is generally used in practice to describe those plans that use a combination of individual contracts in conjunction with an unallocated conversion fund. The conversion fund is sometimes also referred to as the auxiliary fund or the side fund. The objective of the combination plan is to retain, in part, the guarantees and life insurance benefits associated with individual contracts, while at the same time obtaining a degree of the flexibility inherent in unallocated funding instruments.

The mechanics of the plan involve the purchase of a whole life insurance contract (or its equivalent) on the life of each participant, frequently with a face amount equal to 100 times the monthly expected pension benefit. Although paid-up at 65 contracts can be used, the general practice is to purchase ordinary life contracts. Some insurance companies use an endowment-type contract that provides a relatively small fixed cash value as of age 65 regardless of the issue date of the contract: for example, $400 per $1,000 of face value. Standardization of the amount of cash value available at retirement simplifies the calculation of the amounts required in the conversion fund. Ordinary life contracts or the above endowment-type contracts generate the lowest scale of cash values of the various whole life and endowment contracts, and therefore a significant portion of the funding may be provided through the conversion fund. Thus, ordinary life contracts are favored, since the flexibility inherent in the conversion fund is often a prime factor in the employer's decision to use a combination plan. On the average, the cash values of the ordinary life contract will equal about 25% of the net single-premium sum required at normal retirement age to provide the monthly pension benefit, the remaining 75% being provided out of the conversion fund. The exact proportion of the cash value to the principal sum required at retirement will, of course, vary somewhat with the age of issue and the length of time that the contract is in force as of retirement date, unless the endowment-type contracts are used.

The combination plan, like the fully insured individual policy plan, requires the use of a trustee. If the conversion fund is administered by a corporate trustee, the latter party normally also serves as the trustee to own the ordinary life insurance contracts. The conversion fund is often held and administered by the life insurance company that issues the insurance contracts. In this case, the trustee is generally an individual—often one of the officers of the firm. Only one trust agreement is required, regardless of whether the conversion fund is administered by a corporate trustee or an insurance company.

Evidence of insurability may be required with respect to the insurance contracts issued under a combination plan. However, most insurers are willing to issue these contracts on a guaranteed issue basis, subject to certain underwriting restrictions.

Benefit Structure

Retirement Benefits. Combination plans offer considerable flexibility in the choice of retirement benefit formulas. Practically any type of benefit formula can be used under these plans. Even a final-pay provision which bases benefits on the participant's average earnings during the five-year period immediately preceding retirement can be utilized effectively under a combination plan. As indicated earlier in this chapter, it is difficult to estimate precisely the level of compensation to be earned by an employee during his final years of employment, and therefore it is almost impossible to determine the exact face amount of retirement income coverage to be purchased to fund the ultimate retirement benefit. In the case of a combination plan, the problem of estimating the needed amount of ordinary life insurance coverage is not as compelling an issue, since a substantial proportion of the benefit is funded through the unallocated conversion fund. If the employee's final earnings prove to be higher than expected, the additional annuity consideration required can simply be withdrawn from the conversion fund. This cannot be readily done in the case of a fully insured plan, since benefits are funded solely from the cash values under the contracts issued on behalf of that particular employee.

The difficulty of projecting final earnings does present one problem when this formula is used under a combination plan: that is, the problem of determining the amount of ordinary life insurance to purchase for each employee. The approach generally used is not to reflect, for purpose of the ordinary life coverage, the increases in monthly pension benefits resulting from increases in the employee's compensation after age 55 or 60. Of course, any increases in pension benefit after this age could be credited to the employee, but they will be funded exclusively from the conversion fund.

As noted above, the face amount of the ordinary life insurance contract is frequently 100 times the expected monthly pension benefit. Thus, if a pension plan provides a retirement benefit of 40% of compensation, an employee earning $700 a month would be entitled to a pension of $280 a month. The trustee would purchase an ordinary life contract of $28,000 on the life of that employee. Additional contracts will be purchased for increases in pension benefit equal to at least $10 a month to which the employee will become entitled because of future increases in salary. Likewise, reductions in compensation would result in a termination of ordinary life coverage at the rate of $1,000 for every $10-a-month decrease in pension benefit. If the above employee is age 35 as of the issue date of the contract (and assuming no change in compensation), the cash value of a typical ordinary life contract at age 65 would be $14,812. However, the net single-premium sum required for a male, age 65, to provide a 10-year certain immediate life annuity of $280 a month would be $45,024. The difference between the principal sum of $45,024 and the contract cash value of $14,812 would be withdrawn from the conversion fund. In addition, most insurers impose a conversion charge (such as 2½%) on the difference between the net single premium and the cash value under the contract; in this example, a 2½% charge would be $755.30. After retirement, the employee would have an annuity benefit of $280 a month guaranteed for life by the insurance company.

Death Benefits. The preretirement death benefit under combination plans is generally restricted to the face amount of the contract. There is usually no benefit payment from the conversion fund in the event of the death of a participant. Thus, unlike fully insured plans, the death benefit under combination plans remains fixed—usually at 100 times the monthly pension until the date of retirement. Of course, if a lower amount of life insurance is desired, the death benefit can be reduced, for example, to 50 times the monthly pension. In some plans the death benefit is equal to one year's salary but in no case more than 100 times the monthly benefit. At least one writer has suggested that the death benefit under a combination plan can be made comparable to the benefit available under a fully insured plan by providing for an additional payment from the conversion fund upon the death of a participant.[9]

If the participant is uninsurable under the rules of the insurer at standard premium rates, the trustee may be able to purchase a contract at a substandard rate or with a graded or graduated death benefit at the same level annual premium applicable on a standard basis, the amount of the death benefit being determined by the rating assigned by the insurer.

Life insurance coverage may be continued beyond the normal retirement age in plans that permit deferred retirement. If an endowment-type contract is used, the insurer may require satisfactory evidence of insurability before extending coverage in this manner. In that case, the premiums necessary to maintain the

---

[9] Samuel J. Savitz, "The Case for the Combination Plan," *Journal of the Society of Chartered Life Underwriters*, Vol. XX, No. 1 (Winter, 1966), p. 67. Mr. Savitz argues that such benefits are within the limitations prescribed in Rev. Rul. 60–83, 1960–1 CB 157 and Rev. Rul. 61–121, 1961–2 CB 65.

contract in force on the participant's life on a premium-paying basis are generally obtained by the trustee making appropriate withdrawals from the conversion fund.

Disability Benefits. Waiver-of-premium and disability income riders can be provided under a combination plan. Of course, a waiver of premium benefit would apply only to the whole life contracts. Thus, even if the contract were kept in force to normal retirement date as a result of the waiver-of-premium benefit, the cash value would not be adequate to provide the full monthly pension the participant would otherwise have received. The disability income rider, on the other hand, would provide an immediate cash benefit (generally $10 a month per $1,000 of life insurance), with the usual provision that the contract will mature as an endowment at age 65. If a waiver-of-premium or disability income riders were used, the determination of whether a participant is totally and permanently disabled is made by the insurance company in accordance with the terms of the contract provisions.

The typical provision in these plans regarding total and permanent disability, however, is to provide the participant with his share of the conversion fund plus all benefits then available under the contract in force on his life. The determination of disability, in these cases, is generally based on a written certification of a licensed physician, usually selected by the participant and approved by the employer and the plan trustee. The trustee, upon receipt from the employer of such written certification, distributes the appropriate conversion fund share and the contract or its values, in accordance with the terms of the plan, the wishes of the participant, and the rules of the insurer.

Vested Benefits. It is customary, in combination plans, to provide that the participant has a vested interest in the full surrender value of the contract in force on his life. Generally, the participant has no vested interest in any amounts in the conversion fund. Where a terminating participant is to be given a vested interest in his share of the conversion fund, a graduated vesting schedule is often used. The disposition of the cash values of the contracts of a terminating participant depends on plan provisions and generally follows the analysis set forth earlier in this chapter with reference to vested benefits under fully insured plans.

Contributions

The periodic contributions required under a combination plan are composed of premium payments for the whole life insurance contracts and contributions to the conversion fund. The premium rates for purchased contracts are guaranteed and level in amount, subject to reduction on account of dividends. Of course, if an employee's benefits are increased, additional amounts of life insurance will have to be purchased at the rates in effect at the time the contract is actually purchased. In addition to the guarantee of premium rates, the issued contracts also carry an insurer guarantee of the annuity rates applicable at the employee's retirement date. The guaranteed annuity rates apply to the sums withdrawn at retirement date from the conversion fund, as well as to the cash values accumulated under the life insurance contract as of that date. The extent of the annuity rate guarantee applicable to the monies from the conversion fund is normally expressed as some multiple of the face amount of insurance, i.e., at the rate of $10 to $30 of monthly income for each $1,000 of face amount. Some insurers impose a conversion charge, which is normally expressed as a percentage of the difference between the principal sum required at retirement age to provide the pension and the cash value of the policy as of that date. This charge is generally 2% or 2½%, although a higher effective percentage may be imposed where the insurance benefit is less than 100 times the monthly benefit. The higher charge is required in the latter cases to offset the reduced amount of loading available to the insurer due to the relatively lower amounts of insurance.

If the conversion fund is held by an insurance company, the insurer will guarantee that the fund will be credited with a minimum rate of interest and that there will be no capital depreciation. In addition, most insurers will pay interest in excess of the guaranteed rate, as conditions permit. The conversion fund can be administered by a trustee, if the employer desires, in which case there is no guarantee of principal or interest. The significance of the combined annuity rate guarantee and the guarantee of principal and interest with reference to the conversion fund (when administered by an insurance company) is oftentimes not fully appreciated. In these cases, the insurer's guarantees approximate those available under fully insured individual policy plans.[10]

The amount of annual contributions to the conversion fund depends on the actuarial assumptions and the actuarial cost method used. Since the assets in the conversion fund are not allocated to specific employees, the employer can discount in advance for expected mortality and turnover. In practice, a mortality assumption is frequently used, but there is seldom a discount for turnover. Also, the employer has considerable flexibility in his choice of an

---

[10] *Ibid.*, p. 68.

interest assumption with reference to the conversion fund. Thus, one can generate different estimates of the amount of contributions required for the conversion fund based on his choice of assumptions. The effect of mortality and interest assumptions on the required contributions to the conversion fund is illustrated in Table 7–3.

TABLE 7–3
ILLUSTRATIVE ANNUAL CONTRIBUTIONS REQUIRED UNDER COMBINATION PLAN WITH VARYING PRERETIREMENT MORTALITY AND INTEREST ASSUMPTIONS

			Annual Contribution to Conversion Fund ($10 Monthly Income per $1,000 Life Insurance)			
		Annual $1,000 Whole Life Premium (Male)	Based on 1958 C.S.O. Table with Interest at			Based on Interest Only
Issue Age	Retirement Age		3.50%	3.75%	4.00%	4.00%
20........65		$12.58	$ 6.99	$ 6.52	$ 6.06	$ 8.21
30........65		17.15	11.88	11.26	10.67	14.04
40........65		24.76	22.51	21.69	20.90	26.46
50........65		37.72	53.26	52.12	51.01	60.84

The employer also has considerable flexibility in his choice of an actuarial cost method to be used in calculating his contribution requirements for the conversion fund. For example, an individual level cost method with supplemental liability can be used. As discussed in Chapter 4, this method generates a low annual normal cost. The employer is free to fund the supplemental liability as he sees fit, subject to the limitations imposed by the Internal Revenue Service. During periods of financial difficulty, the employer may reduce, or bypass altogether, the amount of contributions to the conversion fund, again within the limitations imposed by the Internal Revenue Service. Thus, the combination plan provides considerably greater flexibility as to the timing of contribution payments than is available under a fully insured plan. Furthermore, the employer has a great deal of investment flexibility with reference to the conversion fund. If the fund is administered by a trustee, the assets can be fully invested in common stocks, if such an investment policy is desired.

However, since contributions to the conversion fund do not constitute premiums as such, responsibility for the adequacy of the fund rests with the employer. If the actuarial assumptions prove to be erroneous, the assets in the conversion fund may not be adequate to provide the promised benefits. Also, it must be remembered, as indicated earlier, that the choice of actuarial cost method has little effect on the ultimate cost of the plan. Lower contributions in the early years must be offset by a higher level of contribution payments in future years. Nevertheless, the flexibility in the timing of contribution payments under combination plans is offered as an important advantage of this funding arrangement over fully insured individual policy plans.

The calculation of the amount of required periodic contributions for the conversion fund generally is performed by the insurance company, although some companies provide this service only if they hold the conversion fund. If the employer desires, he can retain a consulting actuary to perform this service.

GROUP INSURED PENSION PLANS

Insurance companies offer a variety of group contracts that can be used to fund pension benefits. The funding instruments in this category include group permanent, group deferred annuity, group deposit administration, and immediate participation guarantee contracts. Group contracts are generally preferred over individual policies for funding the benefits of larger plans. For example, while group annuity and deposit administration plans account for about 25% of the total number of insured plans, they cover over 5 million employees or about 80% of all employees covered by insured plans.[1] This chapter is devoted to a discussion of the above-mentioned group funding instruments.

GROUP PERMANENT CONTRACTS

Group permanent insurance contracts are basically quite similar to the individual insurance contracts used to fund pension plans. Since individual policy plans were discussed in some detail in Chapter 7, the treatment of group permanent contracts will be restricted primarily to a consideration of the differences between these two funding instruments.

General Characteristics

Group permanent insurance was developed to solve the problem of increasing premium costs under group term life insurance contracts in those instances where employers chose to continue group life insurance protection for their retired workers. The group permanent arrangement, in essence, offered the combined advantages

---

[1] *Life Insurance Fact Book* (New York: Institute of Life Insurance, 1965), p. 37.

of individual level premium life insurance protection for employees and mass or group underwriting. Thus, group permanent contracts, like individual contracts, were developed in response to a life insurance need rather than a retirement or pension need. However, both contracts provide cash values which can be readily converted into annuity benefits at retirement. Therefore, it was quite logical that some insurance companies would adapt their group permanent contracts to meet the needs of the pension market.

Group permanent contracts can be used as the sole funding instrument for a pension plan, or they can be used in combination with a conversion fund. In the case of a fully insured group permanent plan, the nature of the plan is practically identical to an individual policy retirement income plan. If the employer prefers a combination plan, ordinary life or some similar coverage will be issued under the group contract.

Under a fully insured group permanent plan, the insurance company generally issues the group master contract to the employer. Since all rights and obligations of the parties involved, including plan provisions, can be incorporated in the master contract, there is no need for a trust agreement and trustee, although a trust is sometimes employed. The employees receive certificates which indicate, in abbreviated form, the more important provisions of the master contract, and particularly those dealing with benefits and conditions of coverage. In the case of a combination plan, a trustee is appointed, and the group master contract is issued to the trustee.

Since group permanent insurance is a form of group life insurance, this coverage is subject to the group life laws in the various states. For example, in most states these contracts cannot be issued to groups of less than 10 lives. Also, if the pension plan is contributory, at least 75% of the eligible employees must participate in the plan. These requirements must be met throughout the life of the contract, and the insurance company can terminate the master contract if the size of the group or the percentage participation falls below the minimum required. However, group permanent insurance is generally not subject to the statutory maximum limits on the amount of group life insurance on any one life. In addition to the above underwriting requirements, the insurance company normally requires a minimum annual premium and/or a volume requirement for group permanent coverage.

The group permanent arrangement, then, has its greatest appeal in those cases where the employer desires a plan with general features characteristic of individual policy plans and where the number of participants is large enough to enjoy the advantages of group underwriting. The major advantage of the group approach is the lower premium rate attributable to the reduced commission scales, other acquisition costs, and general administrative expense levels. In addition, group permanent insurance is issued without evidence of insurability, subject to the underwriting limits imposed by the insurer. The nonmedical maximum is normally based on the size of the group and the distribution of amounts of insurance on the lives of participants. In some instances, this limit may be more liberal under group permanent than the guaranteed issue limit available under individual policies.

Benefit Structure

The benefit structures under group permanent plans are generally similar to those provided under individual policy plans. The normal retirement benefit formula is usually expressed as a flat percentage of compensation. Pure life insurance protection is available if retirement income or whole life forms of group permanent insurance are used. Therefore, the amount of preretirement death benefit depends on the type of coverage employed, as described in the previous chapter. Postretirement death benefits are normally available in the form of annuity options; the greater the death benefit (extent of annuity guarantee), the lower the amount of the monthly annuity benefit, assuming that a constant principal sum is being applied. Disability benefits and early retirement benefits can also be provided, and on essentially the same bases as these benefits are available under individual policy plans.

Although vested benefit provisions under these plans are essentially similar to provisions found in individual policy plans, there are a few differences that should be noted. Under group permanent plans, a typical provision is to provide the terminating employee with a cash payment or reduced paid-up coverage for the vested portion of the cash value.[2] The paid-up coverage may or may not include the right to surrender. Group insurance laws require that a terminating employee be given the right to convert, to some form of permanent life insurance, the difference between the face amount of his certificate and the amount of paid-up insurance to which he is entitled.[3] If the employee's termination of employment is coincident

---

[2] The cash value schedule under group permanent contracts is often based on the full net level premium reserve. A surrender charge is seldom levied against the terminating employee's vested portion of the cash value; however, such a charge is generally levied if the entire contract is being terminated in its early years. Therefore, other things being equal, the employee's vested benefit under group permanent contracts is somewhat higher (at least in the early years of coverage) than under comparable individual policy plans.

[3] Group permanent contracts generally do not include a loan provision, thereby precluding the alternative available under individual policy plans of the trustee borrowing the nonvested portion and transferring the full coverage subject to the loan.

with the termination of the contract, then the amount of insurance to which he can convert is subject to some maximum, for example, $2,000.

Contributions

The contributions required under a fully insured group permanent plan are composed solely of premiums for the insurance coverage, while contributions under a combination plan are divided between premiums for the group permanent coverage and contributions to the conversion fund.

The premium rate for group permanent insurance is a fixed level premium from date of entry of each participant (or date of increase in benefits) to normal retirement date. The premium rate is lower than the rate for a comparable individual contract, reflecting a lower expense loading in the group permanent rate. Because of the fixed level premium, the fully insured group permanent plan possesses the same contribution inflexibility found in fully insured individual policy plans, particularly if the contract does not contain a loan provision. Likewise, participants near retirement age at the inception of the plan present a significant funding problem under fully insured plans, whether individual policy or group permanent. These problems are minimized in the case of a combination plan.

The premium and annuity rates for all units of group permanent insurance in force are guaranteed. In addition, the contract normally provides that the premium rate guarantee applies to all units of benefit purchased within some period of time, such as three years following the issue date of the master contract. Thereafter, benefits are purchased at whatever rate is in effect at the time of purchase. Thus, the premium rate guarantee is slightly more significant under group permanent contracts than under individual policy plans.

The employer's annual contributions may be reduced by employee contributions, termination and late retirement credits, and dividends or experience premium rate credits. Employee contributions, if any, are usually applied toward the cost of the life insurance protection in order to reduce or eliminate the employee's PS 58 costs. Employer termination credits result whenever there is no vested benefit or when the terminating employee's vested benefit is less than the full surrender value under the contract. However, if the terminating employee elects to convert the coverage being canceled, the employer's termination credit is not available unless the insurer receives evidence of the employee's good health. Typically, the insurer grants an employer credit if: (1) the terminating employee is in good health; (2) the converted policy is surrendered; or (3) the employee is alive at the end of some period such as five years after the conversion. Late retirements could also result in employer credits if the plan does not permit participants to accumulate additional benefits by deferring retirement beyond normal retirement age. Lastly, the employer normally receives a dividend credit at the end of each contract year if experience has been favorable. In group insurance, each contract is experience rated. The effect of experience rating is to recognize, at least in part, the actual experience among participants in a particular plan in calculating the dividend for that plan. The dividends are calculated for the plan as a whole and not for the insurance on each participant's life. The technique of experience rating will be discussed in greater detail later in this chapter, in the section dealing with group deferred annuities.

GROUP DEFERRED ANNUITY CONTRACTS

The group annuity contract, unlike individual insurance and group permanent contracts, was specifically devised to meet the funding needs of pension plans, the first such contract being issued in 1921. Group annuity plans grew very rapidly in the following two decades and constituted by far the most prevalent group insured funding instrument prior to the growth of deposit administration plans in the 1950's.

Although the provisions of a group annuity contract can be tailored to meet the needs of a particular employer, there are certain basic features generally associated with this funding instrument.

General Characteristics

Group annuity contracts provide for the funding of benefits through the purchase of units of single-premium deferred annuities for each participant. However, some insurance companies offer level premium deferred annuities on a group underwriting basis.

The terms of the pension plan are usually incorporated in the master contract issued to the employer. Thus, as is true in the case of any fully insured group plan, there is no need for a trustee. Certificates outlining the benefits and conditions of coverage under the plan are often issued to employees, but there is no requirement that this be done except in a few states that require issuance of certificates if the plan is contributory. These certificates do not constitute a contract between the insurance company and plan participants. Nevertheless, some insurers take the precaution of requiring employees to turn in their certificates immediately prior to receiving benefits under the plan. Also, certificates are sometimes recovered at retirement for the purpose of issuing new certificates which specify the amount of monthly income payable.

Unlike group life insurance, group annuity contracts are subject to very little statutory regulation regarding eligible groups or minimum number of covered lives. However, insurance companies do impose, as a matter of underwriting policy, certain requirements with reference to these contracts. Most insurers require that there be a minimum number of eligible employees (10, for example) in order for an employer to be eligible for a group annuity contract. If the plan is contributory, at least 75% of the eligible employees must participate in the plan, 100% participation being required in the case of noncontributory plans. These underwriting requirements are not imposed so much to minimize adverse selection as they are to produce a sufficient size case to justify the insurer expenses incurred in setting up the plan. A minimum annual premium per participant or for the plan as a whole is also imposed in order to assure the above objective. Also, the insurer imposes an administrative charge if the total premium in a contract year is less than a specified amount, the actual charge being determined by the amount of the annual premium. For example, one insurance company imposes an administrative charge in any contract year in which total premiums, exclusive of any administrative charge, are less than $85,000. The amount of the administrative charge in those years is $600 decreased by an amount equal to 1% of that part of the total premiums paid in such contract year in excess of $25,000.

Benefit Structure

Retirement Benefits. As indicated earlier, benefits under traditional group annuity contracts are funded through the purchase of single-premium deferred annuities. Thus, the inherent nature of this funding instrument suggests the use of a unit benefit formula. Most group annuity plans use a benefit formula of a specified percentage of compensation per year of service. These plans generally provide a different level of benefit for past service as compared with future service. For example, future service benefits may accrue at the rate of $1\frac{1}{4}$% of compensation, with past service benefits being calculated on the basis of $\frac{3}{4}$% of compensation as of the inception date of the plan per year of past service.[4] Unit benefit formulas that provide a flat dollar benefit per year of service are also ideally suited to the group annuity mechanism.

---

[4] The reasons for this benefit differential are discussed at length on p. 40.

Under either of the above benefit formulas, a unit of accrued benefit is associated with each year of service. Thus, a single-premium deferred annuity can be purchased for each employee equal to the future service benefit that accrues with each year of service. If the plan provides a benefit of 1% of compensation per year of service, an employee earning $6,000 a year would accrue a benefit of $60 a year beginning at normal retirement age. The premium that the employer would pay for a *pure* deferred life annuity of $60 a year depends on the sex, the attained age of the employee at the time of purchase, the annuity form, and the normal retirement age. For a male employee, age 35, a typical single premium for a pure deferred life annuity of $60 a year (payable monthly) beginning at age 65 would be $206. If the employee's compensation remains constant during the following year, he will accrue an additional $60 a year of retirement benefit; the single premium, however, will increase to $213.45, reflecting the fact that the employee will be one year closer to retirement.

The past service benefit of a participant is determined by multiplying the participant's compensation as of the inception date of the plan by the past service benefit percentage. Therefore, if the plan in the above examples provides a past service benefit of ½ of 1% of compensation per year of service and the above-mentioned employee earned $6,000 a year at the inception of the plan and is credited with five years of past service, his past service benefit is $150 a year beginning at age 65. The premium required to purchase these past service benefits would be determined by multiplying $150 by the appropriate single-premium rate for a deferred annuity of $1 a year beginning at age 65, the rate being determined by the participant's age at inception of the plan. For a given retirement age, the single-premium rate increases with the age at which the participant's benefits are actually purchased. However, the employer seldom, for reasons noted later in this chapter, purchases the past service benefits of all participants on the inception date of the plan. The typical procedure is to apply past service premiums on an age priority basis, i.e., funding the past service benefits of older workers first.

By retirement date, the participant will have been credited with a series of paid-up deferred annuities. The employee will receive a single monthly pension check upon retirement representing the sum of the units of annuities purchased on his behalf.

Group annuity contracts can also be used without difficulty in the case of defined contribution (money purchase) plans. It will be recalled that under these plans the employer and the employee (if the plan is contributory) contribute specified percentages of annual compensation. The annual contribution can be applied, under a group annuity contract, as a single premium to purchase a unit of deferred annuity. The amount of annuity purchased would depend on the sex, attained age of the participant at the time of purchase, annuity form, and the normal retirement age. As the participant grows older, a given sum of annual contributions would buy smaller and smaller units of paid-up deferred annuities.

Flat percentage of compensation formulas are seldom used with group annuity plans. One reason for this is the problem of imputing a certain amount of the participant's projected benefit to each year of service (or of arriving at an approximately level premium which will provide, in the aggregate, the proper amount of benefit at retirement). Another reason is that in most situations, flat percentage formulas are usually applied to final earnings, which compounds the problem of determining the amount of benefit or premium attributable to any contract year. It is not likely that any benefit or premium estimates required for plans of this type will prove accurate, with the result that additional purchases or cancellations of annuities will be required from time to time. However, a group annuity contract can be used if a flat percentage formula is desired. The projected total retirement benefit can be broken down into units of deferred annuities of equal amounts to be purchased annually on a single-premium basis between attained age and retirement age. As the participant receives increases in compensation and therefore increases in retirement benefits, purchase of the additional benefits will be made in equal installments over the remaining years to retirement. If the insurer offers a level premium group deferred annuity contract, then a flat percentage formula can be accommodated without too much difficulty. However, for the reasons mentioned above, flat percentage of compensation formulas are not generally suitable for group annuity plans. Furthermore, the leveling of deferred annuity units would significantly distort vested benefits—a problem that could be corrected, if at all, only by a complex vesting provision.

Early retirement benefits can be readily accommodated under group annuity contracts. The master contract includes a table of percentage reduction factors for retirements prior to normal retirement date. The appropriate percentage is applied to the total amount of a participant's accrued deferred annuity on the normal annuity form commencing at normal retirement date to obtain the total monthly amount of immediate annuity on the normal annuity form commencing at early retirement date. For a male employee retiring at age 62 under a plan with a normal retirement age of 65, the reduction in benefit is usually about 25%. In addition, this employee sacrifices the additional future service benefits that would accrue between ages 62 and 65 if he continued employment until normal retirement date. Application of early retirement provisions under group annuity contracts assumes that all benefits accrued to the date of early retirement, including past service benefits, have actually been purchased. If past service premiums are applied on an age priority basis, this requirement should present little problem, except possibly in the early years of the plan.

Under most group annuity contracts, a participant whose early retirement date occurs prior to the month with respect to which he expects to receive his first basic monthly Social Security retirement benefit can elect, with the consent of the insurance company, to convert his retirement annuity to provide increased monthly payments up to and including the monthly due date immediately preceding his first Social Security month and decreased monthly payments thereafter. The amount of each monthly payment is generally calculated so that the monthly payment due prior to his first Social Security month is approximately equal to the monthly payment due thereafter, increased by the expected basic monthly amount of Social Security benefits, without regard to any additional Social Security benefits to which he may be entitled with respect to dependents.

If increased late retirement benefits are available under the plan, the percentage increase in benefits for each year after normal retirement date can also be ascertained from a table of late retirement factors set forth in the contract. These percentage factors are applied to the total monthly amount of retirement annuity on the normal annuity form that would otherwise have been payable to him on his normal retirement date. If the plan permits a participant to accumulate additional future service benefits for service beyond the normal retirement date, then the total of the monthly amounts of future service annuity benefits that have been purchased on his life subsequent to his normal retirement date is added to the above figure in calculating his full retirement benefit. If the late retirement benefit is the same as that available at normal retirement date, the employer receives a credit for all late retirements.

Death Benefits. Group annuity contracts are not designed to provide life insurance protection as an integral part of the contract. The contract was designed solely as a vehicle for systematically funding employees' retirement benefits. Therefore, if a participant dies prior to his retirement date, the benefits paid under group annuity plans are generally restricted to a return of an employee's contributions, accumulated with interest at the rate specified in the contract. Preretirement death benefits attributable to employer contributions are seldom provided under group annuity contracts, although benefits of this type can be readily provided if the employer so desires.

Postretirement death benefits depend on the normal annuity form under the plan and the annuity options available to, and elected by, participants. If the plan is noncontributory, the normal annuity form is usually a pure life annuity and, therefore, there is no postretirement death benefit. However, in these cases, participants usually have the option of electing an annuity form that does offer a death benefit, for example, a joint and survivor annuity or a life annuity with payments certain for a specified period. The death benefit inherent in such options, however, is paid for by the participant in the form of a reduction in the amount of monthly annuity benefit. If the plan is contributory, the normal annuity form is generally a modified cash refund annuity. The effect of this annuity form is to assure a retired worker that total retirement annuity payments will never be less than the aggregate of his contributions, usually with interest, to the date of his retirement. If total annuity payments are less than the deceased retired worker's contributions accumulated with interest, the difference is paid by the insurance company, usually in a lump sum, to a designated beneficiary. Optional forms of annuity payment with varying degrees of death benefit are also available to participants under contributory plans. Here again, however, the cost of death benefits under annuity forms other than the normal annuity form is borne directly by the participant in terms of an adjustment of the monthly benefit amount.

To the extent that annuity options provide for increases in death benefits, the insurance company usually imposes some underwriting restrictions on participant elections in order to minimize adverse selection. Elections or changes in annuity options generally must be exercised at least two or three years prior to the effective date of the option; otherwise evidence of insurability will be required.[5]

Disability Benefits. Disability benefits are seldom provided under a group annuity plan. If such benefits are desired, they can be provided through a separate group disability income contract issued to the employer.

Vested Benefits. The benefits available to participants who terminate their employment for reasons other than death or retirement depend on whether the plan is contributory and the nature of the vesting provisions, if any, of the plan. If the plan is contribu-

---

[5] For a further discussion of this point, see pp. 51 and 260.

tory, the participant is always entitled to a return of his contributions, usually with interest. The participant's accumulated contributions can be withdrawn in cash or left with the insurance company to purchase a paid-up annuity on the normal annuity form commencing on his normal retirement date.

Vested benefits are usually available only in the form of a paid-up deferred annuity commencing at normal retirement age, and only if the employee does not elect to withdraw his own contributions. Typically, the vesting scale is applied to the excess of the total of the annuity already purchased for the employee over the amount of annuity his own contributions will provide. For example, assume that a participant terminates his employment at a time when he would be 50% vested. The contributions of the terminating participant that have been paid to the insurance company are applied to the purchase of a paid-up annuity starting at normal retirement date in accordance with the annuity purchase rates set forth in the master contract. The amount of the paid-up annuity so determined is subtracted from the total paid-up annuity benefits that have been already purchased for this participant under the contract. In accordance with the terms of the plan, 50% of the remaining annuity is deemed to be vested in this terminating employee. This amount of benefit plus the deferred annuity purchased by the participant's contributions equals the full amount of the participant's vested benefit.

Group annuity contracts usually provide that the option of paid-up annuity benefits is automatically operative unless and until the option to withdraw the participant's contribution in cash is elected. Few plans permit the participant to withdraw his own contributions and still be entitled to the paid-up annuity provided by employer contributions. However, a terminated employee can always elect, prior to normal retirement date, to withdraw his own contributions.

In the case of noncontributory plans, the availability of benefits for terminating participants, of course, depends solely on the vesting provisions of the plan.

Contributions

Premium Rates. Group annuity plans, as already noted, are funded through the purchase of units of single-premium deferred annuities. The premium rate scale at which annuities are to be purchased is set forth in the master contract. The premium rate scale is generally guaranteed with respect to annuities purchased during the first five contract years under a group annuity contract. Thereafter, the insurance company has the right to revise all rates and values included in the policy, provided that written notice is given to the policyholder some period (such as 45 days) prior to the effective date of any such revision. Of course, any such revision will not affect the premium rates and annuity values applicable to premiums which have been paid prior to the effective date of the revision. Also, the insurance company is not required to give notice to participants of any proposed rate or annuity value changes.

Other factors in the contract, such as early or late retirement and annuity option factors, may also be guaranteed in the same fashion as the premium rates. Often, however, these factors are guaranteed only for a specified period of time (such as 10 years), regardless of when the annuities were purchased. In this latter case, it is customary to have a longer notice period regarding rate changes—for example, three years.

The burden of any rate increase in the case of defined benefit plans generally is borne in full by the employer. Even if the plan is contributory, employee contributions are usually expressed as a fixed percentage of compensation, and these percentages are seldom increased merely to offset the increased cost of an insurer's rate revision. However, in the case of a defined contribution plan, the benefit that can be purchased by both employer and employee contributions is directly affected by insurer rate revisions.

In the typical group annuity plan, employer contributions are used to purchase paid-up units of *pure* deferred annuities and, therefore, no death benefit is provided with respect to these contributions. The absence of an insurer liability for the payment of death benefits can be discounted in the rate calculation, resulting in a reduction of the premium rate per dollar of deferred annuity income. If employees contribute, on the other hand, units of modified cash refund deferred annuities are purchased, and the premium rates are based on the assumption that the participant, or his beneficiary or estate, is always entitled, as a minimum, to a return of his contributions. Obviously, other things being equal, a dollar of contribution will purchase a smaller amount of modified refund annuity as compared to the income benefit available on a pure annuity basis. For this reason, a given amount of benefit under a group annuity plan will cost more if employees contribute.

Group annuity premium rates are calculated on the basis of assumptions regarding expected mortality and investment income, and a loading for expenses and contingencies. In order to assure adequacy of premium rates, insurance companies normally use assumptions that are conservative in relation to the company's current experience. Recognition of actual experience in future years under the plan or among insured lives is reflected in dividend levels and rate adjustments. Currently, most group annuity rates are based on the 1951 Group Annuity Table, with some modification. The basic 1951 table is often modified through the use of a projection scale and/or an age setback. The interest assumption for group annuity rates varies considerably among companies, with rates ranging anywhere from 3¼ to 3¾%. The choice of an appropriate loading for expenses under group annuity contracts presents somewhat of a problem because of the considerable variation in expenses associated with the size of the plan. For example, expenses may range from a low of about 2% for a very large case to a high of about 15% for a small plan. One solution to the problem would be for the insurance company to develop group annuity premium rate schedules that vary by the size of the plan. This, however, would prove to be a rather cumbersome solution. Instead, most companies use a schedule of uniform rates based on a 4% or 5% expense assumption, and adjust the premium through the use of an annual administrative expense charge. Companies that use a 4% loading generally add on any state annuity premium tax imposed. As indicated earlier, the administrative charge generally disappears altogether in any contract year in which the premium exceeds some amount, such as $85,000, leaving the basic loading in the premium rate as the sole expense charge. Of course, dividend experience will reflect actual expenses, which could be more or less than the level assumed in the premium rate.

Annual Contributions. All premiums under group annuity contracts are paid directly to the insurance company by the policyholder, i.e., the employer or, if applicable, a trustee. Since premiums are due in advance, the insurance company will estimate at the beginning of each contract year the amount of total premium due for such contract year. The estimated premium can then be paid on a monthly or an annual basis. The premiums will be increased if payments are made other than on an annual basis. At the end of the contract year, the insurance company will calculate the correct premium for the year, and appropriate adjustments to the estimated premium will then be made. If the plan is contributory, the annual premium basis in effect requires the employer to advance the amount of employee contributions for the year, which he then recovers through payroll deductions. Rather than advance employee contributions, many employers prefer remitting premiums, at least to the extent that they consist of employee contributions, on a monthly basis.

The annual premiums due under group annuity contracts may be subdivided into premiums for future service benefits credited during the contract year and premiums to purchase part or all of the unfunded past service benefits. The premium for future service benefits is simply the aggregate of the single premiums required to purchase the units of deferred annuity income credited to all participants for service rendered during the current contract year. The annual premium for future service benefits will tend to increase for several years after the inception of the plan. This rise in future service premiums is due to the increasing ages of participants and the fact that benefit formulas under group annuity plans are generally related to compensation, which normally increases with years of service. However, the employer's pattern of annual contributions is also affected by changing patterns of the group covered as well as by the rate of funding of past service benefits and the availability of employer credits. Thus, employer contributions for the plan as a whole may not show an upward trend. Indeed, some pension consultants claim that, in practice, the increase in annual future service premiums, if any, tends to be relatively small.

Determination of the premium for past service benefits is somewhat more complex. It will be recalled that past service benefits are credited for service rendered prior to the inception date of the plan. Thus, it is a relatively simple matter to apply the past service benefit formula and determine the exact amount of past service benefits credited to each participant as of the inception date of the plan. The single-premium sum required in the first year of the plan to fully fund all participants' past service benefits would be equal to the sum of the products of each employee's total past service benefit times the appropriate single-premium rates. However, it is not likely that any employer is interested in fully funding all past service benefits in the first year of the plan. The premium expenditure required would be quite sizable. Furthermore, the Internal Revenue Code imposes certain limitations regarding the deductibility, for federal income tax purposes, of contributions applied toward the funding of past service benefits. The maximum deduction in any one year is limited to 10% of the initial past service liability (i.e., the single-premium sum noted above).

Each year that the past service benefits remain unfunded, the single-premium sum required to fund those benefits increases. This point can be best illustrated with reference to an individual participant. The single-premium rate per dollar of deferred annuity income beginning at age 65 increases with the attained age of the participant, since each passing year brings the employee closer to his retirement age. Thus, if the past service benefits of this participant are not purchased in the first year of the plan, the single-premium cost of purchasing his benefits will increase each year.

The same analysis applies with reference to the funding of past service benefits for the plan as a whole.

In applying the annual premiums for past service benefits, the employer may decide to purchase a portion of the past service benefits of all employees, or allocate these premiums toward the funding of the past service benefits of those participants near retirement age. The latter approach is used most frequently, since insurance companies usually require a participant's annuity benefit to be fully purchased by retirement date. If there are several older participants in the plan at inception date, the substantial past service for these employees may preclude any purchases of past service benefits for younger participants for some time. Indeed, if there is a sizable number of older participants when the plan starts, the employer may find the financial burden of past service benefits, even for these employees, to be greater than he is capable of meeting. Many insurance companies now permit a degree of postretirement funding under group annuity contracts, which alleviates some of the financial burdens created by retirements soon after the inception of the plan. However, if the number of older workers at the inception of the plan is very large, it may be necessary to exclude these employees from the plan, to reduce their past service benefit, or to provide their benefits through an alternative funding instrument or on a pay-as-you-go basis. Some insurance companies offer what is called a "deposit administration rider" to a group annuity contract for purposes of funding past service benefits. Past service contributions are paid into a deposit fund, with appropriate sums being withdrawn at retirement age to purchase the past service benefits of retiring employees. This approach minimizes the possibility of employer dissatisfaction that might otherwise result from loss of rather substantial credits if an older participant dies immediately after a sizable annuity has been purchased on his behalf.

Once the employer determines the amount of past service benefits to be purchased for particular participants in a given year, the determination of the premium is identical to the calculation of premiums for future service benefits, i.e., the amount of each participant's deferred annuity income is multiplied by the appropriate single-premium rate for his attained age.

The annual contributions under a group deferred annuity contract, then, are composed of premiums for future service and past service benefits. The employer's share of annual contributions can be reduced by requiring employee contributions. Employee contributions are almost always applied toward the purchase of future service benefits, i.e., past service costs are borne solely by the employer. The employee contribution rate under a group annuity plan is generally related to the benefit formula. For example, if the plan provides a benefit of 1% of compensation per year of service, the employee contribution rate will be expressed as some multiple of that benefit, for example, twice the benefit or, in this case, 2% of compensation. If the benefit formula is $5 per month per year of service, the employee contribution rate may be, for example, three times the benefit or $15 a month in this case. Care must be exercised in the choice of an employee contribution rate, in order to avoid the possibility that employee contributions alone are adequate to purchase each unit of future benefit accruing under the plan. It has been estimated that at the younger ages, a rate of contribution from the employee of three to one or larger will usually buy all of the future service benefits accruing at those ages.[6] This situation is obviously undesirable unless it persists only for the first few years after a young participant enters the plan.

Few group annuity plans permit voluntary contributions in excess of the required rate. The fact that dividends under these contracts are usually credited fully to the employer normally offsets the premium rate advantage available under the group contract.

Under defined contribution plans, employee contribution rates are related to the employer's rate of contribution. A typical provision is to require identical rates of contribution for both employer and employees; for example, each contributes 5% of the employee's compensation.

The employer's share of annual contributions are reduced further to the extent that employer credits are available on premium due dates. Employer credits under group annuity contracts can arise from employee terminations, late retirements, and dividend or experience rate credits. The availability of employer credits due to employee terminations, in turn, depends on the cause of the termination and the nature of the plan's vesting provision, if any. If termination of employment is due to the death of a participant, then no employer credit is available. As mentioned earlier, employer contributions are used to purchase pure deferred annuities. A pure deferred annuity does not provide for a refund of the purchase price if the annuitant fails to live to the specified retirement age. Therefore, mortality has been already discounted in the annuity premium rates used to determine employer contributions. For this same reason, the insurance company requires evidence that participants, terminating for reasons other than death, are in fact in good health. Insurers generally will accept the word of the employer that the terminating employee is in good health, unless substantial

---

[6] John St. John, *Pensions and Profit Sharing* (3rd ed.; Washington, D.C.: Bureau of National Affairs, Inc., 1964), p. 95.

amounts of annuity are involved. In the latter case, the insurer may require evidence of good health, or in the absence of such evidence, may withhold the credit pending the survival of the terminating participant for some period such as five years. Where the employer credit is available, the amount of the credit is generally the full amount of employer premiums paid on behalf of the terminating employee with interest. A charge of 5% is usually levied in those cases where new deferred annuity purchases have been discontinued under the plan. Also, if employee contributions are involved, a charge of 5% of these contributions is usually made against the employer credit. Of course, no employer credit is available if the terminating participant is in poor health or if his benefits are fully vested. If benefits are partially vested, then the employer's credit is based on the nonvested portion of the benefit.

Units of deferred annuity income are purchased under group annuity contracts on the assumption that participants will retire at the normal retirement age. Therefore, an employer credit is generally available whenever a participant defers retirement beyond his normal retirement age, assuming that his benefit is not actuarially increased. Most group annuity plans provide that the same retirement benefit will be paid at a late retirement date as would be payable as of the participant's normal retirement date. Thus, the annuity payments due between the normal retirement date and the late retirement date are credited to the employer. If postretirement death benefits are available, the employer credit will be withheld until subsequent annuity payments exceed the minimum death benefit.

Dividends or retroactive premium rate credits are a third source of employer credits under group annuity contracts. The amount of dividend credited to the employer's account reflects, at least in part, actual experience with reference to participants under the plan. The weight or credibility assigned to the experience of participants of the plan depends on the size of the group and the length of time that the contract has been in force. Initially, the administrative charge and the loading in the premium rate are not adequate to meet all acquisition costs and expenses of setting up the plan. Therefore, the remainder of these expenses must be amortized over the first few years of the plan. Furthermore, the long-term nature of guarantees under group annuity contracts does not permit an accurate testing of the reasonableness of the mortality assumption in the premium rate within a few years after establishment of the plan. For example, if mortality among participants in the first few years of the plan is higher than assumed in the rate, one could not conclude that these savings should be immediately credited to the employer. Meaningful comparisons of actual and expected mortality experience can only be made over a relatively long period of time. In contrast, current experience can be reflected immediately in the dividends or rate adjustments under larger group medical expense plans. This is possible in the group health field, since the insurer's liabilities can be estimated fairly accurately on a contract year basis, and the following year's premium can be adjusted when necessary. The true liability of the insurer under annuity contracts, on the other hand, will not emerge until many years after the inception of the plan. For these reasons, it is not uncommon for a number of years to elapse before dividends become payable under a group annuity contract.

In calculating group annuity dividends, insurers use a fund accounting approach which is usually based on calendar year experience. A separate cumulative experience account or internal record fund account is maintained for each contract. It must be emphasized that this is solely an internal account used for dividend calculation purposes, and has no bearing on the insurer's liability to provide the benefits that have been already purchased. The account is credited with the total earned premium (including the administrative charge) received by the insurer during the year. The account is also credited with an appropriate amount of the actual investment income earned by the insurance company. The internal record fund is debited with any benefits payable during the calendar year with respect to the participants. Examples of these benefits are annuity payments, cash termination payments of vested benefits, and returns of employee contributions with interest in the case of contributory plans. The next item debited is any commission payable on premiums earned during the year. Any state premium taxes incurred are also debited to the account. In addition to the foregoing items, the internal record account would be charged with administrative expenses of the home office, sales expense, and a proportionate share of general overhead.

The account balance, at this point, reflects the excess of income over outgo with reference to the specific group annuity contract. The account must show an excess of income over outgo, since we have not yet considered the extent of the insurer's incurred liabilities under this plan. The insurer is liable for the benefits purchased on the lives of active employees, as well as the guaranteed payments due in future years to already retired workers. The next step in the calculation of the dividend, then, is the valuation of the insurer's reserve liabilities under the plan.

In addition to these reserves for purchased annuities, insurers generally require that each group annuity develop a contingency reserve. One of the main purposes of the contingency reserve is to provide a financial buffer in case of future improvements in longevity and unforeseen contingencies. Another important purpose of the contingency reserve is to provide for mortality fluctuation. On a particular case, it is quite likely that the actual experience will depart from the expected norm, since the norm is based on the exposure of many more individuals. The experience of a small group may vary widely from the norm. The size of the group and the amount of the reserve subject to a mortality risk have a bearing on the size of the contingency reserve. The smaller these items, the greater the chance of random fluctuation and the more the need for the contingency reserve. A third purpose of the contingency reserve is to provide for future expenses. Because of the nature of the annuity business, expenses continue to be incurred for a long period of time after a contract discontinues, and the insurance company has no new premium to provide a loading to help cover these expenses. The ultimate goal as to the size of the contingency reserve may range in the area of from 3% to 8% (or higher in some cases) of the annuity reserves, depending upon the size of the contract; the lower contingency reserve often is required on larger cases. This reserve is usually accumulated on a graduated basis over a period of years.

The amount of the required annuity reserves and contingency reserve is then compared to the fund balance in the internal record account. If the fund balance exceeds the sum of the necessary reserves, a dividend will be credited to the employer. If the reserves exceed the balance of cash income over outgo, then there is no basis for a dividend. The reserve assumptions used by the insurer, therefore, have an important bearing on the pattern of dividends under group annuity contracts. This fact makes group annuity premium rate comparisons fairly difficult.

There are two basic approaches being used by insurance companies today, in calculating the rate of investment income to be credited to the internal record account of each group annuity contract. The traditional approach is to use the net rate of return earned by the insurer on its overall portfolio of investments. This rate is often referred to as the average or portfolio rate of return. To arrive at the amount of investment income to be allocated to a particular case, interest will be credited for a full calendar year at the current dividend interest rate to the balance of the fund outstanding on the previous December 31. Adjustments are then made to reflect the financial activity of the case during the current year.

In the 1950's, a few insurers began questioning the desirability of using the average rate of return method for allocating investment income among group annuity cases. Interest rates on new investments made during this period rose significantly from the low rates of return that prevailed in the 1940's. However, insurance companies held in their portfolios a substantial amount of relatively long-term investments that were acquired in the 1940's and carried the low rates of return in effect during that decade. Thus, the average rates of investment income for most insurance companies were below the yields being earned on new investments acquired in the 1950's, and insurance companies were somewhat at a disadvantage in competing with banks for new pension business, particularly for the larger cases. In the case of a trust fund plan, all contributions would be invested at the prevailing higher rates of return. In addition to the loss of some new cases, insurers found that some employers discontinued purchases of annuities under existing group annuity contracts, while other employers went one step further and withdrew funds from insurers, where possible, and transferred these sums to bank trustees. Therefore, some insurance companies decided to change their basis of allocating investment income for dividend purposes under group annuity contracts, in order to improve their competitive position and to reduce the adverse financial selection they were experiencing under the average rate method. The investment income allocation technique that was devised is generally referred to as the new-money or investment-year method.

Under the new-money approach, an attempt is made to allocate investment income on the basis of the rate of return earned on new investments made in the year in which each block of contributions was received. Since yields on investments acquired each year are seldom identical, the allocation of investment income in dividend calculations for a given year of necessity involves the use of a number of different rates of return. Furthermore, investments made in previous years are constantly maturing and must be reinvested. Therefore, the contributions received, say, five years ago cannot be assumed to be still invested at the yields earned on new investments acquired in that year. Thus, the new-money method required an assumption as to the rate of turnover of investments, with appropriate adjustments in the interest rates applied toward previous contributions.[7]

The new-money method, for this reason, is particularly advantageous during a period of rising interest rates. If investment yields on new investments began to decrease, insurers using the average

---

[7] For a more detailed discussion of the new-money method including an arithmetical illustration, see William K. White, "The New Money Interest Rate Method for Group Insured Pension Plans," *Journal of the American Society of Chartered Life Underwriters*, Vol. XIV (Spring, 1960), pp. 158–70.

rate method for allocating investment income might then have a competitive advantage. During a period of declining interest rates, new-money companies would be faced with the problem of potential adverse financial selection, whereas this problem is more acute for the average rate companies during a period of rising investment yields. In either case, as noted above, insurers make provisions for adverse financial selection through the accumulation of a contingency reserve. It should also be noted that over a long period of time, the amount of investment income allocated to group annuity accounts by either method would be approximately equal, assuming identical patterns of contribution payments. Lastly, apart from the competitive implications of the alternative allocation methods, there is the interesting issue as to which method produces the greater degree of equity among policyholders.[8] However, a discussion of equity considerations involving methods of surplus distribution is beyond the scope of this chapter.

Contribution Flexibility. Group annuity contracts offer the employer a greater degree of contribution flexibility than is available under individual policy and group permanent plans. In the latter plans, it will be recalled that an employee's total benefits (including past service as well as future service benefits) are projected and usually funded on a level premium basis. Group annuity contracts, on the other hand, permit a clear separation, for funding purposes, of past and future service benefits. While the employer has considerable flexibility in the funding of past service benefits, subject to the limitations imposed by the Internal Revenue Service and the insurance company, as discussed earlier, he has little flexibility in the funding of future service benefits. Group annuity contracts provide for the annual purchase of future service benefits on behalf of each participant, as such benefits accrue. While group annuity contracts permit temporary suspensions of annual purchases of future service annuities, the annuities not purchased during such period of suspension are purchased upon the resumption of premium payments.[9] Thus, although suspension of future service annuity purchases is permitted, the objective of the contract provision is to provide relief during periods of financial stress, rather than significant contribution flexibility for the employer. As a result, employers interested in a greater degree of contribution flexibility are prone to favor one of the unallocated funding instruments.

[8] See, for example, White, *ibid.* Also, Edward A. Green, "The Case for Refinement in Methods of Allocating Investment Incomes," *Transactions of the Society of Actuaries*, Vol. XIII (1961), pp. 308–52.

[9] It is assumed in this discussion that such suspensions would not be in violation of the minimum funding requirements imposed by the Internal Revenue Service.

GROUP DEPOSIT ADMINISTRATION CONTRACTS

The deposit administration contract, which first appeared in the 1920's, evolved from the basic group deferred annuity contract. For this reason, it is often referred to as a deposit administration group annuity contract. The deposit administration contract was developed to overcome certain of the inflexibilities associated with the group annuity contract. Although originally developed as a result of interinsurer competition, the growth in popularity of the deposit administration plan began in the early 1950's, largely in response to the increased competition from the trust fund arrangement, which offers a great deal of flexibility in plan design, timing of employer contributions, and investment alternatives.

General Characteristics

The distinguishing characteristic of deposit administration contracts, as contrasted with group deferred annuity contracts, is the fact that employer contributions are not allocated to specific employees until retirement date. Stated differently, the actual purchase of annuities does not take place until an employee retires.

Contributions, other than any administrative charge premium, are credited to an unallocated fund, which is variously referred to as the active life fund, deposit administration fund, deposit fund, deposit account, or purchase payment fund. The contributions credited to the active life fund become part of the general assets of the insurance company for investment purposes. Dividends due under the contract are also credited to the active life fund. The fund is also credited with the rate of interest guaranteed in the contract. The active life fund is debited with the single-premium sums required to purchase immediate annuities for participants retiring during the policy year. If annuities are also purchased as benefits vest, then the fund is debited with the single-premium annuity considerations required to purchase such benefits. Lastly, if the plan provides for death or disability benefits payable directly from the active life fund, then debits to the fund are made as these benefits are paid.

The active life fund is a contractual fund and should not be confused with the internal record account maintained by the insurer for each deposit administration contract for purposes of dividend computations. The nature of the debits and credits to the latter account, as will be noted later, are somewhat different from the above-described charges and credits.

If the plan is contributory, employee contributions may (1) be used to purchase units of paid-up deferred annuities, or (2) be maintained by the insurer in a separate employee fund, or (3) be credited to the overall active life fund under the contract. In any case, a detailed accounting of employee contributions is kept by the insurer, since, as a minimum, these contributions are returned should the employee die or terminate his employment.

Deposit administration contracts originally were only available to larger plans. However, competition and increased insurer experience with this contract have resulted in substantial reductions in minimum-size underwriting requirements for these plans. Many insurance companies will now issue deposit administration contracts to groups as small as 10 lives, with minimum annual contribution requirements of no more than $5,000 being quite prevalent. Of course, an administrative charge is normally levied when annual premiums are less than a specified amount; the charge generally is similar to the schedule imposed by the insurer under its group deferred annuity contracts.

If the plan is terminated, the assets in the fund become fully vested in plan participants. The allocation of plan assets upon termination of the plan presents no problem for retired employees, since single-premium immediate annuities have already been purchased on their behalf. However, there must be a plan provision providing for the disposition of assets held in the active life fund. If the plan is contributory, provision is generally made for a return of employee contributions as a first priority on the assets in the active life fund. The remaining assets are then applied on the basis of a list of priorities established in the plan. Typically, the monies are applied to purchase deferred annuities for the accrued benefits of participants on an age priority basis, starting with employees who have already met the requirements for retirement but have not yet retired as of the termination of plan date.

In some cases, contributions under a deposit administration contract are terminated, but the plan is continued with another funding agency. In these instances, the active life fund may be liquidated through withdrawals as eligible employees actually retire. Also, the deposit administration plan may permit a transfer of the assets in the active life fund to the new funding agency. In the latter case, the insurer usually reserves the right to withhold some amount (usually 5%) of the fund to cover insurer expenses not yet recovered and to offset possible financial antiselection.

Benefit Structure

One major advantage of deposit administration contracts is the flexibility in designing the plan's benefit provisions. Whereas group deferred annuity plans are largely limited to unit benefit formulas, any type of retirement benefit formula can be employed without difficulty under a deposit administration contract. Also, deposit administration contracts may be used without difficulty in plans which base benefits on final average earnings. The fact that benefits cannot be precisely determined until the employee actually retires presents no problem under these contracts, since annuities are not purchased until the date of retirement. Likewise, minimum retirement benefits and the most complex integrated benefit formulas can be readily handled under deposit administration plans. The absence of annuity purchases until retirement date permits considerable flexibility in the establishment of early and late retirement benefit provisions. For example, early retirement benefits may be provided on a more liberal basis than the actuarial equivalent of normal retirement benefits (subject to Internal Revenue Service limitations), while additional benefits may be permitted for service rendered after the normal retirement date.

Deposit administration plans generally do not provide a preretirement death benefit, beyond the return of employee contributions (usually with interest). However, a death benefit not related to employee contributions can be readily provided under these contracts. In the latter case, death benefit payments would be withdrawn from the active life fund. The actuary would have to project the cost of these benefits in estimating the amount of required contributions under the plan. Adjustments in future contribution requirements would be required if future actuarial valuations discovered variations in actual from expected mortality experience. The availability of postretirement death benefits depends on the normal annuity form under the plan and the annuity options available to participants. The nature of the annuity options has been discussed in earlier sections of the text.

Separate and distinct disability benefits are becoming more prevalent under deposit administration contracts. Disability payments under the plan can be charged directly to the active life fund, the procedure being quite similar to that outlined in the discussion of preretirement death benefits. If disability benefits are provided, the determination and policing of the existence of disability is generally the responsibility of the employer. Upon receipt of certification of disability, the insurance company will begin making disability payments to the participant from the active life fund. As an alternative to the above procedure, the employer can choose to make the disability payments directly to disabled workers.

Vested benefits, beyond provision for the refund of employee contributions, can also be provided under deposit administration plans. Where available, these vested benefits are generally treated as an obligation of the plan similar to that of the accrued benefits of participants of the plan—i.e., as deferred annuity credits subject to the requirements that terminated employees be alive and claim the benefit at normal or early retirement age and that the fund will be sufficient to provide these benefits.

It should also be noted that the insurer generally imposes an expense charge for cash payments (for example, for death, disability, or vested benefits) from the active life fund. Therefore, it is advisable whenever possible for the employer to make these cash payments directly to eligible participants rather than from the active life fund.

Contributions

Since contributions are not allocated to specific participants until retirement date, contribution payments to the active life fund are not premiums in the more commonly accepted sense of the term. Therefore, the employer, rather than the insurance company, has primary control over the decision of the amount and frequency of contributions to be made to the plan each year. Of course, the insurance company determines the premium rates that will be charged for the immediate annuities purchased at retirement age.

Guarantees. The insurer specifies a set of guaranteed annuity purchase rates in the contract; the guaranteed rates normally apply to contributions received during the first five contract years, with the rates being subject to revision on an annual basis thereafter. The guaranteed annuity rates may be graduated upward for annuity purchases made in future years. For example, contributions received during the first five years can be used to buy an immediate annuity of $1 a month for a male, age 65, at a guaranteed rate of $137.01 during the first five contract years and a rate of $142.48 for purchases during the second five-year contract period, and $145.36 for purchases made thereafter until the fund is exhausted. The difference in the guaranteed rates reflects anticipated improvements in mortality and the possibility of a decline in interest rates. In recent years some insurance companies have departed from the above-described approach to annuity rate guarantees under deposit administration contracts. In these cases, the contract guarantees the rates for annuities purchased during a specified period of years from the issue date of the contract. In other words, the rate guarantee is based on the date of purchase of the annuity without regard to the date of receipt of contributions.

With reference to the active life fund, the insurer guarantees the principal and at least a minimum rate of interest, regardless of the investment experience of the insurance company. The minimum guaranteed interest rate is usually graded downward, with the passage of time. For example, the contract may provide that the active life fund will be credited at the end of each of the first five contract years with a yearly rate of interest, such as 4% or 4½%, at the end of each of the sixth through the tenth contract years with a rate of interest such as 3½% or 3¾% and thereafter with a rate of interest such as 3¼% or 3½%. Of course, the interest rate guarantees can be changed annually with reference to contributions received after the beginning of the sixth contract year.

Thus, it can be seen that a known set of annuity and interest rate guarantees generally applies to each dollar of contribution, regardless of when annuities are actually purchased. Since the guaranteed rates may vary depending on when the contributions were received, it is necessary to identify the specific contribution dollars being used to purchase annuities as participants retire. The assumption is made, as implied in the discussions above, that contribution dollars are withdrawn from the active life fund to purchase annuities in the order in which contributions were received by the insurance company, i.e., a "first-in, first-out" approach.

Annual Contributions. Under a deposit administration plan, the actuarial calculations can be done by the insurance company, or the employer can hire a consulting actuary to perform this function. In the latter case, the reduction in insurer services required under the plan is recognized through lower expense charges and/or the payment of service fees to consultants. In either case, the employer has considerable flexibility in his choice of an actuarial cost method. He may choose, and usually does, an actuarial cost method that generates a supplemental liability, which in turn offers the employer flexibility in terms of the rate at which the supplemental liability is funded. The deposit administration contract also offers the employer flexibility in the choice of actuarial assumptions. Since contributions are not allocated prior to retirement, the employer may use an interest assumption which approximates the expected rate of return rather than the guaranteed rate, and he may discount in advance for expected terminations of employment or late retirements, thereby permitting lower levels of annual contributions in the early years of the plan. Also, if the benefit formula is related to compensation, projected future increases in the salaries of participants can be reflected in contribution calculations.

The contribution flexibility available under a deposit administration contract is particularly important in the case of collectively bargained plans under which the employer is required to contribute a specified percentage of payroll. Thus, annual contributions to the plan will fluctuate with changes in the amount of covered payroll. It would obviously be difficult to use an allocated funding instrument under these circumstances, unless a defined contribution benefit formula were used.

However, it must be recognized that an increase in the degree of contribution flexibility under an insured funding instrument can only be achieved by a reduction in insurer guarantees. For example, the insurance company does not guarantee that the active life fund will be sufficient to provide the accrued benefits of active employees. Such a guarantee is obviously not possible, since the timing of contribution payments is largely within the control of the employer. Therefore, the adequacy of the active life fund is the responsibility of the employer. The few minimum contribution requirements imposed by insurers under deposit administration contracts are not meant to assure the adequacy of the active life fund. For example, the contract may require that total contributions in any policy year not be less than the minimum sum required by the Internal Revenue Service.[10] Also, if the plan is contributory, the insurer usually requires that the active life fund must always be at least, say, 105% of employee contributions increased with interest, since employee contributions, usually with interest, must, as a minimum, be returned upon death or termination of employment. The additional 5% is required to provide a margin. Lastly, the insurance company requires that the active life fund be sufficient to purchase annuities for participants due to retire.[11] Of course, once the annuity is purchased, the annuitant is guaranteed his pension payments regardless of plan experience.

Generally, there are no employer credits of the type that result under allocated funding instruments, other than a dividend or rate adjustment. This is logical since calculations of contributions under deposit administration plans usually discount in advance for expected mortality among participants, terminations of employment, and late retirements. Any significant deviations of actual experience from expected experience under the plan with reference to the

---

[10] The insurance company may also impose a maximum on the amount of annual contributions permitted under a deposit administration plan. This requirement is imposed to minimize adverse financial selection. The maximum permissible annual contribution could be defined, for example, as the maximum permitted by the Internal Revenue Service as a deductible contribution to the plan.

[11] However, during the early years of the plan, the insurer generally permits a degree of postretirement funding to minimize the financial impact of older participants with sizable past service benefits at the inception of the plan.

above factors can be recognized through adjustments in future levels of required contributions.

Since the insurer guarantees annuity and interest rates under deposit administration contracts, more favorable experience than assumed in the guaranteed rates provides a basis for a rate credit or dividends under these contracts. The procedure for calculating dividends under deposit administration contracts is similar to the procedure described earlier in this chapter for calculating dividends under group deferred annuity contracts. An internal record account is maintained for each deposit administration policyholder. It will be recalled that this account is a cumulative record of the cash income and cash outgo under each contract. The account is credited with contributions received from the policyholder during the policy year, along with the actual investment income allocated to this particular contract.[12] The allocation of investment income will be based on new-money rates or an average rate, depending upon which allocation method is used by the insurer. The internal record account is then debited with all benefit payments made during the year and all expenses directly incurred or allocated to the particular contract. It should be noted that the account is debited with benefit payments actually made during the year and not with the single-premium annuity sums withdrawn from the active life fund to purchase annuities for participants retiring during the year.

A credit balance in the account represents an excess of cash income over cash outgo for the particular contract. The liabilities of the company under the contract are then compared with the cash balance in the internal record account to determine whether a dividend should be paid. The calculation of annuity reserves and contingency reserves is similar to the approach used in dividend calculations under group deferred annuity contracts. However, there may be one difference in the case of deposit administration plans, and that is the calculation of the insurer's liability with reference to the active life fund under the plan. The first, and probably most prevalent approach, is to value the liability for the contractual active life fund as the amount the insurer would then be liable to pay under the liquidation option of the contract. This valuation method is sound if the contract were to be terminated and the monies were

---

[12] Some insurance companies have recently adopted the practice of anticipating a portion of the dividend by crediting the contractual fund with a rate of interest greater than the minimum rate of interest guaranteed in the contract. For example, if the insurer has guaranteed 3¾% interest and expects to earn 4¾% for the year, the contractual fund might be credited with 4¼% interest. Of course, the advance interest credit is taken into account in the calculation of the annual dividend for the contract.

transferred to another carrier, a corporate trustee, or distributed in cash to plan participants.

A second approach is to recognize that each dollar in the active life fund carries some specified annuity rate guarantee. Therefore, at the end of each contract year, the insurer can calculate its liabilities under the active life fund on the basis of mortality and interest assumptions that it deems appropriate at that given time. If the assets in the active life fund exceed the liability calculated on this basis, this would be an additional source of dividend. If the guaranteed annuity rates are currently viewed as being too low, the annuity reserve for active lives may exceed the assets in the active life fund and, therefore, may reduce or eliminate the amount of dividend that would otherwise be available from favorable experience under annuities on retired lives.

GROUP IMMEDIATE PARTICIPATION GUARANTEE CONTRACTS

The deposit administration contract went a long way in providing employers with the desired degree of flexibility not available under the traditional group annuity contract. In addition, the deposit administration contract offers certain interest and annuity rate guarantees. However, the insurance company is able to provide these guarantees only because it accumulates a contingency reserve and because it has control, through dividend computations, over the rate at which actuarial gains pertaining to guaranteed items are credited to the employer. Some employers object to these features of deposit administration plans. These employers prefer an immediate reflection of the actual experience under their plans and are willing to give up the guarantees of the deposit administration plan in order to get it. Thus, insurance companies developed the immediate participation guarantee (IPG) contract,[13] the first contract of this type being issued in 1950. These contracts are generally available only for the larger plans.

In an IPG plan, the employer's account is credited with the contributions received during the contract period plus its share of actual investment income for the year. There is generally no guarantee of principal or a minimum rate of interest under these contracts. The account is charged with all the expenses associated with the particular contract. All benefits, including annuity payments, are charged directly against the account as they are paid. In other words, annuities are not actually purchased for participants at retirement date, as is the practice under deposit administration

---

[13] This type of contract is also referred to as a pension administration contract.

plans. Some insurance companies do charge the account with the gross premium for the annuities of retired workers. However, in these latter cases, the annuities are generally canceled at the end of each year, with the unearned portion of the annuity consideration being credited to the employer's account. Thus, the result is similar to that achieved by insurers that only charge to the account the annuity payments actually made. There is no charge to the account for an allocation toward building up a contingency reserve. Also, since no dividend as such is paid, all the record keeping pertaining to a particular contract can be maintained in one account. Thus, the employer can be quickly apprised of the experience to date under his plan.

Although annuities are not actually purchased at retirement date, the insurer does perform periodic valuations to be certain that the credit balance in the account is at least sufficient to provide lifetime annuity payments to retired workers. If the credit balance approaches the amount of reserves required to provide the benefits of already retired employees, annuities are actually purchased for the retired workers. The reserve basis used in these valuations is more conservative than the assumptions used in valuing liabilities under deposit administration plans, thereby permitting a margin for contingencies.

The IPG contract also specifies a schedule of guaranteed annuity gross premium rates. However, since annuities are not actually purchased at retirement date, these guaranteed annuity rates are only of significance if the plan is terminated.

All of the aspects of flexibility in contribution timing and plan design discussed under deposit administration plans are equally applicable to IPG contracts. The further reduction in insurer guarantees and the immediate reflection of actual experience under the plan, bring the IPG contracts one step closer to trust fund arrangement.

MODIFIED IMMEDIATE PARTICIPATION GUARANTEE

Some insurance companies have developed a contract that possesses characteristics of both deposit administration and IPG contracts and is usually referred to as a modified immediate participation guarantee contract or a direct-rated deposit administration contract. The major characteristic of this latter contract is that the active life fund is maintained on an immediate participation basis, but single-premium immediate annuities are actually purchased for each participant upon retirement. This funding instrument may become increasingly popular as the use of separate accounts funding, discussed below, becomes more prevalent.

SEPARATE ACCOUNTS

As was mentioned earlier, the new-money method of allocating investment income to group annuity cases was developed largely in response to the increased competition in the 1950's from corporate trustees for new pension business. The high rates of return on new investments in recent years and the traditional insurance company investment advantages in the areas of long-term mortgages and direct placement bonds have permitted new-money companies to offer quite attractive yields during this period for pension cases. In spite of the improved rates of return under insured plans, the trust fund approach remained popular with some employers because of the greater flexibility in investment policy permitted under this funding instrument, particularly with reference to the lack of restriction on the extent of common stock investments. The investment policy of insurance companies, on the other hand, is strictly regulated, and investments in common stock are not permitted to exceed a specified percentage (generally 5%) of the total assets of the company.

To overcome this competitive disadvantage, some insurers sought, and have received in many states, permission to establish one or more separate accounts to which part or all of the reserves held in conjunction with a pension plan can be allocated. The assets in the separate accounts are not commingled with the general assets of the insurer, and are exempt from the statutory investment restrictions normally applied to insurance companies. Thus, the insurer can invest all of the assets in the separate account in common stocks, or establish whatever proportions of investments in stock, bonds, and mortgages that it desires. An insurance company can set up one separate account for common stock investments, another for bonds, and still another account for mortgages. In that way, the employer has considerable freedom to designate the percentages of plan assets to be invested in each type of investment. However, most insurers have only set up a separate account for equity investments, since the employer can leave a portion of the fund in the regular active life fund which constitutes, in effect, a fixed income investment portfolio.

Separate accounts funding can be used with deposit administration, IPG, and modified IPG contracts. While the details of separate accounts vary depending on the particular funding instrument involved, the treatment in this text is restricted to a consideration of the broader aspects of this funding technique. Eligibility for separate account funding is further restricted by a Securities and Exchange Commission ruling that limits (if these contracts are to be exempt from the Investment Company Act of 1940) the use of separate accounts to *group plans* covering at least 25 lives at the time the contract is issued. Also, the SEC ruling prohibits the allocation of employee contributions to a separate account. Therefore, employee contributions are always maintained as part of the general assets of the insurance company. Furthermore, state laws generally require that insurance company reserves supporting employee contributions and fixed dollar annuity obligations be invested in the general assets of the company. Thus, as a minimum, amounts equal to the reserves for the benefits of retired employees under the plan and employee contributions must be maintained as part of the general assets of the insurer. If a plan provides a variable annuity benefit (and if permitted by the laws of the particular state), presumably the assets supporting the benefits of retired employees could be maintained in a separate account.

The insurer does not guarantee principal or interest with reference to plan assets held in a separate account. The income and gains or losses, realized or unrealized, on separate account investments are credited to, or charged against, the separate account without regard to the other income, gains, or losses of the insurance company.

Each policyholder's share of the separate account is determined on a proportional value basis or on a participation unit basis. Under the latter method, the value of a participation unit is based on the fair market value of investments in the fund as of the close of business on the valuation date plus cash balances and accruals, less accounts payable and such expenses and taxes as the insurer determines to be allocable to such fund under its regular rules and practices, divided by the number of outstanding participation units in the separate account fund. Allocations to or withdrawals from the separate account fund are usually permitted only on valuation dates (which can be on a monthly or even daily basis). Expenses attributable to the separate account can be handled several ways, depending largely on the type of funding instrument involved. For example, in the case of a deposit administration contract, the amounts allocated to the separate account are usually first reduced by an insurer expense charge attributable to such amount, whereas under IPG and modified IPG contracts, all expenses other than investment expenses may be charged directly as incurred to the employer's regular active life fund. Where expenses are charged when deposits are made, the annuity purchase rates usually reflect this by having a lower loading for expenses than would otherwise be the case.

The monies allocated to the separate account fund can come from annual contributions under the plan or from transfers from the active life fund, or from both sources. The insurer may permit part or all of the annual contributions of the employer to be allocated to the separate account fund. However, some insurers restrict the amount allocable to the separate account fund to a specified percentage of the contributions made during the policy year or a specified percentage of the fund balance. Transfers of assets from the active life fund to the separate account fund, and vice versa, are permissible, but some contracts (particularly deposit administration contracts) might restrict the employer's right to do this because of the possibility of financial antiselection.

In most instances, the assets of all participating employers are pooled in one separate account held by the insurer. However, some insurers are willing to set up an individual separate account for a large employer who might object to pooled accounts.

Separate account funding should not be confused with the concept of variable annuities.

TRUST FUND PLANS

The trust fund arrangement was the first of the existing funding instruments to be used to fund private pension benefits. In addition to being the oldest of the funding instruments, trust fund plans currently account for the bulk of the employees covered and the assets held by private plans. Of the 28 million participants under private plans, about 21 million are covered under trust fund plans, with about 67% of all pension fund assets being held by these plans.[1] The trust fund approach is used extensively in the case of multiemployer plans, with about 85% of the plans, covering about 90% of all participants under these plans, using this funding instrument.[2]

This chapter is concerned with those plans in which all or a substantial portion of the plan assets are accumulated and invested by the trustee. In other words, the discussion in this chapter does not pertain to plans in which a trustee is used, but benefits are funded entirely through insurance company contracts (for example, a trust agreement is generally used with a fully insured individual policy plan). The discussion in this chapter is pertinent to the trust fund portion of combination plans, including trust fund plans that provide for purchases of annuities at retirement or investment of a part of the trust assets in deposit administration or immediate participation guarantee contracts.

GENERAL CHARACTERISTICS

A trust fund plan is an arrangement under which employer and employee contributions, if any, are deposited with a trustee who is

---

[1] *Life Insurance Fact Book* (New York: Institute of Life Insurance, 1965), p. 36.

[2] U.S. Department of Labor, *Multiemployer Pension Plans under Collective Bargaining* (Spring, 1960, Bulletin No. 1326) (Washington, D.C.: U.S. Government Printing Office, 1962), p. 17.

responsible for the administration and investment of these monies and the income earned on accumulated assets of the fund, and who is normally responsible for the direct payment of benefits to eligible participants under the plan. If the trust fund arrangement is used in combination with an insured funding instrument, benefit payments to participants are generally made by the insurance company, with transfers from the trust fund made as required. The trustee is usually a corporate trustee (trust company), although individuals can also serve as trustees of the plan—a rather common practice in the case of multiemployer plans.[3]

Trust Agreement

The duties and responsibilities of the trustee are set forth in a trust agreement which is executed by the employer and the trustee. In the case of a negotiated multiemployer plan, the trust agreement is executed by individuals representing the unions and an equal number of individuals representing the employers, and these persons often compose the board of trustees responsible for the administration of the plan. The board of trustees may retain the task of investing plan assets, or they may choose to delegate this duty to a corporate trustee. In the latter case, a trust agreement setting forth the duties and responsibilities of the corporate trustee is executed by the board of trustees and the corporate trustee.

A typical trust agreement between an employer and a corporate trustee contains provisions, among others, regarding the irrevocability and nondiversion of trust assets; the investment powers of the trustee; the payment of legal, trustee, and other fees relative to the plan; exculpatory clauses pertaining to the liability of the trustee; periodic reports to the employer to be prepared by the trustees; the records and accounts to be maintained by the trustee; the conditions for removal or resignation of the trustee and the appointment of a new trustee; the payment of benefits under the plan; the rights and duties of the trustee in case of amendment or termination of the plan.

The trust agreement, then, is primarily concerned with the receipt, investment and disbursement of funds under a pension plan. The plan provisions may be incorporated in the trust agreement or they can be set forth in a separate plan agreement. The use of two separate agreements is quite prevalent in trust fund plans and is almost always the approach used in multiemployer plans. The advantage of a separate plan agreement is that amendments of the plan can be made without the need to involve the trustee in frequent amendments to the trust agreement.

---

[3] *Ibid.*, chaps. iv and vi.

Administrative Duties of Trustee

The bulk of the record-keeping duties associated with a pension plan is normally performed by the employer under single-employer trust fund plans. If the plan is contributory, the employer generally retains responsibility for maintaining a record of employee contributions. In this case, total contributions are paid to the trustee without reference to any division of employer and employee contributions. The employer also normally assumes responsibility for the maintenance of records of earnings and credited service for each participant. In some cases, the record-keeping function is performed by the consulting actuary for the plan.

Most corporate trustees are able to relieve the employer of the burden of maintaining the necessary records associated with the plans. Corporate trustees normally maintain records in the case of profit sharing plans or defined contribution pension plans and, to a more limited extent, in connection with multiemployer plans. If the trustee performs any record-keeping function, a service charge, in addition to the trustee's investment fee, is levied on an account basis, as explained later in this chapter. The advantages of specialization and the economies of size permit corporate trustees who handle a substantial volume of pension business to perform these services for a reasonable fee. The employer must decide whether it is more economical in his case to maintain these records himself or to have this service provided by the trustee or by a consulting actuary.

In the case of a negotiated multiemployer plan, the board of trustees, rather than the individual employers, are generally responsible for the maintenance of plan records. The record-keeping function is usually performed by a pension fund office created by the board of trustees. If a corporate trustee is retained to manage the assets of the fund, the plan trustees may delegate the task of record keeping to the corporate trustee. In recent years, there has been a significant growth of so-called professional "plan administrators" whose market is composed principally of multiemployer plans. The function of a professional administrator is to keep all the specific records of service and earnings for individual members of the plan and to handle all routine administrative transactions.

Regardless of whether the corporate trustee performs the record-keeping function, he never makes any benefit distributions from the fund without authorization from the employer or retirement committee. In the case of a single-employer trust fund plan, the employer generally appoints a plan or retirement committee generally composed of officers of the company. It is the responsibility of this committee to determine a participant's eligibility for benefits under the plan. Under multiemployer plans, authorization of benefit payments is the responsibility of the board of trustees or a committee of its members appointed by the board, but in some cases, this function is delegated to a professional administrator.

Apart from the above-mentioned administrative aspects of trust fund plans, a corporate trustee is always responsible to maintain accurate and detailed records of all investments, receipts, disbursements, and other transactions involving the trust assets. In addition, the trustee is required to submit an annual statement regarding the above trust transactions to the plan or retirement committee, usually within 90 days of the close of the plan's fiscal year. The trust agreement may require that statements be rendered to the committee more frequently than annually, for example, quarterly or monthly. Also, in some cases, the trustee assumes responsibility for the filing of forms for the trust as required by tax regulations.

Investment Powers of Trustee

The primary function of a trustee is the investment management of trust assets. The trustee invests the trust assets (including contributions and investment income) in accordance with the provisions of the trust agreement and the investment policy desired by the plan or retirement committee. The investment power granted to a trustee by the trust agreement varies among plans; it may range from approval by the retirement committee of every action affecting the fund's assets to full discretion in investment affairs. Furthermore, the corporate trustee does maintain personal contact with the employer, and therefore the latter may influence, directly or indirectly, investment decisions. If the trust agreement fails to specify the investment powers of the trustee, the trustee is restricted to investments that are legal for trust funds in the state in which the trust is established.

The trustee, unless otherwise restricted, can invest trust assets in the securities of the employer. Loans to the employer may also be made from trust assets provided that there is adequate security for the loan and the rate of return is reasonable. However, such investments must be in accordance with Regulations of the Internal Revenue Service, and care must be exercised lest such investments prove to be not for the "exclusive benefit of employees" or are in the class of "prohibited transactions."[4]

The trustee is required to maintain a separate accounting and an actual segregation of the assets of each trust. In other words, the

---

[4] For a discussion of this aspect of trust investments, see pp. 123–127.

assets of a trust generally cannot be commingled with the assets of other trusts or with the general assets of the trustee. Thus, under these circumstances, there is no pooling of the investment experience of a number of trusts. If the investment experience has been exceptionally favorable for a particular trust, the full benefit of that experience is credited to the trust account. On the other hand, the trust must bear the full impact of adverse investment income and capital loss experience. Therefore, a relatively small trust fund plan would be subject to the danger of inadequate diversification of its investment portfolio. To meet this problem, corporate trustees have established common trust funds. A common trust fund permits the commingling of assets of all participating trusts. Although originally established to meet the needs of smaller trusts, corporate trustees have obtained permission to permit pension trusts of any size to participate in common trusts established specifically for qualified pension plans. A trust participating in a commingled fund for investment purposes buys units, or shares, of the fund.[5] Dividends are paid on each unit, each dividend being a proportionate share of the total income earned by the commingled fund. These units fluctuate in value as the value of the assets of the commingled fund fluctuates.

The principal advantage of a common trust fund is to permit any trust to enjoy the investment advantages normally available only to the very large funds. These advantages have been described as follows:[6]

1. Higher rate of return on fixed income investments. Commingled investment permits purchases in amounts large enough to take advantage of private placements and special offerings of securities, which generally carry higher yields than regular market offerings; and in mortgages, lease-back arrangements or other interests in real property.

2. Increased potential through selective stock holding. Commingled investment permits such funds to achieve a degree of selective diversification in equities that would be impossible to attain through individual investment, except in sizable funds.

3. Maximum liquidity of funds for cash requirements. Commingled investment permits redemption of units at the end of any month, at the current market value of units, so that money required for payouts is made available through use of current cash flow rather than having to sell investments, as might have to be done in a separate fund.

4. Dollar averaging on investment purchases. Current cash flow

---

[5] "Trusteed Employee Benefit Plans" (New York: Bank of New York, 1966), p. 10.

[6] *Ibid.*, pp. 10–11.

from incoming contributions, spaced as they are at intervals throughout a given year, has the effect of dollar averaging on investment purchases, which generally works to the advantage of all participating trusts.

5. Lower investment brokerage fees. A commingled trust can purchase stocks in round-lots and in amounts that entail lower brokerage commissions.[7]

Most corporate trustees believe that common trusts offer significant advantages to the larger plans as well as the smaller plans. In one large urban bank, approximately 55% of all of its pension trust accounts participate in the bank's commingled pension trust.

Participation in a commingled pension trust is restricted to qualified plans. Participation by a nonqualified trust could result in loss of the qualified tax status of the entire common trust fund.

Some corporate trustees have established several common trust funds, with each fund designed to provide an investment medium having certain principal characteristics and objectives. For example, one fund may emphasize investments in bonds, notes, debentures, and other fixed income obligations. A second fund may be invested principally in private placements, mortgages, or other interests in real property. A third fund may be invested in a selection of good-quality common stocks with the objective of growth of principal and income over the long term. In addition, a special equity fund may be available for those trusts interested in pursuing a more aggressive investment policy. The multiple common trust funds offer the employer considerable flexibility in the proportion of trust assets to be invested in each of the classes of investments.

Investment flexibility has been an attractive feature of the trust arrangement for many employers. During the past two decades, many employers have expressed a preference for investment of a relatively large proportion of pension assets in common stocks. This preference is evident in the composition of investments of noninsured pension funds set forth in Table 9–1. Insured plans have not been able to offer this investment flexibility until the recent development of separate account funding.[8]

BENEFIT STRUCTURE

Retirement Benefits

The trust fund arrangement offers the maximum degree of flexibility in the design of a retirement benefit formula. Since funds are

---

[7] A small trust fund plan can also obtain the advantages of commingling through investments in mutual fund shares.

[8] See p. 207 for a discussion of separate account funding.

not allocated, even for retired employees, any type of benefit formula can be utilized under a trust fund plan. As is true in the case of deposit administration and immediate participation guarantee plans, retirement benefits based on final earnings can be provided without difficulty under trust fund plans. Likewise, benefit formulas that provide for the integration of Social Security benefits (including Social Security offset provisions) can be readily accommodated under the trust fund arrangement.

TABLE 9–1

ASSETS OF PRIVATE NONINSURED PENSION FUNDS
(As of the End of 1965—Millions of Dollars)

	Book Value		Market Value	
	Amount	Percent	Amount	Percent
Cash and deposits.............	941	1.6	941	1.3
U.S. government securities.....	3,096	5.3	3,011	4.2
Corporate bonds..............	22,703	39.1	21,544	30.2
Own company.............. 967		1.7	851	1.2
Other companies...........21,736		37.4	20,693	29.0
Preferred stock...............	750	1.3	768	1.1
Common stock...............	24,451	42.1	38,924	54.5
Own company.............. 1,712		2.9	4,140	5.8
Other companies...........22,739		39.2	34,784	48.7
Mortgages...................	3,324	5.7	3,330	4.7
Other assets.................	2,822	4.8	2,902	4.1
Total Assets...........	58,807	99.9*	71,420	100.1*

* Failure to add up to 100% due to rounding.
SOURCE: U.S. Securities and Exchange Commission, Statistical Series, Release No. 2132, June 21, 1966, Table 1.

It is true that the more complex the benefit formula, the more difficult will be the task of the actuary in projecting costs and calculating contribution payments under the plan. The fact remains, however, that the trust fund instrument does not of itself present any obstacles to the use of the most complex of benefit formulas. For example, provision for adjustments of retired employees' benefits in accordance with a designated cost-of-living index can be provided under this funding instrument. The actuary can include in his cost calculations an assumption regarding future price level changes, which admittedly is not readily predictable with a great degree of accuracy. However, actuarial gains and losses due to variations of actual from expected price levels can be reflected in subsequent valuations and determinations of contribution payments. Trust fund plans can also provide a retirement benefit that varies with the market value of the assets supporting the pension benefits of retired workers (so-called variable annuities). There are a few trust fund plans that do provide for cost-of-living adjustments and equity or variable annuity benefits.

Defined contribution formulas can be, but seldom are, used in trust fund pension plans. A pension plan generally provides a lifetime annuity benefit to retired employees. Therefore, under a defined contribution pension plan formula, at some point in time the accumulations on behalf of each participant must be expressed in terms of a lifetime monthly benefit (except in cases where lump sum distributions are made). The monthly benefit may be calculated as each annual contribution is received, or annual contributions may be accumulated to retirement date and the determination of the level of monthly benefits may be made at that time. In either case, under a trust fund plan, the plan actuary establishes the set of actuarial assumptions to be used in determining the amount of monthly benefit that can be provided by the contributions for each participant.

In the case of some negotiated plans, particularly multiemployer plans, the employer's financial commitment is expressed as some specified cents per hour worked or as a fixed percentage of compensation. However, these plans are not generally traditional defined contribution plans in that they also provide a defined benefit. The trust fund instrument can accommodate these plans without any difficulty.

Early retirement benefits can be, and frequently are, provided under trust fund plans. The amount of early retirement benefit may be the actuarial equivalent of the participant's accrued normal retirement benefit, or, if the employer desires, a more liberal early retirement benefit may be provided. The additional cost under the latter alternative can be anticipated in computations of contribution payments required under the plan.

Death Benefits

Trust fund plans seldom provide preretirement death benefits, other than a return of employee contributions, if any. In most instances, participants under the pension plan are also covered under a group life contract issued directly to the employer. However, there is no reason why preretirement death benefits cannot be provided under a trust fund plan. A group term contract covering participants can be issued to the plan trustee; or the employer can self-insure the death benefits with payments being made directly from assets of the trust fund. However, few employers choose to self-insure death benefits, because of the potentially great degree of variance between actual and expected mortality except for relatively large groups and because of the adverse tax consequences for beneficiaries.

The availability of postretirement death benefits depends on the normal annuity form under the plan. A pure life annuity is the typical normal annuity form under trust fund plans, or a modified refund annuity in the case of contributory plans. However, in recent years, there has been a trend toward providing benefits for a minimum specified period under these plans. Also, optional annuity forms are becoming increasingly prevalent under trust fund plans. Furthermore, the level of benefits under the optional forms (a joint and last survivor annuity, for example) can be greater than the actuarial equivalent of the normal annuity form. The resultant increased cost can be projected in the actuary's calculations of the periodic contributions required under the plan. Lastly, there has been increasing interest in offering widow's benefits under private pension plans.[9] These benefits can be provided without difficulty under trust fund plans.

Disability Benefits

A great proportion of trust fund plans provide disability benefits. Responsibility for the determination of whether a participant is eligible for disability benefits usually rests with a retirement committee appointed by the employer. In the case of a multiemployer plan, this function is assumed by the board of trustees or a committee composed of board members. The trustee begins payment of disability benefits upon receipt of certification by the retirement committee of a participant's eligibility for benefits. The retirement committee also assumes responsibility for reviewing approved disability claims to determine whether continuance of disability exists or not.

There are several reasons for the prevalence of disability benefits under trust fund plans. First, union leaders strongly favor provision of disability benefits under pension plans, and a substantial proportion of negotiated plans utilize the trust fund approach. Second, disability benefits provide employers with a desirable personnel management tool if control over the determination of disability rests with the employer. A disability pension can be used as a graceful, and often relatively economical, method of retiring unproductive employees. Third, the reluctance of insurance companies (at least up until recent years) to insure long-term disability benefits encouraged the self-insuring of these benefits under trust fund plans.[10] However, the recent liberalizations in the underwriting and

---

[9] See p. 50 for a discussion of widow's benefits.

[10] It should be noted that under deposit administration and immediate participation guarantee plans, disability benefits, when provided, are generally self-insured by the employer in that these benefits are paid directly by the employer or charged directly to the active life fund.

rating of group long-term disability plans has resulted in increased interest in insuring these benefits.[11]

Vested Benefits

The availability of vested benefits under trust fund plans, as is true of other funding instruments, depends upon the provisions of the plan. The majority of the trust fund plans provide some degree of vesting of benefits attributable to employer contributions. Of course, terminating employees are always entitled to a return of their own contributions, usually with interest. If the plan is contributory and if there is no provision for vested benefits, an employee's accumulated contributions are normally paid in a lump sum upon termination of employment. Under most trust fund plans, the availability of vested benefits is deferred until the terminating employee reaches the normal retirement age under the plan. If the plan is contributory, entitlement to the vested benefit is generally conditioned upon the terminating employee leaving his own contributions in the plan; withdrawal of his own contributions results, in these cases, in the forfeiture of the portion of the vested benefit attributable to employer contributions.

Since contributions to a trust fund are not allocated to specific participants under the plan (with the possible exception of a traditional defined contribution plan), vesting is always expressed in terms of benefits rather than contributions. A terminating employee's vested benefits represent a deferred claim against the assets of the trust fund. This claim is conditioned upon (1) the terminating employee living to the normal retirement age (except for his own contributions), (2) making application for the benefit in accordance with plan provisions, and (3) the adequacy of the trust fund to provide the vested benefit. In case of termination of the plan, the priority, if any, of vested benefits is dependent upon plan provisions.

CONTRIBUTIONS

The annual contribution payments under a trust fund plan are determined by periodic actuarial valuations by the plan actuary. The consulting actuary for the plan calculates the amount of contributions to be made to the trust fund on the basis of (1) a given set of actuarial assumptions, (2) a particular actuarial cost method, and (3) the census data for the group of employees covered under the plan. It is the task of the actuary to choose a set of actuarial

---

[11] For a further discussion of this point, see pp. 51–53.

assumptions which, based on his judgment and experience, appear to be reasonable for the particular plan. Generally, the actuary will choose assumptions that are more conservative than the experience actually expected under the plan, in order to provide a margin for contingencies. It is also the responsibility of the actuary to choose an appropriate actuarial cost method to be used in calculations of contribution payments. However, in view of the availability of several different and equally acceptable actuarial cost methods, it is the duty of the actuary to fully inform the employer of the implications of each cost method. Since the choice of an actuarial cost method has a significant impact on the incidence of contribution payments, it is important that the employer have a clear understanding of the factors involved in the final selection of a cost method.

Therefore, under trust fund plans, the employer can participate in decisions regarding the choice of actuarial assumptions and the cost method to be used in calculations of contribution payments. The result is that the employer has maximum flexibility under a trust fund plan in directing the timing of contribution payments. For example, if the employer chooses to use a set of assumptions that appears realistic in relation to expected experience, cost-reducing factors such as turnover and mortality can be discounted in advance. Therefore, the employer's contribution payments can be at a lower level in the initial years of the plan than would be the case under allocated funding instruments. Also, the employer can choose an actuarial cost method that generates a supplemental liability. The creation of a supplemental liability results in a lower annual normal cost. In addition, the employer has considerable flexibility in the rate at which he funds the supplemental liability.[12]

Of course, this does not mean that the ultimate cost of the plan is necessarily lower under trust fund plans. The actuarial gains from turnover and mortality under allocated funding instruments are eventually recognized in the form of employer credits against premiums due in future years. Also, lower levels of contributions in the initial years of the plan must be offset by higher contribution levels in subsequent years. Actuarial assumptions and cost methods do not affect the ultimate cost of the plan, except to the extent that they influence levels of funding and, therefore, the amount of investment income earned on plan assets. The fact remains, however, that the employer has greater control over the incidence of contribution payments under trust fund plans due to the freedom of choice of actuarial assumptions and cost method and the unallo-

---

[12] See p. 105 and p. 106.

cated nature of the funding instrument. It will be recalled that this flexibility is also available, to almost the same degree, under an immediate participation guarantee contract and, to a more limited extent (i.e., with reference to the active life fund), under a deposit administration contract.

Contribution payments under trust fund plans are made at the convenience of the employer. In other words, there are no fixed contribution due dates. The employer may make contribution payments on a monthly, quarterly, or annual basis or even on a non-regular basis. Of course, Internal Revenue Service requirements regarding the timing of contributions must be observed if deductibility of contribution payments is desired.

In addition to the contribution payments necessary to provide the benefits to participants of the plan, the employer must make some provision for the expenses associated with trust fund plans. The major expenses under trust fund plans are trustee, consulting actuary and legal fees, and record keeping and other administrative expenses. A recent survey of trustees' fees under pension and profit sharing plans indicates a considerable degree of variation in fee schedules among corporate trustees.[13] Investment fees of corporate trustees are usually expressed as a percentage of the trust corpus, the percentage being graded downward with the size of the fund. An example of an investment fee schedule for a corporate trustee located in a Middle Atlantic state is: $\frac{1}{2}$ of 1% on the first $100,000; $\frac{1}{3}$ of 1% on the next $900,000; $\frac{1}{8}$ of 1% on the next $4,000,000; $\frac{1}{15}$ of 1% on the next $20,000,000; and $\frac{1}{20}$ of 1% on the balance. Most corporate trustees impose a minimum annual investment fee, ranging anywhere from $50 to $600, with the most frequent minimum charges generally being $150 to $250 per year.

The trustee imposes additional charges if it maintains plan records, makes pension payments to retired employees, or holds insurance and annuity contracts. If the trustee maintains plan records, an annual charge generally ranging from $2 to $6 per participant is imposed. The typical trustee fee for handling pension payments is 25 cents per check. The common charge for holding insurance and annuity contracts is $5 per contract per year, sometimes graded downward with the number of contracts involved. If the employer performs the administrative functions associated with the plan, the cost of performing these duties should be recognized in determining the true cost of a trust fund plan.

With reference to legal and actuarial fees, it is virtually impossible to quote any figures that can be viewed as typical charges

---

[13] "Survey of Fees Charged by Trustees under Pension and Profit-Sharing Plans" (Montclair, N.J.: Kennedy Sinclaire, Inc., 1965).

under trust fund plans, since fees for these services vary so widely among plans. The legal services required for the plan are normally performed by the attorney that handles all other legal work for the employer, and therefore are usually incorporated into the overall legal retainer paid by the employer. A consulting actuary's fee varies with the type and amount of services rendered. The actuary may perform preliminary cost studies or special projects on a fixed fee basis, but most of his services to the plan are billed on an hourly rate basis. The fees for legal and actuarial services can be paid by the trustee out of trust assets or they can be paid directly by the employer. The latter approach is the procedure followed in most cases.

There are no guarantees available under trust fund plans. The trustee cannot guarantee a minimum rate of investment income, nor can it guarantee plan assets against capital losses. Likewise, the mortality risk cannot be transferred to the trustee. The absence of guarantees is consistent with the legal nature of trust arrangements. A trustee's obligation is limited to the management of trust assets in a reasonable and prudent manner and in accordance with its duties set forth in the trust agreement. The adequacy of the fund to provide the benefits promised under the plan is the responsibility of the employer. The high degree of responsibility imposed on the employer under a trust fund plan is consistent with the maximum degree of flexibility available to the employer under this funding instrument. Guarantees must be minimized or eliminated if an employer desires maximum contribution flexibility and complete and immediate reflection of plan experience. Therefore, in choosing a funding instrument, the employer should consider the extent to which guarantees and flexibility are desired. Many large employers have chosen funding instruments that offer a high degree of flexibility and immediate reflection of plan experience. In the case of a trust fund plan, the actual experience of the plan is reflected immediately in the status of the fund. For example, if investment experience has been favorable, the fund receives the full benefit of the favorable experience. Likewise, the full impact of adverse investment experience is borne by the individual trust. However, the investment risk can be spread to some extent through the use of a commingled investment fund. The use of a common trust reduces a plan's investment risk as a result of the greater investment diversification available; but it still does not offer a guarantee of principal or a minimum rate of return. The employer cannot shift the mortality risk under trust fund plans. If the plan covers a large number of employees, the employer may be willing to assume the mortality risk. The mortality risk becomes a more significant consideration as the size of the group covered decreases. Deviations of actual from expected experience with reference to other factors (for example, turnover, disability rates, and actual retirement ages) are also immediately reflected in the status of the trust fund.

Under trust fund plans, actuarial valuations are performed periodically (usually annually, but no less frequently than every five years) to determine the adequacy of the fund. If the actual experience evolving under the plan indicates that the current level of funding is inadequate, actuarial assumptions can be revised to produce higher levels of contributions in future years. Since the liabilities under a pension plan evolve over a long period of time, adequate provision for these liabilities can be made if frequent actuarial valuations are performed and if the employer is willing and able to make the necessary contributions.

TERMINATION OF PLAN

In the event of termination of a trust fund plan, the disposition of plan assets is determined, as is the case under other funding instruments, by the provisions of the plan. Upon termination, all assets of the plan become immediately vested in plan participants. The assets of the plan are then allocated to specific participants in accordance with the order of priorities set forth in the plan. The extent to which liabilities to plan participants can be satisfied depends, of course, on the degree of funding achieved as of the date of termination of the plan. As is true under deposit administration and immediate participation guarantee contracts, unless a trust fund plan is fully funded as of the date of plan termination, some participants must suffer a loss of part or all of their accrued benefits under the plan. However, under deposit administration and usually under immediate participation contracts, the insurance company guarantees continuation of benefits to retired employees. Under trust fund plans, the trustee cannot guarantee the benefits of retired employees. In most trust fund plans, however, plan assets are more than sufficient to meet the claims of retired employees. A few notable exceptions exist in the area of negotiated multiemployer plans.

Upon termination of the plan, the trust can be kept in existence until all plan assets have been distributed to participants. Trustee fees and other administrative expenses are charged to the trust (unless the employer is still in business and is willing to pay these expenses). Also, unless the assets are held in a commingled trust, investment problems develop as the size of the fund shrinks. Thus, it is difficult to project accurately the level of benefits to be provided employees on the lower end of the priority scale. An alternative to continuing the trust is to transfer the plan assets to an insurance company through the purchase of annuities. In that way, the trust can be terminated relatively soon after the termination of the plan, and specific levels of benefit can be guaranteed to participants.

Situations sometimes arise in which an employer desires to switch funding agencies without any intention of terminating the plan. A transfer of assets to another trustee or to an insurance company can be effected without difficulty under trust fund plans. The trust agreement contains no prohibitions against transfers of plan assets (assuming that such transfers are made in accordance with the requirements of the Internal Revenue Service). The trustee may impose a minor charge for the administrative duties associated with a termination of the trust. Of course, losses may be sustained if assets must be liquidated over a relatively short period of time. In some cases, transfers of securities and other assets may be permitted rather than requiring liquidation of investments. The freedom to transfer plan assets and the flexibility that it offers in case of mergers or other circumstances is viewed by some employers as an important advantage of trust fund plans.

SPLIT FUNDING

In Chapter 7 it was noted that the trust fund arrangement can be used in conjunction with group permanent contracts or individual insurance and annuity contracts as one approach in funding pension benefits. This approach is generally referred to as a combination plan. Group pension contracts can also be used in combination with the trust fund arrangement. These latter arrangements are usually referred to as split-funded plans (although the term "combination plan" can be applied to describe any plan utilizing two or more funding instruments).

Split-funded plans generally utilize group deposit administration, or immediate participation guarantee or modified immediate participation guarantee contracts. The decision of the employer to split-fund his pension plan is usually motivated by a desire to obtain, at least in part, the advantages of an insurer's guarantees and/or a possibly favorable investment opportunity. For example, the trust agreement may provide that the trustee administer all assets held on behalf of active employees and that an immediate annuity be purchased as each employee retires. Likewise, an insurer may enjoy relatively high yields on direct placement and mortgage investments, and therefore the employer may decide to invest a portion of plan assets in a deposit administration or an immediate participation guarantee contract.

10

SELECTION OF A
FUNDING INSTRUMENT

An employer who is establishing a funded pension plan must select a funding instrument through which the plan benefits will be provided. Making such a selection is not always easy. To begin with, the employer is faced with a broad choice between the insured or the trust fund approach. Within the concept of insured plans, he may also choose from a variety of individual and group contracts—his choice ranging from the fully insured individual policy plan to a group immediate participation guarantee contract with a separate accounts facility. As pointed out in previous chapters, each of these funding instruments produces certain advantages and disadvantages—but they are relative to the needs and objectives of the employer. A specific advantage of one funding instrument may be of significant value or importance to one employer, yet this same advantage could be of little or no value to another firm.

From the employer's viewpoint, the selection of the appropriate funding instrument is complicated by the differences of opinion that exist among those individuals who are active in the design and installation of pension programs. Some pension consulting firms, for example, have been identified primarily with the trust fund approach. While these firms are usually impartial on the question of insured versus trust fund plans, it must be recognized that the majority of the plans serviced by these firms employ the trust fund approach.

On the other hand, insurance agents and group field representatives quite obviously support the insured plan. Even here, however, there is frequently some difference of opinion between these two groups as to whether individual or group contracts are the best funding instrument.

The authors do not wish to imply that the difference of opinion that exists among pension practitioners is wrong or undesirable. On the contrary, such difference of opinion is a direct result of healthy and vigorous competition between financial institutions—a condition which is highly desirable from the viewpoint of the consumer and for the continued growth of private pension plans. In the long run, both employers and employees benefit from such a competitive environment in terms of broader choices, more efficient administration, lower costs, and innovations in plan design.

In the last analysis, there is no one funding instrument preferable over all others. However, it is generally possible to establish that for a given plan, and under a given set of circumstances and objectives, one or a few funding instruments are more suitable to the needs of a particular employer. The purpose of this chapter is to review the factors that bear on the selection of a funding instrument. While an understanding of the specific characteristics of the different funding instruments is most important in the selection of a funding instrument, these characteristics are not discussed at length in this chapter. For a detailed discussion of the different funding instruments, the reader is referred to Chapters 7, 8, and 9.

PRELIMINARY CONSIDERATIONS

At the outset, it should be made clear that the selection of a funding instrument is not the primary consideration of an employer who is establishing a pension plan. Rather, it is secondary to the more important consideration of the plan provisions. The employer should first determine the class or classes of employees to be covered, the type and amount of benefits they are to receive, and the conditions under which these benefits will be paid. Often, decisions on these matters will influence or even dictate the selection of a funding instrument; in general, the selection of a funding instrument should not dictate the choice of benefits.

One example of the influence of plan provisions and objectives on the selection of a funding instrument would be the case of a small employer who, in his desire to take maximum advantage of the federal estate tax exclusion applicable to qualified plans, wishes to have the death benefit under the plan as large as permitted under federal tax law. The only feasible way of creating an immediate and substantial death benefit is through the use of life insurance. However, the employer's size might be such that the desired amount could not be made available on a group basis from an underwriting viewpoint or, as is often the case, state law might limit the amount of group insurance that could be issued on any one life. Thus, in this situation (and in the absence of other influencing factors), the use of individual life insurance contracts as the funding instrument would be strongly indicated.

Another example might be the case of an employer who wishes to use a flat percentage of earnings formula and to apply this formula to some type of final earnings. While this does not necessarily dictate or suggest the funding instrument he should use, it does, by the process of elimination, suggest that he should not employ a group deferred annuity contract. To carry the example a step further, if the employer wishes to base benefits on the average of an employee's earnings over the final five years of employment, it becomes impractical to adopt a fully insured individual policy or group permanent plan. Other examples could be cited, but the above are sufficient to illustrate the point.

It should also be emphasized that the selection of a funding instrument should not be based solely upon the cost *estimates* furnished to the employer. Estimating the cost of a pension plan can be most complex, and many funding instruments permit a wide choice of actuarial cost methods and assumptions. As was pointed out in Chapter 4, the choice of the actuarial cost method and assumptions will not influence the *ultimate* cost of the plan (except to the extent that investment income will be affected by the incidence of contributions). Unfortunately, however, many employers seem to be influenced in their choice of funding instrument and/or funding agency by the various cost estimates they have received when, in fact, these cost estimates should have little or no bearing on the selection.[1] On the other hand, the employer's choice of a funding instrument might well be influenced by the fact that a particular funding instrument permits a wide choice of actuarial methods and assumptions, thus creating a significant degree of desired contribution flexibility. Nor are the authors suggesting that the ultimate

---

[1] Table 4–3, p. 94, shows the varying cost levels that can be produced for the same plan by simply shifting the actuarial assumptions. The ultimate cost of a plan, of course, will be determined by actual plan experience as to benefits paid, expenses, and investment income, which may or may not be close to the lowest estimated cost produced by the most liberal assumptions. An employer should not choose a funding instrument and/or a funding agency on the basis that the funding instrument with the lowest "cost estimate" is the "cheapest." In fact, this course of action might prove to involve the greatest contribution outlay in the long run, since lower contributions in the early years of the plan could lead to greater contributions in later years, with the likely result that a significant portion of the benefits paid will consist of contributions rather than investment earnings.

cost of the plan will be identical regardless of the funding instrument chosen. Cost considerations in the choice of a funding instrument are discussed later in this chapter.

Finally, it is most important that the employer's own specific circumstances and objectives be carefully analyzed before a decision is made on the funding instrument to be used. The employer's size, for example, is of considerable significance when weighing the cost implications of the various funding instruments. Also of significance is his need or desire for contribution flexibility. The terms of any bargaining agreement in effect could influence this choice and, of course, the employer's tax objectives quite often are an item of considerable importance. These and similar items must all be taken into account.

INSURED VERSUS TRUST FUND PLANS

A most important question for the employer to resolve is whether he should employ an insured funding instrument, the trust fund approach, or a combination of the two. At one time, the employer's choice was a little easier to make—at least, the broad features of the two concepts of funding differed to the extent that the employer could weigh the advantages and disadvantages of each approach and select the one best suited to his needs. Proponents of the insured plan, for example, stressed the guarantees inherent in this approach with reference to both the financial and mortality risks involved. Advocates of the trust fund plan, on the other hand, stressed flexibility and the opportunity to have plan assets invested in equities with the potential of capital gains.[2] In recent years, however, the insurance industry has developed several new products which possess many of the characteristics of the trust fund approach. In particular, group contracts such as deposit administration and immediate participation guarantee contracts, coupled with the new-money method of crediting investment earnings and a separate accounts facility, offer many of the features normally associated with trust fund plans. As a result, an employer's choice between insured and trust fund plans is not as clear-cut as was formerly the case. Indeed, the choice today is quite often between funding agencies, be they banks or insurance companies, rather than between funding instruments.

---

[2] For an excellent discussion of the various arguments, pro and con, on the question of insured versus trust fund plans, see Wendell Milliman, "The Controversy of Insured versus Trusteed Pension Plans," *Journal of the American Society of Chartered Life Underwriters*, Vol. XI, No. 1 (Winter, 1956), pp. 10–15.

It has been suggested that the selection of a funding instrument involves considerations of cost, benefit security, flexibility, and service.[3] Let us review the question of insured versus trust fund plans with these considerations in mind.

Cost Considerations

As indicated in Chapter 4, the factors involved in the cost of a pension plan are the benefits paid, the expenses of plan operation, and the investment earnings on plan assets. Each of these factors must be reviewed in terms of their application under trust fund plans and under the various insured funding instruments.

Benefits Paid. In a trust fund plan, this element of cost will be determined by the level of benefits established in the plan, by the actual number of employees who survive until benefits become payable, and by the length of time they receive benefits. Except to the extent that the employer establishes the benefit level and retirement ages, he has no control over this item of cost under a trust fund plan. Thus, this aspect of his cost will be determined by the plan's actual experience. Dividend and experience rating formulas (in the absence of pooling techniques) will ultimately cause the same result to emerge under most group pension contracts.[4] Where, however, the insured funding instrument involves a pooling of mortality experience, this element of cost will not be determined by the plan's actual experience; rather, it will be determined by the insurer's rate guarantees and by the experience of all contracts in the "pool." (Some insurers use a combination of actual plan experience and the experience of a pool when determining dividends for smaller group pension plans.)

From the foregoing, the general observation might be made that for a larger employer, there will be no difference in cost between an insured and a trust fund plan insofar as the element of "benefits paid" is concerned.[5] For a smaller employer, whose experience under an insured plan will be pooled to some extent, the same observation cannot be made. Here, the employer must decide whether he will assume the cost attributable to the actual experience of his own

---

[3] Dan M. McGill, *Fundamentals of Private Pensions* (2d ed.; Homewood, Ill.: Richard D. Irwin, Inc., 1964), chap. 9.

[4] This result will emerge on a current basis as experience unfolds in the case of a group immediate participation guarantee contract.

[5] It could be argued that this statement is not correct in the case of an insured plan that is terminated in its early years. However, since the selection of a funding instrument is being made on the assumption that the plan will continue indefinitely, the authors feel that in this context, the general observation is properly made.

group of employees, be that experience good or bad, or whether he will obtain the protection of the insurer's rate guarantees and participate in the insurer's pool, thus obtaining experience results which will be reasonably stable and, as a result, reasonably predictable.

Expenses of Plan Operation.   A comparison of expenses between an insured and a trust fund plan is difficult to make. An insured plan will involve certain expenses not present in a trust fund plan. These expenses include the agent's commissions, state premium taxes (where applicable), and, to a slight extent, federal income tax. On the other hand, certain expenses of a trust fund plan (such as actuarial fees) will generally be at a higher level than would be the case in an insured plan.

It has been suggested that a valid expense analysis involves a comparison of development expenses, premium taxes, insurance company administrative expenses, and employer administrative and legal expenses of the insured plan with actuarial fees and the employer administrative and legal expenses of a trust fund plan.[6] This would include any administrative fees charged by the trustee. There is no doubt that these expenses will be greater for an individual policy plan than for a comparable trust fund plan. When comparing a group pension plan with a trust fund plan, however, the difference is much narrower and, for a given plan which includes a comparison of the expense charges of specific funding agencies, the differential could exist in favor of either type of funding instrument.

In group pension and trust fund plans, the expense differential (in the absence of a substantial annuity premium tax) is relatively small in terms of the other cost factors.[7] Thus, when comparing these plans, it would appear that expense levels should not be a significant factor. When individual policy funding instruments are being considered, other factors such as rate guarantees and benefit and tax objectives are often more significant than the relatively higher expense levels of these plans.

Investment Earnings.   Perhaps the most significant item affecting the cost of a pension plan is the investment earnings on plan assets.

---

[6] McGill, *op. cit.,* p. 302.

[7] If the plan is located in a state which imposes a substantial premium tax on annuities, the expenses of the insured plan will almost always be greater. However, a large number of states exclude annuity premiums under qualified plans from premium tax, and at the time this material was prepared, only 11 states imposed an annuity premium tax in excess of 1% on such plans. The states where the annuity premium tax exceeds 1% are: Colorado, Georgia, Illinois, Kansas, Kentucky, Louisiana, Maine, Mississippi, Nevada, North Carolina, and North Dakota.

As noted earlier, an increase in investment earnings of ¼ of 1% could produce a reduction in costs in the neighborhood of from 5% to 6%.

Historically, insured plans placed heavy emphasis on financial guarantees. Premiums collected in connection with pension plans became a part of the insurer's general assets and, because of limits imposed by state laws, were invested predominantly in real estate mortgages, government and high-grade corporate bonds, privately placed corporate securities, and the like. Generally, these state laws are such that an insurer is prohibited from having more than a small percentage of its general portfolio invested in common stocks. As a result, the insured plan was characterized by a guarantee of principal and by a guarantee of some stipulated rate of interest to be credited to funds held by the insurer. Moreover, the insurer's actual earnings in excess of the guaranteed rate, based on its total portfolio, were credited to the plan reserves through the insurer's dividend or experience rating formula. While this produced a substantial degree of financial security for the plan and, to a great extent, a higher rate of return than could be obtained on the fixed income investments of a trust fund plan, the employer did not have the choice of having a portion of his plan assets invested in common stocks with the resulting opportunity for capital appreciation. For this reason, the trust fund plan (or a combination of an insured and a trust fund plan) took on greater appeal during the rising common stock market of recent years. The insurance industry, however, in an aggressive effort to retain a competitive position in the pension field, has been successful in obtaining legislative authority in a large number of states to segregate assets held in connection with qualified pension plans and to invest these assets in common stocks.[8]

In addition to obtaining the authority to invest in common stocks, most insurers active in the group pension field have also adopted the new-money method of crediting interest to group pension contracts, thus reflecting the yields obtainable at the time funds are invested. The net effect of these two changes has been to produce insured funding instruments which are very similar to the trust fund approach in terms of investment yield.

Thus, in the area of certain group pension contracts, the trust fund plan is no longer automatically in a preferential position in terms of potential investment yield. As a matter of fact, advocates

---

[8] At the time this material was prepared, 29 states had authorized insurers to invest funds in this fashion, including such key states as California, Connecticut, Illinois, Massachusetts, New Jersey, New York, and Pennsylvania.

of the insured plan maintain that overall, the investment yield should be higher under a group pension contract with a separate accounts facility than under a trust fund plan. In support of this, they argue that insurance companies, because of factors such as cash flow and investment facilities (including greater opportunities for private placements and advance commitments), have had, and will continue to have, a greater return on fixed income investments than will a corporate trustee. Proponents of the trust fund plan, on the other hand, point out that if the corporate trustee maintains a common trust fund, its opportunities in the area of fixed income investments are similar to those of an insurance company. In any event, if one assumes that in a well-managed investment operation (be it that of a corporate trustee or an insurance company), the selection of common stocks will, in the long run, produce similar results or, alternately, if one assumes that risk factors involved in the selection of common stocks are such that hoped-for performance in this area should not be the basis of selection, the potential return on the fixed income portion of the plan assets takes on greater significance. Advocates of the insured plan make the further observation that in an insured plan, the fixed income portion of the plan assets could be protected by guarantees as to the integrity of principal and as to a minimum rate of return.[9]

It must be remembered that not all insured funding instruments offer the same type of investment flexibility as that just discussed. If a fully insured individual policy plan is under consideration, for example, there will be no opportunity for equity investment. Moreover, the share of the insurer's investment earnings which the plan will receive will be based on the average method of crediting interest to contracts of the type involved.[10] Thus, when comparing a fully insured individual policy plan with a trust fund plan, it must be recognized that the earnings potential of the trust fund plan will be greater.[11]

In the case of a combination plan, the employer will have the opportunity to have a portion of the plan assets invested in common

---

[9] For an excellent discussion of the competitive aspects of the insured plan in this area, see Lawrence W. Snell, Jr., "New Trends in Pension Funding," *Personnel* (New York: American Management Association, Inc., 1965), November/December issue, pp. 34–38.

[10] In the case of a group permanent fully insured plan, the investment earnings credited might be based on the new-money method.

[11] As a practical matter, however, if an employer is considering the adoption of a fully insured individual policy plan, the size of the group will generally be such that the financial and mortality guarantees of the insurer are often of more importance when compared with the risks the employer would have to assume in these areas under a trust fund plan.

stocks, since the conversion fund may be invested in this fashion by the trustee. Alternately, if the employer does not want to accept the financial risk associated with investing funds in common stocks, he may request the insurer to hold this conversion fund. In this event, the insurer will guarantee this fund as to principal and as to a minimum rate of return. Earnings in excess of the guaranteed rate will be credited by the insurer in accordance with its dividend or experience rating formula.[12]

Summary. As the reader has probably observed, comparison and competition between insured and trust fund plans is generally involved only in plans covering large groups of employees. Smaller employers have more frequently adopted insured plans, partly because of benefit and tax objectives and partly because of the financial and mortality protection and stability offered to small groups by the insurer's guarantees and pooling practices. For larger employers, investment earnings are the most significant factor in comparing the costs of group funding instruments and the trust fund plan. The amount of benefits paid will, in the long run, be the same under both funding instruments. The expenses of operation will be very close under both funding instruments—to the point of being insignificant except in the case of a plan in a state which imposes a heavy annuity premium tax on qualified plans.[13] Thus, of the three factors involved in determining the ultimate cost of a pension plan, investment earnings remain as the one item where real cost differences could result. With the new-money method of crediting investment earnings to qualified group pension plans, and with the availability of separate accounts facilities, the insured and trust fund plans are on at least an equal footing in this regard and, in the opinion of some, insured plans have an advantage over the trust fund plan in terms of the ultimate yield that may be produced on plan assets.

Security of Benefits

Ultimately, the benefit security under any pension plan rests with the continued existence and financial strength of the employer, as well as with the continued existence of the plan. Whether a plan is insured or not, there is no guarantee that the employer will remain in business or that the plan will be continued in effect.

---

[12] For the most part, this will be at the insurer's average or portfolio rate, although a few insurers have adopted the new-money method of crediting interest for conversion funds held in connection with individual policy combination plans. Also, in the case of a group permanent combination plan, the interest credited might be based on the new-money method.

[13] See Note 7.

Assuming that the employer will stay in business and that the plan will be continued, there is then the question of measuring the security of benefits under both the insured and trust fund approaches. Under any type of insured funding instrument, allocated or unallocated, a retired employee is protected by the insurer's guarantee that his benefit will be paid regardless of the continued existence of the employer or the plan and regardless of future funding policy of financial experience.[14] In a trust fund plan, such a guarantee cannot be made (unless annuities are purchased for employees when they retire), although if the employer has pursued an adequate funding policy, it is reasonable to assume that retired employees have a significant degree of protection as long as the plan is continued and the employer continues in existence. However, if future contributions to the plan are terminated or curtailed for any reason, future benefits for retired employees under a trust fund plan might be affected, since the existing assets will have to bear any adverse mortality or financial experience, as well as the continued expenses of operating the plan and disbursing benefits. For this reason, it is customary, when a trust fund plan is terminated, to apply existing assets to purchase guaranteed annuity benefits for retired employees. As long as this practice is available, it might be concluded that in an adequately funded trust fund plan, the benefits for retired employees are reasonably secure.

In comparing the benefit security for active employees, it is important to make a distinction between allocated and unallocated insured funding instruments. If an unallocated insured funding instrument is used, then despite certain financial guarantees made by the insurer, the benefit security for active employees will be similar to the security they would have under a trust fund approach, and this security will depend upon the funding policy followed by the employer. Thus, at any given time, the employee's benefit security under an unallocated insured funding instrument or a trust fund plan will depend upon the level of funding achieved and the amount of the plan assets that he would be entitled to receive under the plan provisions if the plan were then to be terminated.

If an allocated insured funding instrument is involved, then the benefit security of active employees is quite different. Here, amounts which have been allocated and applied on behalf of an

---

[14] If the retired employee's benefit is being purchased under a post-retirement funding arrangement, the insurer's guarantees will be limited to benefits that can be provided by premiums received by the insurer. Thus, if the plan is terminated before the retired employee's benefit is purchased in full, his benefit will be limited to this extent.

employee are protected by the insurer's guarantees and, to this extent, the employee has a greater degree of protection than is afforded him either under an unallocated insured funding instrument or a trust fund plan. It might be argued that if an adequate funding policy has been followed, active employees have a reasonable degree of benefit security even under an unallocated funding instrument. This, of course, is true; the difference, however, is that the funding policy might not have been adequate in the case of the unallocated funding instrument, whereas the insurance company has, for all practical purposes, set an adequate funding policy for the allocated insured funding instrument by means of its premium rates and underwriting practices.

In the last analysis, the ultimate benefit security for employees will depend upon the continuation of the plan on an adequately financed basis. On balance, however, the insured plan contains a greater degree of benefit security than does a trust fund plan when amounts have been allocated in any way under a specific guarantee for an employee, be he active or retired.

Flexibility

The flexibility associated with various funding instruments may be considered from the viewpoint of benefit structure, funding policy, investment policy, and the ability to change funding agencies.[15]

Historically, there is no question that in the early development of private pensions, the trust fund plan offered a greater degree of flexibility in all of these areas than did the insured funding instruments. To meet this competitive disadvantage, the insurance industry developed a number of different products, such as group deposit administration and immediate participation guarantee contracts, and, more recently, has made separate accounts facilities available. As a result, several insured funding instruments now offer, for all practical purposes, the same degree of flexibility in these areas that is offered by trust fund plans. However, certain insured funding instruments are still relatively inflexible in this regard.

It should be recognized that flexibility, per se, is not always necessary or desirable. For this reason, it is important, prior to the selection of a funding instrument, that there be a clear understanding of what is needed or desired in the way of flexibility and that this be matched against the degree of flexibility available under the different funding instruments being considered.

---

[15] McGill, *op. cit.*, p. 315.

Benefit Structure. As previously indicated, the determination of plan provisions should precede the selection of a funding instrument. Once the desired plan provisions have been determined, it is necessary that the funding instrument be examined to see if it can be employed to provide the plan benefits.

Individual policy and group permanent fully insured plans are the least flexible of the insured funding instruments. For example, formulas which offset Social Security benefits or which base benefits on final earnings are difficult to employ in a fully insured plan. Likewise, the insurer's contract requirements (both as to minimum amounts of insurance and minimum duration of the contract) might not be adaptable to plan provisions concerning benefit levels and retirement schedules. Individual policy and group permanent combination plans are somewhat more flexible than fully insured plans in this regard; even here, however, a certain degree of relative inflexibility exists.

Among the group insured funding instruments, the group deferred annuity contract is also relatively inflexible. Generally, this funding instrument works well only in connection with plans that base benefits on career average earnings and where benefits may be associated with a particular year of service. The unallocated group funding instruments, such as deposit administration and immediate participation guarantee contracts, are extremely flexible in this respect and, for all practical purposes, are comparable to the trust fund approach. Advocates of the trust fund plan, however, point out that although this flexibility exists, it is available and may be utilized only with the consent of the insurer, whereas in the trust fund plan, the trustee's consent is not required. While this is generally true, it is not usually a matter of significance. In many situations, the plan provisions are not a part of the insurer's contract and, even where they are included in the contract, the insurer will not, as a practical matter, withhold its consent to a plan provision or change unless, possibly, the insurer's liabilities would be affected thereby.

In summary, the trust fund approach offers a great deal of flexibility as to the benefit structure of the plan. Equivalent flexibility is also afforded by the unallocated insured funding instruments. The allocated insured funding instruments, both group and individual policy, are less flexible and, if flexibility is desired or required, the plan requirements in this regard should be compared with the flexibility available to ascertain if the particular funding instrument under consideration may be conveniently employed.

Funding Policy. As is the case with respect to the benefit structure of the plan, the trust fund approach offers considerable flexibility to the employer in terms of the funding policy of the plan. Within limits imposed by the Internal Revenue Service, the employer may select the actuarial cost method and assumptions to be used. His contributions to the plan may vary considerably, and it is not required, for example, that there be sufficient funds on hand to adequately cover expected payments to retired employees.

A similar degree of flexibility as to funding policy exists in the unallocated insured funding instruments; however, there are two notable exceptions. First, apart from a degree of postretirement funding which most insurers will permit at the inception of the plan, the insurer will require that benefits for retired employees be backed by sufficient reserves. The insurer, since it is guaranteeing this benefit to the retired employee, will insist that a sufficient amount of money be in its possession to meet this liability. Second, most insurers will not underwrite a pension plan unless, in the judgment of the insurer, the employer is following a reasonably sound funding policy.

Advocates of the trust fund plan consider the first of these exceptions to be a definite lack of flexibility on the part of insured programs. Proponents of the insured plan, on the other hand, suggest that this is an example of flexibility which is not always necessary or desirable. They point out that at the outset of the plan, when this flexibility is often needed and can be justified, it is available through postretirement funding devices which most insurers offer, but that after the plan has been in effect for a period of time, benefit security is most important and flexibility which permits a funding policy that endangers this security is undesirable.

Allocated insured funding instruments of necessity are less flexible with regard to the employer's funding policy. To a large extent, employer contributions will be determined from year to year by the insurer's rate structure and, while some degree of flexibility is obtained via "stop-and-go" provisions and policy loan features, this does not compare with the flexibility obtainable in unallocated funding instruments.

Investment Policy. With the exception of insured funding instruments that employ a separate accounts facility, an employer has no degree of control over the investment policy in an insured plan. All amounts contributed to the insurer become part of its general assets and are invested by the insurer in accordance with its own investment policies and subject to any statutory requirements as to the investment of such funds. If a separate accounts facility is involved, the employer may establish investment policy to some extent in terms of the portion of the total plan assets that he wishes to be invested in equities; however, many insurers, as an underwriting requirement, will place some limit on the amount of the plan assets that may be placed in the separate account, and statutory requirements may also result in similar limitations.[16] Moreover, even if amounts are placed in a separate account, most insurers will not permit the employer to exercise any direction or control over the specific stocks that are acquired or disposed of in this account.[17]

In the matter of investment policy, then, the trust fund approach must be considered more flexible than the insured funding instruments.

Change of Funding Agency. It is a relatively simple matter, under a trust fund plan, to change the trustee or to transfer assets to another funding agency, such as an insurance company. This applies to the total assets of the plan, including any amounts held with regard to retired employees.

Generally, it will not be possible to transfer the reserves held for retired employees under any form of insured funding instrument. The insurance company, since it has guaranteed these benefits, will continue to make payments and will continue to hold the reserve for these benefits. As a matter of fact, advocates of the insured plan consider this to be one of the advantages of an insured plan—the benefit security for retired employees. As to funds held with regard to active employees, most insured funding instruments permit a change in funding agency without difficulty. Individual policy and group permanent plans are such that coverage may be surrendered and the surrender values may be turned over to the new funding agency. Similarly, the unallocated or active life fund under group deposit administration and immediate participation guarantee contracts may be transferred to the new funding agency, although most insurers generally reserve the right to spread payment of this amount over a period of years.[18] In this regard, group deferred

---

[16] Most state laws authorizing the use of a separate accounts facility require that employee contributions and reserves for annuities purchased be held in the insurer's general portfolio.

[17] If the employer is large enough to have his own separate account (i.e., his plan assets are not in a "pooled" separate account), it is not unreasonable to expect the insurer to recognize the employer's desires in selecting the stocks which comprise the portfolio of the employer's separate account. As a practical matter, however, the practice of establishing individual separate accounts is still relatively uncommon.

[18] See p. 263. The liquidation option generally associated with a group deposit administration contract allows the insurer to retain a small percentage (usually not more than 5%) of the fund being held for active employees. This is sometimes referred to as a "termination" charge. It must be remembered, however, that in such a plan, most of the insurer's loading for expenses will not

annuity contracts are the least flexible, since most such contracts do not contain a surrender privilege. Thus, under a group deferred annuity contract, a change in funding agency may generally be made only with respect to future plan contributions.

Summary. It would seem that the trust fund plan is more flexible than most of the insured funding instruments. In some situations, the need for this greater flexibility will dictate the choice of the trust fund plan as the appropriate funding instrument even though a necessary corollary is that the employer must assume a greater degree of responsibility for the total administration of the plan. As indicated earlier, however, it is first necessary to determine the degree of flexibility needed or desired. Only then can it be determined if the funding instrument under consideration will be satisfactory.

Service

In insured plans, service is normally provided by the home office of the insurance company and by its agency and/or group field offices. In trust fund plans, the employer generally handles the administrative work of the plan or this is performed by an actuarial consultant.

It is difficult to measure the quality of the services performed by the various institutions and firms active in the pension field. Obviously, there can be marked differences in this regard which are not inherent in the different funding instruments. As a general observation, however, it might be said that insured plans have a service advantage over trust fund plans in that the operations of an insurance company extend over a wide geographical area and that it is more efficiently geared to disbursing benefits of the type associated with retirement plans.

Summary

At the outset of this chapter it was stated that there is no one funding instrument preferable over all others, but that for a given plan, and under given circumstances and objectives, a particular funding instrument would be best suited for a particular employer.

---

be received until annuities are purchased even though the insurer has incurred expenses with regard to amounts in the unallocated fund. Thus, one reason for this charge is to reimburse the insurer for expenses already incurred but not yet recovered. In contrast, expenses associated with a trust fund plan are normally paid for as incurred, with the result that if there is to be a change in funding agency, only current unpaid expenses need be deducted from the fund.

By this time, the reader can understand the validity of this statement as applied to the broad question of insured versus trust fund plans. Smaller and medium-sized employers, who are more apt to place greater emphasis on benefit and tax objectives, cost stability, benefit security, and service, have tended to favor the insured plan. Larger employers, who are apt to place greater emphasis on flexibility (particularly as to investment policy and the selection of plan assets), have tended to favor the trust fund plan.

GROUP VERSUS INDIVIDUAL POLICY PLANS

An employer who decides to use the insured approach is faced with a choice between a number of different individual policy and group funding instruments. His choice in this regard may be complicated by the competition that exists within the insurance industry and, on occasion, within the same insurance company.

As might be expected, many life insurance agents have, over the years, favored using the individual policy approach. Group field personnel, on the other hand, have strongly advocated the use of group funding instruments. The situation has been further complicated by the fact that many insurers maintain completely separate and distinct home office pension departments, depending upon the type of coverage involved. Thus, it is possible for the same insurer to issue both individual policy and group proposals to the same employer and for essentially the same plan benefits. Often, the proposals will be issued through different sources—for example, a full-time agent of the insurer will obtain an individual policy proposal while a competing broker consults with the insurer's group field office and obtains a group proposal. When conditions such as these exist, it is not difficult to understand why an employer may become confused as to which is the proper funding instrument for his plan.

Even though already mentioned several times in this chapter, it is worthy of repetition once again that there is no one funding instrument preferable over all others. In some situations, the individual policy approach will be indicated, while in others, some form of group funding instrument will more adequately meet the employer's needs and objectives. The remaining portion of this chapter will discuss some of the more important factors that might affect the choice of a particular insured funding instrument and will review some of the most commonly used individual policy and group funding instruments with an indication of their application to particular situations.

Basic Considerations

Broadly speaking, a comparison of individual policy and group funding instruments should involve the same elements that were previously discussed in terms of insured and trust fund plans—i.e., costs, benefit security, flexibility, and service.

Costs. In the area of costs, it will be recalled, the three elements to be considered are benefits paid, expenses, and investment earnings. As to benefits paid, the individual policy plan offers the employer the protection of the insurer's rate guarantees, as well as participation in the insurer's experience pool. For this reason, the employer may expect reasonably stable and predictable costs in an individual policy plan. Depending upon the employer's size, the group funding instrument involved, and the insurer's dividend or experience rating formula, some or all of the experience of the employer's plan might be pooled with the experience of similar groups. Where such pooling exists, there should be little difference between individual policy and group funding instruments in terms of ultimate cost to the employer of benefits paid. To the extent the group funding instrument takes into account the employer's own actual experience, the employer assumes the risk of this experience, good or bad, and his cost will ultimately reflect this experience rather than the more stable experience of the larger group of lives participating in the insurer's pool.

As to expenses, the individual policy plan will generally run higher than an equivalent group plan. The agent's compensation is one reason for this; other reasons are the lower acquisition and maintenance costs associated with issuing and administering a master contract rather than a number of individual contracts for each employee.

It is a little more difficult to assess the investment earnings aspects of the different insured funding instruments. In a fully insured individual policy plan, reserves will be credited with interest based upon the insurer's average or portfolio rate of interest. In an individual policy combination plan, the same will be true as to the portion of the plan assets consisting of insurance contracts. The conversion fund of a combination plan, however, may be invested in equities, thus affording the opportunity of capital appreciation (along with the attendant possibility of capital loss). Most insurers use the new-money method when crediting interest to reserves held in connection with group funding instruments. If large enough to qualify for a separate accounts facility, a portion of the plan assets may also be invested in equities. Generally, if investment earnings are of paramount importance to the employer, the use of a group funding instrument (or, possibly, an individual policy combination plan) might be preferable. Usually, however, the choice between individual policy and group funding instruments will be influenced by factors other than investment earnings.

It would be well to reiterate, at this point, that a funding instrument should not be selected on the basis of cost *estimates*. This is particularly true when comparing individual policy and group funding instruments, since not only are there the differences which could result from the use of different funding assumptions, but these cost estimates could reflect differences in true costs due to different plan provisions and benefits frequently suggested by the different funding instruments. For example, most individual policy plans automatically include a substantial preretirement death benefit, while such is not always the case when a group funding instrument is involved. Similarly, most individual policy plans are developed so that retirement benefits are paid for life with a guarantee that they will be made for at least 60 or 120 months. In contrast, most group plans (in the absence of employee contributions) provide benefits for life only. Moreover, most individual policy plans are funded on a level premium basis, while most group plans employ a funding method which creates an initial supplemental liability. Since such a supplemental liability may be amortized over a period of time which could extend beyond the normal retirement dates of many of the initial group of participants, a significant difference in the "incidence" of contributions could be produced, creating the impression that the group funding instrument is considerably less expensive. For these reasons, extreme care should be taken when comparing the cost levels suggested in connection with specific funding instruments.

Benefit Security.   As far as retired employees are concerned, there is little difference in benefit security between individual policy and group funding instruments. Since the assets in a fully insured individual policy plan and in a group deferred annuity plan are allocated and since individual policy combination plans are partially allocated prior to retirement, these plans offer a greater degree of benefit security prior to retirement than would be the case in an unallocated group funding instrument. In the latter case, the degree of an employee's benefit security will depend upon the level of funding achieved and the amount of the plan assets that he would be entitled to receive under the plan provisions if the plan were to be terminated.

Flexibility.   Unallocated group funding instruments offer a greater degree of flexibility, particularly in the area of benefit structure, than do individual policy plans. It is no problem under an unallocated group funding instrument, for example, to have benefits based upon final earnings. Similarly, benefit formulas which offset Social Security benefits may be accommodated, along with widow's benefits and various forms of disability benefits. Other examples of this greater flexibility include the ability to establish a wider range of normal retirement schedules, as well as varying levels of death benefits.

The individual policy combination plan is much more flexible in this regard than is the fully insured plan; nonetheless, when compared with the unallocated group funding instruments, it must still be considered as relatively inflexible in terms of designing the plan's benefit structure.

The group funding instruments are also more flexible in terms of the funding policy of the plan. Again, the individual policy combination plan is somewhat more flexible in this regard than is the fully insured plan, since contributions to the conversion fund may be determined by several different actuarial methods and with varying actuarial assumptions. Even so, the group funding instruments permit a wider degree of flexibility as to funding policy than does the individual policy combination plan.

For smaller employers, the individual policy combination plan provides greater investment flexibility than the group funding instruments. For larger employers, flexibility as to investment policy is probably greater under the unallocated group funding instruments.

With the exception of the group deferred annuity contract, the insured funding instruments generally permit a change in funding agency with respect to funds held for active employees. The group funding instruments, however, usually reserve to the insurer the right to spread out payment of this fund over a period of years—at least in the case of larger funds—while such restrictions are not found in individual policy plans.

Service. As far as the home office of the insurer is concerned, there should not be any appreciable difference in the servicing of pension plans funded with either individual or group contracts. There could, of course, be material differences in the case of a given insurer or between different insurers, but this would not be attributable to differences inherent in the particular insured funding instruments.

At the field level, there might be slight differences in service between individual policy and group plans. As noted in Chapter 12, the servicing of individual policy plans will largely be conducted by the insurer's agency office. In group plans, this servicing will be done, to a great extent, directly by the home office of the insurer or through a group field office. Because the servicing of group plans is done under home office direction by salaried employees, there is a greater probability of consistency and continuity of service. The quality of service of individual policy plans will depend more directly upon the individuals involved at the field level and will be more responsive to change if these individuals should retire or terminate their affiliations with the insurer.

Tax Considerations

Before turning to a discussion of the specific insured funding instruments, it is important to recognize that tax considerations often influence the choice between group and individual policy funding instruments.

Most group plans are established so that any death benefit is provided by a group term life insurance contract issued directly to the employer. When death benefits are being provided under a group plan in the above manner, the following tax results occur:

1. The employee does not have to include the cost of insurance as taxable income each year (except to the extent the employer is providing him with total group term life insurance in excess of $50,000).
2. Since the entire proceeds consist of pure insurance, no portion of a lump sum payment will have to be considered as taxable income by the beneficiary.
3. The proceeds of the insurance will be included in the employee's gross estate for federal estate tax purposes.

In contrast, the death proceeds under an individual policy plan will not be includable in the employee's gross estate to the extent provided by employer contributions and if paid to a named personal beneficiary; however, the cash value of the insurance contract, subject to certain deductions, will be taxable as income to the beneficiary, and the employee will be required to include the cost of insurance (offset by his own contributions, if any) as taxable income during his lifetime.[19]

This difference in tax treatment leads to the broad observation that lower-paid employees (i.e., at least those employees who do not

---

[19] The taxation of distributions from a qualified plan is discussed at length in Chapter 6.

have an estate tax problem) are better off, tax-wise, with a plan funded by group coverages. For such an employee, the fact that the proceeds are includable in his estate is not a disadvantage, and the fact that the premium for the life insurance will not be taxable to him while he is alive, coupled with the fact that the proceeds will be received free of income tax by his beneficiary, creates a distinct tax advantage.

For an employee who has estate tax problems, however, the individual policy plan could produce distinct tax advantages. The fact that the entire proceeds could pass completely free from federal estate tax may produce tax savings to such an extent that having to include the cost of insurance as taxable income each year would be relatively insignificant. Moreover, the aggregate of these prior insurance costs, along with the $5,000 employee death benefit exclusion provided by Section 101 (b) of the Code, could be used upon the death of a participant to reduce his beneficiary's income tax liability. Finally, the beneficiary's tax liability would be softened in that any portion of the cash value that is taxable could be treated as a long-term capital gain if certain necessary conditions are met.

While these tax considerations are significant, it must be remembered that federal tax law may be changed at any time. Thus, in a long-range program such as a pension plan, probable tax consequences should not be given undue consideration—particularly when other factors would indicate a contrary course of action.

The Fully Insured Plan

Whether group or individual policy, the fully insured plan offers an employer the greatest degree of guarantees available from an insurance company. The employer has the security that the cost of the coverage in force cannot exceed the premium level stipulated for this coverage.[20] This is so regardless of the actual experience of his plan and regardless of future economic trends.

This is of great significance to some employers. For many, particularly those with only a few employees, this factor alone is enough to warrant the selection of a fully insured plan as the funding instrument for the plan.

Along with this advantage, however, there are certain disadvan-

---

[20] The employer does not, of course, have a guarantee as to the cost of additional benefits that accrue in the future for existing participants or for new participants (except, possibly, to a limited extent under group permanent contracts).

tages associated with the fully insured plan. One of the most notable of these is the lack of flexibility in terms of benefit structure,
funding policy, and investment policy. The basic structure of the
insurance contract is also considered by many practitioners to be a
further disadvantage. It will be recalled that under a retirement
income contract, the cash value increases to the point where it
ultimately exceeds the face amount of the coverage. This leads to a
situation in which the death benefit increases in the years just prior
to retirement—at a time in life when there is usually little justification for an individual to receive (or for an employer to provide)
larger death benefits. Moreover, as previously pointed out, the cash
value of the contract will be considered as taxable income to the
beneficiary when received. In the later years of the contract, this
could mean that all or most of the death proceeds will be taxable as
income.[21] Finally, since the entire amount accumulated to provide
the employee's retirement benefit is paid as a death benefit, there is
no recovery to the trust on account of the employee's death.

For these reasons, the fully insured plan is only infrequently
used for larger groups of employees. Although this type of coverage
may be written on a group permanent basis, the fact that this
approach is used primarily for small groups results in a fully
insured group permanent plan being relatively uncommon. While it
is difficult to draw the line as to what constitutes a small group, it
generally appears that the fully insured plan is used predominantly
for groups of less than 10 covered employees. The fully insured
plan also works quite well in defined contribution (money purchase) plans, where it is often desirable to make a full allocation of
contributions among employees and where it is not desired, for
administrative reasons, to maintain a separate fund and to allocate
investment earnings among employees.

The Combination Plan

The combination plan is one of the most popular of the insured
funding instruments. While it does not offer an employer the complete protection associated with a fully insured plan, there are still
significant guarantees available to the employer—particularly in

---

[21] This aspect could be quite significant. For example, it is not uncommon
for an executive to qualify for a monthly pension of $1,000. Under a fully
insured plan, this would require a retirement income contract with a face
amount of $100,000. In the years just prior to retirement, this death benefit
could increase to an amount in the vicinity of $160,000. Even though the death
benefit could qualify for long-term capital gains treatment, the beneficiary's
tax liability could be quite large if, for all practical purposes, most of the
$160,000 would be considered as a capital gain.

terms of the cost of retirement benefits with respect to insurance contracts in force.[22]

The combination plan is much more flexible than the fully insured plan in terms of benefit structure, funding policy, and investment policy. It is possible, for example, to relate death benefits to earnings or to make the death benefit some multiple (not in excess of 100) of the employee's expected pension. Benefit formulas that offset Social Security benefits or that base benefits on final earnings may also be employed. The existence of the conversion fund permits greater latitude in the choice of actuarial cost methods and assumptions, and in the actual incidence of contributions. Finally, the conversion fund may be invested in equities or in more conservative investments, as the employer sees fit.

Since not all of the reserve being accumulated with respect to an employee's retirement benefit will be paid as a benefit in the event of his death before retirement, it is reasonable to expect that the ultimate cost of a combination plan will be less than under a fully insured plan.[23] Moreover, since the cash value of the insurance contract will be lower than under a retirement income contract, the income tax liability of the employee's beneficiary will not be as great as under a fully insured plan.

The combination plan may be written on either an individual policy or a group permanent basis although, most frequently, individual contracts are used. The combination plan is generally used where the group of employees to be covered is between 5 and 50. This plan may, of course, be used for smaller groups; however, when used for a small group of employees, it is generally desirable not to employ a discount for expected mortality. While occasionally employed for groups of more than 50 employees, this is relatively uncommon because of the cost and flexibility considerations of the group and trust fund approaches.

Group Deferred Annuity Contract

At one time the major form of group funding instrument, the group deferred annuity contract is now used very infrequently. It is relatively inflexible in terms of benefit structure, working well only in connection with defined contribution (money purchase) plans or

---

[22] For an interesting comparison of fully insured and combination plans, where the author concludes in favor of the combination plan, see Samuel J. Savitz, "The Case for the Combination Plan," *Journal of the American Society of Chartered Life Underwriters*, Vol. XX, No. 1 (Winter, 1966), pp. 66–74.

[23] As a matter of fact, this aspect is often reflected in cost estimates which employ a discount for expected mortality insofar as contributions to the conversion fund are concerned.

in defined benefit plans where the benefit is based on career average compensation or where benefits may be imputed to various years of service. For all practical purposes, the group deferred annuity contract offers little flexibility in funding policy (except to the extent of the amortization of supplemental liabilities) and, of course, no flexibility in terms of investment policy.

On the other hand, the group deferred annuity contract offers a greater degree of guarantees to the employer than do the unallocated group funding instruments. Moreover, since it is an allocated funding instrument, record keeping and plan administration are relatively straightforward and simple.

Most insurers will not offer this type of coverage to groups of less than 10 lives. While there is no upper limit as to the size of the group that could be covered, practical considerations tend to limit its use to groups of under 100 lives.[24]

Unallocated Group Funding Instruments

The unallocated group funding instruments include the group deposit administration and immediate participation guarantee contracts and, more recently, the modified immediate participation guarantee or, as it is sometimes called, the direct rated deposit administration contract. Depending upon the size of the group covered, the state involved, and the insurer's underwriting practices, these contracts may also be written with a separate accounts facility.

As has been previously discussed, the unallocated group funding instruments more nearly approach the trust fund plan in terms of the factors the employer might consider when selecting a funding instrument. They offer a wide degree of flexibility in terms of the benefit structure of the plan and the employer's funding policy. With a separate accounts facility, the employer also has a degree of flexibility in determining the portion of plan assets to be invested in equities.

The insurer's guarantees, both from a financial and a mortality viewpoint, are considerably more limited as to duration of time than under an individual policy plan. Typically, these guarantees attach to amounts which become part of the insurer's general assets during the first five years of the contract and continue until the fund so created has been exhausted on a "first-in, first-out" basis to

---

[24] There are, of course, a number of older plans that are still funded with group deferred annuity contracts where the number of employees covered is far in excess of 100. This statement is intended to cover current attitudes and practices with regard to new plans.

provide or purchase benefits. Thus, the insurer's guarantees attach to the fund, rather than to individual employees. For this reason, in a defined contribution (money purchase) plan, the insurer's guarantees under an unallocated group funding instrument are relatively meaningless, except to older employees. Younger employees in such a plan receive little or no protection in terms of the annuity purchase rates that might apply when they retire at some future date.

Most insurers offer unallocated group funding instruments to groups of as little as 10 covered lives. As a practical matter, they are usually employed for groups of 25 lives or more.[25]

---

[25] If an insurer wishes to avoid registration with the Securities and Exchange Commission, a separate accounts facility cannot be offered unless at least 25 lives are to be covered.

UNDERWRITING ASPECTS OF INSURED PLANS

Apart from the usual underwriting considerations applicable to the individual lives or to the group of lives covered under a pension or a profit sharing plan, an insurer must also make the decision of whether or not it is willing to underwrite the plan as a whole. A pension or a profit sharing plan is a long-range undertaking, both for the employer and for the insurance company underwriting the plan benefits. For this reason the insurer must recognize, when it accepts the underwriting risks associated with such a plan, that its commitments will extend well into the future.

From the insurer's point of view, a pension or a profit sharing plan involves sales and administrative costs which are greater than the normal expenses incurred by the insurer in the acquisition and maintenance of its other business. In the sales area, for example, many insurers furnish proposals and cost calculations for pension and profit sharing plans—a service not generally provided in connection with its individual life and health insurance business. In the administrative area, the question of providing special services is also a problem because of the need for periodic actuarial valuations of the plan and because of the information the employer may request or require (such as information to support his claim that plan contributions are deductible for income tax purposes). The expenses associated with services of this type must be taken into account by the insurer when the plan is underwritten.

The purpose of this chapter is to examine some of the factors which bear on the overall underwriting decision of the insurer and to review the broader underwriting aspects of group and individual policy pension coverages. This chapter also discusses the use of the guaranteed issue underwriting technique in connection with individual policy plans.

GENERAL UNDERWRITING CONSIDERATIONS

Early Termination

Before accepting the underwriting risk of the plan as a whole, the insurer must satisfy itself that the plan will be reasonably permanent and that there will not, in all probability, be an early lapse of coverage. The reason, of course, is that the initial cost of acquiring and installing the plan will not be recovered until the plan has been in operation for several years. Thus, one of the insurer's first underwriting considerations is the possibility of early plan termination.

An important factor in this area is the stability of the employer's business and his profit history. If the employer has been in business for only a short period of time, or if his profits have fluctuated widely in recent years, the insurer would be rightly concerned over the possibility that the cost of the plan may prove to be too burdensome, with the attendant possibility of early plan termination. If a profit sharing plan is involved, these factors do not have the same significance so far as the future of the plan is concerned—as a matter of fact, these factors may very well be the reason a profit sharing plan is being considered in preference to a pension plan. From the insurer's viewpoint, however, the fact that a profit sharing plan need not be terminated if the employer is unable to make a contribution is of little solace if coverage is lapsed due to the lack of funds needed to pay premiums due on insurance contracts that might have been purchased through the plan.

Closely related to this problem is the question of whether or not the cost of the plan is too high in relation to the employer's financial capacity. Even though the employer has been in business for a substantial length of time, and even though he has had a stable profit history, the cost of the plan may still be too high for him to undertake on any comfortable basis. Unless the employer has a sufficient profit margin, the future of the plan could be in jeopardy as a result of even a slight shift in business conditions.

Another factor which bears on the consideration of early plan termination is the question of whether or not the plan will achieve a qualified status under federal tax law.[1] Most insurers would be unwilling to underwrite a plan which, in all likelihood, will not be approved by the Internal Revenue Service. However, it is important to distinguish between plan provisions which are grossly unac-

---

[1] This aspect is also important to the insurer in connection with its premium rates and its dividend or experience rating treatment of the plan. See p. 259 and p. 264.

ceptable and those which are marginal. If the plan provisions are marginal and if there is a general understanding between the insurer and the employer that the plan will be changed to conform to any requirements imposed by the Internal Revenue Service, the insurer would probably be willing to underwrite the plan if the potential cost of any contract changes needed to meet the requirements of the Service is not too high.

The insurer will also show some degree of interest in the funding instrument chosen, particularly if circumstances indicate that within a short time this funding instrument might be discarded, possibly at the suggestion of a competitor, in favor of one better suited to the employer's needs.[2] While there is a considerable difference of opinion as to where the line is drawn, there is general agreement that at some point, the use of individual contracts to fund pension benefits becomes questionable. For this reason, the insurer must make an underwriting decision if it is being asked to use individual contracts in a plan where, in the judgment of the insurer, some other funding instrument should be employed. By the same token, the insurer will also be concerned with the choice between a fully insured individual policy plan and an individual policy combination plan and with the choice between the different group funding instruments available.

Administrative Aspects

Another major underwriting consideration for the insurer concerns the administrative requirements and complexities of the plan.

The plan, for example, may include requirements which conflict with the insurer's contract forms, regulations, or procedures. Each plan provision must be checked against the insurer's requirements and any conflict should be resolved before the plan is underwritten. The following list is by no means all-inclusive, but does give some indication of areas where difficulties could arise:

1. Discrepancies between the normal retirement dates specified by the plan and the maturity dates available under the insurer's contracts. For example, the typical retirement income contract used in conjunction with a fully insured individual policy plan will mature on the contract anniversary nearest the insured's 65th birthday. The plan, however, may call for normal retirement to occur on the first of the month coincident with or next following the employee's 65th birthday, with the result that, unless some adjustments are

---

[2] For a detailed discussion of the factors to be considered in the selection of a funding instrument, see Chapter 10.

made, the contract will have either too little or too much cash value on the employee's normal retirement date.

2. Plan provisions which require that coverage be issued at ages when the coverage would not be available from the insurer.

3. Plan provisions which require that coverage be issued for amounts below the insurer's minimums. This is especially significant as it applies to small increases in coverage which accrue after the employee has become a participant in the plan.

4. Plan provisions dealing with late retirement which require the continuation of coverage or the accumulation of funds after normal retirement in a manner which the insurer will not or cannot permit. Many insurers, for example, have developed a special type of contract for individual policy combination plans which matures for a stipulated cash value on the employee's normal retirement date. The plan may require continued life insurance coverage between normal and late retirement, but the insurer may not be willing to continue this coverage after the contract maturity date unless satisfactory evidence of insurability is submitted.

5. Plan provisions which require that certain options be available to a retiring employee. The insurer, however, may not be willing or able to make these options available—or may be able to make them available but only under conditions not included in the plan. The plan, for example, may permit an employee who retires before age 65 to elect to have his benefit adjusted to provide higher payments before 65 and lower payments thereafter, so as to produce an approximately level income when his full Social Security benefits commence at age 65. While this form of payment is readily available under most group pension contracts, it is generally not available in connection with individual policy plans. Another example of the problems in this area would be a plan which permits the election of a certain optional form of payment immediately prior to retirement whereas the insurer, under the funding instrument involved, would require some preelection period before that particular option could become effective.

6. Conflicts between the billing practices of the insurer and plan provisions which could affect the dates and frequency of premium payments. A plan, for example, could permit an employee to become a participant on the day on which he meets all eligibility requirements (which could be any day of any month), and could require that coverage be made effective on that date. This would result in a number of contracts being issued under the plan with different premium due dates. For billing purposes, however, the insurer might want to have all contracts issued with a common premium due date.

7. Plan provisions which require ownership or beneficiary designations which conflict with the insurer's contract provisions and practices. Some insurers, for example, prefer to write contracts under a pension or a profit sharing plan with the trustee as the

owner and beneficiary (with the employee's personal beneficiary designations being filed with the trustee). However, the plan may stipulate that the employee's personal beneficiaries be named in the contract, or many require that the ownership provisions of the contract be split between the trustee and employee, so that the employee has the absolute right, under the contract, to name and change the beneficiary without the trustee's consent or approval.

8. Procedures spelled out in the plan in the event of death, disability, retirement, or termination of employment which require the insurer to do (or not to do) certain things which are in conflict with the insurer's contract provisions or practices. An example of this type of problem would be a plan requirement that the contract be owned by the employee after retirement, along with an additional requirement that any dividends after maturity should be paid to the trustee. This provision could present complications if the insurer's contract stipulates that any dividends after maturity must be paid to the owner of the contract.

Conflicts of the type enumerated are found most frequently in individual policy plans, rather than in group plans. Also, many are of the type that may readily be solved by a simple adjustment to the plan, by the insurer waiving its normal requirements, or by the insurer finding an acceptable alternate solution. Finally, it should also be pointed out that any particular item, while a matter of concern to one company, may be of little or no significance to another. In any event, the insurer will examine each plan with points such as these in mind to ascertain if the plan may be underwritten on a satisfactory basis.

Closely related to the question of potential conflict between plan provisions and the insurer's administrative requirements is the further question of whether the insurer will be required to perform any special services and, if so, the relative cost of these services. For example, does the plan require (or the employer expect) the insurer to furnish any special actuarial services? Does the employer expect the insurer to prepare employee announcement material? Is the insurer expected to supply financial information each year for the covered employees such as insurance (PS 58) costs, a statement of accrued benefits, etc.? Is it expected that the insurer will furnish yearly assistance in the preparation of the employer's tax return or in the preparation of material to be filed under the Federal or any State Disclosure Acts? Will the insurer be required to maintain records relative to the participation of employees, such as a record of their accumulated contributions? If some or all of these services are required, the insurer must evaluate the potential cost involved in determining the acceptability of the case.

Depending upon the coverage involved, many of these services are made available to all employers on a regular basis. Others are readily available as a by-product of the insurer's administrative system at very little additional cost. In any event, the insurer must take these factors into account as a part of its underwriting judgment of the desirability of the plan as a whole.

Exculpatory Provisions

If the plan involves a trust, most insurers will require, as a part of their general underwriting process, that the trust contain provisions which protect the insurer in its relationships with the trustee, the employer, the employees, and their beneficiaries. Similar provisions are usually included in group pension contracts.

A typical provision would establish that the insurer is not a party to the trust and that the insurer is fully protected in relying on any information furnished by the employer or trustee. Such a provision would also establish that the insurer's liability will be measured solely by the terms of its own contracts; that the insurer will be fully discharged in making any payments to the trustee or on direction of the trustee; and that the insurer has no obligation to see that any amount paid in such fashion is properly distributed or applied. It is also common for the exculpatory provision to protect the insurer in dealing with the person who is the trustee in accordance with the latest notification received by the insurer at its home office and in assuming that the trust has not been amended until a copy of the amendment has been received at the insurer's home office.

UNDERWRITING CONSIDERATIONS OF GROUP PENSION PLANS

Apart from the general underwriting considerations already noted, there are several broad concepts specifically related to the underwriting of group pension plans.

The first of these is that group pension coverages (other than group permanent) do not involve immediate life insurance benefits and that the annuity risk assumed by the insurer is relatively long range in nature. For this reason, any mortality antiselection will usually occur at some time subsequent to the effective date of the plan, rather than at its inception. Also, unlike individual annuity contracts where any mortality antiselection is exercised primarily by the annuitant, mortality antiselection under a group pension contract may be exercised both by the employer and by the covered employees.

Another broad aspect of group pension underwriting is the fact that the contract involves the accumulation of substantial reserves over a long period of time and, therefore, insurers are quite concerned about the possibilities of financial antiselection. Thus, the insurer will be particularly concerned with the guarantees that it makes under a group pension contract.

As previously noted, acceptability of the plan to the Internal Revenue Service is a major underwriting consideration. Insurance companies receive federal tax relief with respect to investment income earned on assets attributable to reserves under qualified plans, and it is customary for most insurers to reflect this anticipated tax relief in the form of lower premium rates (or higher interest guarantees) for their group pension contracts. For this reason, the acceptability of the plan to the Internal Revenue Service takes on additional significance to the insurer, since the contract rates could very well be inadequate if the plan does not attain a qualified status and the annuities purchased remain in force.

Finally, because of the nature of group pension contracts and their tailor-made aspects, and because of dividend or experience rating techniques which permit the insurer to charge each case with its own expenses, the insurer is in a position to offer broad administrative services to the employer and to do this on a basis which is equitable to all of its group pension policyholders. Thus, special services to be rendered are not as significant an underwriting consideration in group pension plans as they are in individual policy plans.

Minimum Requirements

Most insurers have established certain minimum requirements which must be met before a group pension contract will be offered. These minimums vary considerably from company to company and will also vary according to the type of funding instrument involved. In some companies, the minimum requirements for the same funding instrument may be different depending upon whether or not the plan requires employee contributions.

A typical minimum requirement for a group deposit administration contract or a group deferred annuity contract is that the plan must cover at least 10 lives and must generate an annual premium of at least $5,000 (possibly $10,000 if the plan is contributory). If employees are to contribute, the insurer may require that 75% of the eligible employees participate. It should be noted that these requirements are not imposed by statute but are usually

established by the companies as underwriting minimums.[3] Other
group pension coverages such as immediate participation guarantee
or separate accounts contracts usually have higher minimum requirements.[4]

Mortality Aspects

The insurer will generally require that the contract be established on a basis which does not permit the employer to individually
select the persons to be covered or the amount of a participant's
annuity. The purpose, of course, is to prevent mortality antiselection.

Just as an insurer is concerned about the maximum amount of
group term life insurance it has in force on any one individual, it
will also be concerned about the maximum amount of annuity it has
in force on any one life. As a practical matter, however, cost
considerations as well as requirements of the Internal Revenue
Service tend to limit this underwriting problem.

Individual mortality antiselection may occur in the choice of
options at retirement—for example, if the basic form of payment
under the plan is a pure life annuity with no death benefit and the
employee has the right to elect to have his benefit reduced and paid
under a joint and survivor option. Obviously, an employee in poor
health could elect this optional form of payment and thus create a
form of death benefit unless some restriction is placed upon his
right to make this election. Thus, most insurers will require that if
an optional form of payment is to be elected, evidence of the employee's good health will be required unless the election is made
prior to some specified period before retirement. The preelection
period varies from company to company, but a requirement of from
two to five years prior to retirement is common. If an election has
been made and if the employee is within this preelection period, he
will not be allowed to change or revoke the option without submitting satisfactory evidence of his good health or, if applicable, evidence of the good health of his joint annuitant.

---

[3] Group permanent coverage is generally subject to the various state group
insurance statutes, with the result that eligibility provisions, schedules of
insurance, the minimum number of covered lives, the minimum percentage of
participation, etc., must also conform to the requirements of these laws.
However, any limitation in the state law as to the maximum amount of group
life insurance usually applies only to group term life insurance and not to
group permanent coverage.

[4] In the case of separate accounts contracts, the insurer may also be
influenced by requirements of the Securities and Exchange Commission which
exempt this type of contract from registration only if it covers at least 25 lives.
SEC Rule 3c–3.

By the same token, the insurer's consent will be required if an employee wants to change his retirement date after having elected an optional form of payment (assuming the plan otherwise permits the employee to change his retirement date). For example, if the employee has elected a joint and survivor option and then finds that he is in poor health and may not live until his scheduled retirement date, it would be to his advantage to elect an early retirement date so as to assure a benefit for his joint annuitant. If, on the other hand, he finds his joint annuitant to be in poor health, he could, if not so restricted, elect a late retirement date. If he did this and if his joint annuitant died prior to the late retirement date elected, this would have the effect of automatically revoking the optional form of payment, thus restoring the higher benefits the employee would receive under the basic form for the payment of his benefit. To prevent the possible antiselection in this latter example, the insurer's consent to the request for late retirement would generally be conditioned upon receiving satisfactory evidence of the good health of the employee's joint annuitant.

Group pension underwriting is also concerned with the mortality aspects of the cancellation of annuities purchased under a group deferred annuity contract. The problem usually arises under a contract written on a deferred pure life annuity or modified cash refund basis (i.e., where there is no death benefit payable before retirement other than a return of any employee contributions) and when an employee terminates employment under such conditions that he is not fully vested. The question, of course, is whether or not there will be a credit made available to the employer with respect to the premiums paid for the nonvested portion of the annuity being canceled. Since the premium rates have been discounted for expected mortality, the insurer will generally be unwilling to make any such credit available unless satisfactory evidence of the terminating employee's good health (at the date of his termination) is received within a specified period of time—usually six months from the date of his termination of employment.

The good-health requirement under any of the situations previously described will vary depending upon the amount of risk involved for the insurer with respect to the particular employee. The evidence may range from a simple employer's statement as to the employee's good health up to a full medical examination of the type normally associated with the issue of new individual life insurance. A factor which also bears on this aspect is the "experience status" the contract has reached under the insurer's dividend or experience rating formula. If the experience of the case is such that dividends are being paid, adverse mortality experience will be borne to a great extent by the employer, since such experience will directly affect the amount of these dividends.

Financial Aspects

As previously indicated, a group pension contract involves the contribution of substantial amounts of money each year which must be held, invested, and reinvested by the insurer over a long period of time. Because of this, the financial aspects of the contract are carefully underwritten.

Most insurers limit their financial guarantees to amounts deposited during the first five years of the contract and reserve the right to change the terms of these guarantees with respect to amounts received after the fifth contract year. The guarantees that attach to the fund or reserve created during the first five years will generally continue in effect as to such amounts until they have been applied or distributed under the contract. For this reason, the initial guarantee may extend for a long period of time, and it is not uncommon to find that by the terms of the contract, the features of the initial guarantee will scale down with the passage of time. For example, under a typical group deposit administration contract the insurer guarantees the rate of interest at which the unallocated or active life fund will accumulate until the fund has been applied on a "first-in, first-out" basis to purchase annuities or to provide benefits. This guarantee will extend until the fund created during the first five years is exhausted, but the rate of interest, although specified, will often decrease with the duration of this initial guarantee. Thus, during the first five contract years the minimum guaranteed rate of interest might be $4\frac{1}{2}\%$ or 4%, reducing to $3\frac{3}{4}\%$ or $3\frac{1}{2}\%$ for the 6th through the 10th years, and reducing once again to $3\frac{1}{2}\%$ or $3\frac{1}{4}\%$ after the 10th year.

The insurer will also be faced with the question of whether or not to extend these guarantees for existing plans at the point when the initial five-year period has expired. Factors the insurer will take into account at that time are the guarantees it is then offering to new policyholders, as well as the "experience status" the contract has achieved under the insurer's dividend or experience rating formula.

Because of these guarantees and the possibility of an adverse change in the investment market, the insurer may also limit the amount which the employer may contribute in any one contract year. Thus, the employer would be prevented from making excessive contributions in a particular year to take advantage of the insurer's guarantees at a time when adverse investment conditions prevail.

Another aspect of investment antiselection is involved in those unallocated funding instruments that contain a "liquidation" provision which allows the employer to transfer the unallocated or active life fund to another insurer or funding agency. The insurer, while generally granting the employer this privilege, will usually reserve the right to spread out payment of the fund over a period of time so as to be able to soften the impact of having to liquidate part of its assets under adverse investment conditions.

UNDERWRITING CONSIDERATIONS OF INDIVIDUAL POLICY PLANS

Individual policy pension and profit sharing plans present an insurer with several underwriting problems that are considerably different from those associated with group programs.

One of the most important distinctions is that practically all individual policy plans include immediate life insurance coverage as well as a deferred annuity benefit. The insurer is, therefore, faced with all of the underwriting considerations associated with individual life insurance. Most insurers will underwrite contracts issued in conjunction with a pension or a profit sharing plan in exactly the same fashion as they underwrite regular individual life insurance contracts—with the exception of utilizing guaranteed issue underwriting if the case meets with the insurer's requirements for the use of this underwriting technique.

A second major distinction concerns the administrative aspects of individual policy plans. While the insurer may classify this entire line of business as a separate class for dividend purposes there is no effective way of charging each plan for its own unusual expenses. Moreover, the insurer, for a number of internal administrative reasons, must make an effort to adopt and maintain uniform rules and practices for the administration of this type of business. As a result, the insurer is generally limited by cost and by administrative and equity considerations as to the extent to which services can be tailored to meet the needs of a particular individual policy plan.

In the past, most insurers utilized their standard contracts in connection with individual policy plans, making only those adjustments absolutely necessary to permit their use in this fashion. However, a number of insurers have now designed a special line of contracts for these plans—thus enabling the development of special contract provisions, the greater use of guaranteed issue underwriting, and the use of special systems and procedures. Special contracts also permit the insurer to classify this business separately for premium rate and dividend purposes.

While most insurers have reflected their federal tax relief directly in rates or guarantees for group pension contracts, this practice is generally not followed in connection with individual policy plans. Here, as the insurer's guarantees are usually for a longer term, this tax relief is passed on either in the form of a special lump sum payment each year or in the form of increased dividends. Because of these added payments or dividends, the insurer, from an underwriting viewpoint, is vitally interested in the acceptability of the plan to the Internal Revenue Service.

The underwriting considerations of investment antiselection under individual policy plans, while of interest to an insurer, do not have the same significance as under group pension plans. The employer is more or less limited by the provisions of the contracts as to how much money may be deposited with the insurer each year, as well as to how much money may be withdrawn. For these reasons, the insurer is not quite as concerned about problems of investment antiselection under individual policy plans as under group programs.

Minimum Requirements

Most insurers do not have any minimum requirements as to the number of lives that must be covered under an individual policy plan. As a result, most insurers will underwrite such a plan even if it involves only one employee.

However, there is some concern over the minimum size of the contracts issued, as well as the average-size contract at the time the plan is established. The majority of insurers will require that their standard minimum-size contract requirement be met with regard to the first layer of coverage an employee receives under such a plan. This requirement is usually relaxed, however, as to the coverage an employee becomes entitled to receive at a later time due to increases in salary. Here, most insurers will usually write a contract with a face amount as low as $1,000, even though this might not meet their normal minimum contract requirements. Because this exposes the insurer to writing a large number of small contracts, it will often require that the total amount of initial insurance generated at the outset of the plan produce an average-size contract which is considerably higher than its normal minimum contract requirements.

Eligibility Requirements

Adequate eligibility requirements are of particular importance to the insurer of an individual policy plan since the lack of them would permit temporary or short-term employees to be included in the plan. This could result in a loss to both the employer and the insurer in the event of an early lapse of contracts due to termination of employment. Most insurers will insist that the plan be designed with reasonable minimum service and age requirements.

Mortality Aspects

An individual policy plan affords the insurer a certain degree of protection as to mortality antiselection since many of the features which permit individual selection in the purchase of life insurance are absent. The insured, for example, cannot select the time that he will be insured. He is either eligible under the plan or he is not, and the amount of his insurance is not subject to his individual determination—rather, it is determined by the benefit formula of the plan. Also the group covered is actively at work. Thus, to a great extent, many of the safeguards of group underwriting are present.

Nevertheless, a certain amount of mortality antiselection may exist. The largest individual amounts of insurance will be on key executives of the firm who may have a voice in establishing the eligibility requirements and benefit formula of the plan. Also, in most instances, the group covered will be small, thus preventing the effective application of true group underwriting principles. Therefore, most insurers will insist that normal medical and underwriting requirements be met before insurance will be issued. The insurer will also look closely at the nature of the employer's business, as well as the occupations of the covered employees, in order to determine whether an undue underwriting hazard exists.

Guaranteed Issue Underwriting

If the group is large and there is a satisfactory distribution of risk by amount and age, most insurers will consider issuing some or all of the coverage on a guaranteed issue basis—i.e., the insurer will issue up to some stipulated amount for each individual employee without evidence of the employee's insurability. The requirements for guaranteed issue underwriting vary considerably from company to company. The following, however, will give some idea of the general practices followed by many insurers.

In most companies, the minimum number of lives required for guaranteed issue underwriting is 10, although a few companies may go lower. If employees contribute, there will also be a minimum participation requirement which ranges from about 75% for larger groups up to as much as 90% for smaller groups.

Many insurers, particularly those who have not developed a special line of contracts for qualified plans, do not automatically use guaranteed issue when their requirements have been met but offer guaranteed issue underwriting only when requested. In these instances, there is usually a reduction in the agent's compensation as well as in dividends if guaranteed issue underwriting is utilized. A number of the companies that have adopted special contracts for qualified plans reserve the right to determine whether or not guaranteed issue underwriting will be used, but tend to use this form of underwriting whenever possible. These companies do not generally distinguish between regularly underwritten and guaranteed issue business insofar as dividends and the agent's compensation are concerned.

A formula of some type is usually employed to determine the maximum amount of insurance that may be issued on any one life under a plan on a guaranteed issue basis. Typically, the formula will be one and one-half or two times the average amount of insurance called for by the plan (after excluding amounts on lives over the maximum age for guaranteed issue coverage and any amounts in excess of some scheduled maximum). Frequently, there is also some inside limit stipulated so that regardless of the result the formula produces, the maximum amount cannot exceed this inside limit. A typical inside limit would be $1,000 or $1,500 multiplied by the number of employees covered under the plan.

The amounts determined by such a formula are usually much lower than would be available under a typical group term life insurance program. One reason for this is that the insurer is in a position to adjust its yearly renewal rates and dividend or experience credits with respect to group term life insurance in the event of adverse mortality experience. In individual policy plans, where the insurer accepts the risk on a long-term basis, a more conservative approach is indicated.

Once the guaranteed issue limit has been determined, the question then arises as to what should be done with respect to the employee who is entitled to an initial amount of insurance which exceeds this limit by only a small amount—say, $1,000. Most insurers recognize this problem by allowing for a "spill-over" which permits guaranteed issue underwriting for small amounts in excess of the stipulated limit. If an employee is initially entitled to an amount which exceeds the total of the guaranteed issue and the spill-over limits, however, his coverage will be regularly underwritten for all amounts in excess of the guaranteed issue limit. The spill-over, in other words, is for the convenience of the insurer, not for the employer or his employees.

One further question arises as to how to handle small increases in coverage that are written in subsequent years due to increases in salary. Usually, there is no problem in issuing these amounts on a guaranteed issue basis until the total amount of insurance in force on an employee's life has reached the guaranteed issue limit (plus the spill-over, if applicable). After this point has been reached, the question is not as easy to resolve, and insurers differ widely in their treatment of this problem. In general, most insurers have worked out some method of issuing small amounts of insurance in subsequent years on a guaranteed issue basis up to some ultimate maximum limit. There will usually be some limit such as $2,000 or $2,500 which the insurer will issue on a guaranteed issue basis at any one time after the employee's total insurance has reached the initial guaranteed issue limit. If an individual is entitled to an increase in benefit of less than this amount, it will be issued on a guaranteed issue basis, but if the amount of his additional coverage exceeds this amount, the entire additional coverage will be subject to regular underwriting.

PLAN INSTALLATION
AND ADMINISTRATION

The advantages that a qualified plan will provide for an employer and his employee has been amply noted in previous chapters. These advantages are most significant, and it is important, from the employer's viewpoint, that they be gained at minimum expense and with minimum administrative effort.

For the most part, the factors involved in the installation or administration of a qualified plan are not complex. However, many of these factors are interdependent, and the relative timing of certain events can be most significant. Moreover, several parties are usually involved in the installation and administration of the program and, very often, these parties have divergent interests. Efficient plan installation and administration requires that the efforts of these parties be coordinated and that there be complete and thorough communication between all concerned. The life underwriter or plan consultant plays an important role in this respect.

This chapter will examine the steps involved in the installation of a qualified plan and discuss the various administrative aspects of such a program. A brief discussion of the Federal Disclosure Act is also included.

PLAN INSTALLATION

Preparation of Legal Documents

The first and most important step in the installation of any plan is the preparation of the necessary legal documents, such as the trust agreement and/or the plan instrument, authorizing resolutions, enrollment forms, etc. The employer's attorney is responsible for preparing the trust agreement, the plan instrument, or both, as the case may be. If a group pension contract is involved, the insurance company will prepare this document, but the employer's attorney should review the contract provisions.

Most insurers and corporate trustees have specimens of the various legal documents involved and will furnish them to the attorney who is working on a specific plan. It is particularly desirable for the attorney to have copies of these specimens (whether he uses them or not), since they generally will contain most of the requirements of the insurer or the trustee for the type of funding instrument involved. By giving the attorney this information, conflicts between the plan provisions and these requirements may be avoided or, at the least, these conflicts may be discussed before the instruments are finalized.

Plans Which Involve a Trust Agreement. It is possible to incorporate the plan provisions in the trust agreement, and this practice is usually followed in individual policy plans (particularly those that are fully insured) or where individuals are acting as trustees. It is also possible to have two separate documents—a plan instrument which establishes the details of the plan and a trust agreement which relates primarily to the duties, rights, and responsibilities of the trustee with respect to the investment and accountability of the plan assets. This latter approach is often used if a corporate trustee is involved, since many employers prefer to limit the role of the corporate trustee in a pension or profit sharing plan to that of an investor of plan assets. Thus, they prefer that the documents clearly establish the fact that administrative duties and responsibilities are vested in the employer or in a committee appointed by the employer. Moreover, a slight degree of flexibility is obtained by having two instruments in that the trustee's signature is not necessary for any changes in the plan instrument alone.

If the plan is insured in any way, it is desirable to submit a draft of all documents to the insurer's home office for review prior to execution. As a matter of fact, this step is required by some insurers as a part of their underwriting process. It is a good practice for the parties involved to do this so as to avoid any possible conflicts between the plan provisions, the insurer's underwriting and administrative requirements, and the trustee's responsibilities. Similarly, if there is to be a corporate trustee, it is advisable to submit a draft of the documents to the bank or trust company for approval prior to execution.

If the employer is a corporation, its board of directors should pass a resolution or resolutions authorizing the plan and appointing the trustee. If applicable, a committee should also be appointed.

Also, if required by state law or the firm's charter or bylaws, it may be necessary that an authorizing resolution be passed by the firm's stockholders.[1]

When all necessary papers have been prepared and are in acceptable form, the trust should be executed. At this time, the employer's first contribution is usually made to the trustee although, if possible, some employers prefer not to make a contribution (or prefer to make only a token contribution) until an approval letter for the plan has been received from the Internal Revenue Service. However, if insurance is to be placed in force, a contribution of an amount necessary to pay the premiums will have to be made. Most insurers will agree to refund this premium, less a risk charge, to the trustee if the plan is disapproved by the Internal Revenue Service within one year.

In an insured plan, the trust agreement generally requires that the insurance or annuity contracts will be applied for by the trustee and that the trustee will pay the first premiums due on such contracts. Since the individual or corporation who is to be the trustee cannot act in this capacity until the trust is in effect, it is important to recognize that the creation of the trust is a necessary condition which must be met before the insurance may be placed in force.

If employees are to be enrolled, the attorney should also prepare the enrollment form that will be signed by employees. If the plan is contributory, this form should include an authorization for the employer to withhold any employee contributions. It might also be desirable for the attorney to prepare a refusal form should any employee elect not to participate. Such a refusal form, signed by the employee, would be a record that the employee had been informed of his rights but had refused to accept them.

Group Pension Plans. A trust agreement is not employed in most group pension plans. The provisions of the plan are contained either in a plan instrument or in the group contract itself. If a plan instrument is involved, the group contract is usually written by the insurer on a "reference" basis—i.e., the group contract, while not spelling out the plan provisions, refers to the actual plan instrument to determine items such as eligibility, retirement benefits, vesting, etc. If a plan instrument is not involved, the group contract itself will contain these provisions. The employer's attorney will prepare any plan instrument involved and will review the terms of the group contract prepared by the insurer.

As in the case of a plan which employs a trust, it will be necessary to have the board of directors (and, where appropriate, the

---

[1] New Jersey and Colorado are two states where the statute requires stockholder approval. N.J. G.C.L., Section 14:9:2. Col. G.C.A., Section 40(b).

stockholders) pass an appropriate resolution authorizing the plan.

When an employer has decided to establish a group pension program, the first step is usually for the employer to submit a letter of application to the insurer for the group contract. This letter of application, along with a premium deposit and all pertinent information relating to the plan (including the plan instrument, if applicable), is forwarded to the insurance company. If all preliminary underwriting requirements are met, the insurer will accept the application and will then prepare the actual group contract. In many situations, particularly if the contract incorporates the actual plan provisions, a draft of the contract will be sent for the employer's approval. Once the final contract has been prepared (incorporating any changes mutually agreed upon between the insurer and the employer), the insurer generally obtains approval to issue the contract from the appropriate state insurance department, if such approval is necessary.[2] After any necessary state insurance department approval has been received, the final contract will be sent for execution by the employer.

Announcing the Plan to Employees

It is necessary, with all qualified plans, that the plan be announced to employees. This announcement may take the form of a letter (usually from the president of the firm), but it is often desirable to have a brochure or booklet printed for this purpose. If desired, most insurers will supply some form of printed announcement material in connection with a group pension program and, prior to the actual printing of this material, will usually furnish copy to the employer for approval. The actual cost of preparing this material is then usually charged to the employer through the insurer's dividend or experience rating formula.

In the case of a trust fund plan or a plan funded with individual contracts, the cost of preparing announcement material is often borne directly by the employer. Most insurers and corporate trustees will assist the employer in developing the actual content of the

---

[2] This is the state where the contract will be delivered and is generally the state in which the employer's principal place of business is located if that state requires that group pension contracts be approved prior to issue. It should be noted that while insurers attempt to standardize the provisions of their group contracts as much as possible, many insurers, because of variations required in a particular case, will submit each contract to the appropriate state insurance department for approval to issue the contract on a "single-case" basis. Since, in this area, insurers do not have the advantage of working with preapproved contract or policy forms, a group contract may take longer to issue than individual contracts.

brochure or booklet, and many will print this material, charging the employer only actual costs.

From the employer's viewpoint, the announcement material should be as attractive as possible, since it is the first as well as the major communication that employees will receive concerning the plan. A well-designed brochure or booklet will do a great deal in helping to obtain maximum employee awareness of the program and appreciation of its value.

The object of the announcement material is to explain the plan in clear and simple terms—but not at the price of accuracy. For this reason, it is important that this material be checked most carefully to make sure that it correctly describes the plan.

Enrollment of Employees

It is generally desirable to enroll employees even under a noncontributory plan. If the plan is contributory or if individual contracts are involved, an enrollment is always necessary. The enrollment usually takes place at the time the plan is announced to employees, or shortly thereafter. This enrollment normally involves the completion and signing of the enrollment form and, if the plan is contributory, the completion of the authorization for the employer to withhold the employee's contributions by payroll deduction. In a group program, the insurer will usually supply the enrollment and refusal cards that should be used. In trust fund plans, the corporate trustee will often be able to supply these forms, if desired.

In an individual policy plan, the application for the employee's insurance or annuity contract will also be completed at the time of enrollment and, if necessary, a medical examination will be arranged. Many medical examiners, when there are several lives to be examined, will agree to conduct these examinations at the employer's place of business. After the enrollment has been conducted, the insurance or annuity applications, appropriately signed by the trustee, should be submitted to the insurance company for underwriting approval. If the trust agreement is satisfactory to the insurer and if all of the insurer's underwriting requirements are met, both as to the plan and as to individual lives, contracts will be issued for delivery to the trustee.

Medical examinations are not generally required for group pension plans, although if group permanent insurance is involved, and if the plan requires amounts of insurance in excess of the nonmedical maximum, it is possible that a few employees will have to be examined.

Other Matters

Evidence of Participation. It is usually desirable that employees be given some evidence of their participation in the plan. Most insurers will provide some form of certificate or statement of participation in connection with both individual policy and group pension plans. In trust fund plans, the consultant will generally arrange to have this material prepared for the employer.

Signature Authority. If there is more than one trustee, the trust agreement will usually state whether actions taken by the trustees must be unanimous or by a majority vote or by one of the trustees. The same is also generally true with respect to the committee of a plan with a corporate trustee. Where unanimous or majority action is required, the instruments may still permit the trustees or committee to delegate to any one of their number the authority to sign documents or to perform ministerial duties on behalf of all. When the instruments contain such a provision, most trustees and committees find it desirable that such a delegation be made for administrative convenience. The insurer or corporate trustee, or both, will require that a copy of any such delegation be in their files if they are being asked to accept less than the full number of signatures otherwise required by the plan.

Checking Account. If individual trustees are involved, it is also desirable for the trustees to open a checking account since they have the responsibility of maintaining adequate records of money received and disbursed. Canceled checks and the accompanying statements are generally accepted as proof of payment or receipt and, for this reason, the trustees' account is most important.

Administrative Records. In addition to the record furnished by the trustees' checking account, it is most desirable that some or all of the administrative records described later in this chapter be established at the inception of the plan.[3] Adequate administrative records, maintained from the very beginning, can prove to be a most valuable adjunct to the smooth administration of the entire program.

TAX ASPECTS OF INSTALLATION[4]

To make sure that an employer receives a deduction for contributions made for the fiscal year in which the plan is established, it is important that all necessary requirements be met within the time

---

[3] See p. 280.

[4] The tax aspects of installation are discussed at greater length in Chapter 5.

allowed under federal tax law. Thus, if the plan involves a trust, the trust agreement should be executed by the close of the employer's fiscal year. If the employer is on a cash basis, the contribution should also be made by this time. If the employer is on an accrual basis, the contribution need not be made until the due date for filing the employer's tax return (including extensions), so long as the liability to make the contribution is established by the close of the fiscal year involved.

If a group pension contract is involved (without a trust), it is not necessary that the group contract be executed by the close of the employer's fiscal year if the employer is on an accrual basis and if the following steps have been taken by the end of such fiscal year.

1. The employer's board of directors has passed a resolution setting forth a definite plan for the purchase of retirement annuities under which a liability is created to provide the benefits.
2. An application has been made by the employer to the insurer for the group contract.
3. The insurer has accepted the application.
4. The group contract or an abstract has been prepared in sufficient detail to define the terms of the contract.
5. The plan has been communicated to employees.
6. An irrevocable part payment on account of the premiums due under the contract has been made.

If these steps have been taken, the actual execution and issuance of the final contract need not take place until the due date of the employer's tax return for the taxable year in which the plan is established (including extensions).

Obtaining an Advance Determination Letter

Regulations promulgated by the Commissioner of Internal Revenue are very specific in listing the information that must be filed in order to obtain an advance determination letter as to the qualified status of the plan.[5] Although it is not absolutely necessary that such an advance determination letter be obtained, it will be necessary to submit detailed information along with the employer's tax return for the first year in which a deduction is claimed. As a practical matter, most employers will file for such an advance determination letter as soon as possible after the plan has been installed. One reason for doing this is the possibility that the Internal Revenue Service will find some feature of the plan to be unacceptable. The Internal Revenue Code permits a plan to be changed retroactively

---

[5] This information is set forth in detail in Chapter 5. See pp. 121–123.

to its effective date if the change is made by the 15th day of the third month following the close of the employer's taxable year.[6] If changes are necessary, the employer may make appropriate amendments to the plan within this period and thereby preserve the deductions he wishes to claim for the taxable year involved. On the other hand, if the employer does not file for an advance determination letter, the qualified status of the plan will be examined by the Service at the time the employer's tax return is audited. Any changes then required by the Service will, in all probability, be at a time which is beyond the period allowed for making a retroactive change. This could result in the employer losing at least one year's deduction.

Substantiating the First-Year Deduction

At the end of the employer's fiscal year during which the plan was established, the employer is required to submit the same type of information that would be required for an advance determination letter, plus the financial and accounting information necessary to establish the deduction limit for contributions, the fact that actual contributions were made, and the amount of these contributions. This material should be submitted with the employer's tax return for the taxable year in question.

Treasury Department Form 2950 may be used for this purpose but, since this form was primarily designed for use in connection with deductions for the second and subsequent years, some practitioners feel that it is much easier to simply update and complete the material initially filed for an advance determination letter.

Taxpayer Identification Number

Under the Revenue Act of 1962, each taxpayer is required to obtain an identifying number. Even though a qualified pension or profit sharing *trust* is tax exempt, it, too, must obtain such a number. Treasury Department Form 3435 is used by the trustee for this purpose.

PLAN ADMINISTRATION

As a generalization, it might be said that the administration of pension and profit sharing plans is divided into two broad areas— actions which relate to the plan as a whole (such as cost calcula-

---

[6] It should be noted that although extensions granted for the filing of a tax return extend the time in which an accrual basis taxpayer may make his contributions to a plan, they do not extend the time during which a retroactive plan change may be made.

tions, tax aspects, etc.), and actions which relate to specific individuals (such as the processing of retirements, terminations of employment, etc.). Actions which relate to individuals may take place at any time during the plan year and often occur without any advance notice. Actions which relate to the plan as a whole generally take place once a year, usually around the anniversary date of the plan.

While group and individual policy pension and profit sharing plans are similar in many ways, they differ considerably in plan administration, particularly in the role played by the life underwriter. Generally speaking, most insurers utilize the same administrative practices for contracts issued in conjunction with individual policy plans as they do for their ordinary life business as a whole. These systems are such that only infrequently will the home office of the insurer have direct contact with the employees or the employer. Thus, most contacts with the employer and employees will be at the field level. For this reason, the role played by the life underwriter and the agency office in the administration of individual policy plans is most important.

In contrast, most insurers will administer their group pension and profit sharing programs in a manner such that the home office is in direct contact with the employer—or the services of the local group field office will be utilized. The life underwriter and the agency office are generally involved only in important or unusual matters. To aid in this concept of direct administration between the employer and the home office, the insurer will usually furnish the employer with an administration manual or guide and a supply of administrative forms at the time the plan is installed. With this manual and supporting material, the employer is in a position to be in direct contact with the home office in most items of plan administration.

In trust fund plans, the plan administration is often handled by the consultant, and the corporate trustee acts primarily as an investor of the plan assets and makes disbursements as directed by the employer or committee. Some larger employers even maintain a full-time staff to administer their employee benefit plans. Consultants are also frequently involved in insured plans, particularly those which employ some form of group pension contract. Here, much of the plan administration and record keeping normally performed by the insurer is handled by the consultant, the insurer to a great extent acting within its contract terms as directed by the employer or consultant.

The following material discusses, very briefly, the major areas involved in plan administration. No attempt has been made to discuss specific administrative procedures, since these vary considerably among insurers, banks and trust companies, and consultants.

Cost and Actuarial Aspects

An important aspect of the administration of any pension plan is the determination of the annual contributions to be made under the plan. For a fully insured individual policy or group permanent plan, this is a relatively simple matter, since the annual contribution will be the sum of the premiums due on existing coverage plus the first premiums due on new coverage then being issued for new entrants or with respect to benefit increases, less any employer credits.

For a group deferred annuity contract, the annual contribution will be the premiums calculated by the insurer to purchase the future service benefits accruing during the year plus, if applicable, a premium toward the liquidation of any unfunded supplemental liability, less any employer credits.

The determination of annual contributions becomes a little more complicated for those plans which employ, in whole or in part some form of unallocated funding instrument. Here, it will be necessary that some form of actuarial valuation be made. For an individual policy or group permanent combination plan, a portion of the annual contribution will consist of premiums then due. The balance will consist of the deposit which must be made to the conversion fund, and this portion must be actuarially determined. Most insurers will perform the calculations necessary to determine the estimated deposits to this fund. A few insurers will do these calculations only when they are holding this fund; however, if not holding the fund, they will supply appropriate tables and instructions to aid in the determination of the annual plan contribution. In any event, certain data must be obtained each year in order to perform these calculations. These data include a revised employee census which indicates new entrants, changed benefits, terminations that have occurred during the prior year, etc.

Most insurers will perform the actuarial valuations needed in conjunction with unallocated group funding instruments, such as group deposit administration contracts, or will accept the actuarial valuations made for the plan by an actuarial consulting firm. In a trust fund plan, the actuarial valuations will be performed by an actuarial firm. For the actuary to perform these calculations, he will need the employee information referred to above. Usually, the consultant or the insurer will have given the employer detailed instructions as to when and how these data should be compiled.

Tax Aspects of Administration

Deductions. Treasury Department Form 2950 is mandatory for use by employers in claiming deductions for contributions made in the second and subsequent plan years. This form is generally filed with the employer's tax return for the taxable year involved.

Cash basis taxpayers must make the actual contribution during the taxable year for which the deduction is claimed. Accrual basis taxpayers need not make the actual contribution during a given taxable year and will be allowed a deduction for the contribution for such year if a liability to make the contribution was established before the close of such year and the actual contribution is made before the due date for filing the employer's tax return for such taxable year (including extensions).

Annual Report—Form 990-P. If a trust is involved, the trustee must file Treasury Department Form 990-P each year within five months and 15 days of the close of the trust's accounting period (usually the plan year). The purpose of this form is to establish that the trust continues as an exempt organization and that the income earned by the trust is not taxable. If a trust has unrelated business income which is taxable, this should be reported by the trustee on Treasury Department Form 990-T.[7]

Annual Information Returns—Forms 1096 and 1099. Treasury Department Form 1099 is an information return which the trustee must file for each beneficiary who receives a payment or distribution from the trust of $600 or more in any calendar year.[8] A copy of this form must be given to the payee before January 31 of the year following the calendar year during which the payment was made. Returns on Form 1099 are in the nature of unverified schedules showing the name and address of the payee, the kind and amount of income paid, and the name and address of the payor. The schedules are summarized on Treasury Department Form 1096, which is the actual "return" for the trust and which must be filed by the payor with the Internal Revenue Service by February 28 of the year following the calendar year in which the payments were made.

It should be noted that these forms must be filed even though the payment is made up in part or in whole by the cash value of an insurance or an annuity contract which is being transferred out of the trust.

In a group pension plan without a trust, it is the responsibility of the insurance company to file these forms.

---

[7] Unrelated business income of a trust is discussed in Chapter 5. See pp. 127–28.

[8] If the insurer makes the payment, it, too, must file this information, with the result that there is some duplication.

PS 58 Costs. When a participant in a qualified plan is protected by level premium life insurance, he is considered, under federal tax law, to be in constructive receipt of the value of the pure insurance protection of his contract.[9] The term cost of this pure insurance protection is, therefore, considered to be additional taxable income to the participant. This cost of insurance (often called the PS 58 cost because the original Treasury Department ruling on the subject was so numbered) in some cases is automatically furnished each year by the insurer or may be readily determined from tables supplied by the insurer.

It should be noted that the PS 58 costs are considered as a distribution from the trust and, if the amount involved (together with any other distributions) is $600 or more, the trustee must report this on Form 1099. In most situations the annual PS 58 cost will be less than this amount, with the result that the trustee will not be required to file Form 1099 for actively employed participants. This fact, however, does not relieve the employee of the obligation of including these amounts as taxable income each year. Failure to include these amounts as taxable income could result in the entire insurance proceeds being taxable as income to the employee's beneficiary in the event of his death.[10] For this reason, many trustees report the PS 58 costs even though the amount involved is less than $600.

Records

A pension or a profit sharing plan can be expected to exist over a considerable length of time, and it is reasonable to expect that during its existence, several different individuals will be responsible for its administration. Thus, it is most important that adequate records be established at the outset of the plan and that these records be maintained in sufficient detail to permit orderly and consistent plan administration.

Records for the plan as a whole should include a list of the names, addresses, and telephone numbers of all individuals who are associated with the plan and its administration. This would include the trustees, any committee members, the life underwriter, the

---

[9] If the plan is contributory and the plan so provides, employees contributions may be first applied to meet the cost of the insurance protection, thus eliminating or minimizing the employee's current tax liability for this benefit. Most plans are written in this manner.

[10] See p. 142.

consultant, the attorney, the accountant, etc. These plan records should also include a complete history of all plan receipts and disbursements. A digest of the major plan provisions would be most helpful to the plan administrator so as to avoid repeated reference to the legal documents constituting the plan. A major portion of the permanent plan records generally includes appropriate memoranda, letters, or minutes which support decisions made in the interpretation of the legal documents or in the exercise of discretionary powers granted to the trustee or committee.

The record maintained for each employee should list such pertinent data as his Social Security number, his date of birth, the type of proof submitted to verify this birthdate, the date of birth of his joint annuitant (if applicable), the effective date of his participation in the plan, his scheduled normal retirement date, his current beneficiary designation (if applicable), etc. This record should show, on a cumulative basis, the employee's earnings (if benefits are related to compensation), his projected benefit under the plan, and his current death benefit (if any). If the plan employs individual insurance or annuity contracts, the record should also include information relating to his contract or contracts such as contract numbers, dates of issue, cash values, rating action, etc.

If employees contribute under the plan, the employee record should include a history of these contributions. Also, if PS 58 costs are involved, a record of these should be maintained, since such costs will be part of the employee's cost basis for any future distributions under the plan.

It is also desirable to maintain, with respect to each employee, a record of each calculation made to determine his benefits. This could be most helpful in producing a consistent application of the plan's benefit formula.

Benefit Payments

Benefits are generally paid out under a pension plan only upon retirement, death, termination of employment, or disability. Under a profit sharing plan, benefits may also be paid out at other times, but most profit sharing plans limit distributions to these contingencies.

It is important to note that the trust or plan instrument will often contain limitations as to what can or cannot be done in the way of benefit payments. Moreover, in an insured plan the insurance company may impose certain limitations consistent with its underwriting and administrative systems. Any such limitations must be carefully observed in paying or providing benefits under any contingency.

Even though certain limitations may exist, the employee will often have a wide choice as to the manner in which his benefit may be paid. His options should be carefully and fully explained, and it should be remembered that tax consequences will frequently play an important role in reaching a decision as to how benefits should be received. In any situation where tax consequences could be of significance, the employee should seek the guidance of his tax counsel before making a decision.[11]

Employee Communications

An important part of the administration of any plan is the manner in which employees are initially informed and then reminded of their plan benefits and the value of these benefits.

The employer's size often indicates the course of action best suited for communicating with employees. For example, if the employer is large enough to have some form of publication for employees, this is an ideal vehicle in which to periodically point out the benefits and value of the plan.

Many employers like to give each employee some type of annual report that shows the employee's accrued and projected plan benefits, as well as their value when this can be ascertained under the funding instrument or actuarial cost method involved. This type of report can be most effective in giving an employee a better understanding of his plan benefits.

Other techniques for publicizing the plan would be bulletin board announcements, payroll envelope stuffers, personal letters, contests, preretirement counseling, etc. The important point to be kept in mind is that the plan should be repeatedly publicized and by the method best suited for the particular employer, taking into account the employee relations pattern that has developed within the firm.

---

[11] Apart from the aspect of securing appropriate advice from tax counsel, there is the further consideration that any advice given to an employee should be full and complete. In *Gediman* v. *Anheuser Busch,* 299 F. 2d 537, the employer gave an employee advice concerning the various options available as to the distribution of his benefit. This advice did not make it sufficiently clear that if the employee elected one of the methods and died before receiving a distribution, his benefits would be considerably smaller than under the other methods. The court held the employer liable for negligence when the employee, in reliance on this advice, elected a method which caused his estate to lose benefits on his subsequent death. The court observed that: "[The employer,] having undertaken to advise, . . . was bound to advise clearly."

FEDERAL DISCLOSURE ACT

The Federal Disclosure Act requires the administrators of certain plans to disclose certain information.[12] The following plans are not subject to this Act:

1. Those plans covering less than 26 participants, both active and retired.
2. Those plans administered by the federal government or by the government or political subdivision of a state or by any of their agencies or instrumentalities.
3. Those plans established and maintained for the purpose of complying with workmen's compensation laws or unemployment compensation disability insurance laws.
4. Those plans administered as a corollary to membership in a fraternal organization described in Section 501 (c) (8) of the Internal Revenue Code and plans of charitable organizations exempt from taxation under Section 501 (c) (3) and (4) of the Code, except those plans administered by a fraternal benefit society or organization representing its members in collective bargaining.

The Act defines the administrator as the person with ultimate or actual responsibility for the control, disposition, or management of the money required or contributed. If this control, disposition, or management is exercised through an agent or trustee, the administrator is the person or persons who have designated such agent or trustee.

Plan Description

If a plan is subject to the Act, U.S. Department of Labor Form D-1 must be filed with the office of Labor-Management and Welfare-Pension Reports. This form must be filed within 90 days of the establishment of the plan. The form is a description of the plan containing, among other items, the names and addresses of those persons having overall responsibility for the plan, their official position with the plan, and their relationship, if any, to the employer or employee organization. The submission of this form will be acknowledged by the Office of Labor-Management and Welfare-Pension Reports, and an identifying number will be assigned. This number must be entered on any documents subsequently submitted.

---

[12] Several states have also enacted disclosure laws. These states include: Connecticut, Massachusetts, New York, Washington, and Wisconsin. For a discussion of these state disclosure laws, as well as a more detailed discussion of the Federal Disclosure Act, see *Pension and Profit Sharing Tax Service* (Englewood Cliffs, N.J.: Prentice-Hall, Inc., n.d.), ¶ 6351, *et seq.*

If the plan is amended, this must be reported to the Office of Labor-Management and Welfare-Pension Reports within 60 days after the change has been made. This can be done in either of two ways—a new and corrected Form D-1 may be submitted, properly identified as a revised filing, or the additional information may be submitted properly executed and labeled "to be incorporated into original submission which has been marked with file number (insert file number)."

Annual Reports

If the plan covers 100 or more employees, the plan administrator, within 150 days of the end of the annual accounting period, must file Department of Labor Form D-2 with the Office of Labor-Management and Welfare-Pension Reports. This form is a comprehensive financial and statistical report on the operation of the plan during such accounting period. If the plan is insured, the insurer must supply and certify the information required from it to the plan administrator within 120 days of the end of the accounting period.

If the plan covers from 26 to 99 employees, Department of Labor Form D-3 is used. This is a very simple form which does not require the reporting detail set forth in Form D-2.

Publication

Besides filing this information with the Department of Labor, the plan administrator must make copies of the plan description and the latest annual report available for examination by any participant or beneficiary at the plan's principal office. Also, if requested in writing by a participant or beneficiary, the plan administrator must mail a copy of the plan description and an adequate summary of the latest annual report to the last known address of such participant or beneficiary. If the plan administrator fails to mail this information within 30 days of the written request, he may be subject to a penalty of $50 for each day of failure to comply (payable to the person making the request), plus costs and reasonable attorney's fees.

The Department of Labor maintains a public documents room where this material is available for examination. Copies of the plan descriptions and annual reports may also be purchased by payment of the appropriate fee. These copies may be obtained by mail if sufficient identifying information is submitted with the request.

Bonding

The Act requires that administrators, officers, and employees of welfare and pension plans who handle funds or property be bonded for at least the greater of $1,000 and 10% of the funds handled. Insurance companies and corporate trustees, and their agents, need not be bonded since they are not, in this context, administrators. In the typical pension of profit sharing trust, the individual trustees (and/or any committee members) should be bonded for at least 10% of the trust funds and at least 10% of the annual employer and employee contributions. If insurance or annuity contracts are involved, they should also be bonded for at least 10% of the cash values of such contracts.

There are few occasions under a group pension plan where bonding is required. In most situations, premiums are paid directly from the general accounts of the employer to the insurer and, in these instances, a bond is not necessary. However, if a group pension contract is issued to a trust, the trustee should be bonded. Also, if employees contribute under a group pension plan, and if these contributions are withheld and deposited to a separate account before they are paid to the insurer, the person with authority to draw on those contributions should be bonded.

Record Retention

The Act requires the plan administrator and any person certifying information to keep all reports and supporting data for at least five years. Microfilm may be used for this purpose if adequate viewing equipment is available and if the microfilmed records are clear reproductions with identifiable dates. Punched cards and magnetic tape may also be used, but the original data to verify such coded data must also be retained.

Enforcement

A person who willfully violates any provision of the law is punishable by fine or imprisonment, or both. In addition, certain offenses are considered as federal crimes and are punishable by fine, imprisonment, or both. These offenses include: (1) an offer, acceptance, or solicitation to influence the operation of an employee benefit plan; (2) a false statement or concealment of fact in relation to documents required by the disclosure law; and (3) theft or embezzlement from an employee benefit plan.

13

PROFIT SHARING PLANS

Profit sharing plans constitute an important component in the overall structure of fringe benefit programs in the United States. Many individuals fail to realize the extent of the popularity of profit sharing plans in employee benefit planning. In 1955, newly established qualified pension plans exceeded by a considerable margin the number of new profit sharing plans—67% versus 37%. However, by 1960, the number of new qualified pension and profit sharing plans were about equal. In the past few years, Internal Revenue Service figures on determination letters indicate a slight preference for pension plans over profit sharing plans—about 56% versus 44%.

The purpose of this chapter is to discuss the basic features of qualified profit sharing plans. Consideration will also be given to the way in which profit sharing funds might be invested in insurance contracts.

DEFINITION OF PROFIT SHARING

Many definitions of profit sharing have been suggested.[1] One expert in this area defines profit sharing as a plan in which the company's contributions are based upon business profits, regardless of whether the benefit payments are made in cash, or are deferred, or are a combination of the two.[2] The above definition suggests three basic types of profit sharing plans which may be defined as follows:[3] (1) current (cash)—profits are paid directly to employees in cash, check, or stock as soon as profits are determined (for

---

[1] For a discussion of these definitions, see B. L. Metzger, *Profit Sharing in Perspective* (Evanston, Ill.: Profit Sharing Research Foundation, 1964), p. 1.

[2] *Ibid.*

[3] *Ibid.*, p. 2.

287

example, monthly, quarterly, semiannually, or annually) ; (2) deferred—profits are credited to employee accounts to be paid at retirement or other stated dates or circumstances (for example, disability, death, severance, or under withdrawal provisions) ; and (3) combination—part of the profit is paid out currently in cash and part is deferred; this can take place under one plan with both current and deferred features, or under two separate plans, one cash and the other deferred, covering, by and large, the same employee groups.

Since this chapter is concerned with qualified plans, let us now turn to a consideration of the definition of a profit sharing plan as set forth in Federal Income Tax Regulations.

A profit sharing plan is a plan established and maintained by an employer to provide for the participation in his profits by his employees or their beneficiaries. The plan must provide a definite predetermined formula for allocating the contributions made to the plan among the participants and for distributing the funds accumulated under the plan after a fixed number of years, the attainment of a stated age, or upon the prior occurrence of some event such as layoff, illness, disability, retirement, death, or severance of employment.[4]

Qualification of profit sharing plans for tax exemption under Section 401 of the Internal Revenue Code, then, is restricted to deferred or combination type plans. Current or cash profit sharing plans, therefore, are not treated in this chapter.

QUALIFICATION REQUIREMENTS

The qualification requirements for profit sharing plans are, for the most part, identical to those applicable to pension plans, a detailed discussion of which can be found in Chapter 5. However, it is appropriate, in this chapter, to discuss these requirements in terms of their application specifically to profit sharing plans.

Coverage Requirements

In order to qualify, a profit sharing plan must be for the exclusive benefit of employees or their beneficiaries. Therefore, a plan will not qualify if the coverage requirements result in discrimination in favor of officers, stockholders, supervisors, or highly compensated employees. Restriction of coverage by type of employment (for example, salaried employees, hourly employees, salesmen) is

---

[4] Reg. 1.40–1 (b) (1) (ii).

permitted, provided that such coverage requirements do not result in the prohibited discrimination.

Most profit sharing plans exclude seasonal and part-time employees. Relatively few plans impose an age requirement, but practically all profit sharing plans specify a service requirement as a condition for participation in the plan. However, the service requirements under profit sharing plans are usually no greater than three years. Also, maximum age requirements, often found in pension plans, are rarely used under profit sharing plans. Lastly, minimum compensation requirements as a condition for participation are seldom found in profit sharing plans.

Thus, the eligibility requirements under profit sharing plans generally tend to be less restrictive than those usually found under pension plans. There are several possible explanations for this fact. First of all, profit sharing plans are often established to provide a direct incentive for employees to increase output and reduce operating costs. If this is the primary objective of the plan, it is only logical that few restrictions on participation be imposed. Second, if the employer is establishing the plan primarily for personal tax reasons, liberal eligibility requirements may produce relatively favorable results for himself. Since the nonvested accumulations of terminating employees are reallocated among remaining participants, the employer may be less concerned about the scope of coverage under the plan. Third, the cost problem of funding a defined benefit for an older entrant under a pension plan is nonexistent in the case of a profit sharing plan. Since a participant under a profit sharing plan is never entitled to any more than the accumulations credited to his account, there is no need to impose a maximum age requirement. Lastly, as will be seen, few profit sharing plans are integrated with Social Security benefits because of limitations imposed on this type of plan under federal tax law.

Contribution Requirements

The Internal Revenue Code does not require, as a condition for qualification, that a profit sharing plan include a definite predetermined contribution formula. However, the Regulations require that "substantial and recurring" contributions must be made out of profits if the requirement of plan permanency is to be met.

Contributions under a profit sharing plan then, may be made on a discretionary basis (for example, as determined annually by the board of directors of the company) or in accordance with a definite predetermined formula. The discretionary approach offers the advantage of contribution flexibility. The board of directors can ad-just contributions in view of the firm's current financial position and capital needs. Also, the discretionary basis precludes the possi-bility of contribution payments exceeding the maximum amount currently deductible for federal income tax purposes (to be dis-cussed later in this chapter). If the amount of contributions is discretionary, the plan often imposes certain minimums and/or maximums. For example, the plan may provide that "contributions cannot exceed 15% of profits, but it is discretionary up to that limit" or "10% to 30% of profits—percentage to be determined by board of directors" or "discretionary, but approximately 25% of profits before taxes."[5]

Several advantages are also offered in support of a definite pre-determined formula.[6] First, a definite formula promotes increased employee morale and feelings of security. Without a definite for-mula, the employee may feel that he cannot count on a share of what he has helped to produce. Second, a definite formula provides a built-in safeguard protecting an accrual basis employer's right to make contribution payments by the fifteenth day of the third month following the close of the tax year and still deduct these contribu-tions on his tax return for that year. Without a definite formula, failure by such an employer to fix his liability for contribution pay-ments before the end of the year could result in a loss of his deduction for the year. Lastly, the Wage-Hour Division requires a definite formula if a company wants to exclude its contributions from regular pay rates in computing overtime. In other words, failure to use a definite formula may result in the payment of extra overtime.

Whether a definite formula or a discretionary contribution ap-proach is to be used, management must still determine the extent to which employees are to share in the firm's profits. In arriving at this decision, management must take into account such factors as the objectives of the plan, the nature of the firm's business, the pattern of profits, the age and sex composition of the employee group, etc. Obviously, a good deal more thought must be given to this matter if a definite contribution formula is used.

The contribution commitment under definite formula plans is generally expressed as a fixed percentage or a sliding scale of percentages of profits. The specified percentages are usually applied to profits before taxes, although the base of after-tax profits is also permitted. The sliding scale formulas provide for higher percent-

---

[5] Metzger, *op. cit.*, p. 47.

[6] *The Profit Sharing Guidebook* (Englewood Cliffs, N.J.: Prentice-Hall, Inc., 1960), p. 38.

age contributions for higher levels of profits. A percentage-of-compensation formula can also be used, if the plan imposes conditions pertaining to levels of profits. Without this condition, a percentage-of-compensation plan would probably be classified as a defined contribution (money purchase) pension plan rather than a profit sharing plan.

Whether a definite formula or discretionary basis is used, the plan usually specifies some limitation on the amount of annual contributions payable. One reason for this is to assure stockholders of a minimum rate of return on capital. Limitations on contribution payments can be expressed in several different ways. For example, the plan may provide that no contribution will be made in years in which dividend payments are less than a specified amount, or unless aggregate profits exceed a stated amount, or if profits are less than a given percentage of the firm's capital funds. Many plans also impose the limitation that contributions in any one year cannot exceed the maximum amount deductible for federal income tax purposes.

Employee Contributions

It is conceptually illogical to require employee contributions under profit sharing plans. Furthermore, in those plans that require employee contributions, the employer's contribution is based on the amount of the employee's contribution, subject to the requirement that there must be profits. For these reasons, contributory plans are generally referred to as thrift or savings plans to distinguish them from the traditional profit sharing plans. However, the tax aspects of thrift plans are determined in accordance with the profit sharing rules of the Internal Revenue Service. Therefore, thrift plans are considered to be profit sharing plans for purposes of the discussion in this chapter.

If employee contributions are required under the plan, full payment of the required amount becomes an eligibility requirement for participation in the plan. Therefore, care must be exercised in setting the employee contribution rate. Employee contribution rates are normally expressed as a percentage of compensation (for example, 5%). If the contribution rate is too high, the Internal Revenue Service may conclude that the requirement will effectively preclude participation by the lower-paid employees, thereby producing discriminatory coverage in favor of the "prohibited" group. An employee contribution requirement of 6% or less will generally be considered by the Internal Revenue Service as not being discriminatory.

Under a contributory plan, the employer's contribution commitment is normally expressed in terms of employee contributions. For example, the employer may match employee contributions or contribute 50 cents for every dollar of employee contributions. In some plans the employer's contribution rate, while related to employee contributions, may vary depending on the level of profits. In that case, the plan more nearly approximates the true concept of profit sharing.

Some profit sharing plans permit voluntary employee contributions in excess of the amount required for participation in the plan. This can be a valuable privilege for employees, since the investment income of a qualified trust is tax free. Furthermore, a substantial portion of the assets of many profit sharing plans will be invested in equities, thereby offering the employee the investment and low-cost advantages of participation in a large investment fund. Of course, the employer's contribution under a thrift plan is expressed in terms of the employee's required contributions and is not influenced by any voluntary employee contributions. Because of the tax-free status of the investment income, the Internal Revenue Service imposes a maximum on the amount of voluntary employee contributions, the limit generally being 10% of compensation. Therefore, if an employee is required to contribute 5% of compensation in order to participate in the plan, he can make additional voluntary contributions of up to 10% of compensation, or a maximum, in this case, of 15% of compensation.

Contribution Allocation Formula

It was noted above that the Internal Revenue Service does not require that the plan include a definite *contribution* formula as a condition for qualification. However, it is necessary that the plan include a definite *allocation* formula in order to become qualified. Since contributions to the plan are generally based on profits, a method or formula is needed to determine the amount to be credited to each participant's account.

The employer must decide the basis upon which the contributions to the plan are to be divided among the various participants. The allocation of contributions to the account of each participant is usually made on the basis of compensation, or a combination of compensation and service. If compensation is used, then allocations are made on the basis of the proportion of each participant's compensation to the total compensation of all participants. For example, if employee "A" earns $10,000 a year and the total annual compensation for all participants is $200,000, "A" will be credited with 5% of the employer's total annual contributions. Under a formula which reflects both compensation and service, for example, a unit of credit might be given for each year of service and an additional unit for each $100 of compensation. If employee "A" had 20 years of service, he would have 20 units for service and 100 units for his compensation of $10,000 a year. His share of contributions will be determined, therefore, by the fraction of 120 over the total number of units similarly calculated for all participants.

The Internal Revenue Service requires a definite allocation formula in qualified plans in order that it may determine whether contributions are shared in a nondiscriminatory manner. In general, allocations based on compensation meet the test of nondiscrimination. However, introduction of years of service into the formula may produce discrimination, in view of the fact that employees included in the "prohibited" group often have long periods of service with the firm. If application of the allocation formula indicates that discrimination might result, then the Internal Revenue Service may require modification of the formula before issuing an approval letter. The most popular allocation formulas are those based on compensation, although many plans use a combination of compensation and years of service.

Lest there be any confusion, it should be noted that the allocation formula is used to determine the employee's share of contributions for accounting or record-keeping purposes. The contribution dollars are not segregated on behalf of each participant. Contributions are received, administered, and invested by the trustee as one common fund. The balance in each participant's account represents his share at that moment of the assets of the fund. Whether he is currently entitled to all or a part of the money credited to his account depends upon the provisions of the plan. An exception to the above view is the case where the trust permits each participant's account to be invested in "earmarked" investments, such as an insurance contract.

Integration with Social Security

As mentioned earlier, profit sharing plans are seldom integrated with Social Security benefits. However, these plans can be integrated with Social Security benefits, subject to the requirements imposed by the Internal Revenue Service. For example, it is permissible to establish a plan in which only employees earning in excess of the Social Security maximum taxable wage base are eligible for participation. In that case, however, the maximum annual amount that can be allocated to each participant's account is limited to

9⅜% of his annual compensation in excess of $4,800. It should be noted that the maximum of 9⅜% pertains to the aggregate of employer contributions and forfeitures during the year of non-vested accumulations. In nonintegrated profit sharing plans, the maximum deductible annual contribution is 15% of compensation. Furthermore, if the plan is not integrated, forfeitures are reallocated among remaining participants without limit (i.e., without reducing the 15% maximum). In an integrated profit sharing plan, forfeitures must be used to reduce employer contributions. Also, non-integrated plans have a credit carry-over feature (to be discussed later in this chapter) which permits, under certain circumstances, annual contributions of up to an additional 15% of compensation. The 9⅜% limitation under an integrated plan is applied without the benefit of any carry-over provision. Lastly, the Internal Revenue Service does not permit an employer to integrate both his pension and profit sharing plan with Social Security benefits if both plans cover the same employees. The objective of this require-ment is to avoid the discrimination in favor of higher-salaried employees that would result.

In addition to the excess formula, stepped-up integration for-mulas can also be used with profit sharing plans. Under a stepped-up formula, eligibility for participation would not be based on compensation. However, a higher allocation rate would be ap-plied to compensation in excess of $4,800 a year. For example, if the allocation rate on the first $4,800 is 5%, then compensation in excess of $4,800 can be credited with contributions of 14⅜%.

Provision for Distributions

As indicated earlier, the definition of profit sharing in the Regu-lations permit distributions "after a fixed number of years, the attainment of a stated age, or upon the prior occurrence of some event such as layoff, illness, disability, retirement, death, or sever-ance of employment."[7]

The primary objective of deferred profit sharing plans is to permit the employee to build up an equity in the fund to enhance his economic security for his retirement years. The Internal Revenue Service requires that the accumulations credited to the employee's account vest in full at retirement date. Most plans also fully vest the amounts credited to the employee upon his death, while a lesser but still significant number of plans provide full and immediate vesting upon the occurrence of disability.

---

[7] Reg. 1.401–1 (b) (1) (ii).

Whether an employee is entitled to a distribution from the fund upon voluntary termination of employment or upon being laid-off depends upon the vesting provisions of the plan. Of course, if the plan is contributory, the employee is always entitled, as a minimum, to a return of his contributions (usually with the investment earnings attributable to his contributions) upon death, disability, or severance of employment.

Most deferred profit sharing plans provide for a degree of vesting in the event of severance of employment. Indeed, it would be difficult to obtain approval of the plan by the Internal Revenue Service if the plan does not provide some vesting upon separation of employment (for reasons other than death, disability, and retirement). The reason for this lies in the fact that under profit sharing plans, the nonvested accumulations of terminating employees are reallocated among the remaining participants. Since employees in the "prohibited" group tend to be long-service employees, the forfeitures of terminating employees would substantially increase the shares of the employees in the former group. Over a long period of time, a very substantial proportion of all employer contributions would effectively accrue to the benefit of stockholders and supervisory and other high-salaried employees. Thus, the absence of a vesting provision in the plan for separating employees would generally be viewed by the Internal Revenue Service as being discriminatory. It will be recalled that employer credits attributable to the nonvested portion of benefits under pension plans are applied toward a reduction of future employer contributions. In the case of a profit sharing plan, the employer is entitled to the full maximum annual contribution without reduction for the amount forfeited by terminating employees. (An exception to the above statement, as noted earlier, is the case of an integrated profit sharing plan in which the maximum annual contribution is reduced by forfeitures reallocated during the year.) The possibility for discrimination under a profit sharing plan due to an absence of a vesting provision should, therefore, be clear. Thus, the Internal Revenue Service will generally require vesting under a qualified profit sharing plan, and at a relatively rapid rate.

There is a considerable range of vesting provisions found in profit sharing plans. Few plans provide for full and immediate vesting. Likewise, very few plans offer deferred and full vesting— for example, no vesting for the first five years, with 100% vesting thereafter. However, a deferred and full vesting provision may be used, if it does not produce discrimination under the circumstances. Graded deferred vesting provisions are by far the most prevalent type of formula found in profit sharing plans. For example, a plan may offer no vesting for the first three years, 30% vesting after three years, increasing 10% each year thereafter so that 100% vesting is reached after 10 years of participation. Typically, the length of time it takes to become fully vested under most plans is 10 or 15 years.

Therefore, under most profit sharing plans, there will still be some forfeited amounts to be reallocated among remaining participants. The reallocations are generally based on the compensation of each remaining participant in relation to the total compensation of remaining participants. The Internal Revenue Service will not permit reallocations on the basis of the account balance of each of the remaining participants if such a procedure would produce discrimination. However, it should be noted that the investment income of a qualified profit sharing trust may be allocated on the basis of the account balances of participants. Thus, it is possible to have different allocation formulas for contributions, forfeitures, and investment income.

Some plans also permit participants to withdraw a portion of their vested benefits in the plan prior to separation of employment. The Regulations permit distributions from a qualified profit sharing plan "after a fixed number of years." The Internal Revenue Service has interpreted this to mean that accumulations cannot be distributed in less than two years.[8] In other words, if contributions have been credited to an employee's account for three years, he can withdraw an amount equal to the first year's contribution and the investment income credited in that year (assuming that the plan permits such withdrawals). Withdrawal provisions are more prevalent in contributory plans. The right to withdraw may be restricted to employee contributions, or it may apply to the vested portion of accumulations attributable to employer contributions. It should be noted that the participant loses the right to investment income and forfeitures with reference to the withdrawn amounts. Of course, the participant must report the withdrawn amounts as taxable income in the year in which it is received, and such amounts will be taxable as ordinary income. The question also arises as to whether the right to withdraw constitutes constructive receipt of allocated annual contributions and investment income, with the possible result that such amounts will be taxable as income whether or not they are actually withdrawn. In general, the loss of investment income and reallocated forfeitures are sufficient penalties to avoid application of the doctrine of constructive receipt to the annual allocations not withdrawn. Although a withdrawal provi-

---

[8] Rev. Rul. 65–178, Part 2(c), IRB 1965–28; Rev. Rul. 54–231, CB 1954–1, 150.

sion may be desirable in a plan, care should be exercised, since a provision that is too liberal could result in defeating the long-term savings objective of the plan.

Loan provisions are also found in a number of deferred profit sharing plans. Under a loan provision, a participant is generally entitled to borrow up to a specified percentage (75%, for example) of the vested portion of his account (plus up to 100% of his contributions, if any). The loan must be repaid in accordance with a specified repayment schedule. The interest rate charged on these loans is usually quite favorable. The loan provision has an advantage over a withdrawal provision in that repayment of the loan will permit achievement of the objective of a long-term program geared toward retirement. However, some employers may prefer the withdrawal provision, since such a provision might help in avoiding possible employee dissatisfaction that could result from the feeling that they must pay interest on the use of their "own" money. The loan provision is also advantageous in that the sums borrowed are not subject to federal income tax. The relatively low interest rates and the deductibility of interest payments enhance the attractiveness of this provision. However, there is a trend on the part of the Internal Revenue Service to be more restrictive in connection with loans to members, and it has requested in some cases that loan durations be limited to two years.[9]

Other Requirements

Qualified profit sharing plans, like qualified pension plans, must be in writing, permanent, communicated to employees, and must preclude diversion or recapture by the employer of contributions to the plan.[10] In the case of profit sharing plans, the Regulations require that "substantial and recurring" contributions be made out of profits as evidence of the permanency of the plan. Unlike qualified pension plans, profit sharing plans always require the establishment of a trust. Also, the requirement that a qualified pension plan provide definitely determinable benefits obviously does not apply in the case of qualified profit sharing plans.

LIMITS ON DEDUCTIBILITY OF EMPLOYER CONTRIBUTIONS

The limits on the deductibility of employer contributions to a profit sharing plan are set forth in the provisions of section 404(a)(3) of the Internal Revenue Code.

---

[9] Samuel J. Savitz, "Guidelines for Decision—Where a Pension Plan Serves Best," *Trust and Estates Magazine*, January, 1966, p. 29, footnote 10.

[10] For a discussion of the nature of these requirements, see pp. 117–119.

The basic principle of these limits is that employer contributions to a qualified profit sharing plan cannot exceed an average of 15% of the annual compensation of participants. In order to permit achievement of the maximum deduction over a period of years, the Code provides for certain carry-over features. Since contributions are based on profits, it is hardly likely that annual contributions will always equal 15% of covered compensation. Therefore, with the availability of carry-over provisions, the employer is able, over a period of time, to secure the maximum deduction (assuming, of course, that the employer seeks to contribute the maximum amount).

There are two types of carry-over provisions: (1) credit carry-over, and (2) contribution carry-over. A *credit carry-over* is created whenever the contribution formula calls for an annual contribution that is less than the maximum allowable deduction (i.e., 15% of covered compensation). This unused credit is carried forward and may be applied in any subsequent year in which contributions exceed 15% of the then current annual compensation of participants. Therefore, deductions for contributions made in a given year can exceed 15% of annual compensation if a credit carry-over is available. However, there is a limit in that the credit carry-over cannot exceed 15% of the current covered annual compensation. Thus, the overall annual limitation, when a credit carry-over is involved, is 30% of current covered payroll—15% of covered payroll for the current contribution and 15% for the credit carry-over.

A *contribution carry-over* is created whenever annual contributions exceed the maximum allowable deduction. The excess of contributions over the deductible limit is not lost forever. Contribution carry-overs can be deducted in subsequent years in which contribution payments are less than the maximum allowable deduction. However, the deduction in any one year, inclusive of contribution carry-overs, cannot exceed 15% of the current covered annual compensation, since this would represent the maximum allowable deduction on a cumulative basis.

If the employer maintains both a qualified pension plan and a qualified profit sharing plan covering the same group of employees, the maximum allowable deduction in any one year for both plans is generally 25% of covered compensation. It should be noted that the limit for profit sharing plans still applies—i.e., if the contribution to the pension plan is only 5% of compensation, this does not mean that the resulting limit for contributions to the profit sharing plan can be 20% of compensation. The 15%-of-compensation limit will still apply. In a situation where both a pension and a profit sharing plan are in effect, the contribution carry-over provision could result in a total maximum deductible amount (for both plans) of 30% of current compensation.

Table 13–1 illustrates the application of the above-described carry-over provisions for a hypothetical profit sharing plan. For simplicity, it has been assumed that the compensation of covered employees will remain constant at $500,000 a year throughout the period indicated. It has also been assumed that the plan specifies a

TABLE 13–1

ANNUAL DEDUCTIONS UNDER A HYPOTHETICAL
PROFIT SHARING PLAN

	Profit before Tax	Contributions to Plan	Compensation of Participants	Amount of Deduction	Contribution Carry-over	Credit Carry-over
1960	$1,000,000	$100,000	$ 500,000	$ 75,000	$25,000	0
1961	600,000	60,000	500,000	75,000	10,000	0
1962	500,000	50,000	500,000	60,000	0	15,000
1963	800,000	80,000	500,000	80,000	0	10,000
1964	900,000	90,000	500,000	85,000	5,000	0
1965	500,000	50,000	500,000	55,000	0	20,000
1966	850,000	85,000	500,000	85,000	0	10,000
	$5,150,000	$515,000	$3,500,000	$515,000	0	$10,000

contribution formula of 10% of net profits before federal income tax. Therefore, contributions of $100,000 to the plan in 1960 exceed the maximum allowable deduction (15% of compensation) by $25,000, thus creating a contribution carryover of this amount. In 1961, profits dropped sharply, producing a contribution of $60,000, which is $15,000 less than the maximum amount deductible. Thus, $15,000 of the excess contributions made in 1960 can be deducted in 1961, leaving $10,000 of contributions to be carried forward to future years. A contribution carry-over, then, can be deducted in subsequent years as long as the aggregate deduction does not exceed 15% of payroll. In 1962, profits dropped further, resulting in a contribution of $50,000, which is $25,000 less than the maximum deduction. The remaining $10,000 of contribution carry-over, then, can be deducted in 1962, producing a total deduction of $60,000, which is $15,000 less than the maximum allowable deduction. Therefore, a credit carry-over of $15,000 exists as of 1962. In 1963, contributions exceed the maximum deduction by $5,000, but the total contribution is deductible because the credit carry-over exceeds this amount by $10,000. The reader should now be able to explain the results for the remaining three years. Reviewing the cumulative results for the seven-year period, we find that net profits before tax amounted to $5,150,000, of which 10% or $515,000 was contributed to the plan. The maximum deductible amount is 15% of the total compensation of $3,500,000 or $525,000. Since total contributions were $515,000, all contributions were deductible, and a credit carry-over of $10,000 is outstanding as of the end of 1966.

Thus, the carry-over provisions permit considerable flexibility in meeting contribution limitations under the law. Furthermore, as noted earlier, the contribution formula can specify that contributions in any one year cannot exceed the maximum amount deductible for federal income tax purposes, if such a result is desired. Also, the reader will recall that the limitations on deductions are different for profit sharing plans that are integrated with Social Security benefits.

TAXATION OF DISTRIBUTIONS

The taxation of distributions from a qualified profit sharing plan is identical to the tax treatment of distributions from a qualified pension plan, which has been discussed in detail in Chapter 6. However, the tax treatment of distributions of securities of the employer should be mentioned here because the practice of investing a portion of trust assets in the securities of the employer seems to be more prevalent under profit sharing plans than under pension plans. Securities of the employer include stock, bonds, and debentures issued by the employer's parent or subsidiary corporations. If a total distribution of the employee's equity is made under conditions entitling him to capital gains treatment, the value of the securities of the employer for the purpose of determining the employee's gain is the cost to the trust and not the fair market value of the securities. In other words, he is not taxed at the time of distribution on the unrealized appreciation. This value then becomes the employee's cost basis should he later decide to sell the securities. However, if he should die before disposing of the securities, the appreciation in value will never be subject to federal income tax. If the securities of the employer are included in a partial distribution not subject to capital gains treatment, then only the portion of the securities attributable to employee contributions can be valued on the basis of cost to the trust.

TERMINATION OF PLAN

Although a qualified profit sharing must be permanent, the Internal Revenue Service does permit inclusion in the trust agreement of a provision giving the employer the right to amend or terminate the plan. However, if the plan is terminated for reasons other than "business necessity" within a few years from its inception, this action will be considered by the Service as evidence that the plan, from its inception, was not a bona fide program for the exclusive benefit of employees in general. If business necessity exists, the employer may terminate the plan without adverse tax consequences. However, it generally will be more difficult to prove "business necessity" in the case of a profit sharing plan as contrasted with a pension plan, since contributions are not required under profit sharing plans during periods of financial difficulties.

If a plan is terminated, all assets in the fund are immediately vested in plan participants. Under no circumstances can any portion of the fund revert to the employer. Since all plan assets are allocated to specific participants, there is no problem regarding any order of priorities in the distribution of the fund. Each participant is entitled to the balance in his account.

Upon termination of the plan, the trustees will determine, in accordance with plan provisions, on a method of distributing the plan assets. The participants' shares may be distributed in a lump sum, in installments over a period of years, used to purchase immediate or deferred annuities, or the assets may be distributed in kind.

USES OF INSURANCE

The trust agreement of a qualified profit sharing plan can be written to permit the investment of part of the trust funds in life and health insurance contracts. Also, all or a portion of trust funds can be used to purchase annuities for participants. Profit sharing funds may be used to purchase insurance on the lives of participants, key men, or stockholders.

Insurance on Participants

The Internal Revenue Service has ruled that trust funds, not otherwise available for distribution, may be used to purchase ordinary life insurance for participants, provided that the premium payments for such insurance coverage are "incidental." The Internal Revenue Service has defined "incidental" as follows:

1. If only ordinary life insurance contracts are purchased, the aggregate premiums in the case of each participant must be less than one half of the total contributions and forfeitures allocated to his account.
2. If only accident and/or health insurance contracts (including

hospitalization, major medical, or similar types of insurance) are purchased, the payments for premiums may not exceed 25% of the funds allocated to the employee's account.

3. If both ordinary life and accident and/or health insurance contracts are purchased, the amount spent for the accident and/or health insurance premiums plus one half of the amount spent for the ordinary life insurance premiums, may not, together, exceed 25% of the funds allocated to the employee's account.[11]

The reason for the requirement that insurance benefits under a profit sharing plan be incidental is obvious. Since the plan is qualified under tax rules pertaining to profit sharing plans, it is inappropriate for the plan to be essentially a life and health insurance plan.

In addition to the above test, the purchase of ordinary life insurance contracts by the trust will be incidental only if the plan requires the trustee to convert the entire value of the life insurance contract at or before retirement into cash, or to provide periodic income so that no portion of such value may be used to continue life insurance protection beyond retirement, or to distribute the contract to the participant.[12]

It should be noted, however, that the above restrictions apply only when the trustee is using funds that have accumulated less than two years and when the form of insurance purchased is ordinary life (or health insurance). If the trustee is using funds which have accumulated for more than two years, or if the life insurance purchased is of an endowment or retirement income variety, these restrictions are not applicable.[13]

Profit sharing trust funds are seldom used to purchase health insurance coverages for participants, since there are no particular advantages in providing such insurance through the trust. The full premiums for health insurance contracts are viewed as current distributions from the trust, and therefore constitute taxable income to participants as these premiums are paid. Furthermore, benefit payments under health insurance contracts owned by the trust offer no special tax advantages. Therefore, the purchase of these coverages out of personal income or through the use of a group health insurance contract outside the trust is generally preferred.

On the other hand, there are many reasons why life insurance

---

[11] Rev. Rul. 65–178, Part 2(n), IRB 1965–28.

[12] *Ibid.*

[13] *Ibid.;* also Rev. Rul. 61–164, IRB 1961–37. Also, see discussion in *Pension and Profit Sharing Tax Service* (Englewood Cliffs, N.J.: Prentice-Hall, Inc.). ¶ 4,121.

for participants under a profit sharing plan might prove advantageous. Life insurance is a convenient method of providing substantial death benefits for participants during their early years under the plan. Over a long period of time, the accumulations in the employee's account available upon death may indeed amount to a very substantial sum. However, during the early years of participation, the accumulations will be rather modest. Also, the young employee with a limited period of participation under the plan is usually the person with substantial life insurance needs. Therefore, life insurance offers considerable flexibility in achieving an objective of substantial immediate and long-term death benefits under the plan. Also, death benefits paid to a named personal beneficiary under a qualified profit sharing plan are accorded favorable federal estate tax treatment. This advantage may be particularly appealing to key employees and stockholder employees. It should be noted at this point that insurance coverages need not be purchased for all participants in order to preserve the qualified status of the trust. The trust agreement should specifically grant each participant the right to direct the trustee as to the purchase of specific investments for the account of each participant. If the trust agreement authorizes the trustee to purchase investments earmarked for the accounts of participants (and all participants have the right to so direct the trustee), then any participant can instruct the trustee to purchase life insurance on his behalf without disqualifying the plan.[14]

Still another advantage in the use of whole life insurance coverage is the guaranteed annuity options available under such contracts. Furthermore, most insurance companies permit the participant to supplement the cash value at retirement with additional sums and convert the total amount to an annuity at the guaranteed rates. (Typically, the insurer guarantees to accept whatever amount is necessary to provide a monthly income at the rate of $20 for each $1,000 of face amount.) Thus, immediately prior to retirement, the participant can direct the trustee to use part or all of the remainder of his share to supplement the annuity benefit that can be provided by the cash value of the contract. Lastly, investments in life insurance contracts can be viewed as the fixed income portion of the profit sharing portfolio. The high degree of security of life insurance investments will permit the trustee to assume a more speculative attitude in the investment of the remainder of trust assets.

In practice the amount used as premiums for ordinary life insur-

---

[14] Rev. Rul. 65–178, Part 5(r), IRB 1965–28.

ance generally do not exceed 25% to 33⅓% of expected average annual contributions. The reason for this practice should be apparent. If premiums approach the legal limit, the annual premium may exceed the limit if contributions fall off in future years. For the same reason, it is often preferable that insurance contracts not be purchased until the plan has been in existence for a period of time. The accumulations in the participant's account will provide a cushion if contributions should drop off in future years.

The participant has a current tax liability when life insurance contracts are purchased for him under a qualified profit sharing plan. The premium for the pure insurance protection (i.e., face amount less the cash value) is viewed as a current distribution from the trust and therefore currently taxable as income to the employee. The amount of reportable income, then, is calculated by multiplying the pure protection portion of the contract by the term insurance premium rate at the participant's attained age.[15]

Any type of life insurance policy can be purchased by a profit sharing trust. A group contract can be issued, with its attendant cost advantage and absence of insurability requirements. However, group contracts are seldom used. The principal problems of using a group contract are the requirements of minimum participation and possible limitations on the maximum amount of insurance on any one life. Of the individual policies, ordinary life, life paid up at 65, or policies maturing for a fixed amount (such as $400 per $1,000 of face amount) are generally used. Of course, retirement annuity contracts can also be used. Since there is no pure insurance protection under these contracts, there is no limit on the portion of contributions that can be applied to the purchase of these contracts. However, once again, since life insurance is normally desired if investments are made in insurance company contracts, retirement annuities are seldom purchased by a profit sharing fund except possibly at a participant's retirement date. With the favorable single-premium immediate annuity rates offered in recent years by many insurers, retiring participants may become more interested in purchasing such annuities.

The insurance contracts purchased on the lives of participants are owned by the trust. The premiums for these contracts are charged directly to the accounts of the particular participants. Likewise, upon the death of a participant, the insurance proceeds are credited in full to the account of the deceased participant or, as is generally the case, the proceeds are paid by the insurer directly to the deceased participant's beneficiary.

---

[15] Rev. Rul. 55–747, CB 1955–2, 228.

Upon retirement, the trustee can surrender the contract and pay the cash value sum to the participant; if the participant desires, the cash value can be converted into an annuity; and, lastly, the trustee can distribute the policy to the participant. If the insurance contract is distributed to the employee, he can keep the contract in force by continuing to pay the premiums required under the contract. If the contract is kept in force, the cash value as of the date of distribution is taxable income to the employee. Capital gains treatment applies if the necessary conditions are met, particularly with respect to the balance of the participant's account.

The disposition of the contract upon severance of employment before retirement depends on the vesting provisions of the plan. If the participant's vested equity exceeds the cash value of the contract, the trustee can distribute the insurance contract, which can be kept in force if the participant so desires. If the vested value is less than the cash value: (1) the participant can acquire the contract by paying the trustee the nonvested portion of the cash value; (2) the trustee can make a loan from the insurer to the extent of the nonvested portion of the cash value and assign the contract, subject to the loan, to the participant; or (3) the trustee can surrender the contract for its cash value and pay the participant his vested interest in cash. The right to keep the insurance contract in force is, of course, quite important for employees who are in poor health.

Life Insurance on Key Men

A profit sharing trust has an insurable interest in the lives of officers, stockholder employees, and key employees of the corporation. Contributions to the plan are dependent on the continued profitability of the business. The future profitability of a business firm may well depend, particularly in the case of small and medium-sized corporations, on the performance of a few key employees. Therefore, a profit sharing trust may wish to protect itself, through the purchase of key man insurance, against reductions of future levels of contributions attributable to the death of such key employees. It would seem necessary, under most state laws, that the trust agreement give the trustee the necessary authority to make such a purchase.

Key man insurance contracts are purchased and owned by the trust. The trust is also named as the beneficiary under such contracts. The premiums for key man insurance are paid by the trustee out of trust assets. Upon the death of the insured, the insurance proceeds are paid to the trust and are usually allocated among participants on the basis of the account balance of each participant.

The purchase of key man insurance creates no current tax liability for participants. Likewise, the tests regarding the "incidental" nature of insurance purchases are irrelevant in the case of key man insurance purchases. Since the purchase is for the benefit of the trust, the percentage limitation on contributions applied as premiums will not be applicable. As a practical matter, the trust is not likely to invest the bulk of contributions in key man insurance contracts. Furthermore, although theoretically permissible, the Internal Revenue Service may question whether the application of a substantial portion of the contributions to the plan for key man insurance is truly in the best interests of all participants.

Life Insurance on Stockholders

Stockholder-employees will, of course, almost always be included as participants under a profit sharing plan. Therefore, such an employee is entitled, like other participants, to direct the trustee to apply a portion of his accumulations to purchase insurance on his life for his own benefit. However, in this section the discussion pertains to the purchase of life insurance on the life of a stockholder-employee for the benefit of the trust. Nor is the objective here key man insurance. The trust, with proper authority given under the trust agreement, may purchase life insurance on a stockholder in order to fund an agreement under which the trust may purchase stock in the corporation from the estate of the deceased.

The trust purchases and owns an insurance contract on the life of the stockholder. The premiums are paid by the trustee, and the contract is considered as a general asset of the trust. Upon the death of the stockholder, the insurance proceeds are payable to the trust. The trust can then use these proceeds to purchase the stock from the estate of the deceased stockholder. Opportunities of this type would most likely arise in the case of small, closely held corporations. The owner may have no heirs or acquaintances interested in operating or purchasing the business upon his death. Therefore, employees, through the financial resources of their profit sharing plan, may be interested in acquiring full ownership or an interest in the business. Life insurance can be used to supplement other plan assets to provide the needed purchase price.

Since an investment of this type involves the purchase of employer securities, approval by the Internal Revenue Service is required. The Internal Revenue Service must be shown that the use of insurance proceeds collected by the trust fund to buy a deceased stockholder's stock is for the exclusive benefit of employees and is not merely to create a market. This could probably be done where the stock is on a dividend-paying basis and its price is no more than the fair market value at the date of death.[16] Also, in order to assure that the investment will be in the best interest of participants, there should be no binding agreement guaranteeing that the stock will be purchased at the death of the stockholder. The agreement should give the trustee the *option* of buying the deceased's share, subject to the approval of the Internal Revenue Service.

PENSION VERSUS PROFIT SHARING PLANS

Qualified pension and profit sharing plans are two extremely effective methods of providing deferred compensation and economic security for employees during their retirement years. Although the broader objectives of both plans might be somewhat similar, the basic characteristics of each method are different in several important respects. Therefore, the employer must carefully evaluate the advantages of each plan in deciding on the program that best suits his needs. Thus, it might be of value to briefly review the characteristics of both plans in the context of the more important factors that an employer must consider in choosing one over the other. Since these features have been discussed at length in other parts of the text, the following discussion avoids detailed consideration of these features.

Objective of Plan

The employer must first decide on the primary objective that he hopes to achieve with the establishment of the plan. If the employer is interested primarily in a plan that offers employees an incentive to perform more efficiently and productively, a profit sharing plan might be the better choice. It is true that a pension plan should also enhance the productivity of employees. However, under a profit sharing plan, the employees are likely to recognize a closer connection between their productivity and their financial rewards under the plan.

On the other hand, if the employer believes that he would be better served by a plan that provides a known level of retirement security for his employees, then a pension plan might best suit his needs.

---

[16] Mark I. Solomon, "Ordinary Life Insurance in Qualified Profit Sharing Plans," *Journal of the American Society of Chartered Life Underwriters* Winter, 1962, p. 27.

Also, the employer may desire a plan that permits the maximum tax advantages to accrue to himself and other key employees. In that case, the tax aspects of both plans should be reviewed with this objective in mind.[17]

Adequacy of Retirement Benefits

The accumulations under a profit sharing plan can grow to a substantial level over a long period of years. However, for short periods of participation, the accumulations, of necessity, must be rather modest. Therefore, employees entering the plan at advanced ages cannot expect much in the way of a retirement benefit. This may be an important factor for stockholder-employees, who are generally advanced in years at the inception of the plan. Although past service may be recognized in the contribution allocation formula under a profit sharing, this factor alone would not offset the adverse effect of a short participation period on the size of the accumulation.

Pension benefit formulas, however, can be designed to provide substantial benefits without reference to the participant's length of participation in the plan. For example, an employee, age 60 at the inception of the plan, may be able to retire with a lifetime benefit of, say, 40% of compensation. As a result of this, older employees at the inception of the plan (often the stockholder employees) will receive a greater proportion of the employer's total contribution under a pension plan than they would under an equivalent contribution made to a profit sharing plan. The appeal of the pension plan for these employees, therefore, is obvious.

Also, the Internal Revenue Service permits integration with Social Security benefits under both pension and profit sharing plans. However, the integration rules are much more favorable under pension plans as compared with profit sharing plans. Thus, the higher-salaried employees generally fare much better under an integrated pension plan.

Death Benefits

A qualified pension plan can provide a death benefit of up to 100 times the monthly pension benefit (or the reserve under an insurance contract, if higher). Thus, a pension plan can provide a substantial amount of death benefit and, in view of the estate tax

---

[17] For an excellent review of the tax considerations from this point of view, see Savitz, *op. cit.*, p. 28, et seq.

advantages, this benefit may be quite appealing to stockholders and high-salaried employees.

Life insurance can also be used in conjunction with profit sharing plans. However, the premium for life insurance must be less than 50% of the total accumulations credited to a participant's account. For the older employees, this limitation is likely to produce a lower level of death benefit (total of insurance proceeds and remainder of account balance) under profit sharing plans.

Timing of Distributions

Pension plans provide a retirement benefit and, in addition, may provide death, disability, and severance-of-employment benefits. Profit sharing plans may permit distributions upon the occurrence of any of the above contingencies and, in addition, may permit withdrawals or loans of part of a participant's account balance while continuing to participate in the plan. Profit sharing plans, then, offer slightly greater flexibility in benefit distributions. The right to withdraw or the right to borrow to meet emergency situations or to build a home may enhance employee awareness and immediate appreciation of the true value of the plan.

The rate of vesting under profit sharing is generally more rapid than under pension plans. Indeed, the Internal Revenue Service usually requires, as a condition for qualification of a profit sharing plan (at least in the case of smaller plans), 100% vesting by the end of a participant's 10th year of participation in the plan. The rapid vesting under profit sharing plans is an important benefit for participant's. However, from the employer's viewpoint, the attitude of the Internal Revenue Service on vesting may encourage the employer to establish a pension plan.

Contribution Flexibility

An important advantage generally offered in favor of a profit sharing plan is the fact that the employer is not committed to a relatively fixed cost under the plan. Contribution formulas can be amended or contributions to the plan can be made on a discretionary basis. However, the Internal Revenue Service does require as evidence of the permanency of the plan that substantial and recurring contributions be made.

Pension plans generally promise a definite benefit and, therefore, the funding must be adequate to provide these benefits. The Internal Revenue Service does permit some flexibility in the timing of contribution payments, but this flexibility clearly is not as great as that available under a profit sharing plan.

However, there are two sides to the coin of contribution flexibility. There is also the question of the maximum limitation on the deductibility of employer contributions under these plans. Under profit sharing plans, the employer cannot deduct aggregate contributions in excess of 15% of aggregate compensation of participants. Under a pension plan, there are no percentage maximums on the deductibility of employer contributions. Therefore, if an employer is interested in contributing as much as possible to a plan, he might find a pension plan to be more desirable.

Appreciation of Participant's Equity

A participant's share in a profit sharing plan is increased by allocations of contributions, investment earnings and appreciation, and reallocation of the forfeitures of nonvested accumulations of terminating employees. The assets of a profit sharing plan can be invested in a wide range of securities, a substantial proportion of which are generally equity investments. Investment gains and losses are reflected in the account balances of participants. In the case of a pension plan, the impact of investment gains and losses are enjoyed or borne by the employer (ignoring the question of possible insurer guarantees) rather than by participants. Also, forfeitures under profit sharing plans accrue to the benefit of the remaining participants, whereas forfeitures under pension plans are applied to the reduction of the employer's future contributions. However, to the extent that more rapid vesting is required under profit sharing plans, the above advantage attributable to forfeitures is somewhat reduced.

PENSION AND PROFIT SHARING PLANS

The above discussion assumes the viewpoint that the employer is faced with the decision of establishing one or the other type of plan. This may well be the typical situation in the small and medium-sized corporation. However, it is quite possible that an employer may wish to establish both types of plans covering essentially the same group of employees. A number of corporations (usually larger firms) have actually established both types of plans. The profit sharing plans in these cases are usually viewed as a supplement to the pension plan. There is no question that the advantages of both plans can be combined to offer an enviable package of deferred compensation for employees.

14

PLANS FOR THE SELF-EMPLOYED

For many years, employed corporate stockholders have been able to enjoy the tax benefits of qualified pension and profit sharing plans. Self-employed individuals, on the other hand, were denied these tax benefits, even though they were permitted to establish such plans for their employees. For approximately 11 years, Congress considered a number of different bills in an effort to remove this tax inequity; the culmination of these efforts occurred in 1962 with the passage of the "Self-Employed Individuals Tax Retirement Act," more popularly known as H.R. 10.

This law permits a self-employed individual to establish a qualified pension or profit sharing plan for himself and for his employees, but with notable restrictions and limitations when compared with the choices and benefits available to an employed corporate stockholder. Briefly, a self-employed individual may establish such a plan if he also covers all of his full-time employees who have been employed for at least three years. The amount he can contribute for his own benefit is limited to 10% of his earned income, but, in any event, this contribution cannot exceed $2,500 a year. A significant limitation is applicable if capital plays a material part in producing the self-employed's earned income. He must make comparable contributions for his employees and, while contributions for employees are fully deductible, he may deduct only 50% of the allowable contribution made for his own benefit. Benefits under the plan may be distributed only under certain circumstances if penalties are to be avoided. Lump sum distributions to self-employed individuals will not qualify for long-term capital gains treatment, and any death benefit paid on behalf of a self-employed individual will be included in his gross estate for federal estate tax purposes, even though paid to a named personal beneficiary.

A comparison of the provisions of H.R. 10, as described in this brief summary, with the provisions of the federal tax law relating to qualified corporate plans indicates the extent to which H.R. 10 falls short of providing self-employed individuals with the same tax benefits available to employed corporate stockholders. Nevertheless, some tax benefits were created for the self-employed under this law, and many individuals have already established plans and are enjoying these benefits. Moreover, it is anticipated that the tax benefits created by H.R. 10 will be expanded and that some of the restrictions and limitations of this law will be eliminated or relaxed.[1]

The purpose of this chapter is to review the major provisions of this law with specific reference to its requirements and limitations in the area of plan provisions, the deductibility of contributions, and the taxation of distributions. The chapter also includes a brief discussion of the different funding instruments commonly being used for H.R. 10 plans and the manner in which approval of a specific plan is obtained from the Internal Revenue Service.

PLAN PROVISIONS

Before discussing H.R. 10 as it relates to actual plan provisions, it is important to recognize that the law distinguishes between *self-employed individuals* and *owner-employees*. All owner-employees are self-employed individuals, but not all self-employed individuals are owner-employees. The key to the distinction is in the amount of proprietary interest held by the individual. An owner-employee is a self-employed individual who owns the entire interest in an unincorporated business (i.e., a sole proprietor) or, if a partner, owns more than 10% of the capital or profit interest of the partnership.[2] Thus, a partner owning 10% or less of the capital or profit interest of the partnership is not an owner-employee, even though he is a self-employed individual. This distinction is important since some provisions of the law are more restrictive for self-employed individuals who are also owner-employees.

One further point to be noted is that if a self-employed individual establishes a plan for his employees but does not cover himself or any other self-employed individual, the rules for qualification and the tax treatment of contributions and benefits are the same as those applicable to plans established by corporate employers. The

---

[1] At the time this chapter was written, for example, Congress already had under consideration several bills to liberalize the provisions of H.R. 10. One of these would remove the maximum contribution provision (except in plans covering only a self-employed individual) and would permit the full contribution for a self-employed individual to be deductible. Another bill would liberalize the present earned income provision.

[2] I.R.C. 401(c)(3); Reg. 1.401–10(d).

requirements and limitations of H.R. 10 apply when a self-employed individual is included in the plan.

Coverage Requirements

If an owner-employee wishes to establish and participate in an H.R. 10 plan, he must cover all of his full-time employees who have completed at least three years of service.[3] He may, of course, cover them as soon as they are employed or after they have completed any period of service up to three years, provided that any service requirement imposed does not discriminate in favor of supervisory or highly paid personnel. Thus, the owner-employee may not establish eligibility requirements such as a minimum or maximum age, nor may he use a minimum earnings requirement. Moreover, if the plan is contributory, an employee cannot be excluded because he refuses or fails to make contributions.

The law does not require the inclusion of part-time or seasonal employees. Thus, an owner-employee may exclude any employee who customarily does not work for more than 20 hours a week or for more than five months a year, regardless of the length of the employee's service.[4]

If the owner-employee has been in business for less than three years when he establishes the plan, the minimum service requirement set must be less than three years if he wishes to participate himself. The minimum service requirement for other employees must be at least as favorable as the requirement chosen to permit the owner-employee to participate.

The above limitations do not apply to a plan that covers only self-employed individuals who are not owner-employees, as would be the case in a large partnership where each partner owns 10% or less of the capital or profit interest of the partnership. In this situation, regular eligibility requirements such as minimum and maximum ages may be used, provided that they do not produce discrimination in favor of supervisory and highly paid personnel.

Limitation on Contributions

The contribution made each year on behalf of an owner-employee is limited to 10% of his *earned income* for such year.[5] Moreover, there is a further limitation in that the annual contribution for an

---

[3] I.R.C. 401(d)(3); Reg. 1.401–12(e).

[4] *Ibid.*

[5] I.R.C. 401(d)(5); Reg. 1.401–12(i). Note, however, that this is not the amount which may be deducted. See p. 322.

owner-employee cannot exceed $2,500.[6] These limitations do not apply to a self-employed individual who is not an owner-employee.

If the plan covers individuals other than owner-employees, and if the plan permits voluntary additional employee contributions, the owner-employee may make a further annual contribution, as an employee, of up to 10% of his earned income or $2,500, whichever is smaller; however, the rate at which he makes these additional contributions cannot be at a rate greater than that permitted for other employees.[7]

The contributions made on behalf of other employees under the plan must be made on a basis which does not produce discrimination in favor of the self-employed individuals or in favor of supervisory and highly paid personnel. This does not mean that contributions for employees must be at identically the same rate as those made for self-employed individuals, just so long as the net effect does not result in the prohibited discrimination. Thus, if a plan employs a defined benefit formula in which the benefits are not discriminatory, the fact that the contributions made for the self-employed individuals are at a higher rate than that for the other employees would not make the plan objectionable. As a practical matter, however, it is expected that most H.R. 10 plans will employ a defined contribution (money purchase) formula because of the manner in which the law is written and because of the overall limitation on the contributions that may be made for self-employed individuals.[8]

Determination of Earned Income

Earned income may be defined as net earnings from self-employment in the trade or business with respect to which the plan is established, to the extent such income is received as compensation for personal services actually rendered.[9] For most self-employed individuals, the determination of earned income will be relatively simple. Where capital is a material income-producing factor, however, the self-employed's annual earned income may not exceed 30%

---

[6] *Ibid.*

[7] I.R.C. 401 (e) (1) (B) (ii) ; Reg. 1.401–13 (b).

[8] A defined benefit formula might have some appeal in a situation where the regular employees are quite young and where the owner-employee is considerably older. Here, for example, a benefit formula producing 20% of compensation might develop a contribution for younger employees which is in the neighborhood of 5% of compensation. In this situation, the contribution for the owner-employee (even though within the limitations of the law) would be higher, when expressed as a percentage of his earned income, than the percentage of compensation he is contributing for other employees.

[9] I.R.C. 401 (c) (2) ; I.R.C. 401 (d) (11) ; Reg. 1.401–10 (c).

of the annual net profits of the business unless the net profits are less than $2,500.[10] If the annual net profit from the trade or business is less than $2,500, the actual net profit may be considered as the self-employed's earned income. If his net profit is between $2,500 and $8,333.33, his earned income may not exceed $2,500, and if his net profit exceeds $8,333.33, his earned income may not exceed 30% of such net profit. It should be noted, however, that the self-employed individual must be rendering personal services on a full-time or substantially full-time basis if any part of his net profits are to be considered as earned income for the purpose of H.R. 10. Thus, for example, a partner who contributes capital but not his personal services to a trade or businesss may not consider any part of his share of the net profits from such trade or business as earned income.

The following examples will help to clarify the provisions of H.R. 10 relating to the determination of earned income:

1. A jeweler whose sole proprietorship has a net profit of $15,000 requires both capital and personal services to produce income. The jeweler's earned income from the business is $4,500 (30% of $15,000).

2. A dentist derives a net income from his practice of $23,000. The entire amount may be considered as earned income.

3. The proprietor of a gift store has a net profit of $3,400 from his business. Here, both capital and service produce income. He can consider a maximum of $2,500 as earned income for purposes of H.R. 10.

4. Jones and Smith are partners in a business in which capital is a material income-producing factor. Jones supplies the capital but no personal services. Smith supplies no capital but performs all services required. The firm has a net profit from all sources of $60,000, which is shared equally between Jones and Smith. Jones has no earned income from the partnership since he performed no personal services. Smith's earned income cannot exceed $9,000 (30% of $30,000).

It should be noted that a self-employed's earned income will be reduced by whatever contributions he is making to the plan for individuals who are not self-employed.[11] For example, if a doctor's earned income otherwise is $25,000 and he is making a $400 contribution to the plan for his nurse, his earned income is reduced to $24,600. However, it is not necessary to reduce his earned income by the amount of the contributions he is making under the plan on his own behalf.

---

[10] I.R.C. 401(c)(2)(B) ; Reg. 1.401–10(c)(3) and (4).
[11] Reg. 1.401–10(c)(2)(iii).

One further limitation on the determination of earned income may be involved if regular employees are covered under the plan. If the contribution for regular employees is related only to their basic compensation (i.e., excluding overtime, bonuses, and other forms of additional compensation), the self-employed's earned income must be reduced. This is done by taking a percentage of his earned income. This percentage is determined by dividing the total compensation paid to all regular employees into the total basic compensation of all such employees.[12] This limitation will not apply if the contribution made for these regular employees is related to their total compensation.

Integration with Social Security

The extent to which plan benefits may be coordinated with Social Security benefits has been considerably modified in the case of H.R. 10 plans. With respect to corporate plans, the limitations for formulas integrated with Social Security relate to benefits or contribution differentials based on compensation levels of participants.[13] For H.R. 10 plans, however, the integration rules take into account the Social Security taxes paid by the owner-employee. Basically, an owner-employee may offset the contribution which would otherwise have been made for an employee by the amount of the Social Security taxes he pays for the employee, the contribution for the owner-employee being similarly reduced by his own Social Security taxes.[14] An important restriction is that this approach may be used only if the contribution made under the plan for all owner-employees is not more than one third of the total contribution under the plan.[15]

If the plan does not cover any owner-employee (i.e., it covers self-employed individuals who are not owner-employees and/or regular employees), the regular rules relating to integration of benefits under a corporate plan will apply.[16]

Excess Contributions

The excess contribution limitations of H.R. 10 do not apply to self-employed individuals who are not owner-employees. However, a contribution for an owner-employee will be considered excessive if it is greater than 10% of his earned income or if it exceeds

---

[12] I.R.C. 401(a)(10)(A); Reg. 1.401–11(d).

[13] See p. 42 and p. 114.

[14] I.R.C. 401(d)(6); Reg. 1.401–12(h).

[15] *Ibid.*

[16] Reg. 1.401–11(c)(2).

$2,500.[17] As previously indicated, voluntary additional contributions may be made by an owner-employee if regular employees are included in the plan and have the same opportunity to make additional contributions. These additional contributions cannot exceed the smaller of 10% of earned income or $2,500.[18]

When the contribution is used to purchase insurance policies, that portion of the premium allocable to the cost of life, accident, health, or other insurance is not taken into account.[19] In a typical insured plan, this means that the cost of insurance (the PS 58 cost) is not considered as a part of the contribution. While this would ostensibly permit the establishment of a fully insured plan where the total premium exceeds the allowable contribution by the cost of insurance, such a plan would ultimately involve an excess contribution because of the constantly reducing cost of insurance element of a retirement income contract. For example, if an owner-employee were permitted to make the maximum contribution of $2,500 and purchased a retirement income contract with a premium of $2,550, he would not have the problem of having made an excess contribution so long as the annual cost of insurance under the contract were more than $50. However, the continued payment of $2,550 will ultimately lead to an excess contribution, since the annual cost of insurance will at some point reduce to less than $50.

A special provision in the law permits an owner-employee to purchase level premium life insurance, endowment, or annuity contracts without fear of making an excess contribution in a year when his otherwise allowable contribution would be below the premium required under his contract. To take advantage of this provision, the contribution for the owner-employee must be limited to the average maximum amount he could have contributed based upon his earned income for the three taxable years preceding issuance of the last contract under the plan.[20] In addition, the premium, including all contract extras such as waiver of premium, cannot exceed $2,500. (If the three-year averaging approach is not used and if the basic premium is $2,500 or less, there will not be an excess contribution if these contract extras bring the total annual premium to an amount in excess of $2,500.)

---

[17] I.R.C. 401 (d) (5) ; I.R.C. 401 (e) ; Reg. 1.401–12 (i) ; Reg. 1.401–13 (b) (2).

[18] I.R.C. 401 (e) (1) (B) (ii) ; Reg. 1.401–13 (b).

[19] I.R.C. 401 (e) (1) ; Reg. 1.401–12 (i) (2).

[20] I.R.C. 401 (e) (3) ; Reg. 1.401–13 (c). If the owner-employee has not had earned income from the trade or business for at least three taxable years when the plan is established, the average may be based on the actual taxable years that earned income was received. Also, even though the owner-employee may make contributions that might otherwise be considered excessive under this provision, his allowable deduction will still be based upon his actual earned income for the year in question. See p. 322.

The penalties that might apply if an excess contribution is made depend upon whether or not these contributions were willfully made and on the length of time taken to repay the excess contribution. If the excess contribution was not willfully made and if it is returned (together with whatever income is attributable to it) to the owner-employee within six months after notification from the Internal Revenue Service that an excess contribution was made, no penalties will attach.[21]

If repayment of an unintentional excess contribution is not made within six months after such notification, the plan will be temporarily disqualified with respect to the owner-employee, and the owner-employee will be currently taxed on the income attributable to his full interest.[22]

If it is determined that an excess contribution was willfully made, the owner-employee's entire interest must be distributed to him, and he will not be able to participate as an owner-employee in any plan for the year in which the excess contribution was made and for the next five years.[23]

Nonforfeitability of Benefits

The contributions made for employees of an owner-employee must be nonforfeitable at the time they are made.[24] This means that no condition can be established in the plan which would deprive such an employee of his benefits even if he is discharged for cause. Thus, the plan must provide for full and immediate vesting; however, payment of a terminating employee's interest may be postponed until his normal retirement date or, if earlier, his death. It should be noted that if the plan does not cover any owner-employees (i.e., it covers only self-employed individuals who are not owner-employees and/or regular employees), this requirement does not apply, and the vesting provisions of the plan may be as desired, so long as they do not produce discrimination in favor of supervisory or highly paid personnel.

Limitations on Distributions

Distributions may not be made to an owner-employee before he has attained 59½ years of age except in the event of his death or

---

[21] I.R.C. 401(d)(8); I.R.C. 401(e)(2). Reg. 1.401–13(d)(2).

[22] I.R.C. 401(e)(2)(D); Reg. 1.401–13(d)(3) and (5).

[23] I.R.C. 401(d)(8); I.R.C. 401(e)(E); Reg. 1.401–12(j); Reg. 1.401–13(e). The penalty tax applicable to premature distributions will also apply. See p. 319.

[24] I.R.C. 401(d)(2)(A); Reg. 1.401–12(g).

his total and permanent disability.[25] This limitation does not apply to regular employees or to a self-employed individual who is not an owner-employee.

If a distribution is made to an owner-employee before he attains age 59½ (other than by reason of death or disability), it is considered a premature distribution and, in addition to a penalty tax being imposed, the owner-employee is barred from participating in the plan for five years.[26] If the amount so distributed which would otherwise be subject to tax is less than $2,500, the tax due will be 110% of the increase in tax as a result of including this amount in gross income for the year in question. If the amount so distributed is equal to or greater than $2,500, the entire distribution will be considered as income in the year in which it is received, but the tax will be 110% of the increase in tax that he would have paid if he had received such amount ratably over the current and four preceding years. In any event, the owner-employee's taxable income for the year cannot be less than the amount of the distribution he has received which is subject to tax less only his personal exemptions (i.e., $600 multiplied by the number of his personal exemptions).[27]

It should be noted that an owner-employee who makes a loan against an annuity or life insurance contract or who assigns any portion of the trust funds before he is 59½ years of age is considered to have received a premature distribution.[28]

The law also requires that distributions to an owner-employee must begin before the end of the taxable year in which he attains the age of 70½, even though he has not actually retired.[29] As long as he is working, however, he can continue to make contributions to the plan, despite the fact that he is drawing benefits.[30] For other employees, including self-employed individuals who are not owner-employees, distribution need not commence until actual retirement, even though retirement is later than age 70½.[31]

There is also a limitation as to the period over which the distribution may be made. This limitation applies to *all* employees, whether or not they are self-employed. Thus, payment of an individual's interest must be made over a period not exceeding:

---

[25] I.R.C. 401 (d) (4) (B) (7); Reg. 1.401–12 (m). Total and permanent disability for this purpose means a disability within the meaning of Section 213 (g) (3) of the Internal Revenue Code.

[26] I.R.C. 72 (m) (5); I.R.C. 401 (d) (5) (C); Reg. 1.72–17 (b); Reg. 1.401–12 (m).

[27] I.R.C. 72 (n) (3); Reg. 1.72–17 (e).

[28] I.R.C. 72 (m) (4); Reg. 1.72–17 (d).

[29] I.R.C. 401 (a) (9) (A); Reg. 1.401–11 (e).

[30] Reg. 1.401–11 (e) (7).

[31] I.R.C. 401 (a) (9) (A); Reg. 1.401–11 (e).

1. The life of the employee,
2. The lives of the employee and his spouse.
3. A period certain not longer than the life expectancy of the employee, or
4. A period certain not longer than the joint life and last survivor expectancy of the employee and his spouse.[32]

If an owner-employee's full interest has not been distributed at his death, the remainder must be distributed within five years or used within five years to purchase an immediate annuity for his beneficiary, payable for life or over a period certain no longer than the beneficiary's life expectancy.[33] Such a distribution within five years is not required if the owner-employee had commenced to receive his interest and the distribution was for a term certain over a period which does not exceed the joint life and last survivor expectancy of the owner-employee and his spouse, determined when the distribution began to the owner-employee.[34] This limitation does not apply to regular employees or to self-employed individuals who are not owner-employees.

Other Provisions

Controlled Business. The plan may not cover any owner-employee, or group of owner-employees, who control either individually or collectively another *unincorporated* trade or business unless a plan is established for the employees of such other trade or business. Control means the full ownership of an unincorporated business by an owner-employee or ownership of more than 50% of the capital or profit interest of a partnership. If the plan provides contributions or benefits for an owner-employee, or group of owner-employees, who individually or collectively control the trade or business with respect to which the plan is established, then the plans established for all such trades or businesses will be taken together and viewed as a single plan for the purposes of qualification. If the owner-employee, or group of owner-employees, do not control the trade or business with respect to which the plan is established, then the plan which they are required to provide for the employees of the trade or business which they control must provide contributions and benefits which are not less favorable than the contributions and benefits provided for the owner-employee or owner-employees under any plan in which they are participating as owner-employees.[35]

---

[32] I.R.C. 401 (a) (9) (B) ; Reg. 1.401–11 (e) (3), (4) and (5).

[33] I.R.C. 401 (d) (7) ; Reg. 1.401–12 (m) (3).

[34] *Ibid.*

[35] I.R.C. 401 (d) (9) and (10) ; Reg. 1.401–12 (l).

The following examples will help to clarify this requirement.

1. Jones owns a 15% interest in the Parker and Jones partnership and also owns a 51% interest in the Jones and Smith partnership. Before he can participate in a plan established by Parker and Jones, he must establish a comparable plan for the employees of Jones and Smith, which he controls. If Jones had only a 50% or less interest in Jones and Smith, he would not have to establish such a plan since it would not be a controlled business. Likewise, had he owned 10% or less of Parker and Jones he would not be required to establish a plan in Jones and Smith (even though he had a controlling interest in Jones and Smith), since he would not be an owner-employee in Parker and Jones.
2. Williams and Ward each own 15% of the Williams and Ward partnership. Each also owns a 26% interest in Baldwin and Associates, a partnership. They would have to establish a comparable plan in the Baldwin firm, which they collectively control, before they could participate in the Williams and Ward plan.

If a controlled partnership owns an interest in another partnership, the partners will be considered to own the same interest in the second. For example, if the controlled partnership had more than a 50% interest in the second firm, the owner-employees controlling the first would also control the second firm.

Owner-Employee's Consent Required. The plan must provide that no owner-employee may be covered without his consent.[36] Note, however, that an owner-employee who is a partner does not have the unilateral right to establish a plan for himself. The plan must be established by the partnership, and each individual partner who is an owner-employee may determine whether or not he wishes to join the plan.[37]

Profit Sharing Plans. H.R. 10 permits the establishment of profit sharing plans as well as pension plans. There must, however, be a definite formula for determining the contribution for employees other than owner-employees.[38] Moreover, this formula may not be changed except for a valid business reason.[39]

The Regulations state that if the employer's contribution for regular employees is related to the earned income of the self-employed individual, the plan will be a profit sharing plan.[40] This would permit a plan which provides for a contribution for the self-

---

[36] I.R.C. 401(d)(4)(A); Reg. 1.401–12(a).

[37] Reg. 1.401–10(e).

[38] I.R.C. 401(d)(2)(B); Reg. 1.401–12(d). A predetermined formula for establishing the amount of contribution under a profit sharing plan is not required for corporate plans. See p. 289.

[39] *Ibid.*

[40] Reg. 1.401–11(b)(1).

employed individual of 10% of his earned income, with a maximum annual contribution of $2,500, and a contribution for each other employee which is a percentage of his salary determined by dividing the contribution for the self-employed individual by the earned income of the self-employed individual. To illustrate, if the self-employed individual's earned income is $50,000 in one year and he makes the maximum contribution of $2,500 for himself, the contribution for each regular employee in that year will be 5% of the employee's salary ($2,500 divided by $50,000).

DEDUCTIBILITY OF CONTRIBUTIONS

A self-employed individual may deduct the full contribution made to the plan for regular employees. And, as previously noted, the amount of these contributions must be deducted from the self-employed's earned income when determining the allowable contribution that he may make on his own behalf.

Of the allowable annual contributions made on behalf of the self-employed individual (regardless of whether or not he is an owner-employee), only one half is deductible, up to a maximum annual deduction of $1,250.[41] That portion of the contribution used to provide life, accident, and health insurance is subtracted from the contribution before determining the amount which is deductible.[42] For example, if the contribution on behalf of a self-employed individual is $2,500, and if the value of his insurance protection is $100, the net contribution is $2,400, of which 50% is deductible. Thus, in this example, the deductible amount would be $1,200.

Although a self-employed individual who is not an owner-employee may make a contribution in excess of $2,500 without such contribution being considered excessive, the $1,250 deduction limit will apply. To illustrate this point, if a self-employed individual who is not an owner-employee receives earned income of $30,000, and if the plan calls for a 10% contribution, the amount that may be contributed for him is $3,000. However, his deduction would be limited to $1,250. Similarly, if a self-employed individual makes permissible voluntary additional contributions, these will not be deductible.

The deduction limit for the contributions made on behalf of self-

---

[41] I.R.C. 404(a)(10); I.R.C. 404(e); Reg. 1.404(e)–1(c). It should be noted that if contributions are being made under the three-year averaging approach, the self-employed's deduction will be based on his actual earned income for the year in question. Thus, the deduction limit for any year will be 5% of the self-employed's earned income for such year, with an overall annual deduction limit of $1,250.

[42] I.R.C. 404(e)(3); Reg. 1.404(e)–1(b)(1).

employed individuals is determined on a year-to-year basis so that no carry-over of unused deductions is permissible.[43] However, a self-employed individual may take advantage of the carry-over provisions with respect to contributions made for regular employees.

One further point is that deductions for contributions on behalf of a self-employed individual may not be used to create or increase a net operating loss.[44]

TAXATION OF DISTRIBUTIONS

As far as regular employees are concerned, distributions will be taxed in exactly the same fashion as distributions made from a qualified plan established by a corporate employer.[45] Distributions to self-employed individuals, however, are taxed in a different manner, the most notable differences being that lump sum distributions will not qualify for long-term capital gains treatment and that death benefits will be included in the self-employed's gross estate for federal estate tax purposes even though paid to a named personal beneficiary.

Retirement and Severance Benefits

Generally speaking, distributions in the form of periodic payments will be taxed as ordinary income in accordance with the annuity rules of Section 72 of the Internal Revenue Code. The self-employed's cost basis for this purpose will be the sum of the amounts which he was not able to deduct.[46] In the case of a self-employed individual who is also an owner-employee, however, his cost basis will not include that portion of his nondeductible contribution applicable to the cost of life, accident, or health insurance.[47] To illustrate, if an owner-employee has contributed $2,000 a year for 20 years as the premium on a typical retirement income contract and if, for this period, the aggregate cost of insurance amounted to $1,700, his cost basis for the purpose of applying the annuity rules would be $19,150, even though his actual nondeductible contributions were $20,850.

As previously mentioned, if a self-employed individual receives his benefit in the form of a lump sum payment, the long-term

---

[43] I.R.C. 404(a)(9)(B); Reg. 1.404(a)–8(a)(2).

[44] I.R.C. 172(d)(4)(D).

[45] For a complete discussion of this subject, see Chapter 6.

[46] I.R.C. 72(d)(2)(B); Reg. 1.72–6(a)(1); Reg. 1.72–17(a).

[47] Reg. 1.72–16(b)(4).

capital gains treatment applicable to qualified corporate plan distributions is not available.[48] Instead, such a distribution will be considered as ordinary income. However, if contributions were made for five or more taxable years prior to the distribution, and if the distribution is not a premature distribution to which a penalty tax would apply, a special averaging device is available.[49] The tax due under this averaging device is the larger of:

1. Five times the additional tax which would be due if 20% of the lump sum distribution were added to the other taxable income of the recipient in the year in which the lump sum distribution is received.
2. Five times the additional tax that would be due if the recipient's income were 20% of the lump sum distribution reduced only by personal exemptions.

This special averaging device will not be available unless there has been a *total* distribution within one taxable year of the distributee.

Death Benefits

If a life insurance benefit is provided by the plan, the beneficiary of a self-employed individual may consider the pure insurance portion of the benefit (i.e., the excess of the face amount over the cash value of the contract) as income-tax-free life insurance proceeds. The cash value of the contract, however, as well as any other form of cash distribution under the plan, will be considered as taxable income to the beneficiary. The beneficiary's cost basis will be the same as the self-employed individual's cost basis at the time of his death, and the tax treatment of the distribution would be the same as that described for distributions to the self-employed. The $5,000 employee death benefit exclusion provided under Section 101(b) of the Code (and available with respect to distributions under qualified corporate plans) is not available to the beneficiary of a self-employed individual.[50] Also, as previously noted, the full amount of the death benefit will be considered as part of the self-employed individual's gross estate for federal estate tax purposes even though paid to a named personal beneficiary.[51]

---

[48] I.R.C. 403(a)(2)(A); Reg. 1.402(a)–1(a)(7).

[49] I.R.C. 72(n); Reg. 1.72–18. This averaging device is not available if the distribution is in the form of a U.S. government bond. I.R.C. 405(d). Bond purchase plans are discussed on p. 327.

[50] I.R.C. 101(b)(3); Reg. 1.101–2(f).

[51] I.R.C. 2039(c); Reg. 20.2039–2.

Other Tax Considerations

The gift tax exemption generally available with respect to qualified corporate plans is not available to self-employed individuals,[52] nor is the sick pay exclusion for disability benefits.[53]

FUNDING INSTRUMENTS

Basically, the funding instruments available in connection with corporate plans may also be used in conjunction with H.R. 10 plans. As a practical matter, however, some of these funding instruments (for example, group pension contracts) will be feasible only when the H.R. 10 program is being adopted by an association or a large firm and the total number of individuals participating warrants the use of the funding instrument.

In addition to these funding instruments, the law authorizes the use of custodial accounts, face-amount certificates, a special series of U.S. government bonds, and the issuance of certain insurance and annuity contracts without the intervention of a trust. While these funding instruments are also available to corporate plans, it is expected that their use will be confined to plans covering self-employed individuals.

Trusteed Plans

If the plan involves a trust agreement, the law requires that the trustee be a bank or a trust company unless all funds are invested in typical retirement income or annuity contracts and all proceeds are payable directly to the employee or his beneficiary.[54] Under these circumstances, an individual or several individuals may be named to act as trustee. In plans which require a bank or trust company to act as trustee, the self-employed individual may still reserve to himself the right to direct investments or to disapprove of proposed investments.

Custodial Accounts

Instead of having a trust, a self-employed individual may use a custodial account if the following conditions are met:

---

[52] I.R.C. 2517(b) ; Reg. 25.2517–1.

[53] I.R.C. 105(g) ; Reg. 1.105–5. If the benefits are attributable to the self-employed individual's own nondeductible contributions, they need not be included in gross income.

[54] I.R.C. 401(d) (1) ; Reg. 1.401–12(c).

1. The custodian is a bank or a trust company.
2. The funds are invested solely in the stock of a regulated investment company issuing only redeemable stock (for example, a
   mutual fund) or solely in annuity, endowment or life insurance
   contracts.[55]

For all purposes under the Code, a qualified custodial account is
considered to be a qualified trust.

It should be noted that even though an actual trust agreement is
not involved, there is still the need for a complete and detailed plan
instrument setting forth such items as eligibility requirements, the
benefit formula, etc.

Nontransferable Annuity Contracts

As previously indicated, it is possible for a self-employed individual to establish a trust and have the trustee invest in retirement
annuity contracts. It is also possible for a self-employed individual
to purchase such a contract directly from the insurance company,
provided the contract is suitably endorsed as "nontransferable"
and provided there is an adequate plan instrument setting forth all
required plan provisions.[56] A typical retirement income contract is
considered as an annuity contract within this provision of the law,
since the insurance protection afforded is considered as "incidental" to the primary purpose of providing retirement benefits.[57]

Face-Amount Certificates

A face-amount certificate is an investment contract between the
purchaser and the company issuing the certificate under which
the purchaser, in return for a lump sum payment or payments over
a specified period of time, receives the certificate's face amount at
maturity. Such certificates are considered as "annuities" under the
law and for this reason may be purchased either by the trustee of
the trust, or directly by the self-employed individual if the certificate is suitably endorsed as "nontransferable."[58] Again, it is still
necessary that the plan provisions be spelled out in an appropriate
document.

---

[55] I.R.C. 401(f); Reg. 1.401-8.

[56] I.R.C. 404(a)(2); Reg. 1.401-9. See p. 146 for a typical nontransferable
endorsement.

[57] Reg. 1.403(a)-1(d).

[58] I.R.C. 401(g); Reg. 1.401-9.

U.S. Government Bond Purchase Plan

A totally new funding instrument for qualified plans, both for corporations and for self-employed individuals, was introduced with the passage of H.R. 10. This is a new series of U.S. government bonds which are sold at par in denominations of $50, $100, $500, and $1,000.[59] The investment yield on these bonds is compounded semiannually, but interest will be paid only upon redemption. The bonds may not be redeemed until the individual is 59½ years of age, dies, or becomes disabled. They are issued in the name of the individual on whose behalf they are bought and are nontransferable.

One interesting feature of a bond purchase plan is that there is no need for a detailed plan instrument. Treasury Department Form 3673, which is the form used to apply for approval of the plan, will constitute the employer's plan when properly completed.

OBTAINING AN ADVANCE DETERMINATION LETTER

A self-employed individual may wish to "tailor-make" his plan. If this is done, and if it is desired to obtain an advance determination letter, the same procedures that are followed for obtaining such a letter for a corporate plan will apply.[60]

The Internal Revenue Service, however, has established procedures under which a sponsoring organization such as an association, a bank, or an insurance company may obtain approval of a master or prototype plan.[61] A master plan is defined as a standardized form of plan, with or without a trust, administered by the sponsoring organization for the purpose of providing plan benefits on a standardized basis. An example of a master plan would be a plan established by some professional association for its members. A prototype plan refers to a standardized form of plan, with or without a related form of trust, which is made available by the sponsoring organization for use without charge by employers who wish to adopt such a plan. The sponsoring organization does not, however, administer the plan. The plans offered by most insurance companies are prototype plans.

In either case, the sponsoring organization submits the plan to the Internal Revenue Service for approval. Once the master or

---

[59] I.R.C. 405; Reg. 1.405.

[60] This subject is discussed in Chapter 5. See p. 121.

[61] Rev. Proc. 64–30, IRB 1964–29.

prototype plan has been approved, a serial number is issued. Individual self-employeds who adopt an approved master or prototype plan need only submit a copy of Treasury Department Form 3673 to the local office of the Internal Revenue Service to determine whether their plan qualifies. This is a very brief form which requires certain general information about the employer and his employees and the plan adopted, including the approval date of the master or prototype plan and its serial number. It should be noted that the adoption of an approved master or prototype plan does not mean that the self-employed individual automatically has a qualified individual plan. It is still necessary that his plan be considered individually with particular reference to his own situation.

NONQUALIFIED
DEFERRED COMPENSATION

In the broadest sense, the term *deferred compensation* embraces all arrangements by which the payment to employees of compensation for past or current services is postponed to some future date. Such arrangements are motivated by the need of employees for income after they retire, and by the employer's need of the goodwill and continued satisfaction of his employees and their families.

However, tax considerations have an important place in the motivation. Indeed, given a choice, there is only one reason why an employee should prefer deferred compensation to a present cash increase in salary. He expects to get more, after taxes, for himself and his beneficiaries by reason of the deferral.

A *deferred compensation agreement* implies nothing more than a contract whereby one person (or legal entity) promises to compensate another for services rendered prior to the date of actual payment. Such a contract is ordinarily reduced to writing. The consideration supporting the employer's promise to pay is the services rendered or to be rendered by the employee.

When such a contract and nothing more exists, we speak of an *unfunded* deferred compensation agreement. When the employer maintains a bank account or other investment, or otherwise establishes a reserve against his future liability under the contract, we speak of an *informally funded* arrangement (with the understanding that such investment of reserve remains the sole property of the employer during the deferral period). The distinction between the two is of no legal significance since, with either, the employee acquires no interest in any specific assets but has merely a right to performance as promised.

On the other hand, a *funded* deferred compensation arrangement refers to a plan to which the employer makes contributions *for the benefit of* an employee. It is distinguishable from an *informally funded* arrangement in that the employee has a beneficial interest in specific funds or property, as contrasted with a mere contractual right.

Because nonqualified, *funded* plans will not ordinarily achieve the tax objectives of the parties (without introducing substantial tax risks), they are rarely used.[1]

To a limited extent, deferred compensation plans follow certain general patterns. Yet, the design of any particular deferred compensation contract will vary substantially from case to case. The underlying motivation of the parties in deciding to have a plan will, to a large extent, dictate its provisions. Thus, a plan may be primarily *benefit oriented* or *deferment oriented*. To a large degree, its specific provisions will depend upon which is the principal orientation. Many provisions of the plan will emerge as the result of arm's length bargaining between employer and employee. Finally, tax considerations will dictate in large measure the basic substance of the plan, as well as the nature of its specific provisions.

GENERAL TAX CONSIDERATIONS

Perhaps the most significant tax characteristic of the *qualified* pension, profit sharing, or stock bonus plan is the fact that such a plan permits the employer to take a current deduction for amounts set aside for the benefit of employees, while employees enjoy the benefit of income tax deferral for such amounts. But such results are unique to qualified plans. Similar tax advantages are not available under *nonqualified* plans.

Generally, under nonqualified plans, if the employer is to obtain a current deduction, the employee must expect current tax liability. If, on the other hand, the employee's tax liability is successfully deferred, it should be anticipated that the employer's deduction will be similarly deferred. Efforts to obtain the best of both worlds (current deduction by employer and deferred tax to employee) may result in failure to achieve either tax objective.

Unfunded Contracts

So long as a deferred compensation agreement encompasses merely the employer's contractual promise to make payments of a

---

[1] Although this chapter will be confined, primarily, to a discussion of *unfunded* or *informally funded* plans (the terms are frequently used interchangeably), some consideration of *funded* plans is necessary to an understanding of the tax effects of certain security devices.

compensatory nature at some subsequent date, the employee will be taxable on such payments only as they are actually received.

Any deduction allowed to a cash basis employer is deferred until benefits are actually paid.[2] If such payments, when viewed together with all payments relating to the employee's compensation prior to that time, are *reasonable* with respect to the overall services rendered, the employer will be entitled to a deduction for the deferred payments to the employee as they are made.

Funded Contracts

If an employer makes contributions to a nonqualified annuity, or to a nonqualified trust, for the benefit of the employee, each such contribution will be taxable to the employee in the year made, if his beneficial interest in the contribution is *nonforfeitable* at the time it is made. It would appear that the same result will follow, whether or not an express trust is created, provided only that the employee acquires a nonforfeitable equitable interest in the fund itself. But if the employee's interest is *forfeitable,* he does not incur current tax liability.

If the employee's rights under a funded deferred compensation contract are *nonforfeitable* at the time the employer makes a contribution, such contribution is deductible in that year. But if the employee's rights to such amounts are *forfeitable,* it may well be that no deduction is allowable for such amounts for *any* taxable year.

This brief characterization of the timing of employer's deduction and employee's taxation is oversimplified. Thus, these generalized observations require examination in greater detail.[3]

---

[2] The discussion in this chapter will be limited to *cash basis* taxpayers, since (1) employees participating in deferred compensation contracts will be reporting their income on a cash receipts basis, and (2) under any plan deferring the receipt of compensation (other than a qualified plan), whether the employer is on a cash or accrual basis, any allowable deduction may only be taken as payments are actually made. *Sol Jacobs, Jr.,* 45 TC—(No. 10, 10/28/65). Reg. 1.404(a)–12.

[3] In dealing with *funded* deferred compensation plans, the Code and Regulations sometimes treat nonqualified *annuity contracts* and nonqualified *trusts* together, and sometimes treat them separately. As an unfortunate consequence of this, a degree of complexity is introduced in comprehending the overall picture. In general, for all practical purposes, the two are treated the same (with one exception applicable to certain tax exempt employers), namely:
1. If the employee's interest in the contribution is nonforfeitable at the time it is made,
    a) he is taxable in the year the contribution is made, (*i*) to a nonqualified *trust* [I.R.C. 402(b)], or (*ii*) to a nonqualified *annuity* [I.R.C. 403(c)] except as I.R.C. 403(b) may apply; and
    b) the employer may deduct the contribution at that time whether it be to a nonqualified *trust* or to a nonqualified *annuity* [I.R.C. 404(a)(5)].

DEFERRAL OF EMPLOYEE'S INCOME TAX LIABILITY

For federal income tax purposes, the term "income" is not confined to money or property actually received, but includes amounts
which for all practical purposes are currently receivable, as well as
the value of economic benefits received by the taxpayer. Thus,
without actual receipt of income, a tax may be imposed under either
the doctrine of *constructive* receipt or the *economic benefit* theory.

Constructive Receipt

Federal tax Regulations contain the following provision with
respect to "constructive receipt":

Income although not actually reduced to a taxpayer's possession is
constructively received by him in the taxable year during which it is
credited to his account or set apart from him so that he may draw upon
it at any time. . . . However, income is not constructively received if
the taxpayer's control of its receipt is subject to substantial limitations
or restrictions. . . .[4]

Thus, income will be constructively received if it is available
upon demand, without substantial restriction. In essence, constructive receipt involves the turning of one's back on available income
for no significant purpose other than the hoped-for deferral of tax
liability.

Economic Benefit

The economic benefit (or cash equivalent) theory of income taxation has been applied by the courts to impose current tax liability
on taxpayers who, although not in constructive receipt of income,
nevertheless receive an economic benefit (for example, something
other than cash, but of measurable value) or receive a cash equivalent (for example, something readily convertible into cash). It

---

2. If the employee's interest in the contribution is *forfeitable* at the time it is
   made,
   a) he is not taxable in the year the contribution is made (by implication
      of the following authorities) nor in the year his interest becomes non-
      forfeitable, (*i*) to a nonqualified *trust* [I.R.C. 402(b) and Reg.
      1.402(b)–1(a)(1)], or (*ii*) to a nonqualified *annuity* [I.R.C. 403(c)
      and Reg. 1.403(c)–1(a)], except in the case of certain tax-exempt
      employers where a change from forfeitable to nonforfeitable is taxable
      [I.R.C. 403(d)] except as I.R.C. 403(b) may apply; but
   b) If the employee's interest (under a *trust* or *annuity*) changes from
      forfeitable to *nonforfeitable*, it would appear that no deduction for the
      employer's contribution is allowable at *any* time [Reg. 1.404(a)–12].

[4] Reg. 1.451–2(a).

would appear that the cash equivalent theory is merely a special case of the economic benefit theory.

In one case, an executive received, in lieu of cash, deferred compensation in the form of a single-premium deferred retirement annuity contract. The executive was the owner of the contract, but it was nonassignable and had no cash surrender value. The court held that although the constructive receipt doctrine did not apply, the executive was currently taxable on the value of the annuity because he received unconditionally the economic benefit of the annuity contract.[5]

Rev. Rul. 60–31

Concepts as broad as *constructive receipt* and *economic benefit*, of necessity, leave much room for doubt and uncertainty on the part of the cautious tax practitioner. But much of the uncertainty was eliminated when, in 1960, the Internal Revenue Service promulgated a ruling (Rev. Rul. 60–31) in which it discussed the application of the doctrine of constructive receipt to five specific deferred compensation arrangements.[6]

It appears from this ruling that a deferred compensation arrangement will not result in constructive receipt of income by the employee (or by a beneficiary of the employee) even though his rights may be nonforfeitable, provided the arrangement is not formally funded and provided he has no right to currently receive the compensation in question. However, a reserve may be established on the employer's books, credited with earnings allocable to it, and earmarked, in an accounting sense, for future performance of the employer's obligation. But no property should be so segregated or set aside as to require that it be devoted to fulfilling the agreement. Any insurance policy or other property acquired by the employer in connection with the establishing of such a reserve should be an unrestricted general asset of the employer. With such an informally funded plan, the employee can safely be given nonforfeitable, unconditional, vested guarantees by the employer, provided there is nothing backing up these guarantees except the unsecured promise of the employer.[7]

---

[5] *Renton K. Brodie*, 1 TC 275 (1942).

[6] Rev. Rul. 60–31, 1960–1 CB 174. While this ruling did not expressly discuss the economic benefit doctrine, it may be inferred that under the specific arrangements considered, application of this doctrine would not have changed the tax results.

[7] If the promise is secured, possible application of the economic benefit doctrine must be considered. See the section on "Security Devices," p. 357.

There seems to be no reason why the employee cannot take a reduction in his future cash compensation for future performance, concurrently with entering into an agreement for deferred payments. But obviously, he could no more forgo salary already due him for past performance than he could repay salary he had actually received, in return for a deferred payment arrangement. Nor must the promisee of the deferred payment be an employee. He may be an independent contractor *provided only* that the agreement to defer applies to compensation not yet earned.[8]

Statutory Considerations

While both the constructive receipt and economic benefit doctrines have been established by administrative and judicial decisions rather than by statute, there is *statutory* authority for the economic benefit doctrine as applied to contributions to a funded, nonqualified plan for the benefit of an employee.

Section 402(b) of the Internal Revenue Code provides that:

Contributions to an employee's trust made by an employer during a taxable year of the employer . . . for which the trust is not exempt from tax under section 501(a) shall be included in the gross income of the employee for the taxable year in which the contribution is made to the trust in the case of an employee whose beneficial interest in such contribution is nonforfeitable at the time the contribution is made. . . .[9]

Yet, surprisingly, the applicable provision of the Regulation states that:

If the employee's beneficial interest in the contribution is forfeitable at the time the contribution is made even though his interest becomes nonforfeitable later, the amount of such contribution is not required to be included in the income of the employee at the time his interest becomes nonforfeitable.[10]

While statutory provisions are expressly applicable only to trusts and annuities, it is reasonable to anticipate that in any case where an employee acquires a nonforfeitable interest in a contribution of the employer, or in property acquired by such a contribution, the government will be able to support a finding of currently taxable income on one of two possible grounds. It may be found that the employee's equitable interest in the contribution amounted to an

---

[8] See *Ray S. Robinson*, 44 TC 20 (1965).

[9] While Sec. 402(b) expressly applies to trusts only, Sec. 403(c) contains generally similar provisions with respect to annuities.

[10] Reg. 1.402(b)–1(a)(1), last sentence, which expressly applies to trusts only. But Reg. 1.403(c)–1(a) contains generally similar provisions with respect to annuities (subject to an exception under I.R.C. 403(d) in the case of certain tax-exempt employers).

interest in trust. Alternatively, it may be found that the general application of the economic benefit doctrine will result in currently taxable income without reference to the statutory provisions.[11]

Summary of Income Tax Deferral

From the foregoing it is evident that with an unfunded or informally funded plan, the employee's income tax on the benefits to be provided will be successfully deferred so long as he is not in constructive receipt nor in receipt of an economic benefit. And both of these doctrines can readily be avoided in a well-designed plan.[12] The possible applicability of one or the other doctrine at any time between the plan's inception and the time that benefit payments to the employee commence should be taken into account, and particular care should be taken that neither becomes applicable at the time benefit payments commence.[13]

It might also seem that even with a funded plan there can be a successful deferral of the employee's income tax merely by making sure that his benefits are *forfeitable*. This is, in fact, the case. Nevertheless, such plans are generally avoided for two important reasons. In the first place, it is no simple matter to determine what conditions or qualifications must be placed on the employee's interests to assure that the Internal Revenue Service will agree that his rights are forfeitable (rather than nonforfeitable). Secondly, under a funded plan, it is the position of the Internal Revenue Service that the employer is *never* entitled to any deduction.[14]

TAX CONSIDERATIONS AFTER EMPLOYEE'S DEATH

Many deferred compensation arrangements provide that upon the employee's death, deferred payments will be made to his estate or to designated beneficiaries. A particular agreement may provide that such payments are to be made in the event of death before retirement, death after retirement, or both. Indeed, some agreements—frequently referred to as salary continuation agreements—

---

[11] See Rev. Rul. 60–31, Example (4).

[12] Provided that there is no trust, escrow arrangement, or other security device. For an excellent Memorandum of Law on constructive receipt and economic benefit, viewed in conjunction with the relevant statutory provisions, see Clark C. Havighurst, *Deferred Compensation for Key Employees* (Mundelein, Ill.: Callaghan & Co., 1964), p. 300 ff.

[13] For example, constructive receipt at termination of employment may occur if the employee will acquire an option to take his benefits in a lump sum payment at that time; or he may receive a taxable economic benefit at that time if, after termination of employment, his benefit payments are guaranteed by an insurance company or are similarly secured.

[14] See the section on "The Employer's Deduction," p. 337.

provide for death benefits exclusively and, usually, only if death occurs *before* retirement of the employee.[15]

Estate Tax

So long as the employee had an enforceable contract at the time of his death, his gross estate, as determined for federal estate tax purposes, will include the value of the promised benefits.[16]

The value of any such death benefits is their commuted value at the date of death. However, under circumstances where the promissor's financial condition is such as to cast serious doubt on its ability to perform as agreed, a reasonable case may be made for a lower value.[17] Conditions of the agreement which might lead to forfeiture during the employee's life, but which become inoperative at his death, have no effect on the valuation.[18]

Income Tax

Such death benefits are taxable to the estate or beneficiaries (as ordinary income) in the year received. However, an exclusion of up to $5,000 is allowed, provided that the employee did not have a nonforfeitable right to receive the amounts in question while living.[19]

The impact of both estate and income taxes being imposed is, to a limited extent, mitigated by a deduction allowable against the income received. The payments received on account of the employee's death will be "income in respect of a decedent." Thus, the payees will receive an income tax deduction for the portion of the estate tax actually paid that is deemed to be attributable to each income payment.[20] It is important to observe that this is a *deduction* against gross income, *not a credit* against the income tax.[21]

---

[15] If a salary continuation arrangement is voluntarily undertaken after the employee's death, rather than pursuant to an agreement, different tax considerations apply. For a discussion of these see the section on "Voluntary Death Payments," p. 360.

[16] I.R.C. 2039(a) and (b). Reg. 20.2039–1(b). See also *Goodman* v. *Granger*, 243 F.2d 264 (CA-3, 1957), *cert. den.* 355 U.S. 835.

[17] See general principles concerning the valuation of property for estate tax purposes in Reg. 20.2031.

[18] *Estate of Wadewitz* v. *Comm'r*, 339 F.2d 980 (CA-7, 1964); *Goodman* v. *Granger*, Note 16.

[19] I.R.C. 101(b)(1)(B).

[20] I.R.C. 691.

[21] On an overall basis, this deduction merely reduces the amount of otherwise taxable income by the amount of estate tax paid on the value of the income right. Thus, it assures that the beneficiary will not pay an income tax on the amount of the estate tax that was paid.

THE EMPLOYER'S DEDUCTION

In computing its income tax liability, an employer is entitled to a deduction for all *ordinary* and *necessary* business expenses.[22] Compensation and fringe benefits paid to (or with respect to) an employee (or former employee) are deductible as ordinary and necessary business expenses to the extent that such payments and the cost of such benefits represent *reasonable* overall compensation for services rendered.[23]

Under a *funded* deferred compensation plan, the employer's deduction is also governed by Section 404(a)(5) of the Code.

Reasonableness of Compensation

While the courts and the Commissioner are not unduly harsh in applying the test of "reasonableness" insofar as supplementary fringe benefits are concerned, they are by no means reluctant to disallow a deduction in an extreme situation. There are numerous decided cases in which the courts have been fairly liberal in allowing deductions for substantial amounts of deferred compensation payments. But the fact that those cases reached the courts is ample evidence that the Internal Revenue Service and employers do not always see eye to eye on the question of reasonableness.

The Service is inclined to give much closer scrutiny to compensation or fringe benefits provided for substantial stockholders. Thus, what may be thought of by the parties as current or deferred compensation may be viewed by the Service as the payment of current or deferred dividends, as the case may be. Nor will the wording of an agreement between employer and employee (which makes a maximum effort to characterize the value of the employee's services as such) be of much help where the substance of the agreement readily evidences that the employee was being furnished benefits that most likely would not have been furnished were he not a substantial stockholder.

This point is well illustrated by the *Willmark* case, which sustained the Commissioner's disallowance of a deduction for payments made to a deceased employee-stockholder's widow, pursuant to a deferred compensation contract.[24] The decedent had owned 50%

---

[22] I.R.C. 162 and 212.

[23] This is made explicit in I.R.C. 162(a)(1), and is clearly implied by I.R.C. 212 and the Regulation thereon.

[24] *Willmark Service System, Inc.*, TC Memo 1965-294 (11/5/65). Taxpayer's appeal to 2nd Cir. pending.

of the corporation's stock. His brother, for whom there was an identical deferred compensation agreement, owned the remaining 50%.

The court observed that the employer had the burden of proving, not only that the payments were made pursuant to a plan deferring the receipt of compensation for past services, but also that the amounts to be paid under the plan constituted reasonable compensation for such services. It held that the employer had failed to establish either. The court was, ". . . unimpressed by the recitals in the preamble to the . . . agreement, which appear to be merely window dressing," and was far from satisfied that the salaries paid the brothers, ". . . were inadequate or that they were consenting to receive unduly low compensation, or that the corporation was in fact entering into the agreement in order to retain their services." "Payments of these substantial amounts,"[25] said the court, "in the absence of any evidence that they had a substantial relation to the value of services rendered by the deceased officer, constituted *extraordinary* and *unusual* expenditures even though petitioner may have been obligated to make them under an agreement with its officers who owned all its stock."[26] (Emphasis added.)

Funded Plans

Section 404(a)(5) of the Internal Revenue Code provides in part as follows:

. . . if compensation is paid or accrued on account of any employee under a plan deferring the receipt of such compensation, such contributions . . . shall be deductible under this section . . . in the taxable year when paid, if the plan is not . . . [a qualified plan] if the employee's rights to or derived from such employer's contribution or such compensation are *nonforfeitable* at the time the contribution or compensation is paid. (Emphasis added.)

But Section 1.404(a)–12 of the Regulations imposes a harsh, and surprising, limitation on the foregoing, as follows: "If an amount is paid during the taxable year to a trust or under a plan and the employee's rights to such amounts are *forfeitable* at the time the amount is paid, no deduction is allowable for such amount for any taxable year."[27] (Emphasis added.)

---

[25] During the years 1953 through 1959, payments to the decedent's widow totaled $133,334 (an average of approximately $19,000 per year).

[26] Note the contrast between the court's words, *"extraordinary* and *unusual"* and the words *"ordinary* and *necessary"* required to support a deduction.

[27] Note, however, that in commenting upon these provisions, Rev. Rul. 60–31 (see Note 6) observed: "In the application of those sections to unfunded plans, no deduction is allowable for any compensation paid or accrued by an employer on account of any employee under such a plan except in the year when paid. Thus, under an unfunded plan, if compensation is paid by an employer directly

The Service may consider such a harsh limitation necessary in view of its interpretation of Sections 402(b) and 403(c) of the Code.[28] In interpreting these sections, the Regulations provide that:

If the employee's rights under the annuity contract in such a case were forfeitable at the time the employer's contribution was made for the annuity contract, even though they became nonforfeitable later, the amount of such contribution is *not* required to be included in the income of the employee at the time his rights under the contract become non-forfeitable.[29] (Emphasis added.)

This would suggest a substantial opportunity for tax avoidance, were it not for the fact that funded plans, initially providing for forfeitable rights which subsequently become nonforfeitable, are discouraged by the Regulation that no deduction is allowed at any time.[30]

There may be a serious question of whether Reg. 1.404(a)–12 is a reasonable interpretation of the statute. In two cases, decided by the U.S. Court of Claims, the Court has held the Regulation to be invalid and has allowed the employer deductions as payments were actually made under the plans.[31]

But the issues before the Court in these cases were narrow ones. And in one of them, the Revenue Service has indicated that it will not follow the decision.[32] Accordingly, until such time (if ever) as the Service revises the Regulation, an employer—however anxious

---

to a former employee, such amounts are deductible under section 404(a)(5) when actually paid in cash or other property to the employee, provided that such amounts meet the requirements of section 162 or section 212."

[28] See p. 334 for text of I.R.C. 402(b). I.R.C. 403(c) reads in its entirety as follows: "If an annuity contract purchased by an employer for an employee is not subject to subsection (a) and the employee's rights under the contract are nonforfeitable, except for failure to pay future premiums, the amount con-tributed by the employer for such annuity contract on or after such rights become nonforfeitable shall be included in the gross income of the employee in the year in which the amount is contributed. The employee shall include in his gross income the amounts received under such contract for the year received as provided in section 72 (relating to annuities)."

[29] Reg. 1.403(c)–1(a). I.R.C. 403(d) makes an exception to this in the case of employers exempt from tax under Sec. 501(a) or 521(a). Reg. 1.402(b)–1(a)(1) (see p. 334) is the corresponding similar provision respect-ing trusts.

[30] But loss of a deduction to a tax-exempt employer is of no consequence. Accordingly, the Internal Revenue Service sought and obtained statutory discouragement of such plans of exempt employers in the form of I.R.C. 403(d), which is an exception to I.R.C. 403(c). See Note 29.

[31] *Russell Mfg. Co.* v. *U.S.*, 175 F. Supp. 159 (Ct. Cl., 1959) and *Mississippi River Fuel Corp.* v. *U.S.*, 314 F.2d 953 (Ct. Cl., 1963).

[32] Rev. Rul. 59–383, 1959–2 CB 456 (in which the Service indicates that it will not follow the decision in *Russell Mfg.*).

he may be to satisfy an employee's desire to avoid current taxation
—will be reluctant to take the risk of never getting a deduction.

Summary

With an unfunded plan, it is logical to expect that the employer's
deduction will be deferred until the taxable years in which benefits
are actually paid out. And with a funded plan, it is logical to expect
that the employer's deduction will be allowed at the time a contribution is made to, or benefits are paid under, the plan if the employee's rights to such contribution are nonforfeitable.[33]

But, with a funded plan under which the employee's rights are
forfeitable at the time the employer makes a contribution, logic is
confounded by the position of the Internal Revenue Service, which
in turn is contradicted (at least in part) by the courts. The only
way to avoid the dilemma is for the employer not to make any
contribution to the plan at a time when the employee does not want
to be taxed; i.e., *formal funding* should be avoided.

The test of reasonableness of overall compensation must, of
course, be satisfied if a deduction is to be allowed for payments
under any compensatory plan.

THE ROLE OF LIFE INSURANCE

Whether life insurance is an essential ingredient of, or merely a
desirable adjunct to, a deferred compensation plan, depends on the
purposes and provisions of the particular plan.

Clearly, if the plan contemplates the payment of substantial
death benefits in case of premature death of the employee, life
insurance is essential. So, also, if the employer contracts to pay the
employee a deferred income for life, the employer should shift the
annuity risk to an insurance company.[34] Where neither of these
elements is present, a life insurance policy may nevertheless serve
as a convenient tool for building a reserve against the deferred
liabilities. And, unlike many other investment vehicles, it offers tax
shelter to the earnings on the reserve.

Ownership of the Policy

Any insurance policy carried in conjunction with the plan should
be paid for by, owned by, and payable solely to, the employer.

---

[33] In both cases (in the absence of a qualified plan), the employer's deduction arises at the same time that the employee's tax liability arises.

[34] By acquiring either an annuity contract or a cash value insurance policy
providing annuity guarantees.

Ordinarily, the deferred compensation contract should be so drawn as to fix the rights and liabilities of the parties entirely apart from the existence or nonexistence of any such insurance policy or the values created thereby.

Indeed, until recently, some writers cautioned against any reference to the insurance policy being made in the deferred compensation agreement.[35] But such caution no longer seems warranted.[36] Perhaps if some useful purpose can be served by referring to such a policy in the agreement, it might be desirable to do so.[37]

However, if there is any such reference, in order to avoid any implication of formal funding, a provision should also be included in the agreement to the effect that the reference to the policy does not in any way collateralize the policy for purposes of the agreement or impose any trust or escrow arrangement upon it, or in any way require that it be devoted to fulfilling the agreement.[38] On the contrary, the agreement should ordinarily specify that the policy is, and shall remain, a general, unpledged, unrestricted asset of the corporation.[39]

Tax Consequences to the Employer

When an employer informally funds a deferred compensation agreement by maintaining an investment account, the employer's tax consequences during the deferral period are identical to what they would be were the same investments made in the absence of any deferred compensation agreement.

Where a life insurance contract is so used, any death proceeds received by the corporation are excluded from its gross income.[40] No deduction is allowed the employer for premiums paid.[41] If the policy matures or is surrendered for cash during the insured's lifetime, any excess of maturity proceeds or surrender value received over the aggregate premiums paid for the policy is taxable to

---

[35] See, for example, Arthur E. Schmauder, "Keyman Insurance in Deferred Compensation Arrangements," *Insurance Law Journal*, June, 1959, p. 365.

[36] This would appear to be a necessary implication of *Casale* v. *Comm'r*, 247 F.2d 440, *rev'g* 26 TC 1020 and of Rev. Rul. 60–31 (Note 6).

[37] See the section on "The Deferred Compensation Contract—Vesting Insurance Policy Values," p. 353, for an example of such a useful purpose.

[38] Unless such a provision would be contrary to a specific undertaking to provide security. See the section on "Security Devices," p. 357.

[39] Such a negative provision may be desirable (in general terms) even when the policy is not referred to in the agreement, in order to avoid a possible holding that the insured has some equitable interest in the policy.

[40] I.R.C. 101.

[41] I.R.C. 264 (a).

the employer as ordinary income.[42] But if the amount so received is less than the aggregate premium paid, no deductible loss is allowed.[43]

If installment or annuity payments are made out of the maturity or surrender proceeds, during the lifetime of the insured, an exclusion ratio is determined in order to arrive at the portion of each payment that is excluded from the employer's gross income as a return of capital; the balance of each payment will be taxable to the employer as ordinary income.[44]

When employer payments to the employee actually commence, it is expected that the full amount paid should be deductible by the employer, and taxable to the employee, as compensation.[45]

Use of Settlement Options

In order to provide a payout over a period of years, while attempting to protect the employee (and his widow) from the uncertainties of the future ability of the employer to make installment payments, it is sometimes suggested that the employee (and his wife) be designated as direct beneficiary of an employer-owned insurance policy. Thus, installment payments could be received under an option of the policy directly from the insurance company.

But the most reasonable tax analysis of such an arrangement would require treating the guarantee of payments by the insurance company as though the policy had been distributed to the employee. Hence, the employee's tax liability would accrue all in one year, thus defeating the tax objective of the installment payments. Therefore, it would seem necessary that the employer be designated as beneficiary for all payments under the contract, receive all such payments, and itself make all distributions to the employee until the payout is completed.

As each periodic installment payment is received by the employer, the employer should draw its own check (or endorse the insurance company's check) to the employee.[46] Or, it may be administratively more convenient for the employer to give the insurance company a revocable instruction to make installment payments

---

[42] I.R.C. 72(e).

[43] *London Shoe Co.* v. *Comm'r*, 80 F.2d 230 (CA-2, 1935).

[44] I.R.C. 72(b).

[45] Note that, since installment payments to the employer may be partially taxable under I.R.C. 72(b), gross installment payments received by it from the insurance company may not be fully available (after taxes) for distribution to the employee.

[46] But see Note 45.

directly to the employee until further notice.[47] So long as the employer reserves the right to redirect all future payments to itself, income tax consequences (to both employer and employee) are the same as if each installment payment were actually received by the employer and distributed by it to the employee.

Improper Accumulation of Surplus

Does a corporation run afoul of the Accumulated Earnings Tax by establishing a reserve against deferred compensation liabilities through an insurance policy on an employee's life with premiums paid from profits?[48] If the deferred compensation agreement is truly compensatory, as in the case of an arm's length agreement with an employee who owns no stock or whose stockholdings are incidental, there is no problem in this regard. However, in the case of an employee who owns a substantial amount of stock, such an agreement might be viewed as not compensatory, but as actually being an arrangement for deferring dividends. Each case will depend upon its own facts.

If it is feared that the agreement might be construed as a deferred dividend arrangement, careful consideration should be given to justifying the insurance from a business purpose viewpoint and to the selection of the plan of insurance. For a substantial stockholder for whom deferred compensation may not be justifiable, the carrying of insurance may, nevertheless, be justified solely for key man indemnification purposes. But to attempt to give the insurance the appearance of key man insurance merely by not referring to it in the deferred compensation agreement, when in reality it is carried for deferred compensation purposes, may be a little unrealistic. Under appropriate circumstances, the Internal Revenue Service and the courts may be expected to make the tie-in.[49]

A retirement income or other endowment plan could be justified *only* on the basis of deferred compensation obligations of the employer. Thus, before deciding on insurance on such a plan, the employer should be satisfied that the deferred compensation agree-

---

[47] But it must be borne in mind that practices of insurance companies vary with respect to the availability of settlement options on policies owned by businesses.

[48] See I.R.C. 531–537. This tax is not imposed unless retained earnings are at least $100,000, and then is imposed only on excess retentions.

[49] Particularly if the policy is taken out at about the same time that the deferred compensation agreement is entered into, and the benefits that the corporation may expect to receive under the policy can, by a little arithmetic, be related to the obligations it assumes under the deferred compensation agreement.

ment can be justified as, *in fact,* compensatory. Under such circumstances, tying the policy in with the agreement may actually be desirable.[50]

But with any type of policy, the justification for the retention of earnings is only as good as the reality of the key man need, or the good faith and reality of the deferred compensation arrangement. In general, it may be better not to have deferred compensation agreements between a corporation and a major stockholder, and thus to have no apparent reason for carrying the insurance (and no attempted justification) except the need of the corporation to be indemnified for expected loss at the death of a valuable officer.[51]

GENERAL CONSIDERATIONS IN PLAN DESIGN

Relative Bargaining Positions

An employer may make a preliminary decision to provide an employee or his beneficiary with specific or determinable benefits upon the happening of certain events. Such a *benefit-oriented* plan is likely to arise as the employer's own idea. He may feel that he needs to do something to minimize the chance that the employee will consider offers by outside firms. Or, he may feel a moral obligation to do more for the particular employee than is available for employees generally under the firm's established fringe benefit plans.

On the other hand, the primary consideration may merely be to defer compensation to some future date rather than to pay it currently. Such a *deferment-oriented* plan is likely to be instigated by the employee who seeks his employer's cooperation in reducing his income tax liability over the next several years. It may involve the passing up of a cash salary increase or bonus, or even a request for reduction in salary. Since, in such instances, the employee is more concerned with a deferral of income than with the specific benefits to be provided, such plans may frequently be of the defined contribution (money purchase) type.

Occasionally, either employer or employee will be in a position to dictate terms to the other. However, more often than not, each party will have sufficient bargaining power to dictate, or at least to

---

[50] See Note 37.

[51] This would rule out any policy on any form of endowment plan. Similarly, it would rule out other forms of investments for informal funding purposes. Perhaps it is such considerations that give rise to the all too often repeated observation that "corporate-owned life insurance is helpful in minimizing any problem of improper accumulations of surplus."

influence, certain provisions of the agreement. The motivation of the parties, and their relative bargaining power, will heavily influence major provisions of the agreement, such as level of benefits, time and rate of vesting, whether vested benefits are to be received in cash on termination of employment, and the like.

Tax Considerations as Design Considerations

Of necessity, tax objectives (and the willingness or unwillingness to take tax risks) will dictate many of the plan provisions. Thus, for example, provisions setting forth conditions under which a forfeiture of benefits may occur may be included principally for tax reasons. Or, a plan may deny the employee the right to assign his interest, or the right to have a lump sum cash benefit at retirement, death, or other termination of employment, for tax reasons.

Vesting

The decision as to whether or not there are to be vesting provisions in a deferred compensation agreement and, if so, what they should be, is a critical one. The ultimate costs of the plan to the employer, and the real value of the benefits to the employee, will depend in large measure on the benefits (if any) that are payable if employment terminates prior to a specified retirement date.

Whether there is a current reduction in salary or a forgoing of an increase that could otherwise clearly be obtained, once a deferred compensation agreement is entered into, it becomes part of the consideration for the future performance of services by the employee. He will not, without careful thought, agree to being deprived of accrued benefits.

When a current reduction in salary (or a forgoing of an increase) is involved, the employee is likely to insist on full and immediate vesting. At the other extreme, where an employer undertakes such a plan without being under any pressure to do so, there may be little or no vesting (except, perhaps, for death benefits). Most cases may fall somewhere between these extremes.

There is much to be said for vesting in case of early termination of employment, particularly where such termination is at the initiation of, or under pressure from, the employer. Perhaps an acceptable compromise for many situations is to provide that there will be no vesting if the employee voluntarily terminates employment before the retirement date but, in general, to provide for vesting under other circumstances.

Cost Considerations

The employer's cost of providing deferred compensation benefits will (as with any other form of pension benefit) depend directly upon: (1) the level of benefits provided; (2) the extent to which benefits are vested; (3) the investment results of any fund that may be established as a reserve against the employer's liability under the contract; and (4) the administrative costs, if any, involved. It may also depend upon the time of the employee's death, and upon the commencement and duration of any disability, if any benefits arise or terminate upon the happening of either such event. But if the deferred compensation is informally funded by an insurance policy owned by the employer, cost considerations based on such contingencies are eliminated. If the benefits are fully insured, the covering of these contingencies becomes a part of the cost of the level of the benefits provided.[52]

And, indirectly, the employer's cost will depend upon any tax consequences to it as a result of undertaking the agreement. Such consequences may include: (1) loss of any current tax deduction that would have been available had cash compensation been paid instead; (2) tax on any investment gains or income on any reserve fund established; and (3) any deduction available to the employer after payment of benefits commences.[53]

Where benefits or costs are arrived at in anticipation of tax consequences to the employer, one may speak of *after-tax funding*. Thus, a plan may be evolved where the level of benefits to be provided, or the net cost of providing them, anticipates the tax consequences to the employer.[54] The impossibility of precise cost

---

[52] So, also, with full insurance funding, the investment results and the administrative costs are in large measure incorporated in the cost of the benefits provided.

[53] See the section on "The Role of Life Insurance—Tax Consequences to the Employer," p. 341.

[54] Suppose, for example, that a corporation is prepared to give a $10,000 increase in salary. However, instead, it is willing to pay into a reserve account whatever amounts, from year to year, would equal the net after-tax cost of such a current salary increase. Thus, in a year in which its tax bracket is 48%, and the after-tax cost of $10,000 of salary increase would be $5,200, it would pay in $5,200 (in a year in which its bracket is 22% it would pay in $7,800).

Assume that the corporation buys a life insurance policy with a $5,200 annual premium and that it contemplates paying out under a deferred compensation agreement what it will net, from what it can receive under the insurance policy, after allowing for its future income tax liability and deductions. If (for the $5,200 annual premium) the corporation will receive $100,000 of tax-free proceeds upon the death of the insured prior to retirement, it can afford to pay a death benefit of $192,300 if it is then in a 48% bracket. For, if the $192,300 is

prediction under such a method is obvious. No one can know what the tax brackets of the employer will actually be during the payout years—or even, before that, during the years of active employment.

Not only can the earnings of a corporation vary its tax bracket from year to year, but legislative changes may introduce further changes.[55] And any allowance made for the expected tax bracket of the employer at the time of payout is, of course, also potentially vulnerable from the viewpoint of whether a deduction will in fact be allowed for the payments as made. If the corporation's deduction should be disallowed, then its net cost would be whatever it pays out, irrespective of its tax bracket.

Thus, clearly, if the magnitude of an employer's contractual commitments is to depend to any significant extent upon anticipated future tax results, it is essential that adequate provisions be included in the contract to protect the employer against unforeseen tax results.[56]

---

deductible, a deduction of this amount at a 48% bracket produces a corporate income tax savings of $92,304. This, together with the $100,000 of tax-free insurance proceeds, provides the total death benefit.

Similarly, if the corporation receives monthly payments under an annuity option of the insurance policy, commencing at the retirement of the insured, its tax liability on the annuity payments can be calculated. Then, when the amount of each monthly payment that it will have left after taxes is determined, it can afford (if it will continue throughout to be in a 48% bracket) to pay 100/52's of the net amount of each such monthly payment.

[55] Any employer who established a deferred compensation plan prior to 1964 and contracted to make specified benefit payments in anticipation of tax deductions at the pre-1964 income tax rates, but did not protect itself by stop-loss provisions under the deferred compensation contract, is in for a rude awakening. The reduction in combined normal and surtax rates introduced by The Revenue Act of 1964 (from 52% to 48%, and from 30% to 22%) will result in a substantial increase in net after-tax cost of providing the promised benefits.

[56] If an employer is to have assurance that the after-tax cost of any deferred benefits it may contract to pay will be equal to the after-tax cost of a current salary increase, an appropriate stop-loss provision is required. Thus for example, the agreement might provide that the employer will set aside as a reserve: "an amount each year which is equal to, one minus the employer's then current top income tax bracket in each such year, multiplied by . . ." a specified amount (i.e., the amount that would otherwise have been paid as a current salary increase).

Similarly, if the employee is to receive whatever benefits can be provided from a specific fund, increased by the amount of any tax deduction available to the employer with respect to the payment of those benefits, the agreement might first describe the "basic benefit" to be payable under various circumstances. It could then further provide that the actual amount payable from time to time shall be: "the basic benefit then due divided by, one minus the employer's then current top income tax bracket."

If a deferred compensation agreement contains such adjustment factors with respect to both costs *and* benefits, it will have the effect of (1) limiting the employer's net after-tax cost of the plan to the after-tax cost of paying the specified amount that might otherwise have been paid as current compensation,

Relating Benefits to Costs in Insured Plans

If a plan is benefit oriented in all respects, then, after the benefits have been determined, costs can be determined with a reasonable degree of accuracy. But they cannot be precisely determined. Conversely, if a plan is deferment oriented in all respects, it will ordinarily be a defined contribution plan. Thus, its cost will be fixed; and while benefits can perhaps be estimated with some degree of accuracy, they cannot be specifically determined.

But there are many instances in which neither orientation dominates exclusively. The employer may want assurance that his costs are fixed. Yet, the employee may be in a position to demand guaranteed benefits without regard for future eventualities that might alter the costs of the plan. Indeed, it is in such instances that the parties may be most likely to look to life insurance for an acceptable solution.

Suppose, for example, that an employer is willing to assume an obligation to pay specified premiums on a life insurance policy of a given size and on a particular plan (irrespective of its tax brackets in the years of premium payments), and to obligate itself to pay benefits under the contract equal to the amount that can be provided by the insurance policy. Hence, an employer prepared to carry a retirement income policy in the face amount of $100,000 might obligate itself under the deferred compensation contract to pay a death benefit of $100,000 in case of death before retirement, or to pay retirement benefits of $1,000 per month. The amount of such benefits can, of course, be specified directly in the deferred compensation contract.

However, if the contract provides for any vesting prior to the designated retirement age, provision should be made for such reduced benefits as would be provided by the value of the insurance policy at the time employment is terminated. Hence, it would appear necessary to: (1) incorporate the values of the insurance

---

and (2) giving the employee the benefit of tax deductions realized by the employer as benefits are actually paid. Thus, in a sense, the employee is compensated for agreeing to let the employer have the equivalent of a "tax deduction" as it puts money into the reserve, by the employer's agreement, in turn, to permit the employee to reap the benefit of any tax deductions actually realized as benefits are paid out of the reserve.

However, it may be best to so anticipate tax results merely as a guide to estimating net costs and benefits, but to have the agreement itself actually provide for specified benefits or for specifically defined contributions. This should result in a better understanding by the parties to the agreement of just what is to happen under its provisions, simplify the drafting of the agreement, and make it simpler to administer.

policy in the deferred compensation agreement by specific reference thereto;[57] (2) reproduce the values of the insurance policy in the deferred compensation contract itself; or (3) include in the deferred compensation contract a scale of benefits to be paid in the event of termination at various times, expressed either in dollars or in terms of a percentage of the benefits that would be payable at retirement age.

These are by no means the only choices available. In fact, any provisions for benefits upon which employer and employee can agree, and which are sufficiently definite or determinable so that the attorney can succeed in reducing their agreement to writing, would be perfectly proper. One could have an agreement with benefits measured in terms of policy values to be in turn multiplied by an appropriate factor determined by the employer's tax brackets in payout years. And the employer's contribution to policy values could itself be a function of his tax brackets in premium-paying years.[58]

THE DEFERRED COMPENSATION CONTRACT

Once employer and employee have agreed on the general nature of the deferred compensation arrangement to be established, their attorneys must then reduce to writing a specific, detailed description of their agreement. The written contract will first recite the purposes of the agreement and the consideration given by each party in exchange for the promises of the other party.

The draftsmen will then attempt to explicitly describe the amount, time, and manner of payment of all deferred benefits. A well-drafted agreement will cover virtually any contingency that can conceivably arise, will be specific as to all amounts of money, will anticipate possible changes in relationship between the parties, and will provide for the manner in which the agreement may be modified or terminated.

---

[57] For further comment on this, see the section on "Deferred Compensation Contract—Vesting Insurance Policy Values," p. 353.

[58] Any such after-tax funding of employer contribution introduces the problem of paying level premiums on an insurance policy out of a variable contribution to the reserve. But, in any event, such a problem must be dealt with in deferment-oriented plans which defer a percentage of income rather than a fixed dollar amount (for example, plans for highly successful commission salesmen).

Among the possible solutions to accommodating such varying contributions to a level premium insurance policy are: (a) use of an auxiliary investment fund for some part of the contribution; (b) use of a flexible premium rider; and (c) discounting premiums in some years while, perhaps, using the automatic premium loan provision of the policy in other years.

Benefit-Oriented Agreements

A benefit-oriented agreement will ordinarily provide for the commencement of specified retirement benefits at a specified time or age (age 65, for example). It may provide that such benefits will be payable for a fixed period of years, or for the life of the payee. It may provide that a minimum number of payments will be continued to a beneficiary or to the estate of a retired employee who dies prior to receipt of a specified number of payments.

It will make provision for any adjustment to be made in the amount of periodic payments in the event employment is continued beyond the designated retirement date. It will fix the benefits (if any) to be payable if employment terminates prior to the retirement date (whether such termination is instigated by the employer or is of the employee's own volition).

The agreement will expressly cover what (if any) benefits are payable in the event of death at any time: i.e., death while employed prior to retirement; death following normal retirement; or death following an early termination of employment.

The agreement may provide for benefits to be payable in the event of the partial or total disability of the employee. It may or may not provide for the circumstances under which employment will terminate in the event of a prolonged disability, and any benefits to be payable under such circumstances.

The agreement, in order to introduce greater flexibility, may provide that in lieu of making specified periodic payments, payment of different amounts for different periods on an actuarially equivalent basis may be made upon mutual agreement of the employer and payee.[59] It would appear that such an alternative election should be available only upon the employer's agreement to do so (rather than as an option of the employee), in order to avoid creating a danger of constructive receipt.

The agreement will ordinarily contain a prohibition against commutation or assignment of any benefits. Such *spendthrift* provisions are included not only as a safeguard against possible application of the economic benefit doctrine, but also to protect the employer from the inconvenience of being forced to deal with the employee's assignees, and to protect the benefits under the agreement from being reached by creditors of a beneficiary.

A provision may be included to negate specifically any inference that the agreement constitutes an employment contract and to ac-

---

[59] It would appear necessary to define *actuarial equivalence*, which clearly has no consistent or universal meaning.

knowledge specifically that any benefits payable under the contract are in addition to, and not in lieu of, any compensation that may be payable outside of the agreement.[60]

If the agreement is informally funded, reasonable caution suggests including specific provisions negating any implication that any insurance policy or other asset acquired by the employer is required to be devoted to purposes of the agreement.[61]

Provision should be included to protect the employee in the event of the merger, consolidation, sale, or termination of the business of the employer.

Customarily, a provision is included which permits the alteration, amendment, or revocation of the agreement by a writing signed by both parties.

Deferment-Oriented Agreements

A deferment-oriented agreement must cover all of the contingencies that are encountered under benefit-oriented agreements. Hence, it will be similar in most respects. However, in one respect it may be considerably simpler, while in another respect it may be more complex.

The greater simplicity will arise because the amount deferred (perhaps enhanced by interest and/or by investment gains) will ordinarily be fully vested from the outset. Thus, the same amount may be payable at a particular time whether or not there is a termination of employment and regardless of whether any such termination arises upon normal retirement, quitting, firing, death, or disability.

A deferment-oriented agreement of the defined contribution (money purchase) type may merely provide that the employee is to be credited with certain amounts annually. It may or may not provide that the account is to be credited with interest, annually, at a specific rate. Or it may provide that the account is to be credited annually with whatever investment earnings are produced by investment of the amounts credited, including gains—whether realized or unrealized.

---

[60] But in a deferment-oriented agreement, it may be desirable to specifically make benefits payable under the deferred compensation agreement *in lieu* of amounts that would otherwise have been payable under certain prior agreements affecting compensation. For example, where the amounts credited are to be in lieu of compensation that would otherwise have been payable.

[61] Such caution is suggested by the case of *Rhodes* v. *Gray*, 175 F. Supp. 208 (1959), which held an insured employee to be the equitable owner of an insurance policy where the employer was the legal owner but where there was a deferred compensation agreement and the insured had physical possession of the policy.

If credited with actual investment earnings, the agreement must contain provisions (similar to those customarily found in a qualified profit sharing plan) respecting valuation of the account. And, unless the benefits are to be fixed in amount as of the time that payment of benefits commences, an annual revaluation will be required during the payout period.

Drafting the Contract

The responsibility for preparing the final agreement between the parties rests with their attorneys. They alone will be responsible for its ultimate substance, its tax results, and its specific wording. In theory, if not always in practice, the contract should be reviewed and approved by both the employer's and the employee's attorney. Unfortunately, in actual practice, separate advisors are not always retained by each of the parties. This, in turn, may lead to unnecessary future litigation.[62]

Not infrequently, those attorneys who have had relatively little experience in this particular area may look to the life insurance man or to the insurance company for guidance with respect to some of the proposed substance, if the plan under consideration contemplates insurance or annuity funding. As a means of offering assistance to such attorneys, many insurance companies make available various specimen deferred compensation contracts.[63] Such specimens cover typical arrangements but are rarely suitable to any particular situation. They by no means replace the attorney's skill and knowledge, thoughtfully applied, nor are they so intended.

The attorney may encounter some difficulty in drafting vesting provisions for certain plans informally funded by insurance contracts, where it is desired to immediately vest in the employee precisely the amount available from a participating insurance policy, including any values arising out of dividends. This may prove to be particularly troublesome if the vested values are not to be distributed immediately upon termination of employment but, instead, there is to be a deferral of payment of the vested amounts until the normal retirement date.[64]

---

[62] Any savings in attorney's fees realized at the inception of the agreement will be trivial when viewed against the costs of litigation at the time of performance.

[63] Such specimens are readily available from many of the larger insurance companies upon request.

[64] Immediate distribution upon termination of employment would, ordinarily, be undesirable since it would confront the employee with immediate tax liability. Also, the employer may not want to provide anything in the nature of a cash quitting benefit, which might tend to induce an early termination of employment.

Vesting Insurance Policy Values

Suppose that an employer wants to provide a package of benefits (for retirement, death, and early termination of employment) that corresponds precisely to the values of an insurance policy.[65] In such a case, all benefits may be measured by the aggregate values of a hypothetical insurance policy independently of whether or not such a policy is in fact kept in force.

The policy (and, hence, its various values) could, of course, be incorporated by reference in the agreement. While reference to the policy is not dangerous in and of itself, too tight an incorporation of specific policy values may introduce a serious danger that the employee will be deemed to have an equitable interest in the policy.

Since it is assumed that a policy is, in fact, acquired by the employer, the agreement might first recite that such is the case, identifying the policy by policy number, date of issue, face amount, and names of insurer and insured. Retirement benefits could then be provided for as follows:

> If the Executive is living on the Retirement Date, the Executive shall be entitled to receive, in monthly installments over a period of ten years, an amount determined according to whichever shall be applicable of subsection "a" or "b" hereof.
>
> *a*) If the Executive has remained continuously in the employ of the Corporation until the Retirement Date, the amount to which the Executive shall then be entitled shall be an amount equal to what the cash surrender value of said Policy would have been at the Retirement Date, plus the then value of all accumulated dividends, and other amounts, *that would then be available if said Policy had been continuously kept in full force* and dividends thereon had been left on deposit.
>
> *b*) If the employment of the Executive with the Corporation shall have terminated prior to the Retirement Date, the amount to which the the Executive shall be entitled on the Retirement Date shall be an amount equal to *what the cash surrender value of said Policy would have been* at the Retirement Date, plus the then value of all accumulated dividends, and other amounts, *had the Policy been kept in full force until the date of termination of employment, and upon the next following anniversary of its issue date had lapsed as paid-up insurance,* and if all dividends on the Policy had been left on deposit.

With such an approach to drafting, it is abundantly clear that the employee acquires no equitable interest in the policy itself, since the agreement will clearly recite that the employer is free to deal

---

[65] This may be particularly desirable in the case of a defined contribution plan, wherein benefits are to be provided in whatever amounts will be produced by an annual commitment of a specified number of dollars.

with the policy as it sees fit and is under no obligation to keep any policy in force.[66]

CHARITABLE CORPORATIONS

Tax considerations respecting certain charitable organizations[67] and their employees are sufficiently different, in three respects, so that special consideration should be given to deferred compensation plans established by such employers. These differences are: (1) such employers are exempt from tax;[68] (2) their employees enjoy a unique deferment of tax liability in connection with employer-purchased annuities;[69] and (3) under nonqualified annuity plans, employees are taxable if their rights change from forfeitable to nonforfeitable.[70]

None of the foregoing considerations would inhibit establishing a plan of the type covered in this chapter.[71] In general, the tax considerations, design considerations, etc., that have been discussed will still apply. But, for charitable employers, the tax differences are such that more can be done to protect the employee without adverse tax consequences to employer or employee.

Tax Exemption of Employer

In contrast to ordinary business corporations, tax-exempt charitable organizations have no concern with whether receipts are taxable income or disbursements are deductible items.[72] Hence, taxes have no bearing on the employer's net cost of providing benefits. The fact that unfunded deferred compensation offers no current tax deduction is of no consequence. And it is of no consequence that a funded plan, under which the employee's rights change from forfeitable to nonforfeitable, puts an employer's deduction in jeopardy.

---

[66] If the plan provides for death benefits, or for benefits to be payable in the event of the employee's disability, the amount of these benefits can be measured in like manner. Such an approach would be equally suitable regardless of the form of permanent insurance policy acquired by the employer, or the nature of the benefits promised.

[67] Those qualifying under I.R.C. 501(c)(3).

[68] I.R.C. 501(a).

[69] I.R.C. 403(b). For a discussion of tax-sheltered annuities, see Chapter 16.

[70] I.R.C. 403(d).

[71] Except to the limited extent that I.R.C. 403(d) might, under some circumstances, bar an arrangement where forfeitable rights change to nonforfeitable, if I.R.C. 403(b) did not apply.

[72] Except to the extent that they may have "unrelated business income" under I.R.C. 511, a matter that is of no concern here.

Guarantees at Retirement

If an annuity contract is purchased for an employee by such an employer, and the employee's rights under the contract are nonforfeitable, the employee, nevertheless, is not taxable until annuity payments are actually made to him under the contract.[73] This deferral of tax liability is subject to an *exclusion allowance,* which limits the size of the annuity in accordance with the length of service of the employee and the amount of his taxable compensation.

Suppose the charitable employer were to purchase an annuity contract in which the employee has no interest, or has a forfeitable interest. If, at a subsequent time (for example, at the date of retirement or termination of employment), the employee obtains a nonforfeitable interest, the situation is viewed as though an annuity contract were purchased for the employee at that time; and no tax liability arises to the employee within the limits of the available exclusion allowance. Thus, unlike the deferred compensation plan of a nonexempt employer, the employee can acquire an absolute right to receive annuity payments directly from the insurance company without fear of there being a taxable economic benefit.

Although this tax shelter is available only for an annuity contract (or an annuity contract with "incidental" insurance), it offers a useful vehicle in connection with deferred compensation contracts informally funded by an employer-owned life insurance policy. Provision may be made in the deferred compensation contract that upon retirement, or earlier termination of employment while living, the employer will fulfill its promises under the agreement by turning over to the employee an annuity contract issued by an insurance company. The employer will expect to accomplish this, at the employee's retirement, by surrendering the insurance policy and electing settlement under one of the options of payment included in the policy. This would technically be an annuity for the employee, under which he would have the right to receive payments directly from the insurance company, as well as direct control of any subsequent death benefits. Or, in the case of early termination of employment with vesting, the employer could exchange the policy for a paid-up annuity contract. Such paid-up contract could provide for either an immediate or deferred annuity.

Thus, when an employee of a qualified charity terminates his employment or retires, the employer can be relieved of all future

---

[73] I.R.C. 403(b). Such so-called tax-sheltered annuities are considered in detail in Chapter 16.

administration of the plan by distributing an annuity contract which fulfills all of the employer's remaining obligations. And, unlike the case of employees of ordinary business corporations, this can be done without fear of tax liability to the employee before receiving actual payments under the annuity contract.[74]

Forfeitable Rights Which Become Nonforfeitable

As previously noted, the general rule is that no taxable event occurs when an employee's forfeitable rights under an annuity contract later become nonforfeitable.[75] But Section 403(d) makes an exception to this in the case of annuity contracts purchased by employers who are exempt from tax under Section 501(a)[76] at the time of such purchase.[77] This exception was added to the statute in order to discourage funded nonqualified plans by tax-exempt employers.[78] But in view of the available tax-sheltered annuity treatment, it offers little discouragement. For, within the limits of the available exclusion allowance, the amount that would be otherwise taxable when rights change from forfeitable to nonforfeitable is deemed to have been applied to the purchase of a tax-sheltered annuity and is, therefore, excluded.

Recommended Plans for Charitable Employers

Notwithstanding the tax-exempt status of an employer, a qualified pension plan offers tax advantages to the employees that are not available under a tax-sheltered annuity or under a nonqualified deferred compensation plan. And, in some instances, tax-sheltered annuities are more attractive than nonqualified deferred compensation.[79] Nevertheless, there are circumstances under which the latter is the most attractive of the alternatives. This may be the case where it is desired: (1) to provide a death benefit that is more than *incidental;* (2) to defer compensation for particular individuals in amounts which would exceed the available exclusion allowance, or which would cause discrimination barring a qualified plan; or (3)

---

[74] See Note 5 and text to which it applies.

[75] See Note 10 and text to which it applies.

[76] Or exempt from tax under I.R.C. 521(a) (relating to certain farmers' cooperatives). Surprisingly, neither the Code nor the Regulations appear to provide any similar exception for nonqualified *trusts* created by tax-exempt employers. Undoubtedly, this was an oversight.

[77] Reg. 1.403(d)–1(b).

[78] Which, for taxable employers, are discouraged by Reg. 1.404(a)–12.

[79] See Chapter 16.

to defer benefits for a payee who is an independent contractor rather than an employee.[80]

Where a nonqualified deferred compensation plan for such an employer is indicated, it will generally be unfunded or informally funded. But formal funding need not be feared if the employee's rights are forfeitable, even if there is deemed to be a trust or annuity plan for his benefit to which the employer contributes. Therefore, it is possible to employ various security devices in such plans without the tax risks involved in such devices for the plan of an ordinary business corporation.

SECURITY DEVICES

One important limitation of the deferred compensation arrangements discussed in this chapter may frequently cause serious concern to the employee. If he agrees to a deferral of compensation that might otherwise have been available to him currently, what assurance does he have that the employer will be financially able to perform its contractual obligations when the date for performance arrives? In general, the answer is, *none*.

One of the risks that the employee takes by entering into a tax-safe, unfunded deferred compensation contract is that of the employer's future insolvency. Indeed, it is the possibility of such insolvency that gives assurance that the employee will have neither constructive receipt nor a taxable economic benefit.[81] Any such risk is trivial if the employer is large and financially sound.

Split-Dollar Insurance

There are situations in which the employee is satisfied that the employer's financial stability is sufficient so that he has no real concern about receiving *his* deferred payments. But he is not satisfied that benefits payable to his widow are as secure as he might like them to be. In the latter case, a ready solution is available in the form of a deferred compensation contract which provides solely

---

[80] While this chapter has been primarily concerned with deferred compensation for *employees*, the concepts discussed are generally applicable to independent contractors also (see Note 8 and text to which it applies). Indeed, in recent years, among those who have manifested great interest in deferred compensation are radiologists, pathologists, and anesthetists. The relationship between such individuals and the hospitals for which they work is, more often than not, one of an independent contractor, rather than an employee.

It should be noted, however, that the provisions of Sections 402–404 of the Code discussed herein, are limited in their applicability to employer-employee relationships.

[81] See *Casale*, Note 36.

(or at least principally) for deferred benefits to the employee himself, with any benefits payable after his death to be provided under a so-called split-dollar insurance arrangement.[82] Under such a supplemental insurance arrangement, the widow will receive her benefits directly from the insurance company. Thus, after the employee's death, the employer's financial stability is no longer relevant.

Collateralized Deferred Compensation

But are there possibilities of greater protection for the employee himself? Has he no alternative but to run the risk of employer insolvency in order to obtain income tax deferral? Not necessarily. He can have substantial protection against the uncertainties of the employer's future ability to pay—but at a price! That price involves introducing a degree of tax risk for either the employer or employee.

The financial risk may be eliminated by the employer pledging specific assets to the employee as security for the performance of the employer's obligations. Such assets should themselves be financially sound (a life insurance policy, for example) and should otherwise be unencumbered. Such arrangements are frequently referred to as *collateralized deferred compensation,* since the asset to be pledged is generally collaterally assigned to the employee as security for the promised performance.

At present, qualified commentators differ as to whether such a secured arrangement will cause current tax liability to the em-

---

[82] See, for example, Bernard M. Eiber, "Deferred Compensation: II," *Trusts and Estates,* August, 1964, p. 752.

The subject of split-dollar insurance arrangements is beyond the scope of this book. Such arrangements generally involve the purchase of a form of permanent insurance by an employer on the life of an employee, with the employer paying the annual premiums to the extent of the yearly increases in the cash surrender value of the policy and the employee paying only any remaining balance of the premiums. Amounts provided by the employer to pay the premiums are generally recoverable by it upon surrender or maturity of the policy, and any additional proceeds upon maturity of the policy are payable to a beneficiary or beneficiaries of the employee.

Prior to November 14, 1964, an employee was held to realize no income from such an arrangement, which was viewed as the same in substance as if the employer annually made loans to the employee without interest. But for such plans established since that date, the employee is taxable annually on an amount equal to the one-year term cost of the declining life insurance protection to which he is entitled under such an arrangement, less any portion of the premiums provided by him (Rev. Rul. 64–328, 1964–2 CB 11). The proceeds of the policy payable upon the employee's death are excluded from gross income under Section 101(a) of the Code. No deduction is allowed to the employer for premium payments made.

ployee if the deferred compensation contract makes unqualified promises of future benefits. In Rev. Rul. 60–31, the Internal Revenue Service observed that: "A mere promise to pay, not represented by notes or security in any way, is not regarded as a receipt of income within the intendment of the cash receipts and disbursements method."

But this Ruling may well contain an implication that a different result would follow if the employer pledges an asset as security.[83] In any event, no useful purpose is served by speculating in this area. Reasonable caution would suggest avoiding such collateralizing if the objectives of the parties can be achieved without taking such tax risks.[84]

If, however, the employee just cannot afford to take the risk of future insolvency of his employer, it may be advisable to eliminate this risk even though other risks are introduced by doing so. In these cases, perhaps, consideration should first be given to whether it is preferable to have any such tax risk fall on the employer or on the employee.

Employer's Tax Risk

If the employer is willing to give the employee security and is willing to take a tax risk in the bargain, tax safety for the employee can be achieved by including in the deferred compensation contract one or more bona fide conditions under which a forfeiture of the employee's benefits will occur.[85] While the employee should thus have little or no risk of current taxation or of loss of benefits arising out of employer insolvency, he does take on a risk of loss of benefits if a forfeiture should occur.[86]

But if the employee's rights are forfeitable, the employer may be denied a tax deduction with respect to any amount paid at any time.[87] Whether the courts will support such a disallowance is uncertain, but the employer may have a fighting chance in view of the *Russel Mfg. Co.* and *Mississippi River Fuel* cases.[88]

---

[83] Probably a taxable economic benefit, rather than constructive receipt.

[84] For a more detailed discussion of this area, see James L. Rivers, "Collateralized Deferred Compensation—Poison or Panacea?" *Journal of the American Society of Chartered Life Underwriters*, Vol. XX, No. 1 (Winter, 1966), p. 37.

[85] See the section on "Summary of Income Tax Deferral," p. 335.

[86] It seems characteristic of the tax field, generally, that one cannot obtain an advantage without a concomitant disadvantage.

[87] See Note 14 and text to which it applies.

[88] See Note 31.

Employee's Tax Risk

The tax risk to the employee is, of course, that any secured contractual promise may be deemed to give rise to a funded plan. In this event, if the employee's rights are *nonforfeitable,* he is subject to income tax liability for each year in which contributions are made. If, on the other hand, his rights are *forfeitable,* he avoids current tax.

Evaluation of Secured Agreements

Secured, unfunded deferred compensation arrangements should be viewed with particular caution until such time as court decisions or further Regulations clarify (1) whether or not they result in currently taxable income in the case of plans where the employee's rights are nonforfeitable, and (2) whether or not an employer forever loses his deduction in the case of plans involving forfeitable rights which later become nonforfeitable.

Nevertheless, in the case of employees of certain *charitable corporations,* such secured plans, providing for forfeitable benefits, would seem attractive (even without further clarification of the law), since (1) a tax deduction is of no consequence to the employer, and (2) any tax impact to the employee when his rights later become nonforfeitable is largely deferred because of the tax-sheltered annuity provisions of Section 403(b).

If such an employer undertakes a deferred compensation contract with an independent contractor (rather than with an employee), all benefits should remain forfeitable until they are actually received, since Section 403(b) applies only to employees.

Whether the agreement be for the benefit of an employee or an independent contractor (and whether the employer is tax exempt or not), the elimination of the employee's risk of the employer's future insolvency at best substitutes a risk of loss of benefits as a result of forfeiture.

VOLUNTARY DEATH PAYMENTS

It is well established that payments made to a widow or other beneficiary of a deceased employee pursuant to a *contract* with his employer are taxable to the recipient as ordinary income.[89] And, ordinarily, they should be deductible by the employer as part of the overall compensation arrangement.

---

[89] Except insofar as the $5,000 exclusion of I.R.C. 101(b) may apply.

But, is a widow taxable on amounts *voluntarily* paid to her by the former employer of her deceased husband, or are such payments received by her tax free as gifts? And to what extent are they deductible? These questions have plagued taxpayers, the Commissioner, and even the courts for many years.

Taxable Status of Voluntary Payments

The issue of taxability reached the Supreme Court of the United States in 1960 in *Comm'r* v. *Duberstein*.[90] But no definitive answer came out of that decision. It held that the issue was basically one of fact, to be decided on a case-by-case basis.

The proper standard, said the Court, is one that inquires concerning the basic reason for the employer's action—i.e., "the dominant reason that explains the action in making the transfer." In short, the Supreme Court held that while a corporation can make gifts, the characterization used by the parties is not binding in determining the character of the transaction for tax purposes. Nor does the corporation, by claiming a business expense deduction for the "gift," conclusively establish that it was not a gift. Each case must be decided on its own facts.

In cases that have arisen since the *Duberstein* case, the Commissioner has generally, but not consistently,[91] been successful in finding a taxable payment to the widow.

Deductibility of Voluntary Payments

Regulations, originally promulgated under the Revenue Act of 1918, which continued unchanged through the 1939 Code, provided in part: "When the amount of the salary of an officer or employee is paid for a limited period after his death to his widow or heirs, in recognition of the services rendered by the individual, such payments may be deducted."[92]

Indeed, in 1939, the Commissioner ruled that voluntary payments over a two-year period, even though nontaxable gifts, were nevertheless deductible.[93]

But the Revenue Service was actually (and properly) more concerned with the amount of salary continued, rather than the period of continuation. In a 1954 Ruling it stated that the above-

---

[90] 363 U.S. 278.

[91] For example, see *Laura H. Greeley* v. *U.S.*, 247 F. Supp. 37 (1965), and see *Fanning* v. *Conley*, 243 F. Supp. 683, *aff'd* 357 F.2d 37 (CA-2, 1966).

[92] Regs. 111, Sec. 29.23(a)–9.

[93] I.T. 3329, 1939–2 CB 153.

quoted sentence of the Regulations "should be liberally construed so as to reflect the true purpose of Section 23(a) (1) (A),[94] namely, that the words 'for a limited period' should be regarded as relating to the rules of reasonableness employed by the statute, rather than the length of time during which payments may be made."[95] The Ruling observed that an amount equal to $2\frac{1}{2}$ years of compensation paid over a 12-year period would meet the tests set forth in the Regulations. The present Regulations are substantially equivalent to those promulgated under the 1918 Act, but speak of continuing salary for a *reasonable* period rather than a *limited* period.[96]

The applicability of the foregoing would now appear to be limited solely to payments that are *compensatory* in nature; for a recent statutory change makes it clear that *gifts* are no longer deductible as business expenses to the extent that in any taxable year of the business they exceed $25 to an individual donee.[97]

Postdeath Planning

If there is to be even a reasonable hope of having a tax-free gift to the widow, it would seem that the decision to benefit her must be made subsequent to her husband's death. Such payments are not ordinarily includable in the deceased employee's gross estate for estate tax purposes, because he will have had no property rights in the payments at the time of his death, nor will he have made any transfers.

The extent to which the employer will be allowed a deduction for amounts so paid is questionable unless the aggregate amount in-

---

[94] Dealing with ordinary and necessary business expenses under the 1939 Code.

[95] Rev. Rul. 54–625, 1954–2 CB 85.

[96] The present Regulations under Sec. 162, pertaining to the deduction of business expenses, promulgated in 1958, omitted the language found in the earlier Regulations. The basis for the deduction is now to be found in Reg. 1.404(a)–12, which reads in part as follows: "Similarly, if amounts are paid as a death benefit to the beneficiaries of an employee (for example, by continuing his salary for a reasonable period), and if such amount met the requirements of section 162 [relating to trade or business expenses] or 212 [relating to expenses for production of income], such amounts are deductible under section 404(a) (5) in any case where they are not deductible under the other paragraphs of section 404(a)."

Although the Internal Revenue Service has not explained the reasons for its change of approach in the Regulations, it appears that such changes were made in an effort to support the position of the Service that under the 1954 Code all payments, voluntary or otherwise, are in the nature of deferred compensation rather than gifts. And, further, that a deduction will only be permissible if it *is* in the nature of compensation, but not if it is in fact a gift.

[97] I.R.C. 274(b), which was added by the Revenue Act of 1962.

volved is severely limited. And while the income tax treatment of the widow does not control the issue of deductibility by the employer, it should be expected that the Revenue Service will attempt to limit the deduction to $25 per year if the payee has received tax-free gift treatment (or is likely to so prevail).

Such postdeath planning is, of course, not ordinarily within the province of the life underwriter. Rather, he concerns himself primarily with arrangements to anticipate the financial impact of death well in advance of its occurrence and, hence, with salary continuation arrangements involving agreements made prior to death.

THE USE OF NONQUALIFIED DEFERRED COMPENSATION

No individual whose spendable income is inadequate to meet his current needs will have any interest in a deferred compensation plan. It is only when current income substantially exceeds current expenses that a deferral of income may be desirable from his viewpoint.

Clearly, the deferred compensation concept has little appeal unless the individual is in a fairly high tax bracket and anticipates that he will continue to be in a high bracket for some time. Yet, if his bracket is likely to remain continually high (or to increase), deferral of income may be unprofitable. Income should be deferred voluntarily only when one may reasonably anticipate that the payee's bracket will be lower at the time the income is actually received than it would have been if income had been received at an earlier date.[98]

Yet, excessive current income and a reasonably anticipated reduction in tax bracket at a future date, are not enough to indicate the desirability of income deferral. The individual must have a relatively high degree of assurance that the deferred payments will in fact be paid in full. He must have a high degree of confidence in the company employing him and its future solvency before he will be enthusiastic about accepting the employer's unsecured contractual commitment.[99] The employer, on the other hand, must have a high regard for the employee in order to be willing to pass up the current income tax deduction for compensation currently paid. In-

---

[98] It is often pointed out that every individual taxpayer is entitled to an additional $600 exemption after age 65 (two if his spouse is over 65), and, hence, savings may be anticipated by virtue of this factor alone. It seems doubtful that the savings realized thereby will be truly significant, in the absence of a significant reduction in gross income.

[99] And, as indicated under the section on "Security Devices," p. 357, a secured commitment may introduce tax risks.

deed, there must be a high degree of mutual good faith. Good draftsmanship can give both parties reasonably adequate assurance that each will perform as agreed. But draftsmanship alone will not suffice. Though neither party would knowingly contract for a future lawsuit, many a contract (particularly one of long duration) is ultimately construed in court. Good faith, then, may be equal in importance to draftsmanship.

Nor should a nonqualified deferred compensation arrangement be undertaken unless it is clearly demonstrable that a *qualified* plan is not feasible under the circumstances.[100] Also, where they apply, tax-sheltered annuities should be considered as a possible alternative.[101]

---

[100] For, with a qualified plan, a number of advantages are available that cannot be achieved through a nonqualified plan, namely: (1) current deduction to employer without current tax to employee, (2) tax-exempt earnings on reserves held for future benefit payments, (3) capital gains opportunities for certain lump sum distributions of retirement, termination, or death benefits, and (4) estate tax advantages.

[101] See Chapter 16 for their advantages.

TAX-SHELTERED ANNUITIES

In some respects, the so-called "tax-sheltered annuity" resembles the deferred compensation plans discussed in Chapter 15. The motive of income tax deferral is, of course, the same. And, while the applicability of tax-sheltered annuities is considerably more limited, where they do apply they offer some significant advantages. In other respects, tax-sheltered annuities resemble qualified pension plans, with the added advantage that they can be discriminatory. But they by no means offer all of the tax advantages of a qualified plan.

STATUTORY ASPECTS

Background

Ever since 1942, the Internal Revenue Code has contained a provision which permitted certain tax-exempt charitable employers to purchase annuity contracts for their employees without current income tax liability to the employees. Eligible employers are those that qualified under Section 101(6) of the 1939 Code, or Section 501(c)(3) of the 1954 Code. Under the original statutory provision: ". . . if an annuity contract is purchased for an employee by an employer exempt under Section 101(6), the employee shall include in his income the amounts received under such contract for the year received. . . ."[1] In the absence of such a statutory provision, taxable income would arise as premiums are paid.

As the public became aware of this provision in the Code, some individuals began to avail themselves of this tax advantage to a far greater extent than the Commissioner of Internal Revenue felt proper. Thus, the Commissioner attempted to limit the circum-

---

[1] Section 22(b)(2) of the 1939 Code.

stances under which, and the extent to which, the statutory provision would be deemed applicable.[2]

The Internal Revenue Code of 1954 made no modification in the statutory provisions. However, by the Technical Amendments Act of 1958, a considerably more detailed provision (Section 403 (b)) was enacted which established the concept of a 20% exclusion allowance.[3] Then, by the Revenue Act of 1961, Section 403(b) was amended to extend tax deferral with respect to such annuity purchases to employees of public school systems. And, finally, after a number of years, Regulations were promulgated interpreting the new provision.[4]

The Present Statute

Section 403(b) of the Code, as amended, now provides in part that,

If an annuity contract is purchased for an employee by an employer described in section 501(c)(3) . . . , or for an employee . . . who performs services for an educational institution (as defined in section 151(e)(4)), by an employer which is a State, a political subdivision of a State, or an agency or instrumentality of any one or more of the foregoing, . . . and the employee's rights under the contract are non-forfeitable, except for failure to pay future premiums, then amounts contributed by such employer for such annuity contract . . . shall be excluded from the gross income of the employee for the taxable year to the extent that the aggregate of such amounts does not exceed the *exclusion allowance*[5] for such taxable year.

Thus, the essential requirements to achieve the desired tax shelter are as follows:

1. The annuitant must be employed by a duly qualified charitable organization or by a public school system.
2. The annuitant must be a bona fide employee.
3. The annuity contract must be *purchased* by such employer.
4. The annuitant's rights under the contract must be nonforfeitable except for failure to pay future premiums.

---

[2] Rev. Rul. 54–267, 1954–2 CB 58; 26 CFR 1.403(a)–1(3) (TD 6203, 9/24/56). And see the section on "Current Salary Reductions," pp. 377–378.

[3] While the Congressional Committee Reports indicated that the new, objective statutory tests were to replace the arbitrary position of the Commissioner (Senate Finance Committee Report #1983, 85th Cong. 2d Sess.), several years passed before the Internal Revenue Service appears to have acknowledged the edict of Congress. See Note 4.

[4] Reg. 1.403(b)–1, TD 6783 (12/23/64).

[5] Emphasis added. The *exclusion allowance* will be examined in great detail subsequently.

5. The amount of the premium paid in any year should not exceed the exclusion allowance for the year in question (and will be currently taxable to the extent that it does exceed such allowance).

While these are the *essential* ingredients of a tax-sheltered annuity, each of these requirements calls for examination in considerable detail.

REQUIREMENTS OF A TAX-SHELTERED ANNUITY

Qualified Employers

If the employee is to qualify for tax-sheltered annuity treatment his employer must be:

a) A charitable organization qualified under Section 501 (c) (3) of the Internal Revenue Code (for example, a tax-exempt hospital, church, school, or other such organization or foundation), or

b) A public school system (for example, one operated by the state, or by a county, city, town, school district, or other political subdivision or agency of a state).

Note that not every tax-exempt organization is a qualified employer, but only those which qualify under Section 501 (c) (3).

Note also that not all types of publicly operated facilities can qualify, but only public *school* systems. Certain other publicly operated facilities (hospitals or other charities, for example) may or may not qualify. For the qualification of such organizations, a ruling should be obtained from the Internal Revenue Service.[6]

Eligible Employees

To be eligible for the tax shelter, the individual most be an *employee* of a qualified charitable organization or of a public school system. He may be the top executive or the lowest-paid clerk. He may be a seasonal, part-time, or full-time employee. But he must be an *employee*—not an independent contractor. This point requires particular attention in connection with certain professional people (such as radiologists, pathologists, and anesthesiologists) who may or may not, in a given set of circumstances, in fact be employees.[7]

---

[6] If the activity of the facility is such that if it were not publicly operated it could qualify under Section 501 (c) (3), and if it has sufficient independence from the state, etc., it may be able to obtain a ruling that it is a *counterpart* of a Section 501 (c) (3) organization. See Rev. Rul. 55–319, 1955–1 CB 119, as (radically) modified by Rev. Rul. 60–384, 1960–2 CB 172.

[7] Some professionals in the service of tax-exempt organizations may be barred by ethical or legal considerations from meeting the tests for the

Clerical, administrative, supervisory, and custodial employees of public school systems qualify, as well as teachers.[8]

Unlike qualified pension and profit sharing plans (and certain stock option plans), Section 403(b) and the Regulations pertaining thereto contain no prohibitions whatsoever against discrimination. Thus, a tax-sheltered annuity plan may be adopted for the benefit of any one or more favored employees, even though clear discrimination in their favor results.

Annuity Contract Purchased by an Employer

In speaking of "an annuity contract . . . purchased . . . by an employer . . . ," the statute gives no indication of what constitutes "an annuity contract" or a "purchase . . . by an employer."

Presumably, an annuity contract refers to a contract to pay annuity benefits issued by an insurance company regularly engaged in the business of issuing such contracts.[9] It would appear to make no difference whether such a contract is a single-premium or annual-premium contract or whether it provides for fixed or variable annuity payments, immediate or deferred, with or without a refund provision.

For many years the Internal Revenue Service took the position that a contract which provided a life insurance benefit would not qualify as a tax-sheltered annuity. But the Regulations now provide that "an individual contract issued after December 31, 1962, or a group contract which provides incidental life insurance protection may be purchased as an annuity contract," to which Section 403(b) applies.[10] The expression, *incidental life insurance protection*, presumably has the same meaning as it has with respect to insurance purchased under qualified trusts.[11]

---

required employer-employee relationship. For a discussion of this see Charles C. Hinckley, "Tax Sheltered Retirement Plans under I.R.C. Section 403(b)," *Journal of the American Society of Chartered Life Underwriters*, Vol. XX, No. 1 (Winter, 1966), pp. 5, 9.

[8] In addition, the Regulations provide that one who is elected or appointed to certain public offices may qualify if there is a requirement that to hold the office such person must be trained or experienced in the field of education. For example, a regent or trustee of a state university, or a member of a board of education is not eligible. But a commissioner or superintendent of education will generally be eligible. Reg. 1.403(b)–1(b)(5).

[9] Including fraternal benefit associations. It seems doubtful that the term would include a contract issued by the charitable employer itself, even though such an employer may upon occasion enter into an annuity contract for other purposes. It is questionable as to whether annuity guarantees of a funded state system, existing as a separate entity, would satisfy the statutory requirement.

[10] Reg. 1.403(b)–1(c)(3).

[11] For a discussion of the meaning of "incidental" life insurance under qualified plans, see p. 119.

Also, after December 31, 1962, the term "annuity" includes a so-called face-amount certificate, but does not include a contract or certificate issued after that date which is transferable.[12] The Regulations spell out in some detail what is meant by the term "nontransferable," and their language has been used as a guide by insurers in appropriately endorsing their contracts.[13]

Thus, any annuity contract,[14] individual or group, ordinarily issued by an insurance company may be used to provide a tax-sheltered annuity, provided it contains an appropriate restriction respecting transferability.

In recent years, new contracts have been developed by many insurers to accommodate the needs of the tax-sheltered annuity market. One can now find contracts with premiums payable for only 9 or 10 consecutive months during a year, in order to meet the needs of payroll schedules of educational institutions. There are also available contracts which permit variations in the amount of premiums paid each year and are therefore readily adaptable to varying incomes (hence, varying annual exclusion allowances).

There are no guidelines as to the meaning of "purchased by an employer." It is generally considered advisable for the employer to apply for the contract and to pay all of the premiums on it. However, while payment of the premiums by the employer would appear to be mandatory, it is questionable if tax consequences would be controlled to any extent by whether or not the employer appears on the application as applicant. It is the opinion of some practitioners that payment of premium will satisfy the "purchase" requirement. Thus, a qualified employer who merely assumes the payment of premiums on an individual annuity contract already owned by one of his employees presumably will be considered as having "purchased" a tax-sheltered annuity for him in each year that premiums are so paid, to the extent of the available exclusion allowance, and provided that the contract contains the requisite restriction as to transferability.

---

[12] I.R.C. 401(g), which reads in its entirety as follows: "For purposes of this section and sections 402, 403, and 404, the term 'annuity' includes a face-amount certificate, as defined in section 2(a)(15) of the Investment Company Act of 1940 (15 U.S.C. sec. 80a–2); but does not include any contract or certificate issued after December 31, 1962, which is transferable, if any person other than the trustee of a trust described in section 401(a) which is exempt from tax under section 501(a) is the owner of such contract or certificate."

[13] Reg. 1.401–9(b). Nontransferable contracts are also employed to postpone income tax liability when contracts are distributed from qualified corporate plans and in connection with H.R. 10 plans. For a typical nontransferable endorsement, see p. 146.

[14] Including so-called retirement income or income endowment contracts, issued after December 31, 1962, that satisfy the incidental insurance benefit test.

Employee's Rights Nonforfeitable

Attempted definitions of nonforfeitability are elusive. Without a trust, the employee's rights under the contract would appear to be nonforfeitable if ownership of the contract is vested solely in him.[15] The same would appear to be true if there is some form of joint ownership of the contract,[16] together with an agreement between employer and employee whereby the employee could not be deprived of benefits provided by annuity premiums previously paid, even though the employer could exercise control over the time of enjoyment of those benefits.

As a practical matter, it would appear that ownership is ordinarily vested solely in the employee, thus leaving him free of any restrictions or problems that might arise by virtue of insolvency or change of management of the employer. As sole owner of the contract, the employee is free to exercise any of his contractual rights with the insurer, subject, of course, to restrictions on transferability. Thus, he may be free to elect a reduced paid-up annuity, to change the contract for a reduced annuity with an earlier maturity date, to surrender the contract, or to borrow against its cash value from the insurer.[17]

Exclusion Allowance

The *exclusion allowance* for an employee for the taxable year is defined as:

. . . an amount equal to the excess, if any, of—
(A) the amount determined by multiplying (i) 20 per cent of his includible compensation, by (ii) the number of years of service, over
(B) the aggregate of the amounts contributed by the employer for annuity contracts and excludable from the gross income of the employee for any prior taxable year.[18]

Thus, in general, the measure of the premium that an employer may pay for a nonforfeitable annuity for an employee—without current income tax to the employee—is determined in the following

---

[15] There is little evidence that trusts are in fact used in this area.

[16] Or, perhaps, even ownership by the employer.

[17] While the Regulations make it clear that a contract satisfies the requirement of nontransferability even though it may be assignable to the insurer as security for indebtedness (see Note 13), they give no indication of the tax consequences if a policy loan is actually made.

[18] I.R.C. 403(b)(2).

manner. First, 20% of the current year's compensation is multiplied by the total period of employment (expressed in years). From the product, there is deducted the sum of prior amounts so expended and certain other similar employer expenditures. The excess difference is the permitted tax-sheltered premium for the current year.

If the maximum exclusion allowance as so determined is *fully* utilized in the current year (for example, by purchase of a single-premium annuity), the exclusion allowance available for future years will ordinarily be merely 20% of his then current compensation.

Any contributions of the employer to any other tax-sheltered annuity, qualified pension, profit sharing or annuity plan, qualified bond purchase plan, etc., would be charged against the current year's exclusion allowance—if the employee has previously not been taxed thereon for any reason.[19] Thus, for example, if contributions are being made by the same employer to a qualified plan, the amounts so contributed would reduce the 20% available under Section 403(b).

If the employer has never made any prior tax-free payments with respect to a particular employee (whether by payment of annuity premiums, by contributions to a qualified plan, or otherwise), the amount described in "B" above will be zero. If this is the employee's first year of employment, the exclusion allowance will be merely 20% of his includable compensation for the current year.[20]

The computation of the exclusion allowance can be an exceedingly easy or an exceedingly difficult matter, depending upon (1) the mathematical facility of the one undertaking it, and (2) the complexity of the facts involved. Complicating factors may be introduced by part-time employment, salary reduction agreements, or other benefit plans being currently funded by the same employer which provide tax-deferred compensation. Such complicating factors will be considered subsequently in this chapter.[21]

The initial application of the exclusion allowance formula for an employee with past service may produce a very large exclusion allowance.[22] Ordinarily, a single-premium annuity intended to fully utilize this allowance immediately is not feasible. If less than the full allowance is used, the unused portion will increase the allow-

---

[19] Reg. 1.403(b)–1(d)(3).

[20] If less than one year of service has been completed, years of service is taken as *one*. I.R.C. 403(b)(4).

[21] See the section on "Arithmetic of the Exclusion Allowance," pp. 379–383.

[22] For example, with $15,000 of current includable compensation, and 10 years of past service, the exclusion allowance is $(.20) \times (\$15,000) \times (10) = \$30,000$.

ance available in future years over what it would have been had the entire "past service allowance"[23] been fully used.[24]

As a practical matter, it is frequently desirable to purchase an annual-premium annuity, so selecting the amount of gross annual premium that: (1) by the normal retirement date, full benefit will have been taken of the "past service allowance"; and (2) in each year the available exclusion allowance will be equal to or greater than the premium payable. In other words, we wish to determine the *maximum* level premium that may be paid by the employer each year that will take full advantage of the "past service allowance" over the remaining years of employment.

To do so, first determine the total number of years that will have elapsed between the employee's date of employment and his projected retirement date and *assume* that this present rate of annual includable compensation will continue until retirement.[25] The maximum annual premium will then be 20% of includable compensation times *total* years of service (past and future) divided by *future* years of premium payments.

This may be expressed algebraically as:

$$P = \frac{.20 \times S \times T}{F}$$

where P is the maximum annual premium, S represents salary, T represents total years of service (both past and future), and F represents future years of premium payments.[26] This may be simplified to:

$$P = \frac{S \times T}{5F} \tag{1}$$

---

[23] No reference to *past service allowance* is made in either Section 403 (b) or in the Regulations. However, use of such an expression will be helpful in examining the operation of the exclusion allowance. It refers to the exclusion allowance that would be available to an employee, as a consequence of past service with the same employer, which has not otherwise been utilized.

[24] If the full $30,000 exclusion allowance was used after the 10th year of employment, the 11th year exclusion allowance (assuming includable compensation continues at $15,000) is (.20) × ($15,000) × (11) − $30,000 = $33,000 − $30,000 = $3,000. However, if only $5,000 of the initial exclusion allowance had been used, then the 11th year exclusion allowance would be (.20) × ($15,000) × (11) − $5,000 = $33,000 − $5,000 = $28,000.

[25] This assumption will prove to have been too conservative if compensation is subsequently increased. Conversely, it will have been too liberal if compensation decreases. See the section on "Caveat re Future Salary Reductions," p. 378.

[26] Thus, in effect, we are finding his total working lifetime exclusion allowance and prorating it over his remaining working years.

If premiums are paid other than annually, the sum of the periodic premiums should not exceed the level premium so determined.[27] If the years of service is actually less than one, the number of years of service should be taken as *one*.[28]

INCOME TAXATION OF BENEFITS

Income Tax Consequences during Lifetime

During his lifetime, and prior to actual receipt of any benefits under the contract, the employee will incur no income tax liability if: (1) the annuity contract contains no element of insurance protection; and (2) all premiums paid by the employer in each year are within the exclusion allowance available for the particular year.

Where the contract provides an incidental insurance benefit, the employee will be taxable in each year on the value of such incidental benefit.[29] Also, any premiums will be currently taxable to the employee to the extent that they exceed the exclusion allowance for the particular year.[30]

When the employee actually commences receiving benefits under the annuity contract, the amounts received are taxable to him under Section 72 of the Internal Revenue Code. However, *capital gains treatment is not available* with respect to any lump sum payments. If the employee himself contributed nothing to the cost of the contract, and if all contributions of the employer were within the limits of the exclusion allowance in each year, so that the employee was previously subject to no income tax on such contributions, everything received by him under a true annuity contract[31] will be includable in his gross income as received.

---

[27] It is the *sum* of the periodic premiums actually paid by the employer during a year that should be kept within the limits of the year's exclusion allowance. So, if premiums are to be paid, for example, monthly, the size of the annuity or insurance contract will be slightly smaller than if premiums were paid annually.

[28] See Note 20.

[29] I.R.C. 72(m)(3)(B); Reg. 1.403(b)–1(c)(3), and 1.72–16(b). Presumably, the so-called PS-58 (term) costs of the amount at risk under the contract (expected proceeds minus cash value) will be the appropriate measure of his currently taxable benefit.

[30] If a maximum tax-sheltered annuity, using a contract providing an incidental insurance benefit, is desired, should the premium be limited to the amount of the exclusion allowance? Or, may it exceed such allowance by the (PS-58) cost of the insurance benefit for the year in question? The latter would appear to produce no undesirable results. The amount by which the premium exceeds the exclusion allowance will be currently taxable. But, even though it may be taxable either (*a*) because it exceeds the exclusion allowance by the amount in question, or (*b*) because the insurance protection element is a currently taxable economic benefit, it cannot be taxed twice.

[31] That is, one with no insurance element.

If the employee made any contributions (or if he is deemed to have made contributions), he will be entitled to a tax-free recovery of such contributions.[32] The employee will have made, or will be deemed to have made, contributions to the extent that: (1) he actually made such contributions out of his after-tax money; (2) employer contributions were taxable to him by virtue of having exceeded the exclusion allowance for one or more years; or (3) incidental insurance costs were taxable to him.

If the benefits are received in one sum, he will have *ordinary income* to the extent of the excess of the amount received over his aggregate contributions. If he receives installment payments, an *exclusion ratio* will be determined, and a portion of each annuity payment proportional to the employee's contributions will be excludable from gross income. The balance of each payment is includable in gross income as received.

But if the employee's aggregate contributions are small enough so that the total *guaranteed* amount of annuity payments receivable by him during the first three years of such payments will exceed the aggregate contributions, the so-called *accelerated recovery-of-cost rule* is used in lieu of the exclusion ratio (as in the case of retirement benefits under a qualified plan).[33] Thus, under such circumstances, the employee excludes all *guaranteed* annuity payments from gross income until he has received a tax-free return of his cost (any dividends being fully taxable). Thereafter, all amounts received are taxable to him as ordinary income.

Income Tax Consequences after Death

In the case of a true annuity contract, taxation of benefits paid after the employee's death depends upon whether the employee had, or had not, actually commenced to receive annuity payments prior to his death. If such payments had not already begun, the beneficiary would be taxed as if he were the employee in the manner described above.

If the employee had already commenced to receive annuity payments, taxation of the beneficiary would depend on the particular mode of payment applicable at the employee's death. If the only amounts payable after his death are in the nature of refund payments, such amounts will be taxable as ordinary income, but only after the amounts so received by the beneficiary, together with all amounts received tax free by the employee during his lifetime,

---

[32] Reg. 1.72–16 (b) (4).

[33] I.R.C. 72 (d).

exceed the aggregate contributions of the employee. On the other hand, if the amounts payable to the beneficiary are a continuation of installment certain payments (without life contingency), or are payments to a surviving annuitant under a joint and survivor annuity, the beneficiary continues to exclude a portion of payments received each year in accordance with the exclusion ratio determined for the employee.[34]

Beneficiaries under contracts which provide an incidental insurance benefit are taxed in virtually the same manner as beneficiaries of a deceased insured under a qualified pension plan; *but capital gains treatment is not available* with respect to lump sum payments.[35] The death benefit is composed of Section 101 proceeds and Section 72 proceeds, the former being the amount at risk under the insurance contract as of the date of death and the latter being the cash value of the contract determined as of that date.

The Section 101 proceeds will be treated the same as regular personal life insurance: income tax free if received in one sum; or, if received in installments, taxable to the extent that installment payments in any year exceed a pro rata portion of the one-sum proceeds, with the spouse's $1,000 exclusion applicable.

The Section 72 proceeds (i.e., the cash value as of the date of death) will be taxable in the same manner and to the same extent as if the employee had received such proceeds during his lifetime, with the single exception that the $5,000 employee death benefit exclusion of Section 101(b) will be applicable under certain circumstances. To the extent applicable, such $5,000 death benefit is deemed to increase the employee's contributions for purposes of determining the beneficiary's taxable income.

The $5,000 death benefit exclusion applies to tax-sheltered annuities only under the same circumstances that it would be available with respect to deceased participants of qualified plans. The benefit must be paid, by reason of the employee's death, within one taxable year of the distributee. But this tax-free death benefit is not available for employees of public school systems. Nor is it available for employees of every Section 501(c)(3) organization, but only to a certain *subclass*.[36] If the individual was employed by an organiza-

---

[34] Reg. 1.72–4(a)(4); Reg. 1.72–11(c)(1); Reg. 1.72–11(c)(2), Exs. (1) and (4).

[35] See Chapter 6. Also, see Robert J. Lawthers, "Federal Income Taxation of an Employee and His Beneficiaries under a Qualified Pension or Profit-Sharing Plan," *Journal of the American Society of Chartered Life Underwriters*, Vol. XII, No. 2 (Spring, 1958), p. 130.

[36] That *subclass* consists of those Section 501(c)(3) organizations exempt from tax under Section 501(a) which are referred to in Section 503(b)(1), (2) or (3): namely, schools (not publicly operated) having a student body in

tion of the latter type, the choice of how death benefits may best be received will involve a balancing of factors.[37]

ESTATE AND GIFT TAXES

Estate Tax

Unless the employee is employed by an organization which is a member of the previously mentioned subclass of Section 501 (c) (3) organizations, the value of all amounts payable after his death will be includable in his gross estate for federal estate tax purposes, whether payable to his estate or to a named beneficiary.[38] Where, however, the employer is a member of this subclass, the estate tax benefits available for qualified plans will be available with respect to any death benefit under a true annuity contract.[39] Thus, if such payments are to or for the benefit of the estate, they will be includable in the gross estate.

On the other hand, if payments are to a named beneficiary, at least some portion of them will be excluded. If the employee made no contributions to the cost of the annuity (and none were attributed to him), nothing will be includable in his gross estate upon his death. Where contributions were made by (or attributed to) the employee, there will be included in his gross estate only such fractional part of the value of the death benefit payable to the beneficiary as corresponds to the ratio of the employee's contributions to the total cost of the annuity.[40]

---

attendance; churches, or conventions or associations of churches; or organizations receiving a substantial part of their support from the general public or from some governmental body.

[37] If proceeds are not taken in one sum, any otherwise available $5,000 exclusion will generally be lost, but the tax liability of the beneficiary is spread out over the years of payment. If proceeds are taken in one sum, then (provided the employer was a member of the above-mentioned subclass), tax liability will all arise in one year, but an amount of up to $5,000 may entirely escape taxation.

[38] There is no possibility of an employee escaping estate tax liability by transferring his rights to another, as any such transfer is barred by the restrictions on transferability required by Section 401 (g).

[39] I.R.C. 2039 (c) (3). At present it is not clear what the estate tax situation will be (assuming the employer is a member of the subclass) where the contract provides an incidental insurance benefit. It may be that the estate tax treatment of the entire death benefit will be determined as above described. However, the government may claim that the entire amount at risk is includable in the gross estate (under the incidents-of-ownership rule of Section 2042), and that only the "annuity portion" of the death benefit (i.e., the cash value as of date of death) will be entitled to the exclusion treatment applicable to death benefits under true annuity contracts. In either event, it does not appear that employer contributions that were taxable to the insured solely as PS-58 costs would be treated as employee contributions for estate tax purposes.

[40] See last sentence of Note 39.

The favorable estate tax treatment just described is inapplicable to employees of public school systems.[41]

Gift Tax

Where an employee who is employed by a member of the *subclass* previously mentioned designates a beneficiary to receive refund payments under a tax-sheltered annuity, or elects a joint and survivor annuity, such designation or election will not constitute a transfer within the meaning of the gift tax laws.[42]

SALARY REDUCTIONS

Current Salary Reductions

At one time the Commissioner took the position that the postponing of tax liability would apply only where the annuity is "merely a supplement to past or current compensation," and that, therefore, there would be no postponing of tax liability if the annuity premiums were paid in lieu of existing salary, or even "in lieu of an increase in current compensation" if this were done at the employee's request.[43]

Under the Regulations, this position still stands for amounts paid by an employer during taxable years beginning before January 1, 1958.[44] But for taxable years beginning thereafter, a salary reduction in the amount of the annuity premium is permitted, and the annuity premium paid out of what would otherwise have been paid as salary will not be constructively received, provided only that:

1. There is an agreement between employer and employee for the latter "to take a reduction in salary, or to forgo an increase in salary, but only to the extent that amounts are earned by the employee after the agreement becomes effective." Such an agreement must be legally binding and irrevocable with respect to amounts earned while the agreement is in effect;
2. The employee must not be permitted to make more than one such

---

[41] It appears that they were overlooked in this and certain other respects (see discussion of $5,000 death benefit, p. 375, and see the following section on "Gift Tax,") when they were first brought under the statutory provisions of Section 403(b) by the Revenue Act of 1961. Perhaps this will be rectified by future statutory amendments.

[42] I.R.C. 2517 (which also applies to a participant in a qualified plan). Note that such a designation is not a "transfer" prohibited by the restrictive endorsement required by Section 401(g).

[43] See Note 2.

[44] Reg. 1.403(b)–1(b)(3).

agreement with the same employer during any taxable year of the employee; and

3. "There may be no substitution of annuity premium for salary *already earned.*"

Also, it is now perfectly clear that the arrangement may be instigated at the request of the employee.

Salary Reduction Agreement

While, from the tax viewpoint, the employee may instigate a salary reduction, there must be a real *reduction* in his compensation. For the employee to merely request that his employer *deduct* a specified amount from his compensation to be applied as an annuity premium will *not* suffice.[45] The distinction between a *reduction* and a *deduction* cannot be overemphasized. The former will produce the desired tax deferral. The latter will *not*.

Thus, the employer must enter into a written agreement with the employee with respect to the salary reduction, such agreement to be applicable to compensation for services thereafter rendered until such time as the agreement shall have been terminated by either party.[46]

Caveat re Future Salary Reductions

In the normal course of events, it is unlikely that an employee's compensation will continue without change until his retirement, although such an assumption might be made for purposes of determining the maximum annual annuity premium that may be paid without exceeding his projected exclusion allowances.[47] No difficulty will be encountered (with respect to the adequacy of exclusion allowances for future years to cover fully level annual premiums) if he receives periodic *increases* in compensation.[48]

In the remote event, however, that an employee should, in the future, find it necessary to take a cut in his compensation, the situation will require a careful review in the first year such a reduction occurs, in order to ascertain the effect upon the current year's (and, perhaps, subsequent years') exclusion allowance.

When and if the reduced compensation problem arises, there

---

[45] As, for example, in a typical "salary savings" plan.

[46] The drafting of such an agreement for any given case is a matter for the attorneys representing the parties.

[47] See Note 25, and text to which it applies: and see the section on "Maximum Premium—Negotiated Salary Reduction," p. 379.

[48] As a matter of fact, it may be well to review the picture from time to time to see whether the increase in compensation is sufficient to warrant the purchase of an additional annuity.

would appear to be three possible alternatives: (1) take a reduced paid-up annuity; (2) have the employer continue to pay the annuity premium, recognizing that the premium paid will be currently taxable to the employee (but only to the extent that it exceeds the exclusion allowance for the year in question); or (3) the employee can pay the premium himself. The possibility of the reduced compensation problem arising is not serious. And, if it does arise, satisfactory solutions are available. It would, therefore, seem that this possibility should never discourage one from taking advantage of this provision of the law. However, the possibility should be recognized.

ARITHMETIC OF THE EXCLUSION ALLOWANCE

We have previously considered the problem of determining the maximum level premium, P, that may be safely paid by the employer each year in order to take full advantage of the *past service allowance* over the remaining years of employment. We noted that:

$$P = \frac{S \times T^{49}}{5F}. \tag{1}$$

But we have made two major assumptions that may not be valid in a given situation, namely: (1) that the premium is paid from the employer's own funds without reduction in the employee's current compensation, and (2) that there is no other tax-deferred contribution (for example, to a qualified pension plan) currently being made by the employer with respect to the employee. Now, let us consider the situation when one or both of these factors *is* present.

Maximum Premium—Negotiated Salary Reduction

One important caution must be observed where there is to be a salary reduction while attempting to take advantage of the maximum exclusion allowance. The exclusion allowed is based on 20% of the employee's *includable compensation*, i.e., his compensation exclusive of amounts received tax free. Therefore (ignoring past service for the moment), one cannot take a 20% reduction in salary and have the reduction applied to annuity premiums, since this would produce annuity premiums equal to 25% of the *remaining includable compensation*. If, however, the salary reduction is limited to one sixth of that paid prior to reduction, then that one sixth

---

[49] Where S represents salary, T represents total years of service (both past and future), and F represents future years of premium payments. See Note 26 and text to which it applies.

of salary will give the maximum excludable annual annuity premium for a future service annuity.[50]

Suppose an employee (with independent income sources) wishes to take the maximum reduction in salary that would be possible in order to have the largest possible future annual annuity premium that would utilize his exclusion allowance, based on both *past and future service,* up to the limit.

Assume that there are no prior contributions to be deducted (or future contributions to any other tax-exempt plan or trust for his benefit) and that his salary prior to any reduction, S, would (except for the negotiated reduction) remain constant throughout his remaining years of employment. Then the maximum annual premium, P, that can be paid and still be excludable can be expressed as:

$$P = \frac{.20 \times (S - P) \times T}{F}$$

(noting that "(S − P)" represents *includable compensation* after S has been reduced by P). This may be simplified to:

$$P = \frac{S \times T^{51}}{5F + T}.\tag{2}$$

Maximum Premiums—Other Tax-Deferred Contributions

Where the premium is paid solely from the employer's own funds, i.e., no salary reduction is involved but other tax-deferred contributions are involved (for example, pension contributions), the maximum annual premium, P, is determined by subtracting the aggregate amount of such tax deferred contributions, C, from 20% of includable compensation times total years of service, and dividing the difference so determined by future years of premium payments. Thus,

$$P = \frac{.20 \times S \times T - C^{52}}{F}.$$

---

[50] Since one sixth of salary before reduction is equal to 20% of the five sixths of salary which remains after the reduction.

[51] See Note 49 for meaning of symbols. To illustrate the application of the formula, assume a 55-year-old employee with a present salary of $15,000. Suppose that he has 10 years of future service and 30 years of past service. Thus, $S = \$15,000$; $T = 30 + 10 = 40$; and $F = 10$. Therefore, the maximum premium (and hence, the maximum salary reduction) would be:
$$P = \frac{S \times T}{5F + T} = \frac{\$15,000 \times 40}{(5 \times 10) + 40} = \$6,666.66.$$

[52] Thus, in effect, we are finding his total working lifetime exclusion allowance by first subtracting the total of other tax-deferred contributions and *then* prorating it over his remaining working years.

This may be simplified to:

$$P = \frac{S \times T - 5C}{5F}. \tag{3}$$

Suppose that the ratio of the employer's pension contributions to the employee's salary prior to reduction is known, as in the case of a defined contribution (money purchase) pension plan. Designate this ratio as Q. Then if $C = Q \times S \times T$ (i.e., if the aggregate of pension contributions during the working years equals a constant percentage of S times total years of service), Formula (3) may be expressed in the form:

$$P = \frac{S \times T - 5(Q \times S \times T)}{5F},$$

i.e.,
$$P = \frac{(1 - 5Q)ST}{5F}. \tag{4}$$

Salary Reduction and Other Tax-Deferred Contributions

It will be recalled that in cases where there is to be a salary reduction (and ignoring past service), the employee's current cash compensation should be reduced by not more than one sixth, if the annuity premium paid via the salary reduction is not to exceed 20% of includable compensation after salary reduction.

Suppose that the employer is making current pension contributions with respect to the employee (but has not previously done so). If the ratio of the employer's pension contribution to the employee's salary prior to reduction is Q, then the maximum permissible salary reduction, P, to be devoted to the tax-sheltered annuity must be such that:

$$P + Q \times S = .20(S - P),$$

i.e., the sum of tax-deferred contributions equals 20% of includable compensation (after salary reduction). Solving for P, this may be reduced algebraically to the formula:

$$P = \frac{(1 - 5Q)S^{53}}{6} \tag{5}$$

---

[53] It will be observed that if $Q = 0$ (i.e., if there is no employer contribution to a qualified plan with respect to the employee), we would have

$$P = \frac{(1 - 0)S}{6} = \frac{S}{6}.$$

In other words, we arrive at the familiar salary reduction of one sixth.

In Formula (5), no past service was taken into account. In Formula (4), no salary reduction is involved. Where both such factors must be considered,

$$P = \frac{.20(S - P)T - Q \times S \times T}{F},$$

i.e.,

$$P = \frac{(1 - 5Q)ST^{54}}{5F + T}.\tag{6}$$

Employer Pension Contributions Unknown

Frequently, the actual amounts previously contributed by the employer to provide pension benefits for a specified employee are not known. The plan may expressly describe the retirement benefits to be furnished, leaving the amount necessary to fund the plan to be actuarially determined, without allocation of actual contributions among individual employees. For such situations, the Regulations provide explicit rules for the computation of the excludable amounts to be charged against the employee's annual exclusion allowance.[55]

Part-Time Employees

If an employee is a part-time employee, or is a full-time employee for only part of a year, he is allowed only an appropriate fraction of a year in computing his "number of years of service." The fraction to be used is the ratio of the time spent by the employee in the employer's service during that year to the time that would be spent on a similar job for the same employer by a full-time employee.

For example, a full-time instructor at a college with the usual nine-month year is a full-time employee; but a librarian employed by an organization whose employees normally work the year round (and get no vacation) is a three-quarter-time employee if he works for the organization for only nine months during the year. If the normal teaching load at a college is 12 hours per week, a part-time instructor carrying a 9-hour load for the nine-month academic year would be a three-quarter-time employee. If he carries a nine-hour load for only four and one-half months during the year, he is a three-eighths-time employee.

These fractional years of service are then aggregated to find the

---

[54] The mathematically astute reader will note that Formula (6) is a generalized form of Formulas (2) and (5), all involving salary reductions. Also, Formula (3) is a generalized form of Formulas (1) and (4), neither of which involves salary reductions.

[55] Reg. 1.403(b)–1(d)(4), discussion of which is beyond the scope of this chapter.

"number of years of service."[56] This is then multiplied by 20% of "annualized compensation" in order to arrive at the exclusion allowance. But if the employee's part-time work is constant—for example, if he works one-quarter of a year every year, and his salary in that one-quarter of a year is the same for at least the previous four years, or as many years as are necessary to aggregate one full year of employment, we can completely ignore his part-time status and treat him for purposes of the formulas as though he were a full-time employee.[57]

SOME FURTHER TAX CONSIDERATIONS

The Dual Nature of Tax-Sheltered Annuity Premiums

Where an employer, of his own initiative, decides to provide one or more employees with a tax-sheltered annuity and to bear the cost of so doing, no particular problems arise. It is clear (at least from the viewpoint of federal income taxation) that the employee's current compensation or wages do *not* include the premium on the tax-sheltered annuity (if the annuity contract is nontransferable and the premium is within the available exclusion allowance).

But the concept of providing the annuity premium by a salary reduction voluntarily agreed to by the employee had no precedent in our tax laws. If the employee merely agreed to a salary reduction and nothing more, or even if he agreed to a reduced salary and a deferred compensation agreement, his reduced current compensation should be his salary for all tax purposes. But when the amount by which his salary is currently reduced is put into an annuity contract of which he is sole and immediate owner, certain tax consequences are less clear. Is the annuity premium *his* money or is it the employer's? Does the answer to this question control other tax results?

Social Security Taxes and Benefits

In 1953 the Revenue Service ruled that the payment of a premium by the employer, on a tax-sheltered annuity for an employee,

---

[56] But if the number of years of service thus computed for a part-time employee is less than one whole year, the number of years of service should be taken as *one*. See Note 20.

[57] Assume a half-time employee earned $5,000 per year for half-time employment during five successive calendar years. His aggregate number of years of service is two and one-half, and his annualized compensation is $10,000. Therefore, his exclusion allowance is: $.20 \times (\$10,000) \times (2.5) = \$5,000$. But since his fractional employment time and his compensation were uniform throughout the period in question, we can treat him as though he were a full-time employee with five years of service, earning $5,000 per year. Hence, $.20 \times (\$5,000) \times (5) = \$5,000$.

does not constitute "wages" as defined under the Federal Insurance Contributions Act and, therefore, that such payment was "not subject to withholding for federal employment or income tax purposes."[58] This ruling also held that the employer was not required to file an information return Form 1099 with respect to such payment.

A recent ruling, while reaffirming the prior ruling generally, distinguished it, insofar as FICA considerations are concerned, where voluntary salary reduction agreements are involved.[59] Amounts used by the employer pursuant to a salary reduction agreement to purchase an annuity for the employee are now considered as "wages" for purposes of the FICA, even though such amounts are excludable from gross income. The prior ruling still applies to a situation where the employer *uses its own funds,* rather than one where the employee takes a voluntary salary reduction to provide the necessary funds.[60] Thus, for FICA purposes, a salary reduction to purchase a tax-sheltered annuity is treated as though the annuity premium was currently received as wages by the employee.

Wage Withholding

The position that any annuity premium excludable from gross income under Section 403(b) is not subject to withholding of income tax (whether or not a voluntary salary reduction agreement is involved) has recently been reaffirmed.[61]

Measure of Pension Benefits

An employer who maintains a qualified pension plan may define compensation covered by the plan to include premiums on tax-sheltered annuities, as well as cash compensation paid. Even though a salary reduction is effected to provide for the purchase of a tax-sheltered annuity, other retirement benefits provided by the employer may be measured by the amount of *unreduced* salary.[62]

---

[58] Rev. Rul. 181 CB 1953–2, 111.

[59] Rev. Rul. 65–208, IRB 1965–35, 6.

[60] This is in accord with Social Security Ruling 64–59, October, 1964, which made a similar distinction.

[61] Rev. Rul. 65–209, IRB 1965–35, 8.

[62] Special Ruling dated 3/29/65, issued to the Board of Education of Rye, N.Y., *Pension and Profit Sharing Tax Service* (Englewood Cliffs, N.J.: Prentice-Hall, Inc., n.d.), ¶ 12,043.

Pension Reserves

An insurance company is entitled to a tax reduction with respect to its so-called qualified pension plan reserves. At present this reduction may amount to approximately ¼ of 1% of the contract reserve, which is ordinarily passed on to the policyholder in the form of an increased annual dividend or a reduced premium. The reserves held in connection with tax-sheltered annuity contracts enjoy this favorable tax treatment.[63]

CONSIDERATIONS OF LOCAL LAW

Employees of Public School Systems

When the use of public funds is involved in the proposed purchase of a tax-sheltered annuity, many questions of state law arise. May such funds be used to purchase a tax-sheltered annuity? If so, is an incidental insurance benefit permitted or prohibited? Is a voluntary salary reduction agreement allowed? Unfortunately, these questions have not been answered in many states; and, where they have been, the answers have varied considerably from state to state.

Merely as an illustration of the substantial disparity between the various states, it may be noted that in Nevada only group annuity contracts are permissible. In New York, the situation is rather confused. It appears that a salary reduction may not be permitted.[64]

Where a voluntary salary reduction agreement is permitted, does such a reduction also require a reduction in the teacher's benefits under the state retirement system? This may be an open question in some states. However, several have specifically ruled that no such reduction is required, among them, Arizona, Florida, Indiana, and North Carolina. Curiously, California has similarly ruled insofar as *teachers* are concerned but has reached an opposite conclusion respecting *nonteaching* employees of school districts who are covered under the state retirement system.

Each of these rulings, either expressly or by implication, was concerned with a voluntary salary reduction agreement. It may be inferred that state law may not permit the use of public funds to purchase tax-sheltered annuities except on a voluntary salary reduction basis. Otherwise, there may be a violation of salary scales established by law.

---

[63] I.R.C. 805(d)(1)(D).

[64] With a limited exception for employees of the University of the State of New York.

State Income Taxes

No uniform pattern has as yet developed as to the tax status of tax-sheltered annuities for state income tax purposes, whether they be purchased for employees of Section 501 (c) (3) organizations or public school systems. The few states that have ruled on the question again serve to illustrate a disparity of positions. For example, California and Indiana have ruled that the annuity premiums would be excludable from a teacher's gross income under the state income tax law to the extent excludable under the federal income tax laws. On the other hand, Arizona and Georgia have ruled that local law makes no provision for the exclusion of such amounts from state income taxation and, accordingly, they will be currently taxed. No assumptions should be made respecting income tax treatment in other states. Indeed, it is likely that many states have not as yet taken a position on this question.

State Premium Taxes

A significant portion of the total tax burden imposed on life insurance companies arises out of the premium taxes imposed by the states. However, only about one half of the states impose such a tax on *annuity* premiums. Where such taxes are imposed, the current rates range from 1% to 2.5%. While the majority of states which impose a tax on annuity premiums give no special relief to tax-sheltered annuity premiums, six states do give them preferential treatment.[65]

THE FUTURE OF TAX-SHELTERED ANNUITIES

The long-range outlook for any tax advantage that favors a relatively small portion of the populace is ordinarily somewhat speculative. Congress giveth, and Congress taketh away. Indeed, the logical foundation for the tax opportunity available through tax-sheltered annuities may be relatively weak. But the political foundations seems strong.

Western culture has generally held the teacher in high esteem. And while the United States has been somewhat delinquent in this respect until recently, there appears to have been a reversal of the trend. So, also, has the need for the cultural and social contribu-

---

[65] California and Washington have a reduced rate for tax-sheltered annuity premiums, while in Idaho, Missouri, Nebraska, and Tennessee they are exempted from the annuity premium tax.

tions that are made by our charitable organizations been recently emphasized.

It seems unlikely, then, that legislation that had its roots over 20 years ago, in a less favorable environment, will readily be uprooted. It would appear that the tax-sheltered annuity is becoming, and will remain, an integral part of our overall scheme of providing pension benefits.

Many of the detailed problems should disappear over the next decade. The states will gradually fall in line—not necessarily a very straight line—in taking a more uniform viewpoint respecting the applicability of local income taxation. Enabling legislation will be enacted to remove some of the barriers that exist with respect to the use of public funds.

INDEX

*This book has been set in 10 and 9 point
Century Expanded, leaded 2 points. Chapter numbers are 30 point Spartan Medium;
chapter titles are 18 point Spartan Medium.
The size of the type page is 27 by 45½
picas.*